MW01180686

OXFORD ENGLISH MONOGRAPHS

General Editors

John Lydgate's
Fall of Princes

Narrative Tragedy in its Literary and Political Contexts

NIGEL MORTIMER

CLARENDON PRESS • OXFORD

*This book has been printed digitally and produced in a standard specification
in order to ensure its continuing availability*

OXFORD
UNIVERSITY PRESS

Great Clarendon Street, Oxford OX2 6DP

Oxford University Press is a department of the University of Oxford.
It furthers the University's objective of excellence in research, scholarship,
and education by publishing worldwide in

Oxford New York

Auckland   Cape Town   Dar es Salaam   Hong Kong   Karachi
Kuala Lumpur   Madrid   Melbourne   Mexico City   Nairobi
New Delhi   Shanghai   Taipei   Toronto
With offices in
Argentina   Austria   Brazil   Chile   Czech Republic   France   Greece
Guatemala   Hungary   Italy   Japan   South Korea   Poland   Portugal
Singapore   Switzerland   Thailand   Turkey   Ukraine   Vietnam

Oxford is a registered trade mark of Oxford University Press
in the UK and in certain other countries

Published in the United States
by Oxford University Press Inc., New York

© Nigel Mortimer 2005

ISBN 978-0-19-927501-4

Acknowledgements

The *Fall of Princes* by the Benedictine writer John Lydgate (*c.*1370–*c.*1450) is a translation of Boccaccio's *De casibus virorum illustrium* (1355–60) via an intermediary French prose version by Laurent de Premierfait, the *Des Cas des nobles hommes et femmes* (1409). Lydgate's debt to his immediate source text has never before been systematically studied: this book analyses the significance of the *Fall* with reference both to the *Des Cas* and also to the contexts (literary, political, monastic) in which the work was composed. Additionally, because the *Fall* was repeatedly imitated by admiring readers in the century and a half after Lydgate's death, attention is given to the ways in which subsequent writers respond to and manipulate the poem.

This study is a revised version of my doctoral thesis. My two supervisors at the time, Professors Helen Cooper and Douglas Gray, not only provided innumerable insights into medieval literature in general (and strategies for responding to Lydgate's work in particular), but also read my work at every stage with a fastidious attention to the detail of its argument. I am grateful, too, for their constant encouragement of my project and for their unflagging conviction that Lydgate deserved better treatment than he had received during preceding decades. It was Helen Cooper who patiently encouraged me to revive my excitement for the 'Monk of Bury' and pursue plans for publication. Ten years, an embarrassingly long time, have passed since the completion of the thesis; however, fashions change and even the most cursory glance at English Faculty websites suggests a growing appetite for Lydgate among a new and open-minded audience. It is these readers in particular I hope will find this book of value. However, I am aware that it may strike the reader as a series of disconnected discussions, as a pot-pourri rather than a single, unified argument. If this proves to be the case, I apologize; as those who are familiar with Lydgate's poems will agree, the encyclopedic nature of the *Fall* to an extent makes such an approach inevitable.

I am deeply indebted to the staff of several Libraries: in Oxford, the staff of the Bodleian Library (especially those of the Upper Reading Room and of Duke Humfrey's Library) and the Taylor Institution; the archivist of Corpus Christi College, Mrs Christine Butler, and the Librarians of Exeter College and Pusey House; in London, the staff of the Manuscript Students' Room at the British Library and of the Warburg Institute; in Cambridge, the staff of the University Library, of the Fitzwilliam Museum Library Reading Room, and the Manuscript Librarians of the Pepys Library at Magdalene College, of Trinity College, and of St John's College; in Edinburgh, the staff of the National Library of Scotland.

The British Academy funded my research. I am additionally most grateful to the Rector of Lincoln College and the Master of St Peter's College for appointing me to Lectureships, and to the relevant Fellows of Lady Margaret Hall, Brasenose, St Hilda's, University, and Pembroke Colleges for providing opportunities for teaching. A graduate scholarship from Lady Margaret Hall and minor research assistantships for Professors C. David Benson and Yoshihiro Masuya provided further financial support.

The career of John Cranewys amply proves that Sacristans of the Abbey at Bury St Edmunds were respected men of considerable authority and intelligence; sadly, modern-day sacristans rarely attain these heights: by far the greater part of my research was conducted while I was Sacristan of Pusey House, the library of which provided an invaluable resource. I am very grateful indeed to the former Principal of Pusey House, the Revd Philip Ursell, for his unstinting support, for his generous hospitality, and distinctive humour. I also thank successive Members of the Pusey Chapter for their patience and good fellowship.

Thanks are also due to the following: Dr Helen Barr and Professor Anne Hudson (whose inspiring teaching first led me to consider research in the medieval period), Dr James Clark, the Revd Dr Peter Groves (for his Thomistic discussions and domestic camaraderie), Dr Alexandra Gillespie and the Revd Dr Nicholas Heale (for allowing me to consult their doctoral theses), Dr Tony Hunt (who corrected certain of my lengthier translations of Premierfait's French), Ashley Law (who kindly drove me to Bury St Edmunds, Long Melford, and Lidgate), Andrew McNeillie and his colleagues at OUP, Dr Francis O'Gorman, Professor Malcolm Parkes (who taught me palaeography and gave advice on MS Bodley 263), Dr Corinne Saunders, Dr M. C. Seymour (who sent me a copy of his work on the manuscripts of the *Daunce*), Dr Nicholas Shrimpton, Dr Angus Tallini (who generously accommodated me on my research trips to Cambridge), Dr Matthew Townend, and Barry Webb. Ann Thompson and the Revd William Davage nobly undertook proof-reading and I am grateful to them for their attention to detail; the responsibility for any errors which remain is my own. On a personal note, I owe more to my mother and to the sustaining friendship of Edward and Emma Balfour than I could ever adequately acknowledge.

Textual references:
References to the *De casibus* are by book and chapter, citing throughout the 1520 Paris edition of the A-version, followed by cross-reference to Louis Brewer Hall's 1962 facsimile; references to the *Des Cas des nobles hommes et femmes* are to Nicholas Couteau's 1538 Paris print of Laurent's second redaction, entitled *Bocace des nobles malheureux*.

Unless otherwise acknowledged, translations are my own.

Contents

Contents   xi

Abbreviations

ANTS	Anglo-Norman Text Society
AV	Authorized Version
BAV	Biblioteca Apostolica Vaticana
BCP	Book of Common Prayer
BIHR	*Bulletin of the Institute of Historical Research*
BJRL	*Bulletin of the John Rylands Library*
BL	British Library
BLR	*Bodleian Library Record*
BN	Bibliothèque Nationale de France
BQR	*Bodleian Quarterly Record*
ChauR	*Chaucer Review*
CS	Camden Society
CT	*The Canterbury Tales*
CUL	Cambridge University Library
CUP	Cambridge University Press
DBF	*Dictionnaire de Biographie Française*, ed. J. Balteau et al. (Paris: Librairie Letouzey et Ané, 1933–)
DCP	*De consolatione Philosophiae*
DDC	*Dictionnaire de Droit Canonique*, ed. R. Naz, 7 vols. (Paris: 1931–65)
DNB	*Dictionary of National Biography*
EETS OS/ES	The Early English Text Society Original Series / Extra Series
EHD	*English Historical Documents, iv. 1327–1485*, ed. A. R. Myers (London: Eyre and Spottiswoode 1969)
EHR	*English Historical Review*
ELH	*English Literary History*
ELN	*English Language Notes*
HLB	*Huntington Library Bulletin*
HLQ	*Huntington Library Quarterly*
IMEV	*The Index of Middle English Verse*, ed. Carleton Brown and Rossell Hope Robbins (New York: Columbia University Press, 1943)

JEBS	*Journal of the Early Book Society for the Study of Manuscripts and Printing History*
JEGP	*Journal of English and Germanic Philology*
JEH	*Journal of Ecclesiastical History*
JMRS	*Journal of Medieval and Renaissance Studies*
JWCI	*Journal of the Warburg and Courtauld Institutes*
LGW	*The Legend of Good Women*
MED	*The Middle English Dictionary*, ed. Hans Kurath, Sherman M. Kuhn et al. (Ann Arbor, Mich.: University of Michigan Press, 1956–)
MLC	*Medieval Literary Criticism. Translations and Interpretations*, ed. O. B. Hardison et al. (New York: Frederick Ungar, 1974)
MLN	*Modern Language Notes*
MLQ	*Modern Language Quarterly*
MLR	*Modern Language Review*
ModPhil	*Modern Philology*
MP	*The Minor Poems of John Lydgate*, ed. Henry Noble MacCracken, EETS ES 107 (1911) and OS 192 (1934)
MS Addit.	Additional Manuscript
MV	George Cavendish, *Metrical Visions*, ed. A. S. G. Edwards, RETS 5th ser. 9 (Columbia, SC.: University of South Carolina Press, 1980)
N&Q	*Notes and Queries*
n.d.	No date of publication given
n.p.	No place of publication given
NS	New series
NeuphilMitt	*Neuphilologische Mitteilungen*
OUP	Oxford University Press
PhilQ	*Philological Quarterly*
PIMS	Pontifical Institute of Mediaeval Studies
PL	*Patrilogia Cursus Completus: Series Latina*, ed. J-P. Migne, 221 vols. (Paris: 1844–91)
PMLA	*Publications of the Modern Language Association of America*
PPC	*Proceedings and Ordinances of the Privy Council of England*, ed. N. H. Nicolas (London: 1834–7)
RES	*Review of English Studies*

RETS	Renaissance English Text Society
RP	*Rotuli parliamentorum*, ed. J. Strachey et al. (London: 1767–77, 1832)
RS	Rolls Series
SATF	Société des Anciens Textes Français
SCH	*Studies in Church History*
SP	*Studies in Philology*
SSL	*Studies in Scottish Literature*
STC	*A Short Title Catalogue of Books Printed in England, Scotland and Ireland and of English Books Printed Abroad, 1475–1640*, ed. A. W. Pollard and G. R. Redgrave, 2nd edn. (London: Bibliographical Society, 1986–91)
STh	*Summa Theologiae*
STS	Scottish Text Society
TB	*Troy Book*
TC	*Troilus and Criseyde*
TCBS	*Transactions of the Cambridge Bibliographical Society*
TEAS	Twayne's English Authors Series
TLS	*Times Literary Supplement*
TRHS	*Transactions of the Royal Historical Society*
TWAS	Twayne's World Authors Series
YES	*Yearbook of English Studies*

'When the bad bleeds, then is the tragedy good'
(*The Revenger's Tragedy*, III. v. 205)

I

The Fortunes of John Lydgate

John Lydgate's *Fall of Princes* is undoubtedly one of the most significant literary texts of the later medieval period, and yet critical assessment of the poem has unfortunately tended to be conducted in the spirit of Callimachus' observation that a big book is a great evil. At 36,365 lines the work is undeniably vast;[1] moreover, it is perhaps the longest poem in the English language, with only Spenser's *The Faerie Queene* (34,650 lines with the 1590 version of Books I–III) and Gower's *Confessio Amantis* (32,356 lines in the Fairfax manuscript) approaching its bulk.[2] Lydgate's poem has suffered from neglect more than any other text of its scope or influence, and this neglect has gradually fathered contempt. Even though manuscript witness indicates that the *Fall* was one of Lydgate's most popular works (surviving complete in more manuscripts than any other of his texts, excluding the *Dietary* and *Life of Our Lady*), it has yet to attract scholarly attention on the same scale as other of his longer poems, such as the *Troy Book* and the *Siege of Thebes*.

The inspiration for this study grew from my desire to offer a reconsideration of the *Fall* that would counteract the damaging tradition that sees its author as a talentless drudge. So ingrained are these responses to Lydgate, in fact, that readers are in the anomalous situation of hearing some of the more extravagant dismissals of the poet (as an unthinking and tedious poetaster)

[1] Schick gives the total as 36,316 lines (Lydgate ed. Schick 1891: clv).
[2] Lydgate's *Troy Book* has 30,117 lines, *Cursor Mundi* 29,555 lines in the Cotton Galba MS and Browning's *The Ring and the Book* perhaps comes next (after Lydgate's *Pilgrimage of the Life of Man*) with 21,133 lines. The Cotton Caligula version of Laȝamon's *Brut* runs to 16,095 lines, *pace* Bennett and Gray (1986: 68). If one judges length by number of lines alone and ignores vexed problems of syllabics, the poem is nearly four times longer than the *Aeneid*, over four times longer than Wordsworth's 1805 *The Prelude*, and well over three times as long as both Ovid's *Metamorphoses* and Milton's *Paradise Lost*.

from critics who are also among his scholarly admirers. Derek Pearsall, the author of several articles, a bio-bibliography, and the most influential of the four book-length studies of Lydgate's work, has repeatedly pointed out the poet's supposed inadequacies:

When he has to select for himself . . . the result is flatulence . . . he is driven by a daemon of inclusiveness . . . He can vary but he can never truly develop . . . criticism is silenced as the mind is battered into submission.[3]

From poem to poem the same stimulus triggers off the same response . . . Lydgate characteristically freezes the processes of life into non-physical abstraction . . . all the complexities of human behaviour are resolved into a remorselessly simple series of polarities[4]

Lydgate's method . . . is always to add, never to alter . . . [he has] a total lack of originality . . . [he has at his disposal] no style—but only a raw, barren, arid waste of words . . . [H]is mind never probes or questions, but slithers instantly into the apt generalisation . . . he gropes forward as if every breath will be his last . . . In Lydgate there is no mystery and no search . . . Lydgate is not a poet at all[5]

[W]ords and sentences slip away from him, blurred and out of focus, just as eloquence gives way to grandiloquence, sonority to bombast, and moral seriousness to maudlin platitude . . . enclosing Chaucer in a capsule of medieval commonplace . . . Lydgate has no sense of governing poetic structure but that of the encyclopaedia . . . Lydgate's habits of mind were too profoundly medieval to respond to novelty[6]

Lydgate [is] a marvellously *useful* writer, in whom medieval preoccupations, themes, and conventions are represented in full without the complicating intermediacy of genius, individuality, or even, sometimes, of thought . . . Lydgate gives us the Middle Ages in slow motion . . . Chaucer is the sharp-pointed object; Lydgate is the sticky bun . . . he did not understand the point of the poetic tradition within which he was working . . . he turns backward rather than forward, reencapsulating the protohumanism of Boccaccio within a hermetically sealed medievalism . . . it must have been like trying to reverse the direction of a driverless steamroller . . . all he knew was how to lay one line beside another[7]

Although Pearsall's work has yielded many interesting and valuable insights (especially in helping us to understand how Lydgate mediated the work of Chaucer to the fifteenth century), it is sadly

[3] Pearsall (1966a: 210, 211, 217, 220).   [4] Pearsall (1969: 28, 37).
[5] Pearsall (1970: 153, 172, 176, 195, 209, 212, 298).
[6] Pearsall (1977: 228, 229, 231; see Chaucer ed. Edwards, 1985a: 34).
[7] Pearsall (1992: 5, 6, 7, 10, 11, 12, 22).

his more robust caricatures of the poet, rather than his subtle understanding of Lydgate's methods, that have until very recently held critical sway.[8]

ENCOMIUM TO AMBIVALENCE: EARLY CRITICAL ASSESSMENTS

Nearly every account of Lydgate's critical fortunes includes the deadening judgements of Joseph Ritson, who in 1802 famously branded Lydgate 'this voluminous, prosaick, and driveling monk'.[9] However, even those who incline towards Ritson's views concede that responses to the poet have not always been so dyspeptic: indeed, the disjunction between early popularity and subsequent dismissal (or ignorance) is one of the enigmas that still bewilders Lydgate study.[10] Contemporary readers and poets were almost unanimous in their praise of Lydgate's achievements: Dunbar's 'monk of Bery' (the fit companion of Chaucer and Gower), 'Ludgate laureate' occupied a privileged position in the canon of poetic authority,[11] and this is a position others were quick to accord him also. Dunbar's references to Lydgate neatly exemplify the later medieval representation of the poet both as disciple of Chaucer and as illuminator of the English language: this early tradition of encomium lasts for about 120 years after Lydgate's death. At the beginning of the sequence stands the poet's immediate follower Benedict Burgh, whose poem 'In Praise of Lydgate' lists the Monk's literary merits (notably his 'Innate sapience' and 'verray price of excellence'), contrasting them with his own untalented efforts.[12]

---

[8] While there are certainly aspects of his verse which one might wish to criticize (such as its thinness of texture or metrical unevenness), many attacks on Lydgate reveal a wider prejudice against fifteenth-century poetic practice; to blame Lydgate for his encyclopedic aspirations, for his 'wearisome drone' (Pearsall 1966*a*: 220), or for being more of 'a pedantic scholar . . . a Holcot, a Trivet or a Whethamstede' than a Chaucer (Pearsall 1977: 230), is in effect to criticize him for being medieval in the first place.   [9] Ritson (1802: 87).

[10] Edwards (1977; 1983: 15, 23, 26); Ellis (1811: 276–7: 'Few writers have been more admired by their contemporaries; yet none have been treated with more severity by modern critics.' Ellis concludes that Lydgate's popularity in the 200 years after his death was 'excessive and unbounded'.

[11] 'Lament for the Makaris' ('Timor mortis conturbat me'), l. 51; 'The Goldyn Targe', l. 262, in Dunbar ed. Kinsley (1979), 179, 37.

[12] 'In Praise of Lydgate', ll. 22, 24 in Lydgate ed. Steele (1894: xxxi–xxxii).

Towards the end of Lydgate's life (c.1448-9) the poet John Metham, observing that Lydgate was 'both a poyet and a clerk', also praises his aureation:

> Hys bokys endyted with termys off retoryk
> And halff chongyd Latyne, with conseytys off poetry
> And craffty imagynacionys off thingys fantastyk.[13]

The copyist John Shirley (ob.1456) is well known for his preservation and circulation of Chaucerian texts, and his commonplace books (namely Trinity College, Cambridge, MS R. 3. 20; BL MSS Additional 16165 and Harley 2255; Bodleian, MS Ashmole 59) are frequent repositories of Lydgate's poems as well as, of course, famously energetic rejoinders to Lydgate's more anti-feminist passages.[14] Shirley's doggerel readily praises the poet he did so much to popularize:

> *Lydegate* þe Munk cloþed in blacke
> Ijn his makyng þer is no lacke
>
> .   .   .   .   .   .
>
> Boþe with his laboure and his goode
> God wolde of nobles he hade ful his hoode.[15]

The Suffolk Augustinian Osbern Bokenham (c.1450) salutes 'Lytgate' as 'fresh rhetoryens' in his *Legendys* and is the first to slot Lydgate into an English poetic triumvirate.[16] George Ashby also speaks of Lydgate's role in joining Chaucer and Gower in extending the expressive and metrical range of the language, in his *Active Policy of a Prince* (c.1470):

> Primier poetes of this nacion,
> Embelysshing oure englisshe tendure algate,
> Firste finders to our consolacion
> Of fresshe, douce englisshe[17]

---

[13] *The Romance of Amoryus and Cleopes*, epilogue ll. 2197, 2193-5 in Metham ed. Craig (1916: 80).

[14] Hammond (1927: 79, 191-4; 1905; 1907); Brusendorff (1925: 453-71); Schirmer (1952, trans. 1961: 251-3); Doyle (1961); Pearsall (1970: 73-6); Edwards (1983: 19-21). See also the sections on Shirley and Lydgate in Lerer (1993: 36, 47-8, 55-6, 116, 120-43).   [15] Hammond (1927: 196).

[16] Bokenham, *Legendys of Hooly Wummen*, ll. 416-17, 1403-4, 4058, 10,532-3, in Bokenham ed. Serjeantson (1938).

[17] *Active Policy*, ll. 2-5 in Ashby ed. Bateson (1899: 13).

Similarly, Caxton acknowledges the superior skill of Lydgate in his epilogue to the second book of *The Recuyell of the Histories of Troye* (c.1471) when he refers to the *Troy Book*:

that worshifull [*sic*] 7 religyous man dan Iohn lidgate monke of Burye dide translate hit but late after whos werke I fere to take vpon me that am not worthy to bere his penner 7 ynke horne after hym.[18]

Caxton is equally effusive in his version of the *Book of Courtesye* when he regrets Lydgate's death ('Pety hit is that suche a man shulde die') and commends Lydgate's works to his young reader:

Redith is volumes that ben so large and wyde
Souereynly sitte in sadnesse of sentence,
Elumynede wyth colouris fresshe on euery syde,
Hit passith my wytte; I haue no eloquence
To yeue hym lawde aftir his excellence.[19]

If Burgh is Lydgate's most devoted follower, then Stephen Hawes joins Caxton in being among his most fulsome. In his *Passetyme of Pleasure* (1503) he repeatedly praises Lydgate's eloquence, seeing him as 'the moste dulcet sprynge | Of famous rethoryke', and Hawes is held not only to have known much of Lydgate's verse by heart but also to have entertained Henry VII with his recitations of it.[20] Hawes also marks the revival of Burgh's tradition of regarding 'master Lidgate' as a wise author of valuable counsels when he carefully expounds the meaning of the *Fall* as a reflection on 'mutabylyte'.[21] Equally, he differentiates the three poetic giants in his *The Example of Vertu* as follows:

O prudent Gower! . . . O noble Chauser! . . . O vertuous
Lydgat much sentencyous.[22]

The model of 'sentencyous' Lydgate quickly takes root and coexists alongside the tradition of Dunbar's 'angel-mouth[ed]' stylist 'most mellifluate':[23] in the prologue to his *The Complaint*

---

[18] Caxton ed. Crotch (1928: 6). Caxton printed Lydgate's 'Churl and Bird', 'Horse, Goose and Sheep', and *Temple* in 1477, and the *Pilgrimage* and *Life of Oure Lady* in 1483 and 1484 (Blake 1969: 70-2, 163-8, and *passim*; 1985).

[19] *Courtesye*, ll. 374, 386-90 in Caxton ed. Furnivall (1868).

[20] Hawes ed. Mead (1928: l. 1373); see also ll. 26-35, 1317-407 for references to the triumvirate.   [21] Ibid. ll. 1345-51; Hammond (1927: 96).

[22] Hawes ed. Gluck and Morgan (1974: 3).

[23] 'Targe', l. 265, in Dunbar ed. Kinsley (1979), 37.

of A Lover's Life (1509) Thomas Feylde, describing Chaucer as 'pleasaunt and meruayllous' and Gower as 'herde and delycyous', says that Lydgate's 'workes are fruytefull and sentencyous, | Who of his books hathe redde the fyne | He will hym call a famous rethorycyne.'[24]

However, there are dissident voices in these early years also. An anonymous 'Reproof to Lydgate', surviving only in Bodleian Library, MS Fairfax 16 (fos. 325^r–327^r), spends nine *Fall* stanzas (*ababbcc*) taking the Monk, who would otherwise be a worthy successor to Chaucer, to task for his hostility towards women and the arts of love. Against the backdrop of short courtly love poems the writer attacks Lydgate's views as 'an eresy':

> Wher as ye say that loue ys but dotage   (fo. 326^v)
> Of verey reson that may not be trew
> ffor euery man that hath a good corage
> Must louer be thys wold I that ye knew
>
> .   .   .   .   .
>
> A fye for schame O thou envyous man   (fo. 327^r)
> Thynk whens thou came and whider to repayr
> Hastow not sayd eke that these women can
> Laugh and loue nat parde yt is not fair
> Thy corupt speche enfectyth alle the air
> Knoke on thy brest repent now and euer
> Ayen therwyth and say thou saydyst yt neuer
>
> .   .   .   .   .
>
> O thou vnhappy man go hyde thy face[25]

More famously, Lydgate finds a critic in John Skelton, who cruelly parodies his more encrusted aureation in 'Garlande of Laurell', and whose Jane Scrope says of the Monk that

> It is dyffuse to fynde
> The sentence of his mynde
>
> .   .   .   .
>
> He wryteth to haute.

[24] Feylde ed. Dibdin (1818; pp. unnumbered).

[25] 'Reproof', ll. 36–9, 64–70, 75. See Hammond (1927: 198–201) for a printing of the whole poem and a summary of the theories of authorship. It should perhaps be said that Lydgate is usually only anti-feminist when forced to be so by his sources; indeed, at one stage of the *Fall* he omits misogynist comment given by 'Bocace' at the end of I. ch. 17, and later defends good women from criticism (I. 6707–34; see also his treatment of the remarried Cleopatra with that of Premierfait: *Des Cas* VI ch. 4/*Fall* VI. 1352–8), although he does, of course, later omit a chapter on noble women (*Des Cas* VIII ch. 23). (See Renoir 1961a; Edwards 1970b, 1972b.)

Skelton's criticism here is not solely levelled at Lydgate, for he later also dismisses Gower as being 'of no value'.[26] The movement away from late medieval encomium in the sixteenth century coincides with a new ambivalence towards the poet; formal 'academic' responses to Lydgate begin against the backdrop of mid-Tudor religious conflict and enthusiastic activity at the presses. (After Pynson's *editio princeps* of 1494 the *Fall* was next printed by Pynson in 1527, then, in the reign of Mary, by Tottell in 1554, and twice by Wayland in ?1554.)[27] John Leland's *Commentary* (c.1545), which includes the first attempt to reconstruct a biography of Chaucer, makes no mention of Lydgate,[28] but the radical Protestant John Bale's 1548 *Index* (which often draws closely on Leland's work) includes a section on the Monk.[29] The tradition of 'sentencyous' Lydgate's regiminal (that is to say, offering political advice to rulers) respectability gains strength in the middle decades of the sixteenth century; Bishop Hugh Latimer omits Lydgate from his 1549 attack on the reading of idle literature (such as *The Canterbury Tales* and stories of Robin Hood), although this can hardly be supposed to grant everything Lydgate wrote a tacit Protestant imprimatur. Comfortably into the reign of Elizabeth, Meredith Hanmer's 1577 translation of Eusebius, *The Auncient Ecclesiasticall Histories*, is able to celebrate 'the Monke of Burie full of good stories', but does so with praise that is significantly qualified. Lydgate may be among the most advisable kinds of secular literature (and much to be preferred to 'the stories of Kinge *Arthur*: The Monstrous fables of *Garagantua* . . . Reinard the Fox with many other infortunate treatises and amorous toies'), but is nonetheless only a poor substitute for godly reading of early Christian writings.[30] Only four years after Hanmer, John Lawson concedes the 'wordye

---

[26] 'Garlande', ll. 386–441, 'Phyllyp Sparowe', ll. 804–7, 812, 785, in Skelton ed. Scattergood (1983: 322–4, 91–2).

[27] Respectively *STC* 3175, 3176, 3177, 3177.5, and 3178.

[28] Leland (1709).

[29] Bale, ed. Poole with Bateson (1902, repr. 1990: 228–31). Interestingly, Bale's list of Lydgate's work includes a 'De arturio rege' (which must certainly be *Fall* VIII. 2661–3164), possibly reflecting the popularity of the Arthur section of the longer poem (see Lydgate ed. Schick 1891: cli).

[30] 'Epistle Dedicatorie' to *The Auncient Ecclesiasticall Histories of the First Six Hundred Yeares After Christ* (1577), pp. unnumbered (see Spurgeon 1920, rev. 1925: i. 112–13).

praise and everlastynge meade' of 'maister John lydgaite ... |
Thoo he was a monnke'.[31] William Webbe in 1586 is the first
to voice openly an arch-Protestant distrust of the Benedictine
writer:

Chawcer ... alwayes accounted the God of English Poets ... Neere in
time vnto him was Lydgate a Poet, surely for good proportion of his
verse, and meetely currant style, as the time affoorded comparable with
Chawcer, yet more occupied in supersticious and odde matters, then was
requesite in so goode a wytte: which, though he handled them com-
mendably, yet the matters themselves beeing not so commendable, hys
estimation hath beene the lesse[32]

Ownership of a copy of the *Fall* (now MS Bodley 263) by the
high-profile recusant Sir Francis Englefield supplies further
evidence of an increasingly sectarian readership of the poet.[33] It
is not surprising, then, that Philip Sidney, himself allied with the
Protestant Leicester/Essex faction at court, should fragment the
poetic triumvirate in his *An Apology for Poetry* (printed 1595),
mentioning Chaucer and Gower but passing over Lydgate in
silence[34] nor that the highly partisan 1595 tract against divination
and astrology by the anonymous 'W. C.' (now thought to be one
William Covell), *Polimanteia*, should in its accompanying 'Letter
from England to her Three Daughters' provide the first example of
the subtly patronizing assessment of Lydgate that has since become
the modern norm, saying that Lydgate wrote as 'simplie and pure-
lie' as his age would allow, but that his 'vnrefined tongue [is] farre
shorte of the excellencie of this age'.[35] The falling-off from
Richard Sherry's praise of Lydgate in 1550 as a proponent of the
very best style is striking.[36]

Appetite for Lydgate does not, however, die out with the onset of
the Reformation. Although there are understandably few references

---

[31] *Lawsons Orchet* (see Spurgeon 1920, rev. 1925: i. 120).
[32] Webbe (1586: pp. unnumbered).
[33] See ch. 6, pp. 254–9 for a fuller discussion.
[34] Sidney ed. Shepherd (1965/73: 96). Puttenham (c.1584–8) describes '*Lydgat*
[as] a translatour onely and no deuiser of that which he wrate, but one that wrate
in good verse' (Puttenham ed. Willcock and Walker 1936: 62).
[35] Covell (1595: pp. unnumbered). Covell here, interestingly, disagrees with
Gabriel Harvey, who found Chaucer and Lydgate 'much better learned than owre
moderne poets' (see Spurgeon 1920, rev. 1925: i. 127).
[36] *A Treatise of Schemes and Tropes very profytable for the better vnderstanding of good authors* (1550–1) (STC 22428), 'Epistle', fo. Aiii (see Renoir 1967: 4).

to Lydgate's aureate and Marian writings, his ethical and regiminal works—the *Fall of Princes* in particular—and his chronicles remain in vogue: indeed, the *Mirror for Magistrates* group of texts manifests a lively and creative engagement with the *Fall* in the middle decades of the century. So it is that the early years of the seventeenth century produce a modernized version of the *Troy Book* (as *The Life and Death of Hector*, previously thought to be by Thomas Heywood)[37] and, in the same year, Thomas Freeman includes Lydgate in his praise of the philosophical stature of the members of the English poetic triumvirate, claiming that they 'equal'd all the sages | Since these three knew to turne perdy | The Scru-pin of Phylysophy | As well as they'.[38] In 1615 and 1624 Lydgate appears among the poets in masques by Jonson and Webster.[39] Openly Catholic encomium finds its voice in 1619 when the Wykehamist recusant John Pits, following Bale, adds a short account of Lydgate's life and works in his *Relationum historicarum de rebus Anglicis*:

Erat autem non solum elegans Poeta, & Rhetor disertus, verum etiam Mathematicus expertus, Philosophus acutus, & Theologus non contemnendus. Multum etiam ornatus patriae linguae contulit, imitatus in hoc Chaucerum nostrum.

(He was moreover not only an elegant poet and eloquent rhetorician, but also a proven mathematician, acute philosopher, and was not to be scorned as a theologian. He also contributed much of eloquence to the language of our native land, having imitated our Chaucer in this.)[40]

The depiction of Lydgate as a theologian here only confirms the impression that responses to the poet at this period were to some extent sectarian: the question of how great an influence was wielded by such accounts of the poet is an intriguing one. It does *not* seem to be the case that the Monk of Bury ever became solely associated with any one ecclesiastical party, favoured though it seems he was by those who remained loyal to the old religion.

[37] *The Life and Death of Hector* (1614) (*STC* 5581.5, 13346a) (see Rouse 1928; Ellis 1811: 298).
[38] 'Rvnne, And a great Cast. The Second Bowle', epigram 14 in Freeman (1614) (*STC* 11370).
[39] Jonson, *The Golden Age Restored* (*STC* 14751), (Jonson ed. Herford et al. 1925–52: vii. 425) (Lydgate, Chaucer, Gower, More, and Sidney); Webster, *Monuments of Honour* (*STC* 25175) (Webster ed. Lucas 1927: iv. 319).
[40] Pits (1619: 632–4).

Indeed, it is unlikely that Pits's own views (possibly because they had been printed in France) affected readers of Lydgate widely.[41]

Despite some notably sympathetic appraisals of the poet, Lydgate's fortunes wane during the period of the Enlightenment. Thomas Chatterton shows an idiosyncratically enthusiastic regard (his 'Rowley' addresses a 'Song to Ælla' to the Monk); Thomas Gray draws attention to a quality not before acknowledged in the writer—his manipulation of pathos—but tempers his praise of Lydgate's 'stiller kind of majesty' with a measured awareness of his weaknesses ('They loved, I will not say tediousness, but length and a train of circumstances in a narration').[42] Thomas Warton, similarly, recognizes that the Monk can be 'verbose and diffuse . . . tedious and languid', but commends his descriptive skill, remarking that 'no poet seems to have possessed a greater versatility of talents' and saluting Lydgate as a poet not only 'of his monastery, but of the world in general'.[43]

This background of comparative neglect makes the survival of an eighteenth-century sales catalogue in the Bodleian Library (Mus. Bibl. III. 8°. 187) all the more interesting. The catalogue, entitled *Bibliotheca Westiana, a Catalogue of the Curious and truly Valuable Library of the late James West*, lists the lots of a public auction held in Covent Garden over several days in March and April 1773 and enables us to chart with accuracy the extent of Lydgate's decline.[44] Marginal annotation in the Bodleian copy records the price raised by each lot and so fortuitously supplies a commercial reckoning of the perceived value of the books sold. Whereas a folio copy of Caxton's first print (undated, but presumably that of 1478) of Chaucer's *Works* (billed as 'the only

---

[41] In his account Pits corrects the widely held belief (which he attributes to Bishop Josephus Pamphilius) that Lydgate was an Augustinian canon, but the discredited view persists (see Phillips 1675: 113).

[42] 'Some Remarks on the Poems of John Lydgate', in Gray ed. Gosse (1884: i. 292, 397–402). Rowley's 'To Johne Ladgate' elicits Chatterton's reply, 'Lines by John Ladgate, A Priest in London' (Chatterton ed. Taylor and Hoover 1971: i. 60–3). Rowley has been described as a 'Bristol Lydgate' by Meyerstein (1930: 170). It must be admitted that Chatterton seems to have admired Lydgate on grounds of obscure medievalism—and for exactly the characteristics which lie behind Ritson's attack. A pseudo-Chattertonian pastiche appeared in *Literary Museum* (1789): 'Onne mie Maister Lydgate, his travellynge ynnto Fraunce'.

[43] Warton (1774–81: ii. 52–8). Warton echoes the Pits formula ('not only a poet and a rhetorician . . .'); it is coincidentally interesting that he was the first to unmask Chatterton's Rowley deception. [44] Paterson (1773).

perfect copy known in England') is sold on Saturday 10 April for
£42 15s. 6d. (and is 'Bought for the King'),[45] and copies of
Caxton's *Troylus* and 1483 print of *Confessio Amantis* reach £10
10s. and £9 9s. on the same day,[46] Lydgate raises rather less interest. Wynkyn de Worde's quarto of *The Temple of Glas* (which
attributes the poem to Hawes) is sold for eleven shillings, and on
Friday, 9 April the not inconsiderable Pynson 1527 and Wayland
(undated, but ?1554) prints of the *Fall* raise only £1 5s. and eleven
shillings respectively.[47] These prices gain significance when
comparison is made with more recent books: on the following
Monday *Sidney's Arcadia modernized by Mrs Stanley* (1725),
Spenser's *Works* (1679), and a third edition of Shakespeare of
1664 are sold for eleven shillings, fifteen shillings, and £1 12s.
respectively.[48] Financial valuation articulates an emerging canon-
ical hierarchy.

NINETEENTH-CENTURY ACADEMIC REVIVAL: THE IMPACT OF EMIL KOEPPEL

The nineteenth century opens with Ritson's blistering venomous
comments on Lydgate's 'stupid and fatigueing productions . . . and
their still more stupid and disgusting author'.[49] Elizabeth Barrett
Browning's praise of the poet ('when he ceased his singing, none
sang better; there was silence in the land'[50]) aside, popular evalu-
ations of Lydgate never recover from Ritson's diatribe. However,
the closing years of the nineteenth century see revived academic
study of Lydgate as the result (at least as regards the *Fall*) of a
renewed interest in Boccaccio. Attilio Hortis's 1879 *Studij sulle
opere latine del Boccaccio* (which included discussion of the
De casibus and, though its conclusions have been subsequently
challenged by Zaccaria, made an important contribution to

---

[45] Lot no. 2274 (p. 130).   [46] Lot nos. 2280 (p. 130), 2297 (p. 131).
[47] STC 3176 and 3177.5/3178: lot nos. 1684 (p. 104), 2104, and 2105 (p. 124).
In 1556 Sir William More of Loseley House, Surrey, records the price of four
shillings for his 1554 Tottell print (Bennett, 1950–1: 175).
[48] Lot nos. 2486, 2487, 2488 (p. 141).
[49] Ritson (1802: 88). Ritson also attacked Lydgate's 'leaden pen' over twenty
years earlier in 'A Historical Essay on the Origin and Progress of National
Song' (1783).   [50] Browning, 'The Book of the Poets' (1863: 121).

discussion of the dating of the two versions of the text[51]) had considerable influence on the most significant piece of writing of any length that has yet appeared on the *Fall*: Emil Koeppel's 1885 Munich thesis 'Laurents de Premierfait und John Lydgates Bearbeitungen von Boccaccios *De Casibus Virorum Illustrium.* Ein Beitrag zur Litteraturgeschichte des 15. Jahrhunderts'.[52] The significance of Koeppel's work has by no means been as widely recognized as would have been helpful: the situation has not been helped by the fact that the thesis was never published. Koeppel's work is not of importance for any aesthetic evaluation of the poem; indeed, in his claim that there is not a single ray of sunshine in the whole work Koeppel takes a place among the most curmudgeonly of Lydgate's critics.[53] Instead, the value of the thesis is exactly in its careful discussion of questions which had never before been asked about the text and in its refreshing willingness to treat the relation between the *Des Cas des nobles hommes et femmes* and the *Fall* as worthy of serious analysis.

Koeppel is the first to provide an assessment of the significance of Laurent's two versions of the French text and to catalogue the French author's characteristic alterations of the Latin work: its addition of the very circumstantial detail (historical, mythological, geographical) and exegesis (e.g. in its reorganizations of faulty chronology, etymologies, and genealogies) that does so much to distend Boccaccio's dense Latin text into the encyclopedic treatise which was to confront Lydgate, yet which also invests the *Des Cas* with claims to factual accuracy and increases its value as a work of reference. His list of some of Laurent's misunderstandings of the Latin and his catalogue of many of the sources for Laurent's additions to the text are evidence of his careful scholarship.[54] His comments on the Frenchman's use of Ovid have, in particular, been ignored at some cost by twentieth-century critics of the *Fall*: I have endeavoured to assess some of the wider implications of his

[51] Hortis (1879: 133 n. 1, 134 nn. 1 and 2).

[52] Koeppel (1885: 37), for example, draws on Hortis's discussion of the question of Lydgate's knowledge of Boccaccio in which he raises the question of certain passages seeming closer to Boccaccio than to Premierfait.

[53] Koeppel (1885: 3). In his obituary of Koeppel, Friedrich Brie celebrates the positivistic disregard Koeppel had for subjective questions of hypothesis, ideology, or aesthetics, and praises him for being a master of detail rather than of 'zusammenfassende Darstellungen' ('overarching interpretations').

[54] Koeppel (1885: 10–35).

comments in my discussion of Lydgate's understanding of the workings of Fortune and tragedy.[55] Koeppel's examination of Laurent's ecclesiastical bias has similarly failed to receive the attention it deserves.

Koeppel's introduction to Lydgate's reworking of Laurent is a masterful rhetorical display intended to induce feelings of dismay at what lies ahead:

Nicht ohne Mühe, gewiß ohne Genuß, durchlesen wir Laurents schwerfällige Paraphrase der Schrift des Boccaccio; der Gedanke aber, dieses ungefüge, langweilige Sammelwerk in Verse umsetzen zu müssen, würde wohl auch dem mechanischsten aller modernen Reimschmiede Entsetzen einflossen.

(We read through Laurent's ponderous paraphrase of Boccaccio's text not without some exhaustion and certainly without enjoyment; but the thought of having to translate this clumsy and boring catalogue into verse would probably fill even the most mechanical of modern poetasters with horror.) (p. 35)

What does follow, however, is over one hundred pages of sensitive and thorough analysis of Lydgate's sources (classical, biblical, Judaic, and vernacular) and his manipulations of the French text. Bogus critical canards are calmly laid to rest (especially that of Lydgate's Italian travels and knowledge of Italian, current at least since Pits) and Lydgate's antipathy towards the classical cult of noble suicide is demonstrated (pp. 76–83, 103–4). Ultimately, however, Koeppel's attitude towards the English poet is ambivalent; harbouring few illusions about Lydgate's poetic merit or accuracy in factual detail (speaking of his 'gewohnter Ungenauigkeit' and demonstrating his misapplication of biblical and other material),[56] he also shows respect for Lydgate's learning and extraordinary breadth of reading (describing him as 'einer der bestunterrichteten Männer seiner Zeit und seines Landes').[57] In the final analysis, Koeppel disagrees with those who dismiss the poem as being of little value (p. 111).

It is clear that the inaccessibility of Koeppel's thesis has been responsible for its eclipse; I have traced his arguments in some

---

[55] Ibid. 25–6.
[56] e.g. Lydgate's misreading of his source, Aulus Gellius, in his story of Marcus Manlius at *Fall* IV. 260–2, his introduction of coffins into the Constantine legend, and his frequent numerical errors (ibid. 72, 73; see 53, 60, 65, 77, 90).
[57] Ibid. 46. For Lydgate *contra paganos* see Dwyer (1978).

detail here in an attempt to reinstate him as the pioneering critic of the *Fall of Princes*. Koeppel's contemporaries freely acknowledge his pre-eminent position in the field; on his death in 1917, Friedrich Brie—himself author of an important but forgotten article on Lydgate—asserted the ground-breaking character of both Koeppel's thesis and of his 1884 study of the sources of the *Siege of Thebes*.[58] Furthermore, just as he himself had been influenced by Hortis and Julius Zupitza, Koeppel's work provided the catalyst for others' research into Lydgate, much of which was undertaken by German scholars working in a positivist tradition.[59] In 1891 Josef Schick, aged just 22, edited the first Lydgate text to be issued by the Early English Text Society, the *Temple of Glas*. In a long introductory essay Schick attempts the first chronology of Lydgate's works and includes a re-dating of the poem which takes issue with Koeppel's belief that it was written between 1424 and 1433.[60] Schick's suggested 1430–8/9 (not, it should be pointed out, argued very convincingly for the *terminus ante quem*) has since been regarded as the period within which the *Fall* was produced, even though Schick's combination of analysis and guesswork is rarely acknowledged as the source of this particular scholarly insight (pp. civ–cvii). Though Schick reveals his attitude towards the *Fall* when he describes his 'terror' (p. cvii) in the face of the poem's bulk, his importance in the development of Lydgate criticism is that he holds this opinion without the vitriol of earlier critics: indeed, he attacks Ritson for this reason ('He found it easier to revile the monk than to know him') (p. cliii).

Interest in Lydgate, however, is otherwise in these years confined to continental Europe, and sometimes even then only as the corollary of work on Premierfait or Boccaccio. Important work was done on the French reception of Boccaccio's *De casibus* by Henri Hauvette at the start of the twentieth century.[61] Hauvette extended Hortis's remarks on the existence of differing readings of certain passages of the *De casibus* into the hypothesis that these in fact represented two distinct redactions of the work (the versions

---

[58] Brie (1917–18: 467).

[59] Zupitza, editor of *Guy of Warwick*, *Aesop*, and the *Fabula duorum mercatorum*, is credited by Koeppel for encouraging him to research into Lydgate (Koeppel 1885: 112).

[60] Schick seems not to have been familiar with Koeppel's thesis (Lydgate ed. Schick 1891: xiii, c n. 1, cv).   [61] Hauvette (1901: 279–97).

which are now dated as 1356–60 and 1373, and which I shall for convenience label respectively A and B).[62] Furthermore, Hauvette is also the first to notice from the evidence of extant manuscripts that Boccaccio's extended B-version seems to have been far *less* popular than the curt A-version it was intended to supplant:

Ce que l'histoire de ces remaniements présente de singulier, c'est que, contrairement à l'intention évidente de l'auteur, la seconde rédaction n'a nullement fait oublier la première; bien plus, la première rédaction paraît avoir été beaucoup plus répandue, surtout hors d'Italie.

(What is unusual about the history of these revisions is the fact that, contrary to the author's obvious intention, the second version in no way supplanted the first; moreover, the first version seems to have been the much better known, especially outside Italy.)[63]

Hauvette extended this work in his Latin doctoral thesis on Premierfait's renderings of the *Decameron* and the *De casibus*,[64] in a series of articles, and also in a full-length study on the Italian author.[65] Hauvette in many ways continues Koeppel's pioneering work to reinstate the Latin works of Boccaccio in general (all of which he notes have been 'longtemps abandonnées aux vers et à la poussière des bibliothèques'), and the French translation of the *De casibus* in particular, as worthy of serious academic attention.[66]

THE TWENTIETH CENTURY

A number of research projects at this time testify to the continued influence of Koeppel at Munich, and several German editions of Lydgate's shorter works are published in this period.[67] This

[62] Ibid. 282–8: see Hortis (1879: 127). The datings are taken from Serafini-Sauli (1982: 102): other critics differ (e.g. Gathercole 1956: 304). Cf. Vittorio Zaccaria's introduction to the Zaccaria/Ricci edition of the B-version of the *De casibus* (Boccaccio 1983: xv–xx), and also Ricci (1985). It is useful to note that the arguments for the dating of the two versions are not as simple as Ricci assumes, and that the Mainardo B-version dedication is found in 12 of the surviving 27 A-version manuscripts (see Zaccaria 1977–8). [63] Hauvette (1901: 289).
[64] 'De Laurentio de Primofato qui primus Joannis Boccacci opera quaedam Gallice transtulit ineunte seculo XV' (Ph. D. thesis, 1903).
[65] See Hauvette (1903b; 1907; 1908; 1909; 1914: 347–58, 391–6).
[66] Hauvette (1903b: 1). Regrettably, Hauvette's work always stops short of studying the *Fall of Princes* and he seems not to have known Koeppel's thesis.
[67] Perzl (Ph. D. thesis, 1911: 9); Werner (Ph. D. thesis, 1914); Beutner (Ph. D. thesis, 1914). Editions include Carl Horstmann's of 'S. Giles', 'S. Margaret', and

burgeoning interest in Lydgate's work is matched in the English-speaking world by the editions of the EETS which steadily appear from 1891 (the year of Schick's *Glas*) to 1935,[68] by Henry MacCracken's 1907 Harvard thesis, his establishment of the Lydgate canon in his edition of the minor poems,[69] and his 1911 edition of *The Serpent of Division*,[70] and in 1927 by Eleanor Prescott Hammond's *English Verse between Chaucer and Surrey*.[71] Even among all this productivity, however, it is noticeable that Lydgate's longest work is the last to be furnished with an edition.

Until the 1920s work on Lydgate was necessarily preoccupied by the essential foundation-laying of establishing the canon and printing accurate texts of the poems. Yet aside from the editorial activity, two further articles emerge from Germany before the Second World War which remain of significance for Lydgate scholarship, but which have not received the kind of attention they deserve. Max Förster's notice in *Deutsche Literaturzeitung* in 1924, however, marks a return for *Fall* criticism to the sort of interpretative and source-based response to the English poem which Koeppel offered thirty-nine years earlier. Partly in response to the first volume of Bergen's EETS text, Förster describes the poem as a reflection on earthly instability (a manifestation of 'ein Lieblingsthema mittelalterlich-klerikaler Lebensanschauung') and offers some preliminary remarks on the differences between the Latin, French, and English texts. Boccaccio is seen as a 'hot-blooded

SS Edmund and Fremund in *Altenglische Legenden: neue Folge* (1881: 371–5, 446–53, 376–445), and his *S. Albon und Amphabel, ein Legendenepos* (1882). Zupitza and Schleich edited *Lydgate's Fabula duorum mercatorum* (1897).

[68] EETS ES 60 (Lydgate ed. Schick, *Temple of Glas*, 1891): 66 (Lydgate ed. Steele, *Lydgate's and Burgh's Secrees*, 1894): 69 (Lydgate ed. Triggs, *The Assembly of Gods*, 1896): 77, 83, 92 (Lydgate ed. Furnivall and Locock, *Pilgrimage of the Life of Man*, 1899, 1901, 1904): 80 (Lydgate ed. Glauning, *Two Nightingale Poems*, 1900): 84 and 89 (Lydgate ed. Sieper, *Reson and Sensuallyte*, 1901, 1903): 97, 103, 106, 126 (Lydgate ed. Bergen, *Troy Book*, 1906, 1908, 1910, 1935): 107 and OS 192 (Lydgate ed. MacCracken, *Minor Poems*, 1911, 1934): 108 and 125 (Lydgate ed. Erdmann, *Siege of Thebes*, 1911, 1930): 121, 122, 123, 124 (Lydgate ed. Bergen, *Fall of Princes*, 1924, 1924, 1924, 1927): and 181 (Lydgate ed. Warren, *The Dance of Death*, 1931).

[69] EETS ES 107 (Lydgate ed. MacCracken 1911*b*: v–lviii). For previous attempts at formulating the canon see Hammond (1927: 99).

[70] Lydgate ed. MacCracken (1911*a*).

[71] Hammond (1927: 77–187). Hammond (whose 1898 Chicago doctoral thesis was on *The Dance of Death*) is also highly critical of Lydgate as a blunderer, digressive, pedantic, and verbose, with 'little or no structural sense' (ibid. 80); but see her important articles on the poet (Hammond 1914; 1927–8).

Mediterranean', his severe and incautious intolerance of the failings of princes as a product of his republicanism. By contrast, Premierfait's pusillanimity is seen as a reflex of his dependence on his royal patron, Jean, duke of Berry.[72] Whereas Boccaccio's text is seen as 'a beacon to shake humanity from its indolence' ('ein Fanal, die Menschheit aus ihrer Trägheit aufzurütteln'), Premierfait must tread more carefully:

Dementsprechend tritt er [der nordfranzösische Klerikaler] den Großen mit Ehrerbietung gegenüber und ist mit den bestehenden sozialen und politischen Verhältissen im Grunde einverstanden. Wo seine Vorlage von Tyrannei redet, wagt er kaum zu tadeln

(Accordingly, he—the northern French cleric—regards powerful men with deference and basically agrees with existing social and political conditions. When the original text discusses tyranny, he hardly ever dares to voice a rebuke)

Lydgate, however, treads the middle path in his social criticism, his own royal patronage not inhibiting his criticism of the vices of the great:

Das hindert ihn aber nicht, den Großen mit männlichen Stolz gegenüberzutreten, ihnen Ratschläge zu erteilen und, wenn nötig, sie auch zu tadeln. Niemals so leidenschaftlich kühn wie Boccaccio, ist er aber auch niemals so untertänig ergeben wie der Franzose.

(That does not prevent him, however, from confronting powerful men with manly pride and giving them pieces of advice and, if necessary, even rebuking them. Never as passionately bold in this as Boccaccio, neither is he ever as submissively humble as the Frenchman.) (col. 1945)

Lydgate's voice is defined as an explicitly clerical one, his even-handed treatment of the sins of nobility springing from his belief in the superior authority of the Church.[73]

Friedrich Brie follows Förster in 1929 with a longer discussion of the relationship between the medieval and the ancient in the

[72] Förster (1924): 'Der heißblütige ... trat den Großen dieser Welt mit Feindschaft und bitterer Verachtung gegenüber, ohne jede Sympathie oder auch nur Achtung. Ihrer Herrschsucht, Habgier und Sinnlichkeit, ihrem Stolz und ihrer Rachsucht glaubte er alle Übel der Welt zuschreiben zu dürfen.' ('The hot-blooded [Boccaccio] ... approaches the powerful men of this world with enmity and bitter contempt, with neither sympathy nor even respect. He believed all evils of the world could be attributed to their domineering nature, greed and sensuality, their pride, and their vindictiveness') (col. 1944).
[73] For a fuller treatment of this, and related, issues see Ch. 4.

Fall. In many ways this is the first extended critical discussion of some of Lydgate's central ideas and characteristic attitudes: though its audience seems to have been small, it is still one of the finest and most balanced pieces of *literary* criticism of the *Fall*. As his starting point Brie laments the fact that the thirty years since Schick's edition have not fulfilled the expectations in Lydgate research which that volume seemed to promise; he then moves on to demonstrate the ways in which Lydgate's poem engages with a branch of the humanistic project, here represented by his attitude towards pagan antiquity:

> Wir hoffen zeigen zu können, daß seine Bedeutung eine größere ist, als die Kritik bisher anzunehmen geneigt war, mit anderen Worten, daß wir in dem FP einen der wichtigsten Meilensteine auf dem langen Wege von Chaucer bis zu Thomas Morus vor uns haben.

> (We hope to be able to show that its importance is greater than criticism had hitherto tended to assume; in other words, that in the *Fall* we have before us one of the most important milestones on the long road from Chaucer to Thomas More.)[74]

Although more recent opinion might cast doubt on some of Brie's assumptions (in particular, perhaps, the view that attitudes towards antiquity can always be so easily focused along clerical/lay coordinates),[75] his argument is a timely caution against the more pejorative critical pigeon-holing of Lydgate as 'typical of his age' that can so easily forestall not only further critical enquiry, but academic interest altogether.[76] Brie's comments on Lydgate's playful erudition ('eine Spielerei mit Gelehrsamkeit') and his discussion of the *Fall* in terms of its innovative qualities ('gegenüber allen früheren Dichtungen in englischer Sprache stellt der FP etwas Neues und Epochemachendes dar') blow a fresh breeze through the history of Lydgate scholarship: his lively and open-minded appreciation of the *Fall* strikes a note in formal academic criticism which recalls the enthusiasm of Hawes and which has never been

---

[74] Brie (1929: 262).
[75] Ibid. 265–6. See Reuss (1909) for the view that Lydgate's Benedictinism ruined his ability to respond to nature.
[76] Brie (1929: 261–2): 'neuere Kritik hat sogar behauptet, daß er seine Zeit so zusammengefaßt habe wie Pope oder Samuel Johnson die ihrige' ('more recent criticism has even claimed that he represented his time just as Pope or Samuel Johnson did theirs'); see Pearsall's comparison of the medieval poet and his humanist patron (1970: 224).

heard before—or, indeed, since.[77] Brie's discussion of pagan virtue, and of the presentation of Caesar, and his rejoinder to Koeppel's remarks on Lydgate's attitude towards noble suicide are significant and impressively argued positions which have deserved a better hearing.[78]

Even though the volume of published work on Lydgate still bears very little comparison with the body of research into Chaucer, Gower, or—more recently—Hoccleve, interest in Lydgate gradually grew in the second half of the last century, even if at first much of this discussion was descriptive and rather cursory and (until the very final years) the impression was still that of lone individuals working in a landscape of indifference or hostility. The *Troy Book* and *Siege of Thebes* have attracted more attention than the *Fall*,[79] and Premierfait's prose translation has profited from far fuller analysis than the English poem it inspired.[80] Despite the publication of four book-length studies of the poet (by Walter Schirmer, Alain Renoir, Derek Pearsall, and Lois Ebin),[81] a clutch of new editions, and a bio-bibliography in this period,[82] only three

[77] Brie (1929: 267, 268). See pp. 293–4, where Brie points out Lydgate's 'geistiger Freiheit' ('intellectual freedom').

[78] In my view Brie goes a little too far in his claims that the poem is the *first* in English to present pagan heroism on its own terms and that 'der FP unzweifelhaft das erste Werk in englischer Sprache ist, das antike und frühmittelalterliche Geschichte in leidlicher Vollständigkeit und mit Ansätzen zu einer humanistischen Auffassung bietet' ('the *Fall* is unquestionably the first work in the English language which presents antiquity and early medieval history in reasonable completeness and with the first signs of a humanist outlook') (1929: 273): see work on this topic by Minnis (1982) and Spearing (1985). Elsewhere Brie usefully argues for the Monk's understanding of the value of ancient ethics of shame and courage (1929: 284).

[79] Ayers, Parr, Patterson, and Renoir wrote in this period on *Thebes* (the last submitting a doctoral thesis in 1955 at Harvard), Atwood and Benson on the *Troy Book*. The shorter poems received more attention than the *Fall*: Mooney has written on the 'Kings of England' (1989); Hagen (1990) took the *Pilgrimage* as her starting point.

[80] Gathercole produced an edition of the first book of the 1409 *Des Cas* in 1968 and fourteen articles on Premierfait in the period from 1954 to 1973. Other key articles are those by Purkis (1949; 1955), Simone (1971), and Morse (1980).

[81] Schirmer (1952, trans. 1961), Renoir (1967), Pearsall (1970; 1997), Ebin (1985). See also Schirmer (1950; 1951) and Ebin (1977; 1984).

[82] *Life of Our Lady*, (Lydgate ed. Lauritis, Klinefelter, and Gallagher 1961); SS *Albon and Amphibalus* (Lydgate ed. Reinecke 1974, repr. 1985), from his 1960 Harvard doctoral thesis; van der Westhuizen also edited *Albon* in 1974. Unpublished editions of *Edmund* have been offered as theses by Schofield (MA thesis, University of London, 1957) and Miller (Ph. D. thesis, 1967). Norton-Smith's Clarendon Press anthology appeared in 1966.

articles (those by Johannes Kleinstück, Richard Dwyer, and David
Lawton) on the *Fall* as a literary text have approached the sophistication of Brie's 1929 essay.[83] However, vital bibliographical and
codicological work was undertaken by A. S. G. Edwards in the
decade from 1969 to 1978,[84] and 1975 saw Tamotsu Kurose's
analysis of the epithets used in the poem to qualify Fortune. It is
incidentally noticeable that Lydgate has been increasingly popular
with church historians.[85]

REHABILITATION

By far the most influential discussion to focus on Lydgate in
the past twenty years is that by David Lawton on 'dullness' and
fifteenth-century poets: if any single article can be said to have
kick-started the rehabilitation of these writers, Lawton's must
surely be it. Unmasking professions of poetic incompetence not
merely as conventional *captatio benevolentiae* modesty claims but
also as shrewd political self-defence mechanisms, Lawton considers
the political voices of Hoccleve and Lydgate in their public and
advisory poetry, urging for a recontextualization of Lydgate's
work in particular.[86] Aware that the image of 'Lydgate as hero'
may strike many students as rather odd, Lawton touches on the
'potentially dangerous' *de casibus* genre and hints at Lydgate's
ambivalent attitudes towards his patron.[87]
    In the wake of Lawton's essay there has been considerable
interest in later medieval vernacular writing that locates itself at
the intersection between literature and political power; issues such
as the attitudes of poets to their patrons, or the relationship
between texts and the uneasy Lancastrian dynasty they would
appear to serve, have attracted growing attention. Lydgate has

---

[83] Kleinstück, 'Die mittelalterliche Tragödie in England' (1956); Dwyer,
'Arthur's Stellification in the *Fall of Princes* (1978: 155–71). (Dwyer also includes
brief comment on Lydgate in his *Boethian Fictions* (1976: 35–49)); Lawton,
'Dullness and the Fifteenth Century' (1987); see Lawton (1985: 130.)
[84] Other important Lydgate manuscript work is that undertaken by Dorsten
(1960), Robbins (1967-8), Scott (1968), Doyle and Pace (1975), Seymour (1985),
Horrall (1988), and Keiser (1991).
[85] e.g. Knowles (1955: ii. 273–6); Rubin (1991: 28, 100, 103, 106, 152, 158–9,
229–32, 238); Duffy (1992: 173, 178, 223, 253, 304). See also Heale (D. Phil.
thesis, 1994).   [86] Lawton (1987: 787, 777–9).
[87] Ibid. 782–7.

benefited from this line of enquiry. Seth Lerer has offered an innovative approach to Lydgate's clerkly understanding of literary history and *auctoritas* and his engagement with his political milieu.[88] Lee Patterson's work on the poet's complicity with the world of the court suggested that Lydgate's role as an apologist for the Lancastrian machine is compromised by his scepticism about the legitimacy of the dynasty. Arguing persuasively that the *Siege* contains a subversive 'antiwar message' against the French campaigns in the months leading up to Henry V's early death in 1422, Patterson's contention that the conventional view of Lydgate as a dutiful Lancastrian functionary needs to be re-examined has become influential.[89]

Paul Strohm, one of the most important voices in Lydgate's critical rehabilitation, has declared that 'these are exciting times for fifteenth-century studies, and for Lydgate studies in particular'. Detecting hesitant and subversive moments in the 'Complaint for my Lady of Gloucester' (a lyric written in response to Humphrey of Gloucester's politically injudicious pursuit of the territories of Holland, Hainault, and Zeeland), Strohm has extended Patterson's discussion of Lydgate's role as an apologist for the Lancastrian dynasty, drawing attention to the poet's apparent nervousness about the unstable and barely legitimate succession.[90] Again, James Simpson has fruitfully 'historicized' Lydgate in the context of discussions of the *Siege of Thebes* and of the *Troy Book*, where he explored Lydgate's modification of the view of historical event as contingent and rooted in 'human passions and decisions' that he encountered in his source, Guido delle Colonne's *Historia destructionis Troiae*.[91] The work of these critics has helped to foster a

---

[88] Lerer (1993: 25, 38–55).

[89] Patterson (1993); the influence is seen in Straker (1999; 2001), Strohm (2000), and Simpson (2001).

[90] *MP* ii. 608–13; Strohm (2000: 115). Strohm's attention turned to Lydgate's ambivalent and evasive complicity with the Lancastrian succession (1998: 186–95); this discussion is helpfully reproduced in (1999: 640–61). Strohm's early work on Lydgate includes (1977), (1982), and (1988).

[91] Simpson (1997; 1998). Simpson has elaborated on Lydgate's wider literary importance in the section 'The Energies of Lydgate' in his Oxford English Literary History volume (2002: 37): 'Lydgate is a critical figure in the economy by which Middle English literature is placed and received as "medieval" in cultural history.' Professor Simpson informs me that a forthcoming collection of essays on Lydgate (*John Lydgate: Poetry, Culture, and Lancastrian England*) will include an essay by Jennifer Summit on the *Fall*, ' "Stable in Study": Lydgate's *Fall of Princes* and Duke Humphrey's Library'.

climate in which what might be termed the 'naivety' of Lydgate has been challenged; whereas formerly readers would have been amazed at the suggestion that Lydgate was self-aware enough to use his poems to advance opinions of his own, there is now an openness to the idea that these texts are thoughtful, daring, even radical.

Strohm's belief that 'Lydgate's writing is more challenging, and exciting, and more rewarding to close attention than previously supposed'[92] is clearly shared by four critics (Alexandra Gillespie, Joseph Dane, Irene Basey Beesemyer, and John Thompson) who have examined Lydgate's career at the presses from the incunabular to the Marian period, tracing patterns of reception by drawing on bibliographical evidence and exploring the sectarian assumptions of his post-Reformation English readership. The prints of the *Fall* have been seen as particularly significant, and so it is from study of the early history of the printed book, especially in the work of Alexandra Gillespie, that a new focus on the *Fall* is now emerging.[93] Gillespie's doctoral thesis examined the (often unstable) location of Lydgate in the printed canon during the middle decades of the sixteenth century and his disappearance from print in the period from 1534 to 1553. Her work analyses the conditions behind the production of the editions of the *Fall* in the reign of Mary, exploring their bibliographical relationships to the suppressed 1554 print of the *Mirror for Magistrates*, and fascinatingly considers the 'construction' of 'Lydgate' as a printed author in these years.[94]

Lydgate scholarship moves slowly—perhaps even as slowly as the 'breathless snail's pace' of which the Monk of Bury has been found guilty.[95] Although interest in poets of the Lancastrian period has gained momentum over the past decade and enthusiasm for the Monk has now revived, study of his longest poem is intermittent and many elements of the *Fall* remain unexamined.[96]

---

[92] Strohm (2000: 130). Some recalcitrant voices persist: 'Lydgate's *Fall* is dead on arrival' (Wallace 1997: 334).

[93] Gillespie (2000*a*; 2000*b*; 2001*b*; 2003); Dane and Beesemyer (2000); Thompson (2001).

[94] Gillespie (D. Phil. thesis, 2001): publication (as *Print Culture and the Medieval Author: Chaucer, Lydgate, and their Books, 1473–1559*) is pending. I am grateful to Dr Gillespie for waiving restrictions on access to her thesis and allowing me to consult it.   [95] Pearsall (1970: 7).

[96] Christa McCay produced a doctoral thesis on the *Fall* in 1972. Computer-aided work has been undertaken at the University of Alberta to establish the

As Edwards pointed out in 1984, there are still uncertainties about the conditions under which the poem was composed and, among other things, about the involvement of Duke Humphrey in the production of the *Fall*; additionally, the manuscript tradition of the text, Edwards's own area of expertise, has yet to be studied systematically.[97] Most pressingly, the need for a detailed study of the *Fall* (and in particular one that examines Lydgate's treatment of his French source) has become obvious. Mindful of David Lawton's call for a recontextualization of fifteenth-century verse, in the chapters that follow I endeavour to offer a study of various aspects of the *Fall of Princes* in both its literary and its political contexts, hoping that critical discussion of this neglected poem will find itself on a more informed footing than it has yet known.

In Chapter 2 the Latin and French predecessors of Lydgate's poem, the ways in which they seem to have been received by contemporary readers, and Lydgate's characteristic readings of his French source are discussed: consideration is also given to the impact Lydgate's stay in France in the 1420s may have had on his work. Chapter 3 looks more closely at the involvement of Lydgate's patron Humphrey of Gloucester in the composition of the poem and also of the prose work *The Serpent of Division*: certain of Lydgate's substantial additions to the poem, in particular the moralizing 'envoy' passages and the fascinating narrative of the rape of Lucretia, are considered. Chapter 4 analyses Lydgate's poem as an expression of Benedictine orthodoxy, and, in particular, discusses the ways Lydgate adapts his poem so that it more clearly articulates the relationship between spiritual and secular authority: contextual evidence for the significance of these issues in Lydgate's home monastery at Bury St Edmunds is given. Chapter 5 analyses the *Fall* as a work of tragedy, evaluating the influence of Chaucer's *Monk's Tale* and the role and presentation

Lydgate canon through analysis of the corpus of 380 poems carrying scribal attributions to the poet, but the Canon Project has yet to turn its attention to the *Fall*. Initial testing of the Project's statistical methods was reported in Lancashire (1993), and a progress report was presented at the International Congress on the Fifteenth Century at Salzburg in July 1995. The production of an electronic text of the *Lives of SS Edmund and Fremund* has been one of the most important fruits of the project to date. A project at the University of Victoria, British Columbia, has digitized the Victoria *Fall* fragment and made this available on the Internet.

[97] Edwards (1984: 35).

of Fortune in the narratives: again, the differences between the poem and its French source are documented and provide vital evidence for an accurate assessment of Lydgate's achievement. In the final chapter the uses to which later readers put the poem are discussed, analysing extracts from the *Fall* copied in surviving manuscripts, evidence of ownership (including that of Catholic recusants), and later imitations of the poem for what they show us of the expectations fifteenth- and sixteenth-century readers brought to their reading of the *Fall*. The chapter concludes with an exploration of the impact of Reformation reactions to the poem and the subsequent disappearance of the *Fall* from the printed canon. The inclusion of a conspectus of the line numbers of the poem alongside the chapter headings of the Latin and French texts (listing the component narratives of the French chapters and noting Lydgate's larger alterations to these) for the first time makes it possible for readers to move through the *Fall* with a sense of its relationship to its underlying source texts.

The chronicler of Battle Abbey claims that the monks who listened to the twelfth-century abbot Odo of Canterbury 'did not scorn any prolixity on the part of the preacher—though sometimes he spoke rather wordily—for they were charmed with the sweetness both of his person and his words'.[98] Our knowledge of the decline in Lydgate's fortunes tells us that a modern audience would not be quite as tolerant of verbosity. However, the *Fall of Princes* is a valuable and intriguing text, one which was read with excitement and, at least in the one hundred and fifty years after Lydgate's death, repeatedly imitated by admiring readers: we ignore such a powerful and influential work at our cost.

---

[98] *Chronicle of Battle Abbey* ed. and trans. Searle (1980: 308); see Spencer (1993: 9, 92, 101).

2

The French Context of the *Fall of Princes*

THE *DE CASIBUS* IN FRANCE AND THE *DES CAS DES NOBLES HOMMES ET FEMMES*

The *De casibus* seems to have found its most receptive audience not in Boccaccio's native Italy but instead in France, where his shorter (1355–60) version was translated in 1400 and again in 1409 by Laurent de Premierfait.[1] Evidence for the popularity of the Latin text in France before Laurent's two translations is scanty, but there survives a citation from the work in Christine de Pisan's last long political treatise, the *Livre de la Paix* (composed in 1412 for Louis, duke of Guyenne). Louis, the third son of Charles VI, became dauphin at the age of four on the untimely death of his older brother in 1401 (Charles's eldest son had died in 1386); the book Christine presents to the fifteen-year-old prince is regiminal in intent: a presentation of the seven virtues necessary in a good ruler.[2] Christine seems to have used the Latin *De casibus* in a manner similar to that of later readers of Lydgate's poem, raiding it for useful ethical advice.[3] At the head of her forty-first chapter

[1] Premierfait's authorship, now universally accepted, was previously questioned on the grounds that his name appears only once in the surviving manuscripts of the two versions of the *Des Cas* (in a signing to the explicit to Book I in the early BN MS fr. 226): for a description of the manuscript see Branca (1999: iii. 86–90); see Gathercole (1956: 304). The 1400 version was dedicated to Louis, duke of Bourbon (brother-in-law of Charles V), the expanded 1409 version to Jean, duke of Berry (brother to Charles V).
[2] Christine de Pisan ed. Willard (1958: 28). Louis was to die shortly after Agincourt, aged eighteen.
[3] For this characteristic use of the *Fall* by its readers see ch. 6, pp. 224–51.

(devoted to 'the great evil that may befall a prince' if he succumbs to the sin of sloth) she quotes the *De casibus* as follows:

O nunc virtutum mollicies et sicius estati sit adversa adolescencie tamen prejuiciosisiam hostis est que si blandiciis actracta fuint cui exciciali tamen peius excrescendo delabitur. Bocacius in *Libro de Casibus Virorum Illustrium*.[4]

Possibly as a result of the degenerate state of the text Christine quotes, this citation has gone unnoticed by readers of Boccaccio, and unidentified by the editor of the most recent edition of the *Livre*. Patient reading of the *De casibus*, however, reveals that the passage Christine has in mind is located in the chapter 'De Mithridate Ponti rege' in Boccaccio's sixth book:

O nouerca virtutu*m* mollities: etsi cuius etati aduersa | adulesce*n*tiae quide*m* perniciosissim*us* hostis est. Nam si fuerit eius blanditiis adtracta: & eius refederit inclinata in gremio: Non ipsa periclitatur tantum: Verum de reliquo vitae actum est. Quae si etiam protrahatur longissima | confecta huius exitiali tabe semper in peius excrescendo dilabitur.

(O soft living, stepmother of virtues—though she is the adversary of every age, yet is she in particular the most pernicious enemy of youth. For if your youth has been led on by her flatteries *and sits leaning on her bosom, your youth itself is not just in danger, but all is finished with the remainder of your life. Even if your life is extended to being very long,* finished off by the fatal corruption of this behaviour, you will continually slide to the worse as you grow older.)[5]

In a work aimed at a young reader, the content of this extract (from Boccaccio's account of Mithridates) is particularly appropriate, and, even though it is possible that Christine may have come across this passage in a florilegium of moralistic maxims, it is not surprising that the Boccaccian work should be known to a woman who in 1400–3 produced her own long examination of the workings of Fortune, *Le Livre de la Mutacion de Fortune*, presented to Laurent's patron, Jean, duke of Berry.[6]

The most celebrated use of Boccaccio's text in France at this time is, however, that by Jean Petit in defence of political assassination.

---

[4] Christine de Pisan ed. Willard (1958: 177). Boccaccio is quoted just once in the work.

[5] *De casibus* Paris 1520 A-version, fos. 61ʳ–61ᵛ; repr. Louis Brewer Hall (1962: 147–8): text not cited by Christine in the *Livre* is here italicized.

[6] Christine de Pisan ed. Solente (1959–66; vol. i, p. xi). The *De casibus* is not listed by Solente as a source for the *Mutacion* (ibid. i. xxx–xxxi).

On 23 November 1407 Louis, duke of Orléans (the second son of Charles V and brother to the officially reigning, but mentally unstable, Charles VI), was murdered by Raoul d'Anquentonville at the instigation of Jean sans Peur ('the Fearless'), duke of Burgundy and Louis's cousin: the attack was a result of Burgundian discontent at the influence Louis wielded over the weakened king, although one Norman chronicler believed that sexual jealousy also played a part.[7] In March 1408 Jean Petit preached for four hours before the royal family, making a public apology for Jean the Fearless, but justifying the murder on the syllogistic grounds that 'it is permissible and meritorious to kill a tyrant', that Louis had indeed been a tyrant, and therefore that 'the duke of Burgundy did well to kill him', adding the breathtaking claim, among many corollaries and disputational articles, that the duke of Orléans had been guilty of *lèse-majesté* and was an Absalom whom David (in the figure of the King) needed a Joab (Burgundy) to kill.[8] The *Justification du duc de Bourgogne*, which has been described as 'one of the most insolent pieces of political chicanery and theological casuistry in all history',[9] cites many authorities to support its defence of tyrannicide: the Bible, Cicero, Augustine, Gregory the Great, John of Salisbury, and Bonaventure are all plundered by Petit.[10]

Alongside these passages there is also a maxim from Boccaccio's *De casibus*: 'il n'est plus agréable sacrifice que le sang du tyran'.[11] In the fifth chapter of Book II ('In fastosam regum superbiam') Boccaccio, whose views on the legitimacy of killing tyrants are clear-cut, writes (possibly adapting a Senecan dictum): 'Quum nulla fere sit deo adceptior hostia | tyranni sanguine' ('Scarcely any offering is more acceptable to God than the blood of a tyrant'.)[12] The passage occurs in a chapter on the proper relationship between a

[7] Vaughan (1966, repr. 2002: 44–8).

[8] Ibid. 69–70; see Simone (1971: 18, 24–6); Boccaccio trans. Brewer Hall (1965: xv); 'le duc de Bourgogne avait été le lion qui avait combattu ce loup, le Joab qui avait tué cet Absalon' (Guenée 1992: 197).   [9] Vaughan (1966, repr. 2002: 70).

[10] Monstrelet provides a detailed version of the *Justification* in his *Chronicle* (see Monstrelet trans. Johnes 1810: i. 109–48 (ch. 39)). The passage Petit takes from the *Policraticus* is from II. 15, but John of Salisbury is notoriously energetic in his support of tyrannicide elsewhere: see VIII. 17 (John of Salisbury ed. Webb ii. 345: § 778a), VIII. 18 (ii. 364: § 788d), VIII. 20 (ii. 376: § 795a).

[11] Monstrelet, *Chroniques* vol. i, ch. 39, p. 73.

[12] *De casibus* fo. 15ʳ (p. 53); Boccaccio trans. Brewer Hall (1965: 50); see Seneca, *Hercules furens*, ll. 922–4.

ruler and his subjects; Boccaccio argues that the power of an
earthly prince is not held absolutely, but that royal authority
instead derives its force from its relationship with the populace
(on which it is to some extent conditional), for it is the sweat of
the people that adds lustre to regal eminence ('Na*m*, vti ex sudore
pop*u*lorum regius fulget honos').[13] Rulers who pervert this self-
validating relationship lose the right to govern. This section of the
chapter is translated closely by Laurent—so closely, in fact, that
it has been suggested that Petit drew his (French) quotation from
the *Des Cas* rather than from the Latin.[14] Lydgate has little time
for Boccaccio's political theory and not only draws on the
Policraticus for a rather more orthodox organic view of political
relationships in the community, but also softens the venomous
detailed attack on the vices of princes which he found in his
French source.[15] The issue of bad government does not have the
same significance for Lydgate as it does for his two predecessors.
Whereas Boccaccio and Laurent use their discussion of tyranny as
an opportunity to sketch out the extent to which it is permissible
for subjects to check abuses of power, Lydgate's passage is more
conventionally advisory: the emphasis is turned away from subject and back to prince because the issue at stake in the *Fall* is
not how subjects may constrain bad government, but rather how
the erring prince should regulate his own moral behaviour.
Disenfranchising the victims of tyranny of any kind of directly
corrective authority (rather as Aquinas—citing 1 Peter 2: 20—had
done over a hundred and fifty years before),[16] Lydgate's version
of this chapter is an exercise in caution: no mention is made of
Boccaccio's recommendation that *tyrannical* princes be killed.[17]

[13] *De casibus* fo. 14ᵛ (p. 52).
[14] Coville (1932, repr. 1974: 201 n. 76; see 186, 217). Laurent translates the
maxim as 'car il nest sacrifice a dieu ta*n*t aggreable co*m*me est le sang du tyra*n*t
et mauuais prince' (fo. 27ᵛ).
[15] *Fall* II. 806–917. Laurent dilutes Boccaccio's impact a little in his fifth chapter by prefacing the assault on princes with comments on Rehoboam (the subject
of the preceding chapter), as if to suggest that the invective should be seen partly
in the light of that biblical narrative.
[16] 'On Princely Government, to the King of Cyprus', ch. 6 in *Aquinas* ed.
D'Entrèves (1948: 28–35). Note that Lydgate does admit the adage at III. 4005–11
when he finds it in Laurent's III. ch. 15 ('Aphri quidam queruli'), fo. 68ᵛ: there is
no parallel for this in the Latin, *De casibus* fo. 32ᵛ (p. 90).
[17] Lydgate does, of course, extend the brief references to Mucius Scaevola,
Lucretia, and Virginia into over five hundred lines of verse, but the political impact

Petit's citation of Boccaccio and—as importantly—his attribution of the quotation to the *De casibus* seems to have imbued Boccaccio's work with a certain notoriety. The *Justification*, although perhaps not the best publicity for Boccaccio's text, certainly became popular: the Abbé de Cerisy's Orléanist reply to Petit in September 1408 contained a sniffy reference to Boccaccio as 'ung poëte nouvel', and Jean Gerson's counterblasts also seized on the passage from the *De casibus*.[18] The verbatim account of the *Justification* given by Monstrelet (favourably slanted towards Burgundy) ensured a wider readership for Petit's defence: the enthusiasm for the text is shown by the survival of copies of Monstrelet's account made separately from the rest of his *Chronicle*.[19] So widespread were the shock waves caused by Petit's treatise that, partly as a result of Gerson's obsessively anti-Burgundian machinations,[20] the matter was debated by the Council of Constance at the end of its fifteenth session (6 July 1415), when, after condemning the views of Wyclif and Hus, the Fathers roundly attacked Petit's propositions as 'erroneous in the faith and with regard to morals . . . heretical, scandalous, and seditious . . . leading the way through perjury to frauds, deceptions, lies, and betrayals'.[21]

This cause célèbre aside, Laurent's translations of the *De casibus* do seem to have been the medium through which most French readers encountered Boccaccio's text. Laurent de Premierfait (actual surname Guillot) describes himself as 'clerc du diocèse de Troyes';[22] although little is known of him before 1397, the evidence of his subsequent career shows this self-description to be an

of these sections is curiously treated (see Ch. 3). For Boccaccio's typically hostile attitude towards princes, see *Fall* ed. Bergen vol. i. p. xviii. Philip II of Spain is thought to have owned five copies of the *De casibus* (Wright 1957: 3 n. 9).

[18] Coville (1932, repr. 1974: 187, 240, 186); see Simone (1971: 25).
[19] Coville (1911: 71).
[20] Connolly (1928: 164–7, 181, and *passim*).
[21] 'erroneam esse in fide et in moribus, ipsamque tamquam haereticam, scandalosam, seditiosam et ad fraudes, deceptiones, mendacia, proditiones, periuria vias dantem' (*Decrees of the Ecumenical Councils* ed. Tanner 1990: i. 432); see Coville (1932, repr. 1974: 503 ff); Morrell (1960: 13–14, 95, 123); Loomis ed. Mundy and Woody (1961: 248, 256–7). Lydgate's patron acquired from the executors of the bishop of Worcester in 1433 a copy of the proceedings of Constance in which this decree is reported: BL MS Cotton Nero E. v, fo. 58ʳ. Jean the Fearless was himself assassinated in 1419 at Montereau (Vaughan 1966, repr. 2002: 67–84, 210–12).
[22] Smith (1934: 512–13); Purkis (1949: 22–3). Comparatively little is known of Laurent's life: see *DBF* xix. 1430–1; Koeppel (1885: 5); Gathercole (1956: 304 n). Famiglietti (1983) offers the clearest biography of Laurent.

understatement. Laurent was at the papal court at Avignon from possibly as early as 1390 and it was there that he became the secretary to Amédée, Cardinal of Saluzzo. Avignon was an international melting pot where a hungry French audience could come into contact with Italian humanist influences and texts, and Laurent seems to have made good use of the opportunity. The facility with which he composed stylish classical Latin earned him both the commendation 'poeta et orator eximius' and the praise of Giovanni Moccia, who placed the Frenchman in the pantheon of Roman writers after Cicero, Virgil, Ovid, Seneca, and Horace.[23] Laurent's translations are not confined to the *De casibus*, although the A-version of the *Des Cas* (finished in November 1400 for Charles VI and surviving in seven known copies, the oldest of which is Paris, BN MS fr. 24289[24]) does seem to have been his first work: unable to read Italian, he also translated Boccaccio's *Decameron* (as *Cent nouvelles*, 1411–14)[25] from 'a rather clumsy' intermediary Latin version produced for the purpose by the Franciscan Antonio d'Arezzo,[26] and possibly the *De mulieribus claris* (as *Des cleres et nobles femmes*).[27] He translated Cicero's *De senectute* and *De amicitia* (the latter being one of the two texts Dante had read to console himself at the loss of Beatrice) in 1405 (20 manuscripts extant) and 1416 (12 manuscripts) respectively,[28] and in the last year of his life Laurent translated Aristotle's *Economics* (surviving in 6 copies); there is debate over his authorship of a French translation of Seneca's *De quattuor virtutibus*.[29] Arguing that Laurent's exposure to Livy formed 'une sorte d'étape préparatoire à sa seconde rédaction du *De casibus*',[30] Marie-Hélène Tesnière has suggested that a revision of Bersuire's translation of Livy surviving in one Paris manuscript (copied for Jean Chanteprime) may also be Laurent's work:[31] certainly, Laurent was

[23] Purkis (1949: 23).   [24] Branca (1999: iii. 67–8).
[25] Ibid. 29; Gathercole (1955: 14).
[26] Purkis (1949: 29). See Gathercole (1954: 246); Purkis (1955: 2); Gathercole (1958: 262); Bozzolo (1973: 25–9).
[27] Gathercole (1958: 269; 1960: 370 n.; 1962: 41); Bozzolo (1973: 91–100, 149–55, 180–3).
[28] Gathercole (1958: 263–4; 1954: 245; 1960: 366–8). For Dante's use of the *De amicitia* see *Convivio*, II. xii [xiii] §§ 2–4 (Dante ed. Vasoli and Robertis n.d.: v.1b. 201–3).
[29] Purkis (1949: 33); Gathercole (1954: 245 n.; 1958: 265–6; 1960: 369).
[30] Tesnière (1986: 280).
[31] BN MS fr. 264-265-266; Tesnière (1986: 274–5, 280–1).

adviser to the royal counsellor Chanteprime by 1400,[32] and the
political interests of Livy's history would make it a congenial text
for him.[33]

Laurent's works passed through the hands of the powerful: the
Cent nouvelles survives in fifteen manuscript copies,[34] one of
which, the lavishly illustrated presentation copy (Vatican, BAV MS
Pal. lat. 1989), passed from the dedicatee Jean of Berry to Jean
the Fearless.[35] Jean's son, Philippe le Bon ('the Good'), commissioned his own copy (now Paris, MS Arsenal 5070), and by 1467
(the year of his death) the Burgundian library at Bruges held a
third copy of the work (now Oxford, Bodleian Library MS Douce
213).[36] Humphrey of Gloucester's copy of the *Cent nouvelles*—a
gift from Richard Beauchamp, thirteenth earl of Warwick—is now
Paris, BN MS fr. 12421,[37] while one of the three London manuscripts (BL MS Royal 19 E. 1) may have been copied for Edward
IV.[38] Aristocratic ownership of the work continues in England well
into the sixteenth century: BL MSS Additional 35322–3 belonged
to Edward Seymour, duke of Somerset.[39] The *Cent nouvelles* were
printed at least eight times between 1485 and 1541, spawned many
imitations, and remained popular until Margaret of Navarre commissioned Antoine Le Maçon to make a new French translation of
the work (appearing 1545).[40]

[32] Hauvette (1903: 35); Purkis (1949: 26); Smith (1934: 513).

[33] The political usefulness of Livy was valued highly in the Middle Ages: Nicholas
Trevet produced a commentary on the work for Pope John XXII in c.1318 (now
surviving in only one manuscript), which was known to Boccaccio and quoted by
him in his commentary on Dante: see Dean (1945) and Smalley (1960: 58–65). In
1427 John, duke of Bedford, gave his brother Humphrey a copy of Bersuire's translation of Livy (now Paris, Bibliothèque Sainte-Geneviève MS fr. 777); see Sammut
(1980: 122); Cosimo de' Medici sent a copy of Livy to Alfonso il Magnanimo in
order to forestall hostilities between Florence and Naples; see Ullman (1973: 57–8).
Petrarch's acquisition of a copy of Livy (BN MS lat. 5690) in 1351 comes soon after
the discovery of the apocryphal epitaph to Livy at Padua; see Ullman (1973: 53–4).
On the use made of Livy by the *Des Cas* see Koeppel (1885: 12–14).

[34] See the stemma constructed by Cucchi and Lacy (1974: 483–502).

[35] Branca (1999: iii. 205–14); Bozzolo (1973: 163–5); Vaughan (1966, repr.
2002: 234).

[36] Branca (1999: iii. 218–25, 235–6); Bozzolo (1973: 100–2, 163–5, 160–2); see
Purkis (1950: 67; 1955: 9–10).

[37] Branca (1999: iii. 230–5); Bozzolo (1973: 107–8); Purkis (1955: 9–10);
Gathercole (1961: 314).

[38] Branca (1999: iii. 243–4); Bozzolo (1973: 159–60); Gathercole (1958: 268;
1961: 314); Reynolds (1988: 151–3).

[39] Branca (1999: iii. 240–3); Bozzolo (1973: 157–8).

[40] Cucchi (1975: 6–9); see Purkis's number (1949: 32; 1955: 1).

But if the *Nouvelles* were popular, the *Des Cas* was more so: it has long been recognized that both Boccaccio and Petrarch were better known for their Latin ethical works in the medieval period than they were for their vernacular 'humanistic' or amorous compositions.[41] The number of the surviving manuscripts of the *Des Cas* has been revised several times in recent years,[42] but the greater part are copies of Laurent's later redaction: for example, of the ten manuscripts held in British libraries, all but one (London, BL MS Additional 11696) contain the B-version of the work.[43] In the Bibliothèque Nationale alone there are fourteen copies of the B-version of the *Des Cas*, while the A-version survives in just three.[44] The success of the Laurentian translations may clearly be seen in the paucity of surviving manuscripts of the original Latin work: it is possible that it was as a result of the greater abundance of copies of Laurent's translation that Lydgate based his verse translation on the French *Des Cas* rather than on the Latin original. As A. S. G. Edwards has shown, seven of the eight copies of the *De casibus* now held in British libraries were already in England in the medieval period: of these, three offer extracts only.[45] The four complete British texts, held in Oxford by Lincoln, Magdalen, and New Colleges, and by Cambridge University Library, present an unusual picture, for only one is a copy of the A-version (CUL MS Ll. ii. 8), which as we have seen, was normally more popular than the longer 1373 B-version. While it is incautious to suggest too much from

[41] Although it is not as generally realized that this binary opposition falsifies the picture; for in France, at least, the *Decameron* was read moralistically—an approach made easier by Laurent's ethically oriented translation of the work (Norton (1972); Cucchi (1975); see Olson (1982: 222–3, 229)).

[42] Florence Smith gave the number as 47 in 1934, Purkis as 50 in 1949, while Patricia Gathercole gave 65 in 1955 and 1958, but updated this in 1962 to 68; in 1973 Carla Bozzolo raised the total to 69. Note that Gathercole's claim (1955: 14) that George Sarton (1948: 1805) gave the number of *Des Cas* manuscripts as 30 is based on a misreading of the passage: Sarton is, in fact, speaking here about the *Fall*. Pearsall (1970: 232), states that there are 'over a hundred' manuscripts of the *Des Cas*: I have not been able to find evidence for this claim.

[43] Branca (1999: iii. 155–7). The other manuscripts are Glasgow, Hunterian MSS 208, 371–2; London, BL MSS Additional 18750 and 35321, MS Harley 621, MSS Royal 20 C. IV, 18 D. VII, and 14 E. V; Oxford, Bodleian MS Bodley 265; see Gathercole (1955: 19) and Bozzolo (who gives the number of manuscripts as ten) (1973: 129–40).

[44] Branca (1999: iii. 364–6): the A-version copies are nos. 20, 43, and 49.

[45] Edwards (1977: 426–7). Bodleian MS Laud Misc. 721 contains the Templar narrative from the *De casibus* (IX. ch. 21) with a fragment of the following chapter (fos. 337^r–9^r).

so small a field of evidence, it is interesting that among the few Englishmen we know from their surviving books to have owned the *De casibus* in its original Latin versions there should be the notable early English humanist Robert Flemmyng (who owned the copy now held as Lincoln College MS 32). Flemmyng (ob.1483), dean of Lincoln and nephew of Bishop Richard Flemmyng, who founded Lincoln College, travelled and studied widely on the Continent, and was a pupil of Guarino da Verona: it is possible that he may have acquired his copy of Boccaccio's work during his two long visits to Italy.[46] An owner of New College MS 263, John Russell, bishop of Lincoln and Chancellor to Edward V, was also a man of considerable humanist learning.[47]

If there is a difference between the way the *De casibus* is received by the English and the French, it is that in England the *De casibus* seems to have been read by the scholarly, while in France the Laurentian versions of the work appear instead to have been popular with the powerful. The copies belonging to Jean the Fearless (the lavishly illustrated Paris, MS Arsenal 5193), the imprisoned Jean of Orléans, count of Angoulême (Paris, BN MS fr. 231), and Laurent's patron Jean of Berry (the oldest surviving copy of the 1409 version, given to the duke in 1411 by the Archbishop of Chartres and now Geneva, Bibliothèque publique et universitaire MS fr. 190) have all been identified.[48] What, however, did the French readers of the *Des Cas* make of the work? Franco Simone has suggested that the political misfortunes of the French in the opening decades of the fifteenth century made the work strangely attractive to its contemporary readers: the catalogue of laments was attuned to the spirit of the age.[49] Although this impression would seem to make sense, there is little hard evidence to suggest what Laurent's audience expected from the text; perhaps the clearest insight we have into the ways in which these readers regarded the *casus* genre may be seen in the copy of the B-version of the *Des Cas* now held in Munich (Bayerische

---

[46] Weiss (1957: 97–105); see Reiss (1974: 22–3).

[47] Weiss (1957: 177), see Wright (1957: 5).

[48] Branca (1999: iii. 76–80, 150–2, 68–72); see Martin (1911); Bozzolo (1973: 52, 68, 146–7); Callu and Avril (1975: 56); Hauvette (1903: 56–8). Jean of Orléans also owned copies of the *Cent nouvelles* (BN MS fr. 1122) and *Des cleres* (BN MS fr. 1120). For further owners see Ch. 6.

[49] Simone (1971: 28): 'l'ouvrage de Boccace qui se révéla le plus en harmonie avec les exigences culturelles de la France de cette époque'.

Staatsbibliothek MS Gallicus 6, *olim* 369). This manuscript was copied in 1458 and on folio. 2ᵛ a full-page illustration of the *Lit de Justice* of Vendôme of the same year is given.⁵⁰ The illustration shows Charles VII presiding at the trial of Jean, duke of Alençon, who had been accused of conspiracy with the English and who was condemned to death by the *Lit* on 10 October 1458: it has been suggested that the illustration in the Munich manuscript captures the exact moment of the judgement.⁵¹ The codex appears to have been copied for Laurens Gyrard, secretary to Charles VII, and, later, a high-ranking official in the exchequer:⁵² that the *Des Cas* should have continued to excite the interest of powerful men is of interest, of course, but just as significant is the fact that a depiction of so topical and recent an event should be felt appropriate to illustrate the work. The Munich illustration says something important about the standing of the *De casibus/Des Cas* in the middle of the fifteenth century: far from seeing the text as static or limited in its impact to the narratives it contains, the illustrator of this manuscript 'updates' the cautionary aspect of the work with the contemporary (and highly public) fall of a nobleman, a 'sujet de brûlante actualité au moment où le manuscript a été exécuté' ('a subject of red-hot topicality at the time the manuscript was being composed').⁵³ Just as Vives was to praise Petrarch for shaking the dust off the figures of the past, so the *De casibus* narratives of the fallen figures of mythology, the Bible, antiquity, and recent history appear to have been used in France to comment on the political events of the present.⁵⁴

The changes made to Boccaccio's austere Latin treatise by its French translator have received close study.⁵⁵ Laurent's learned

⁵⁰ Durrieu (1909: 7–12, 51–5). The illustration has been reproduced in McLeod (1969: fig. 8). For a description of the manuscript, see Bozzolo (1973: 124–6) and Branca (1999: iii. 125–30 (fig. 183).
⁵¹ Durrieu (1909: 52): 'la sentence de condamnation est lue au roi par un personnage de l'ordre judiciaire'.
⁵² Ibid. 15: 'le haut fonctionnaire qui avait en France . . . la charge de contrôleur de la recette générale des finances'.   ⁵³ Ibid. 52.
⁵⁴ For Vives's remarks see Coogan (1971: 281). In 1431 Jean Lamelin, a councillor to Parliament, selected narratives from Laurent's A-version to produce an abridged *Des Cas*, now Paris, Bibliothèque Mazarine MS 3880 (Branca 1999: iii. 201; see Callu and Avril 1975: 55–6).
⁵⁵ Koeppel (1885: 10–35); Hauvette (1903: 40–55); Smith (1934); Gathercole (1967); Premierfait ed. Gathercole (1968); Purkis (1949: 31), Schirmer (1952, trans. 1961: 208–9); Pearsall (1970: 232): Pearsall gives the French source cursory attention.

encrustation of the work with fuller historical detail, geographical description, and clarified chronology bespeaks a serious academic approach to Boccaccio's text: Koeppel's thesis shows the impressive range of Laurent's reading of classical and medieval literature. Laurent's second redaction is considerably longer than the shorter (A-version) *De casibus* it purports to translate, and his additions have been seen variously as 'useless padding [which] vitiates the whole book', 'inept and colourless' with 'no grasp of antiquity',[56] and also as a model of early humanism.[57] Laurent has an idealistic understanding of the function of literature that reveals a little of the importance he attaches to his own translation of the *De casibus*. When Boccaccio speaks of poetry in his third book (III. ch. 14: 'Auctoris purgatio, & poeseos commendatio') in positive, but relativistic, terms (as an inspired task, but just one of many in a balanced community), Laurent speaks at length of the sacred quality of the art. And yet, Laurent's heavy-handed earnestness sometimes fails entirely to capture the elegance of Boccaccio's prose, as is clearly seen in his laboured exposition of Boccaccio's evocative summary of the numinous force of poetry. Boccaccio ends his chapter:

Latrent igitur canes. & luna fulgida caeli more suo percurrat lympidas regiones.

(Hounds, then, may bark, but the bright moon runs its accustomed course through the limpid expanses of the night.)[58]

Laurent's desire to be unambiguous destroys the aphoristic impact of the Latin:

Ie vueil doncques que les chiens | cestassauoir les enuieux des Poetes abayent contre eulx et contre poesie et si vueil q*ue* la lune rousse | cestassauoir poesie coure et voise par les cleres regions du zodiaque ainsi co*m*me elle a acoustume. Cest a dire que poesie nonobstant ces blasmeurs ne vault ia pour ce moins ne que la Lune ne vault moins pour les chiens qui contre elle abayent ou glatissent.

(So by 'dogs' I mean all those who, envious of poets, bark against them and against poetry itself; the April moon (that is to say, poetry) runs on, sailing through the bright celestial regions of the zodiac, as is her custom. This all goes to show that poetry pays no more attention to its detractors than the moon takes heed of those dogs who bark at or rail against her.)[59]

---

[56] Smith (1934: 515, 519).   [57] Gathercole (1954: 252).
[58] *De casibus* fo. 32ʳ (p. 89).   [59] *Des Cas* fo. 68ʳ.

That Laurent entertained serious ambitions for his second translation of the work may be seen in his long dedication of that version to Jean of Berry. After a conventional disclaimer for his text, and an explanation of the role of Fortune in the falls of the great, Laurent devotes long passages to the current state of the three orders of French society: 'la*u*cteur parle du cas de leglise presente et des prestres', 'du cas de noblesse', and 'du cas des laboureux champestres'. In each Laurent lists contemporary evils which he sees as consequent on the Fall of Man: clergy are ignorant, sexually impure, and over-involved in worldly power, 'la seignorie du monde'; nobles disregard the path of virtue and fail to protect the innocent; city workers have given themselves up to dissension and riot. Even rural labourers ('simples inno-cens sans cruaulte et sans armes, qui nuit et Iour demeurent en poures maisonettes si sobrement'), who work for the common good and whose life of honest simplicity and frugality has throughout past ages been commended by princes and philoso-phers, have been falsely tried in ecclesiastical courts, been oppressed by wicked men and driven from their lands, their daughters and wives defiled.[60] Contemporary France has slipped into vice, injustice, and disregard for the will of God; in paint-ing these abuses Laurent has no doubt that the diseases of the wider social body are the result of the collapse of private virtue. Laurent shows that he has taken seriously Boccaccio's initial dec-laration that the *De casibus* is offered for the benefit of the state ('reipublicae vtilitatis adferre'). This awareness of the larger impli-cations of personal self-government is reflected in a quartered illustration found at the start of four surviving copies of the *Des Cas*. A miniature of Laurent's presentation of his book to his patron is accompanied by depictions of the three orders of society—in this fourfold image the book occupies a significant and privileged place alongside the representatives of the very community (clergy, nobles, and labourers) it is intended to reform.[61]

---

[60] *Fall* ed. Bergen vol. i, pp. lviii–lxv.
[61] MSS BN fr. 131, the oldest codex of the four (fo. 1ʳ); Bodley 265 (fo. 2ʳ); Royal 18 D. vii (fo. 1ʳ); Addit. 18750 (fo. 3ʳ). See Branca (1999: iii. 83–6, 96–8, 104–5, 197–8). The disfiguration of the faces of the Pope and two cardinals, leav-ing the face of the Bishop untouched, in the Bodley illustration points to an anti-catholic response by at least one reader.

LYDGATE'S READING OF THE *DES CAS*

Lydgate's reading of the *Des Cas* produces a fundamentally different work from its French predecessor: in verse, rather than prose, its narrative viewpoint is also moved from the first person into the third. This displacement of viewpoint, while diminishing the dramatic quality of the work (as we are *told* that figures present themselves before 'Bochas', rather than seeing the complainants through the eyes of the musing poet), introduces a third layer to the work—the voice of the studious Benedictine joining those of his 'auctor' and the laments (rarely themselves in *direct* speech) of the fallen *elati*. Lydgate sometimes exploits this displacement skilfully, most notably in narratives where he wishes to dissociate himself from the nationalistic bias of his French source (as when he undermines the praise of France as the noblest of countries in his version of the narrative of Charles of Jerusalem):[62] the continuing struggles of the Hundred Years War can be detected behind the *Fall*.

The most sensitive passages in the *Des Cas* come in its final narrative—that of the downfall of John II ('le Bon') of France after his defeat by the English at the battle of Poitiers. John's reign was one of the least successful seen in medieval France: the years of his rule (1350–64) were marked not only by military disaster, territorial loss, and administrative incompetence, but also by the ravages and aftermath of the Black Death. Nonetheless, John seems to have had an active interest in the theory and effective exercise of political power: soon after his accession he commissioned Pierre Bersuire to translate Livy's *History*. Bersuire's preface makes clear the appeal of the work for the king:

excellent princes, the wiser they are, the more they will want to learn about the virtuous deeds and remarkable works of the princes of antiquity . . . so that modern princes can in the same way defend and govern their lands, defeat and dominate foreigners, discomfit enemies[63]

---

[62] *Fall* IX. 1877–88.

[63] Patterson (1987: 197). On Bersuire's translation see Smalley (1960: 262) and Lucas (1970: 239–40). John II seems to have encouraged several translation projects: he initiated plans for a vernacular Bible and Jean de Vignai translated the *Échecs Moralisés* for him (Green 1980: 149–50). The King introduced Bersuire to Petrarch in Paris in 1360 (Wilkins 1961: 175).

John's interest in the *speculum* tradition of advice to princes is easily understood; as the son of the first Valois monarch, Philip VI, he was the inheritor of a precarious dynasty. Accounts of princes who ruled successfully (or, perhaps more cogently, of those whose reigns were troubled and unhappy) would undoubtedly have struck a chord with him. His promulgation of rules to ensure the Valois succession and his establishment of the neo-Arthurian Order of the Star in 1351[64] both suggest a nervousness about the security and legitimacy of his rule: the chivalric rhetoric and pageantry of the latter sits naturally alongside the urgent political manoeuvring of the former. However, John had little time to emulate the models of good government he would have found in Livy. After his defeat in 1356 he was destined to spend much of the rest of his life on English soil: imprisoned for four years after Poitiers, John was released (for a crippling ransom) on the completion of the Treaty of Brétigny in 1360. His return to France was both inglorious and brief (he chose to return to England when his son Louis, duke of Anjou, broke parole) and he died in captivity in 1364.

In his *De casibus* Boccaccio reads John's career as a highly pitiable modern *casus*. His account in his final chapter (IX. ch. 27: 'Pauci flentes et libri conclusio') is short and pointed:

Ioannes Francorum Rex execrabile infortunium suum damnabat quod ab anglis inertissimis adque pauidis et nullius valoris hom*in*ibus regnum suum rapinis exhaustum | occupationibus diminutum | incendiis adque caedibus passim foedatum sit. Postremo infausto certamine fusis fractis consternatisque viribus suis c*ae*sisque nobilibus multus ip*se* Edvardi Regis hostis sui captiuus effectus & vinctus in Angliam deportatus sit.[65]

(John, king of the French, bemoaned his own accursed misfortune because, at the hands of the most base and fearful English, who are men of no valour, his kingdom was impoverished by plunderings, diminished by occupations, and disfigured far and wide by fires and slaughter. At last, by an unlucky contest, his own noblemen having been dispersed, broken, confused, and slaughtered, he himself, great man though he be, was made a captive of his enemy King Edward and, defeated, was deported to England.)

The emphasis of the narrative (which in its Latin version already presents the English in a poor light) differs in Premierfait's

[64] Evans (1925, 3rd edn. 1969: 140).   [65] *De casibus* fo. 116ᵛ (p. 240).

Des Cas: the English are no longer simply the ignominious agents of a malevolent fortune, but are now accredited with deplorably inhuman behaviour. Their infamous character ('des angloys hommes faillis et vains & de nulle valleur') is carefully translated, but John II's compatriot strengthens the account with the addition of a lengthy description of the battle of Poitiers, of the captivity of the king, and of the payment of the ransom (emotively the 'payement de tresgrant somme dor baillee pour sa rancon'). The whole concludes with an energetic assertion that John was shamefully murdered at the hands of his English captors:

il sans estre deliure mourut soub3 la puissance de son ennemy par vne maniere de mort indigne 7 miserable et incongneue a plusieurs

(Without being freed, in the hands of his enemy he met an undignified and miserable manner of death unheard of by most people)[66]

Given that Laurent's dedicatee for the 1409 version was one of John II's sons, it is not really very surprising that the French account should contain unashamedly partisan adaptation: under the guise of a direct translation from the Latin, Laurent inserts his own interpretation of John's career and, furthermore, adds damaging accusations (with which a French audience may have been familiar) about the circumstances of John's death. The literary consequences of this authorial interposition are subtle: by strengthening the atrocities of the English enemy, Laurent in effect undermines Fortuna. John is not now the luckless victim of an anonymous universal force, of a superhuman cause operating through the English opponent, but is instead made to seem a very particular victim of an equally particular, and very human, evil—the soldiers of Edward III. In short, the cathartic impact which is generated by the *casus* form (and, chiefly, the fear aroused in the reader lest a similar fate should befall him) is subverted. The English themselves become the primary cause of John's downfall, and this specificity works against the more general emotional force of the account: when detail and accusations are so particular, it is difficult for a reader to feel that the same misfortune could happen to him or her. Boccaccio's tale of undeserved suffering has, then, become Premierfait's political protest. The reader of the Latin text finishes the last narrative of the work with a sharpened awareness of the contingency of Fortune

---

[66] *Des Cas* fo. 219ᵛ (misnumbered as fo. 218).

and of his own vulnerability; the reader of the French *Des Cas* has
only a sense of patriotic outrage.

Lydgate's version of the narrative is strikingly different.
Demonstrating an awareness of the ways in which the past can
be manipulated and realigned to accord with personal bias, he
querulously (and humorously) takes issue with the version of
events he finds in 'Bochas':

> Thouh Bochas yaff hym fauour bi langage,
> His herte enclyned onto that partie,
> Which onto hym was but smal auauntage:
> Woord is but wynd brouht in be envie.
> For to hyndre the famous cheualrie
> Of Inglissh-men, ful narwe he gan hym thinke,
> Lefft spere and sheeld[e], fauht with penne & inke.

> Thouh seide Bochas floured in poetrie,
> His parcial writyng gaf no mortal wounde

> .   .   .   .   .

> In his report, men may his writing see;
> His fantasie nor his oppynioun
> Stood in that caas of noon auctorite:
> Ther kyng was take; ther knihtis dide flee;
> Wher was Bochas to helpe at such a neede?
> Sauff with his penne he made no man to bleede.

> Of rihtwisnesse euery cronicleer
> Sholde in his writyng make non excepcioun;
> Indifferentli conueie his mateere;
> Nat be parcial of non affeccioun[67]

For all his sense of injustice at French bias, the *Fall of Princes* is
one of the most consistently partisan poems Lydgate ever wrote.
As the 'laureate' of the Lancastrian dynasty, Lydgate was deeply
complicit in national politics; as a dutiful member of the community at Bury St Edmunds, he was caught up in ecclesiastical
politics of a very particular kind: both of these aspects of the
poem are explored in later chapters.

Smoke-screening references throughout the *Fall* to 'myn auctor
Iohn Bochas' conceal the poem's immediate source, and so thorough
is Lydgate's camouflage of the influence of the *Des Cas* in his

---

[67] *Fall* IX. 3162–70, 3177–86. These lines have been called 'among the most
vigorous in the *Fall*' (*Fall* ed. vol. Bergen iv. 396).

work that he refers to Laurent by name on only three occasions in his poem: twice in his prologue, and once in the later narrative of Charles of Jerusalem.[68] Lydgate's suppression of his source is almost complete, although on two occasions he inadvertently allows his guard to slip, revealing that he has worked from a French intermediary and not, as he consistently claims, from 'Bochas': in the account of the Roman emperor Vitellius he informs us that 'In Frenssh my*n* auctou*r* recordeth thus, parde' and he later surveys his nine-book achievement, referring to his source as 'The Frenssh vnkouth co*m*pendyously co*m*pyled'.[69] Elsewhere it is possible to see that Lydgate is working in close contact with French (rather than Latin) material: when relating the way in which the Persian king Sapor used the Emperor Valerian as a mounting block, he anglicizes Laurent's word for the object and informs us that it 'is in Frensh callid a mou*n*tweer'.[70]

Although Laurent necessarily wields the strongest literary influence over the *Fall*, Lydgate's poem also testifies to his wider reading. References to Josephus throughout the work (none of which has a parallel in the French source) show Lydgate's knowledge of the *De antiquitatibus* and of the *De bello Judaico*;[71] his frequent citations of Ovid, particularly in the earlier books of the *Fall* (where mythological narratives make Ovidian analogues possible), often seem to be used to authorize substantive departures from Laurent's text.[72] References to the *Aeneid*, (allusively) Martianus Capella's *De nuptiis*, Vincent of Beauvais, and the *Pryke of Conscience* are all original to Lydgate, as, too, are his many citations of Chaucer.[73] However, one of the most significant influences

---

[68] *Fall* I. 3, 79; IX. 1886.   [69] Ibid. VII. 966; IX. 3329.

[70] Ibid. VIII. 460: 'et apprestast son dos a guyse de montouer pour monter le roy sapor sur son cheual' (*Des Cas* fo. 172ᵛ). Only once in the poem does Lydgate's eagerness to convince his reader that he has been working from the Latin text cause him to slip up: in the narrative of Atreus and Thyestes he allows Atreus, who is addressing 'Bochas', to cite Boccaccio as an authority ('As seith Bochas . . .', I. 4126). This slip seems to have arisen from a hasty reading of the words 'mais Jehan Boccace dist atreus considere se tu peulx lhorreur', (fo. 9ʳ), where *Atreus*, and not *Jehan Boccace*, is the subject of the verb *dist*.

[71] *Fall* II. 728, 2367, 2605; VII. 1502, 1662–3.

[72] References at I. 324, 1672, 1945, 2136, 2243, 2383, 2411, 2442, 2542, 2666, 4708, 4717, 4920, 5475, 5704, 5792, 5905, 6628; II. 2151, 3450; IV. 94; IX. 3404.

[73] *Fall* IV. 67–91 (the copy of the *Aeneid* belonging to Lydgate's Abbot, William Curteys, survives as Trinity College Cambridge MS R. 3. 50), III. 66 (see *MP* i. 73); VI. 3162–74; IX. 3413–14; Chaucer: I. 246–357, 1783–806; II. 974–1001; III. 3860; VI. 3620–30; VIII. 666–79; IX. 3405–27.

claimed by the English poet is that of Petrarch. Although Lydgate found references to Petrarch in two chapters of the *Des Cas*,[74] he introduces further references of his own at four places in the *Fall*.[75] Of these, the list of Petrarch's Latin works at the start of Book IV is well known, and it is certainly possible that Lydgate's access to 'excellent monastic libraries' may have enabled him to derive (even if only cursory) familiarity with these works.[76] Plainly regarding Petrarch as an important model for the *De casibus* genre, Lydgate writes in the closing sections of the *Fall*:

> The Fal of Prynces gan pitously compleyne,
> As Petrark did, and also Iohn Bochas;
> Laureat Fraunceys, poetys bothe tweyne,
> Toold how prynces for ther greet trespace
> Wer ovirthrowe, rehersyng al the caas,
> As Chauceer did[e] in the Monkys Tale. [77]

While it is possible that Lydgate may have the *De viris illustribus* in mind here, it seems more probable that he is referring to the *De remediis*, Petrarch's 'book . . . Off too Fortunys, welful and peruerse'.[78] (Interestingly, Lydgate fails to include the *De viris* in his catalogue of Petrarch's works in the Prologue to Book IV, but mentions the *De remediis* in some detail in the Prologue to Book I.)

Boccaccio himself knew and admired Petrarch's dialogues (completed 1366),[79] and, as J. B. Trapp has noted, the work was frequently copied and became 'the cornerstone of his reputation, especially outside Italy, in the century following his death'.[80] In France, however, the career of the *De remediis* took a slightly different route, for, although the work was popular, comparatively

---

[74] Namely VIII. ch. 1 ('Et primo viri clarissimi Francisci Petrarche in auctorem obiurgatio') and IX. ch. 1 ('Et . . . inde de Brunichilde Francorum regina').

[75] *Fall* I. 257–66; III. 3859; IV. 106–26; IX. 3422–7.

[76] Gray (1989: 36). However, Schirmer (1961: 217) follows Hammond (1927–8) in believing that Lydgate encountered Petrarch primarily through Humphrey; certainly, Humphrey donated seven volumes of Petrarch to Oxford in 1439–44, two of which were copies of the *De remediis* (*BQR* 1 1914–16: 134; Mann 1975b): 282–3. Humphrey owned the incomplete *De remediis*, now surviving as BN MS lat. 10209 (Pellegrin 1961: 405–6); (Bodleian Library 1970: 8–9); (Sammut 1980: 64, 79, 119–20).   [77] *Fall* IX. 3422–7.

[78] Ibid. I. 258–9. See Haas (1987: 55, 65).

[79] Boccaccio praises the *De remediis* in his *De generatione deorum Gentilium* XIV. 10: 'herein all that is clear and holy in the bosom of moral philosophy is presented in so majestic a style that nothing could be uttered for the instruction of mankind more replete, more mature, nay, more holy'.   [80] Trapp (1996: 68).

few copies of it seem to have been available after Charles V commissioned an early French translation from Jean Daudin (completed 1378) which quickly displaced the Latin original.[81] Although its influence was wide among both scholars and nobles, it is not known how familiar Laurent himself may have been with the translation; however, one of the seven surviving manuscript copies of Daudin's text was acquired by Laurent's patron Jean of Berry in 1403.[82]

Vastly popular, and owned by Lydgate's patron, this dialogue seems to have made a strong impression on the Benedictine writer: he says of it that its 'mater is wondirful delectable'.[83] It is not unusual that Lydgate should have understood the *De remediis* to be an analogue for the *De casibus* tradition, for the apophthegmatic warnings and rebuffs given by *Ratio* to *Gaudium* and *Spes* in their prosperity in the first volume and the consolation offered to *Dolor* and *Metus/Timor* in their adversity in the second inculcate similar moral lessons to the laments uttered by the fallen *elati* of Boccaccio's text: life and good fortune are fragile things, the pleasures of this world are so inconstant, its rulers so variable, and its justice so elusive, that the individual has no hope of gaining happiness unless he acquire a virtuous and stoic disposition.

Lydgate may have encountered the work in either France or England, for sixteen of the forty Petrarch manuscripts in England in the medieval period were copies of the *De remediis*:[84] the earliest manuscript of Petrarch in England is a fourteenth-century copy of the work in an English hand (later owned by John Blodwell, dean of St Asaph's, and now Cambridge, Corpus Christi College MS 40),[85] a copy was bequeathed to York Minster in 1414,[86] a quotation from the work was held in Peterhouse as early as 1418,[87] and a copy of the work was the only humanist text in the University Library in Cambridge in 1475.[88] Charles of Orléans had a copy of the work during his imprisonment in England.[89]

---

[81] Mann (1969: 2).   [82] Ibid. 6, 11.

[83] *Fall* 1. 267. 'At least 150' manuscripts of the complete work survive and another 94 abridged, translated, or excerpted copies are extant (see Mann 1971: 57). Humphrey's copy survives as Paris, BN lat. 10209.

[84] Mann (1975: 139–40).

[85] Mann (1971*b*: 178; 1975*a*: 140; 1975*b*: 280–1).

[86] Mann (1975*b*: 286).

[87] Now Peterhouse MS 133 (see Mann 1975*b*: 281).

[88] Mann (1971*b*: 178).   [89] Now BN MS lat. 6498 (see Mann 1969: 3).

The first ten dialogues of the second book of the *De remediis* were the only Latin Petrarch text to be translated into English in the period.[90]

Although Petrarch may have been popular among the English, this sentiment was not reciprocal: Petrarch makes his view of the English victory at Poitiers clear in a letter and in the last of his *Bucolicum carmen*, which he adapted in 1357 for this polemical purpose.[91] In 1360, as an envoy of the Visconti, who were to provide funds for the ransom of John II, Petrarch travelled to the French court: Petrarch's sympathy for the defeated king emerges in the oration which he delivered before John on the subject of Fortune.[92] Petrarch's consolation could not be further in spirit from the partisan alterations Lydgate makes to the narrative of John II in the last book of the *Fall*.

LYDGATE IN FRANCE

Lydgate was in France in the mid-1420s. The exact reason for his going and the precise duration of his stay have never been determined, but the date 28 July 1426 has been deciphered from astronomical data in the 'Title and Pedigree of Henry VI' (which was written in France) and taken as the poem's date of commission,[93] and by the time of Henry VI's Westminster coronation in November 1429 (and possibly earlier) Lydgate had returned to England.[94] While in France Lydgate produced two major works—the

[90] Surviving as CUL MS Ii. vi. 39 (see ed. Diekstra 1968).

[91] *Epist. Famil.* XXII. 14; Petrarch, trans. Bergin (1974: 196–213, 250–2): lines 148–58 were added by Petrarch. The same eclogue was exploited by Thomas Bekynton, Humphrey's former Chancellor of twelve years, in 1450 in a defence of the French claim of the kings of England, *De iure regum Anglorum ad regnum Francie* (Mann 1975a: 141; 1975b: 283; 1980: 294).

[92] Wilkins (1961: 173–5).

[93] *MP* ii. 613–22, ll.287–323. MacCracken reads the dating as 20 July 1426 (*MP* ii. 621); Schirmer (1961: 118) and Pearsall (1970: 166) conclude 28 July 1427: Pearsall (1997: 25) confirms the 28th of the month, but moves the year to 1426. Lydgate was absent from Hatfield Broad Oak, the cell of Bury of which he had been made Prior in June 1423: if this date is reliable, then Lydgate is the 'prior de Hatfeldbrodehoke' who is rebuked by the Chapter of the Black Monks for failing to excuse himself from the Northampton Chapters in July 1423 and July 1426 (see Pantin, ii. 138, 161).

[94] Lydgate produces the 'Roundel' for this coronation, as well as the 'Soteltes' for the coronation banquet and the celebratory 'Ballade to King Henry VI upon his Coronation' (*MP* ii. 622–30; see Pearsall 1997: 28–9).

translation of Guillaume de Deguileville's *Pélerinage de la Vie Humaine* (the *Pilgrimage of the Life of Man*) and the *Daunce of Machabree*—as well as the shorter 'Title and Pedigree'. The 'Devowte Invocacioun to Sainte Denys', which survives in only one manuscript (Shirley's MS Ashmole 59, fos. 65ʳ–66ʳ), is rather more problematic,[95] while the date of Lydgate's only other lengthy translation from a French source, *Reson and Sensuallyte*, is uncertain.[96]

Whatever the reasons for his going to France, Lydgate's stay there brought him into contact with men of considerable importance in the Lancastrian administration. When John, duke of Bedford, commissioned the French notary Laurent Calot in 1423 to produce a poem in demonstration of Henry VI's descent from St Louis (Louis IX, *regn.* 1226–70), he only partly did so in defence of the young king's dual monarchy of France and England. The poem seems to have been a very shrewd exercise in diplomatic relations: as J. W. McKenna has documented, Bedford was well aware of the importance of the Anglo-Burgundian alliance to the English cause.[97] It is clear that the poem functioned partly to cement the vital political relationship with Philippe the Good (duke of Burgundy since the assassination of his father, Jean the Fearless, in 1419). As Lydgate's translation records, Calot's poem vilified the Montereau murder:

> Thurgh feyned falshed caused cursidly
> By the Dolphyn, that so horribly
> Made sleen *without*e drede or shame,

---

[95] *MP* i. 127–9. The difficulty with this poem is one of dating: the headnote to the poem states that Lydgate produced it for 'Charlles þe Frenshe kynge', but there is no internal evidence to support this claim. If the poem was produced for Charles VI ('the Mad')—and it is surely unthinkable that it would have been written for Charles VII, the enemy of the Lancastrian administration—then Charles's death on 21 October 1422 supplies a very early *terminus ad quem* for the work. As it is improbable that Lydgate was in France at this time, either the putative patronage of the poem or its composition in France must be in doubt. Compare Pearsall's confidence (1970: 166) that the poem was produced for Charles VI and Schirmer's contrasting belief (1961: 126, 189) that it was produced for Charles VII.

[96] *Reson* survives in only two manuscripts (Bodleian, MS Fairfax 16 and BL MS Additional 29729): neither provides evidence of dating (or even medieval evidence of Lydgate's authorship). In his discussion of the poem Sieper suggests that it was composed before the *Troy Book* (that is, before 1409), but he has no hard evidence that would not permit its composition immediately after the *Troy Book*, during Lydgate's French period (i.e. 1422–6) (Lydgate ed. Sieper 1903: 5–9).   [97] McKenna (1965).

At Monstreux, a toun of grete fame,
Iohn duc of Burgoyne, by grete violence

.   .   .   .   .   .

. . . alas! þat was to grete a ruth[98]

The inclusion of these lines attacking the Dauphin in a vindication of Henry's succession to the French throne is a shrewd political manoeuvre, and Lydgate's translation illustrates the degree to which he was involved in Lancastrian propaganda. The commission for the translation of Calot's verses came, as Lydgate tells us, from Richard Beauchamp, thirteenth earl of Warwick, the Agincourt veteran who had been tutor to the young Henry VI and who was in 1437 appointed Lieutenant-General of France.[99] The exact extent of Lydgate's familiarity with Warwick is not known, although Lydgate does write his *Guy of Warwick* for Margaret Talbot, Warwick's eldest daughter, and his 'Fifteen Joys of Our Lady' for Isabelle, Warwick's second wife.[100]

The chief importance of Lydgate's visit to occupied France lies, however, in his exposure to literary, rather than political, influences. Of these the most significant for a reading of the *Fall of Princes* is undoubtedly the text of the *Danse macabré* which adorned an arcade in the Cemetery of the Saints Innocents in Paris. The anonymous 'Bourgeois de Paris' records the construction of the fresco in 1424–5:

Item, l'an mil quatre cents vingt-cinq fut faite la Danse Macabré aux Innocents, et fut commencée environ le mois d'aoust, et achevée en caresme ensuivant.[101]

---

[98] *MP* ii. 616, ll. 83–7, 91. The sensitivity of the Anglo-Burgundian alliance to the assassination may be seen when, in 1420, Henry V captured Montereau and supervised the exhumation and reburial of John's corpse (Strohm 1998: 241 n. 4). In 1429—ten years after the event—his brother Bedford staged a dramatic reconstruction of the assassination for Burgundy, possibly to stiffen Burgundian opposition to the coronation of the Dauphin at Rheims later that month (see McKenna 1965: 156). For the intriguing suggestion that the assassination of John the Fearless was an indirect result of the success of Petit's arguments for tyrannicide on the duke's behalf in 1408 see Guenée (1992: 281).

[99] Griffiths (1981: 52–3, 205, 250); for the commission see p. 219. See also Rowe (1932–3), but note that Rowe—who is followed by Scattergood (1971: 73), Griffiths (1981: 219), and Wolffe (1981: 52)—is mistaken in her belief that Bedford's donation was hung in Notre Dame: see Stratford (1993: 115–16).

[100] Pearsall (1970: 167–8): Pearsall suggests that Lydgate went to France 'presumably at Warwick's instigation' (p. 166). Isabelle was not, as Pearsall claims, Warwick's third wife.

[101] *Journal d'un Bourgeois de Paris sous Charles VI et Charles VII* ed. Mary (1929: 188).

Lydgate's translation of the verses on the cemetery mural did much to open up the European 'Dance of Death' tradition to an English audience: his text was used to accompany a cycle of pictures for a cloister on the north side of St Paul's Cathedral in London which survived until its demolition in 1549 by Edward Seymour, Protector Somerset, to provide building materials for the construction of Somerset House in the Strand.[102]

The European tradition has been carefully catalogued by Hellmut Rosenfeld in his study *Der Mittelalterliche Totentanz*; it seems to have taken its origins from a Latin *Dance* text of the mid-fourteenth century (*c*.1348–50),[103] which may have been a response to Benedict XII's bull *Benedictus deus* (1336) on the debated issue of the admission of departed souls to the beatific vision. Rosenfeld has seen the *Dance* tradition as marking a seminal moment in the emergence of the mindset of the Renaissance, while Johan Huizinga felt that the *Dance* marked a key point in the evolution of later medieval sensibilities.[104] Lydgate's poem *Daunce of Machabree* survives (in two versions) in fifteen manuscripts and was first printed at the back of Tottell's 1554 print of the *Fall*; Bergen appends a revised version of Totell's text to his edition of the *Fall* in 1924.[105] In the poem Death addresses in turn thirty-five representatives of human society, both clerical (Pope, Cardinal, Patriarch, Archbishop, Bishop, Abbot, Abbess, Canon, Carthusian, Benedictine Monk, Curate, Franciscan Friar) and lay (Emperor, King, Constable, Baron, Squire, Baily, Astronomer, Juror, Minstrel, Child): some of these Lydgate adds to his French source.[106] Although the figure of Death sometimes seems to rebuke his victims for the distractions of their life or office, there

---

[102] Stow's 1598 account of the cloister in his *A Survey of London* ed. Kingsford (1908 repr. 1971: i. 327) states that the verses had been translated 'by Iohn Lidgate, Monke of Bury' (see Lydgate ed. Warren 1931: xxii–xxiii), and subsequent commentators have accepted this claim (e.g. Douce 1833: 51–2; Mâle 1922: 370; Eisler 1948: 216; Rosenfeld 1968: 120).   [103] Rosenfeld (1968: 45).

[104] Ibid.: 'Somit wird die Subjektivität der gotischen Epoche auch vom Dogma her begünstigt und letzten Endes ermöglicht, daß Renaissance und Reformation das Individuum in den Mittelpunkt der Welt stellen' ('In the event, it was in this way that the mindset of the Gothic age, previously so hampered by dogma, made it possible for the Renaissance and the Reformation to put the individual at the centre of their world-view'); Huizinga (1924: ch. 11: 'The Vision of Death').

[105] 1554 print, fos. 221ʳ–225ᵛ; *Fall* ed. Bergen vol. iii. 1025–44; Seymour (1985: 22–4). See also Simpson (2001) on the poem.   [106] e.g. Princess, Abbess, Tregetour, Nun, Canon Regular, Juror.

is no sense in which death meets the protagonists as a punishment
for vice. The worldliness of the Archbishop, the vanity of the
Abbess, the covetousness of the Merchant and Usurer, and the
corruption of the Juror are all incidental to their invitation to join
the dance, as too are the humility of the Archbishop and disciplined piety of the Carthusian. A sense of wasted opportunities for
amendment of life and a regret for frustrated aspirations under-
score many of the speeches, and nowhere more powerfully than in
the encounter with a new-born child who pitifully mumbles:

> A, A, A, a woorde I cannot speake;
> I am so yonge; I was borne yesterday.
> Death is so hasty on me to be wreake,
> And list no lenger to make no delaie.
> I come but now, and now I go my way[107]

The significance of the *Daunce* for Lydgate's longer poem is clear,
for both deal (although to differing effect) with the laments of the
fallen. Crucially, however, the *Daunce* and the *Fall* differ in
the reaction they may be held to induce in their reader: whereas
the *exempla* of nobles who have fallen into misfortune and
poverty as a result of personal failings can be exploited to voice
a stern ethical warning lest the same fate should befall the reader,
no amount of admonition or virtuous living can alter the
inevitability of death. However, in his original prologue to the
Daunce Lydgate presents Death in terms which he will later characteristically use of Lady Fortune (as Death eclipses the bright sun
of the powerful with his showers of rain) and Death's victims
lament their *chauntepleure* ('singing-then-weeping') reversal of
fortunes as the victims of the *Fall* will later do.[108] The arousal of
pathos, rather than the correction of specific vices, is the intention of the *Daunce*, and in this respect it functions rather as do
those *elati* in the *Fall* who are the innocent victims of Fortune.
The pathos of undeserved misfortune, as I will demonstrate, is one
of the chief additions Lydgate made to the *Fall* as he worked his
way through Laurent's prose.

Lydgate's stay in France comes at an interesting time for students
of the *Fall*, because these years confirm his close involvement
with men and women of influence which the commission of the

---

[107] *Daunce*, 585-9.   [108] See *Fall* III. 660, 3599; IV. 1644, 2903; VI. 21.

Troy Book for Henry V had initiated: it is possible that Lydgate was known to Henry V (as the Prince of Wales) as early as his time at Gloucester College, Oxford.[109] The French years, therefore, see an increase in Lydgate's engagement with matters of secular politics and confirm his status as the Lancastrian 'laureate': indeed, it was in France that Lydgate produced his most politically sensitive text, in the form of his translation of Calot's defence of Henry's dual monarchy, and, if these years saw the production of his *Reson and Sensuallyte* (a translation of the first 4873 lines of the anonymous French poem *Les Échecs Amoureux*) which C. S. Lewis saw as a 'beautiful and important' work, then the stay in France also results in Lydgate's first large-scale attempt at politically advisory literature.[110]

The *Échecs* is an allegory based on the *Ludus scaccorum* by the Lombard friar Jacobus de Cessolis (*fl.* 1288–1322), an advisory work strongly influenced by Giles of Rome's popular *De regimine principum* of the 1270s, in which the narrator, finding himself in the landscape of the *Roman de la Rose*, is schooled in love by Venus and in reason by Diana. In the Garden of Deduit he plays a game of chess in which the pieces (their designs and the materials from which they are fashioned) form a complex allegory.[111] The game itself, which Lydgate only partly translates, unfolds as a serious moral and sexual challenge: the narrator's opponent, a maid, finally checkmates him. Throwing his lot in with the god of Love, the narrator requests a further game, but is rebuked by Pallas for abandoning the paths of reason: the text concludes with thirty-five remedies for love, a thorough analysis of the orders of society (kings, councillors, judges, clergy, artists, peasants, and so on), and some practical advice on marriage, child-rearing, education, physical exercise, and elementary economics. Although the incomplete English *Reson* (as its two

---

[109] See a letter from Henry (when Prince of Wales) to the Abbot of Bury interceding for the continued studies of 'Dan J. L.' at Oxford, in All Souls MS 182, repr. Legge (1941: 411–12). For details of Gloucester College see Rashdall (1936: iii. 184–6; Pantin (1946–7); Pearsall (1997: 56–7).

[110] Lewis (1936: 277). The *Échecs* should not be confused with the conflation of Jean de Vignai's and Jean Farron's translations of the *Ludus* which formed the source of Caxton's *The Game of Chess* (1474 and 1483).

[111] The symbolism of the chessmen is clearly tabulated by Legaré et al. in (1991: 78–9). There has been little published discussion of the *Échecs* which is Lydgate's source; but see Sieper (1898: 1–94) and the material given by Galpin (1920).

surviving manuscripts witness) omits the more openly political material of the *Échecs*, Lydgate's close exposure to advisory literature of this nature has an influence on the ethical envoy sections he intersperses through his translation of the *Des Cas*. The French models of both the *Danse macabré* and, more broadly, the *Échecs*—the literary legacy of Lydgate's experiences of the 1420s—lie behind his major production of the 1430s, the *Fall of Princes*; the pathos of the one and the political valency of the other combine to allow him to synthesize exempla of the frailty of the human condition with loosely regiminal instruction. What kind of appeal this synthesis may have held for Humphrey of Gloucester, Lydgate's patron, will form part of the investigation of the next chapter.

3

'Lancastrian' Lydgate: Poet and Patron

The notion of 'Lancastrian' Lydgate—that is, of Lydgate as a preferred court poet in the reigns of Henry V and Henry VI—continues to intrigue modern readers; much of the force of this interest seems to arise from the perceived paradox that the Monk of Bury should, while a member of the Benedictine Order, have been granted access to the society of some of the most powerful men of his age, accepting commissions from dukes, princes, and nobility.

The image of Lydgate as closely engaged in the politics and personalities of the Lancastrian dynasty finds its origins in Eleanor Hammond's suggestive reconstruction (from internal evidence in the *Fall* and from an eight-stanza verse letter) of the economic dynamic between Humphrey and Lydgate: this article (the content of which Hammond incorporated into her anthology *English Verse between Chaucer and Surrey*) claimed that the relationship between the two may have been more interactive than had previously been imagined. Poet and patron, she suggested, enjoyed not a dry relationship of commission and delivery, but rather one of bargaining and exchange.[1] Schirmer discusses the commission for the *Fall* by the 'Lieutenant and Warden of England', hinting that a close professional relationship existed between Lydgate and Duke Humphrey: 'Humphrey . . . not only commissioned this work but also supervised its progress'.[2] In 1970 Derek Pearsall offered several pages of reconstruction of 'Gloucester's actual influence on Lydgate's translation' and devoted a whole chapter to 'laureate Lydgate', the 'poet-propagandist to the Lancastrian

---

[1] Hammond (1914); see also (1927–8: 149–50).
[2] Schirmer (1952, trans. 1961: 209, 215).

dynasty'.[3] More recently Pearsall has suggested that Lydgate is arguably 'the first poet writing in English to fashion his poems as instruments of royal policy'.[4] John Scattergood treated Lydgate as a 'major court poet' in 1971, speaking of his 'unofficial laureateship', and the same idea resurfaces in R. F. Green's impressive study, *Poets and Princepleasers*: 'for some years after 1425 Lydgate performed a semi-official role as apologist for the Lancastrian government'.[5] Revisionist readings during the 1990s fruitfully problematized straightforward notions of Lydgate as a dutifully diplomatic mouthpiece for the Lancastrian court. In the context of a discussion of the *Siege of Thebes* Lee Patterson has detected Lydgate's 'skepticism towards his identity as a spokesman for Lancastrian interests' and suggested that the poem confronts Henry V's French campaigns with 'an antiwar message'; James Simpson has suggested that Lydgate was 'deeply critical of the English military project'.[6] Articles by Paul Strohm have identified hesitant and subversive notes in Lydgate's apparent complicity with 'an illegitimate and insecure dynasty', while Scott-Morgan Straker has argued that Lydgate is more politically 'audacious' than Chaucer, reading the *Troy Book* as a steely challenge to its patron, Henry V, to choose peace rather than further conflict in France.[7]

Exciting as the emergence of this portrait of Lydgate's intelligent and occasionally daring political understanding has been, the tantalizing tension between cloister and court seems to have been resolved, with the Monk of Bury of fifteenth-century readers becoming a civil servant for their modern successors; in a discussion of the relationship between the Benedictines and Henry V's suppression of heretical activity Patrick Horner even contends that 'one might, understandably of course, regard Lydgate more as a spokesman of the Lancastrian court than as a representative Benedictine voice'.[8]

---

[3] Pearsall (1970: 227, 160–91). Stephen Hawes presents Lydgate almost as an adviser to Henry V in his 'Ioyfull Medytacyon', ll. 8–14 (*The Minor Poems* 1974: 85).   [4] Pearsall (1992: 15).
[5] Scattergood (1971: 145, 73); Green (1980: 189).
[6] Patterson (1993: 93, 96); Simpson (2001: 234).
[7] Strohm (2000: 130); Straker (1999; 2001: 16).
[8] Horner (1990: 217). The sixteenth century saw another Black Monk, Alexander Barclay, performing a similar role for Henry VIII: in 1520 Barclay is ordered to 'deuise histoires' for the banquet hall on the Field of the Cloth of Gold (see Trapp 1955: 1 n. 5).

The next chapter reconsiders the impact of ecclesiastical polity on the *Fall*, but this chapter re-examines Lydgate's relationship with Duke Humphrey by considering those aspects of the *Fall* which reflect the expectations and concerns of its patron (notably the refrained envoy sections and other passages which were included in the poem as a result of Humphrey's intervention), and suggests how far the Lydgatean emphases of these narratives accord with what is known of Humphrey's character and interests; *The Serpent of Division*, a prose treatise attributed to Lydgate (which was possibly commissioned by Humphrey), is also discussed. Elizabeth Salter and Felicity Riddy have both shown the difficulties of establishing historical allusion and topical reference in poetry of the later medieval period:[9] mindful of these cautions, readers should tread warily in tracing possible connections between Lydgate's work and contextual event or the biography of his patron.

HUMPHREY OF GLOUCESTER

In his translation of the French *Livre de Melibée et de Dame Prudence* in the *Canterbury Tales* Chaucer omits after line 1199 of his version a powerful biblical formula: 'Dolente est la terre qui a infant à seigneur'.[10] The resonances of this line for a Ricardian poet are obvious; however, the sentiment is one that would also have been apposite for the first decade of the reign of Henry VI, in that the early death of Henry V and the accession of his infant son left England without a strong leader at a particularly urgent stage of its dealings with post-Troyes France. Lancastrian Normandy required careful supervision and the relationship between the two parties of the Anglo-Burgundian alliance was precarious; the abrasive character of Humphrey of Gloucester, uncle to the boy-king and younger brother to the duke of Bedford, did little to ease the delicate position of foreign policy in these years. His politically incautious marriage to Jacqueline, countess

⁹ Salter (1978); Riddy (1986).
¹⁰ Cf. Eccles. 10 : 16; see Walsingham ed. Riley (1863–4: ii. 344); *Piers Plowman* Prol., B. 195–6; Lindsay, *Dreme*, ll. 1009–11; Christine de Pisan *Treasure of the City of Ladies*, III. 7 trans. Lawson (1985: 166), and *Othéa* LXXX trans. Scrope (1970: 98). For the topical use of this proverb in 1400 see Griffiths (1981: 241).

of Hainault, endangered the vital alliance,[11] and his decision to invade the Low Countries in October 1424 in order to claim Flemish territories from the duke of Brabant (who had Burgundian support) shows a disregard for the intricacies of political life. Humphrey's violent quarrels with his uncle Henry Beaufort, bishop of Winchester (*regn.* 1404–47) and cardinal (from 1426), similarly bespeak a rash and headstrong personality.[12]

Frustrated ambition, among his other manifest faults, most clearly characterizes Humphrey in the decade of the minority.[13] His petulant persistence with claims to the full regency of England (which he maintained to be rightly his as a result of a promise made to him by Henry V)[14] in these years reveals his willingness to allow personal ambition to jeopardize the wider good of the kingdom. Despite Humphrey's citation of a deathbed codicil to Henry V's will in his demands for the titles of Protector and Tutor to the infant king, the Parliament of November 1422 denied him these honours (which brought not only the power to summon, preside over, and dissolve Parliaments, but also an extremely privileged influence over the growing king). The lords debated Humphrey's role on 5 November and finally styled him

le puissant Prince Humfrey Duc de Gloucestre son Uncle, Protectour & Defensour de les Roialme et Esglise d'Engleterre, et son Principal Conseillour en l'absence de l'excellent Prince John Duc de Bedeford[15]

[11] Vickers (1907: 92–6, 124–5, 130–7 and *passim*); Wolffe (1981: 38–9); Griffiths (1981: 30, 36, 70–1, 179); Strohm (2000); Vaughan (1970, repr. 2002: 33–53).

[12] For the *praemunire* crisis launched by Humphrey at his enemy in 1432 see Griffiths, (1981: 41–2); Wolffe (1981: 67–9). Humphrey's long-standing rivalry with Beaufort even resulted in 'the most severe domestic crisis of the protectorate' (Griffiths 1981: 36), including armed confrontation in the streets of London between the supporters of the duke and the bishop in October 1425 (ibid. 70–81). For details of Beaufort's claims against Humphrey and the contentious position he held with regard both to the papacy and the authority of the English crown ('the pope's man in England, the king's man at Rome') see Harriss (1970: 142; 1988: 94–9, 115–18, 134–49, 150–3). See also Harriss (1991); McFarlane (1945); Holmes (1973); Richard Davies (1977).

[13] Vickers (1907: 95, 106, 124, 125, 168–9, 228, 318, 333–9). Bergen has commented on the irony that Laurent and Lydgate's translations should have been made for two such unethical princes (*Fall* ed. Bergen vol. i. p. xvi).

[14] Rymer (1816–30: IV. iii. 146); Roskell (1953: 203–26).

[15] *RP* iv. 175; see Rymer (1816–30: IV. iv. 83–4). As the lords clarified in 1427, the titles chosen did not include the 'name of Tutour, Lieutenant, Governour, nor of Regent, nor no name yat shuld emporte auctorite of governaunce of ye lond' (*RP* iv. 326–7).

Even these titles, then, had to be surrendered whenever Humphrey's elder brother John, duke of Bedford and regent of France, was in the country.[16] It was not to be until Henry VI's departure to France for his Paris coronation on 16 December 1431 that Humphrey finally realized his ambition to be the King's Lieutenant—and even this hard-won power was limited to the period of Henry's absence from England (from 23 April 1430 to 9 February 1432).[17]

The absence of a regent had in effect instituted conciliar rule during the minority, a situation at odds with the ambition and dirigiste politics of Lydgate's patron: Humphrey chafed under the rule of the lords, and did not do so passively. Once Henry's coronations had taken place (in 1429 and 1431), Humphrey seems deviously to have declared an open season of hostilities against his pro-conciliar enemies.[18] The fundamental principle upon which the minority Protectorate (and the lords' frustration of Humphrey's regency ambitions) had rested was that the king's rule had been deemed to have started upon the death of his father—no other individual could exercise regal authority on the monarch's behalf. Once Henry had been anointed and crowned, then, Gloucester turned the same much-hated principle back on his opponents: now that the minority was over, the conciliar powers of the lords had no legitimacy. John Watts has shown that Gloucester played the council off against the young king in these years, arguing that he 'inaugurated a new politics' and was the first to exploit 'the dependence of the monarchical system upon the private person of the king'.[19] Certainly Gloucester does seem to have manipulated the weak position of the lords after the premature coronations: in 1432 he orchestrated a coup in an attempt to transfer government away from the council to the court, wielding his influence to secure the replacement of men closely associated with Bishop Beaufort with partisan appointments, thereby using constitutional change as a tool in his struggle with his old enemy.[20] It is even possible that he may have been

---

[16] For fuller accounts of Humphrey's claims see Griffiths (1981: 17, 19–24); Wolffe, (1981: 29–32); Butt (1989: 495–516).

[17] Rymer (1816–30: IV. iv. 160); see Wolffe (1981: 65); Butt (1989: 515).

[18] The Protectorate terminated with Henry VI's Westminster coronation in November 1429 (RP iv. 336–7; EHD iv. 245).   [19] Watts (1996: 120).

[20] On his return from France Henry reshaped the council, replacing the Chancellor (Archbishop John Kemp), Keeper of the Privy Seal (Bishop William

responsible for goading the twelve-year-old Henry VI into challenging the authority of the lords in 1434, a crisis which led to the embarrassing confrontation between boy and Parliament at Cirencester in November of that year.[21]

It is intriguing that Humphrey should commission a translation of the De casibus from Lydgate at the start of the 1430s: an anthology of narratives of tyranny, tragic downfall, and political mismanagement must have wielded a powerful appeal at a time when Humphrey's own real constitutional influence was in decline. Ultimately, Humphrey's career reads much like one of the casus of the Fall: the trial of his second wife, Eleanor Cobham, for witchcraft in 1441 when Humphrey was heir presumptive to the throne,[22] his subsequent loss of royal favour and removal from the Privy Council in 1445, and his arrest and suspicious death in St Saviour's Hospital during the Bury St Edmunds Parliament in February 1447 all chart his fall from influence.[23] Eventually Humphrey himself is inscribed into the de casibus tradition which his commission did so much to foster: he received a pseudo-Lydgatean versified epitaph[24] and features in George Chastelain's 1463 continuation of the De casibus (the Temple de Bocace), in cautionary verses for Archbishop William Booth,[25] and again in the sixteenth-century continuation of Lydgate's poem, the Mirror for Magistrates.

Although Humphrey emerges as an elephantine and politically clumsy figure, he is an ambiguous one also. Without overstating

Alnwick), Steward of the Household (John, Baron Tiptoft) and Treasurer (Walter, Lord Hungerford) with Bishop John Stafford, Bishop William Lyndwood, Sir John Babthorp, and John, Lord Scrope of Masham—these appointments considerably strengthened Gloucester's 'grip on the government of the realm and his influence over the upbringing of the king' (Griffiths 1981: 41; Vickers 1907: 230; see Watts 1996: 155–8). It was in 1432 that Humphrey launched the praemunire crisis, attempting to secure Beaufort's downfall.

   [21] Wolffe (1981: 79–80). The lords had in fact compromised any personal exercise of regal authority as early as November 1433 when Bedford was reinstated as an adviser, and in December the Council was revived (RP iv. 423, 446; see Watts 1996: 121–2).   [22] Griffiths (1968–9).
   [23] Vickers (1907: 290–4); Wolffe (1981: 17, 242); see the account of Humphrey's fall in Hall's Chronicle; Containing the History of England (1809: 209–10).
   [24] The Epitaphium, ascribed to Lydgate by Stow at the end of Speght's 1598 edition of Chaucer, was dismissed by MacCracken (MP vol. i. p. xl); it survives in MSS Harley 2251 (fos. 7ʳ–8ᵛ) and Addit. 34360 (fo. 65ᵛ), and has been printed by Rossell Hope Robbins (1955).   [25] Wright (1859|61: ii. 228).

the case,[26] Humphrey was a remarkable patron of English and Italian poets and scholars during these same years. Aside from commissioning work from Lydgate, his employment of Tito Livio Frulovisi and friendship with Zeno da Castiglione, bishop of Bayeux,[27] his literary correspondence with Pier Candido Decembrio and Piero del Monte (the papal collector in England from 1434–9),[28] and his extraordinarily generous donations of 274 books to the University of Oxford (in 1439, 1441, and 1444) all attest to an engagement with issues of scholarship and the humanist project of recovering the work of the ancients.[29] Humphrey seems to have been particularly enthusiastic in his reading of classical moral and political theory: not only did he own Bruni's Latin version of the *Ethics*, but he also personally received a translation of *The Republic* from Decembrio and (impatiently) commissioned another of the *Politics* from Bruni.[30] He owned copies of the influential *De regimine principum* of the Augustinian Aegidius Romanus (Giles of Rome), written in the last quarter of the thirteenth century for the future Philip IV, and of Hoccleve's English adaptation of it for the future Henry V, the *Regement of Princes* (1412).[31] Granted, book ownership may reveal less about medieval owners than some scholars would care

[26] As perhaps Weiss (1957a: 39), Schirmer (1952, trans. 1961: 210), and Renoir (1967: 71) have been prone to do: nonetheless, Aeneas Sylvius Piccolomini did salute Humphrey for having 'zealously received polite learning into England' Harriss (1995: 119).

[27] Weiss (1957a: 40–5, 47 and *passim*); see Weiss (1957b).

[28] Weiss (1957a: 45, 51–61); Vickers (1907: 340–82); see Petriberg (1895) and Borsa (1904).

[29] Accounts of the donations are given by Henry Anstey (1898: i. 179–84, 204–5, 232–7), and also in *BQR* 1 (1914–16: 131–5) and Sammut (1980: 60–84). See Ullman (1973); Bodleian Library, *Duke Humfrey's Library and the Divinity School 1488–1988* (1988: 18–25). An older attempt to catalogue the books owned by Humphrey is in Vickers (1907: 426–38).

[30] Weiss (1957a: 51–7, 46–8). Humphrey's copy of Decembrio's *Republic* survives as MS Vat. lat. 10669; see Bodleian Library (1988): 45–9.

[31] Two sheets of a French translation of Giles survive with Jean de Vignai's French Vegetius in CUL MS Ee. ii. 17, fos. 1r–2r; Humphrey's inscription is on fo. 36v. Humphrey donated an unidentified Giles manuscript to Oxford in 1444 (Anstey 1898: i. 237; Sammut 1980: 84). A copy of the work was held at Bury Abbey in the fifteenth century (now Gonville and Caius MS 113), an inscription on fo. 152v revealing that it was donated by the sacrist John Cranewys (1426–41): other owners of Giles include Charles V and Henry Percy, second earl of Northumberland (now Bodleian MS Laud misc. 702) (see Delisle 1907: 258–60; Cavanaugh, Ph.D. thesis, 1980: 647).

to admit (every bookshelf, after all, displays unread, or cursorily read, volumes).³² Furthermore, men in positions of power can be notoriously bad at accepting wise counsel: King John famously interrupted St Hugh of Lincoln on Easter Day in 1199 with the wry comment that long sermons on bad kings delayed his meals,³³ while refusal to take counsel was listed as one of Richard II's failings in the deposition documents of 1399.³⁴ However, advisory literature has an obvious educational power: in 1428 the lords instructed Henry's tutor, the earl of Warwick, to instil morality into his young charge with historical exempla,³⁵ and on receiving Decembrio's translation of the first five books of *The Republic* Humphrey himself claimed that 'they shall be to us as companions or counsellors for ruling our life'.³⁶

Although there is evidence that Humphrey owned several works by Boccaccio, his own copy of the *De casibus* does not survive.³⁷ However, given his developed interest in advisory literature, it is interesting to ask what kind of appeal Lydgate's poem might have held for its patron. What, in short, is the political impact of the *Fall*? The clearest example of Humphrey's intervention into Lydgate's composition of the poem comes in the poet's claim at the start of the second book that his patron asked him to insert a 'remedie' after each narrative, an envoy section directed at 'noble pryncis' so that 'Bi othres fallyng thei myht themsilff correcte'.³⁸ Humphrey's intention seems to have been that Lydgate's version of the *De casibus* should highlight the regiminal value of the work. Study of the sixty-nine envoys reveals that Lydgate followed the terms of Humphrey's request

³² Note Green's cautions (1980: 91–2).
³³ Hugh [de Avalon] ed. Dimock (1864: 292–3).
³⁴ *EHD* iv. 411 (§ 23). The copy of the *De regimine* belonging to Richard's tutor, Simon Burley, survives as Cambridge, Pembroke College MS 158.
³⁵ *PPC* iii. 299.   ³⁶ Green (1980: 142); see Borsa (1904: 516).
³⁷ Humphrey donated two copies of the *De genealogia deorum* and one each of the *De casibus*, *De montibus*, and the *De mulieribus* to Oxford (Anstey 1898: i. 183, 235; Sammut 1980: 70, 78–9) and owned the French *Decameron* discussed in Ch. 2. Antonio Beccaria, his Italian secretary, translated the *Corbaccio* into Latin for him: the book possibly survives as Bodleian, MS Lat. misc. d. 34 (Sammut 1980: 128–30, 162–5; Weiss 1957a: 45–6).
³⁸ *Fall* ii. 150, 153–4. Wilhelm Kleineke mentions the addition of the regiminal envoys in his *Englische Fürstenspiegel* (1937: 13), but offers no discussion of them. Watts gives a succinct analysis of the theoretical function of advisory literature in this period (1996: 23–31).

closely: fifty-eight of the passages consciously expound the significance for princes of the preceding narrative.[39] What emerges clearly, however, is that Lydgate's advisory idiom is broadly ethical rather than specifically political or legal. Rulers are frequently exhorted to avoid vicious behaviour, be it pride (I. ch. 4), lust (I. ch. 12; III. ch. 4), adultery (I. ch. 16), anger (I. ch. 19), or sloth (II. ch. 13), and are instructed to obey God and honour his Church (II. chs. 1, 19). Practical advice on statecraft sometimes arises from more general moral guidance: the heroism of the Roman consul Marcus Attilius Regulus (v. ch. 3) teaches princes 'to supporte & meynteene rihtwisnesse' in their kingdoms, and the sins of Machaeus of Carthage (III. ch. 15) demonstrate that rulers should not oppress their subjects 'Lik bestial tigres, lik leouns vntretable' (v. 838; III. 4030).

Certain envoys do offer more theoretical advice: Boccaccio's chapter on credulous princes, 'Adversus nimiam credulitatem', is given an envoy advising readers to be wary of liars and flatterers and to be slow in pronouncing judgement, his chapter on Lucretia and Virginia (II. ch. 5) advises rulers to suppress rebellion, the Cyrus envoy (II. ch. 21) advises that princes should be merciful rather than tyrannical or bloodthirsty (cf. IV. ch. 7), while those of Jugurtha, Mithridates, and Nero (v. ch. 20; VI. ch. 5; VII. ch. 4) dilate on the evils of oppressive and tyrannical rule. Rulers are advised not to trust the commons (III. ch. 5) and are warned of the evil of corrupt judges (III. ch. 9; cf. III. ch. 10: 'In leguleos imperitos'). Fraternal discord and internal division are shown to be the ruin of many princes (I. ch. 9; III. ch. 19; IV. ch. 11; VI. ch. 9; VIII. ch. 19).

However, if Humphrey had hoped for systematically theoretical regiminal teaching from Lydgate he must have been disappointed in the *Fall* envoys, for their advisory material is largely ad hoc, moralizing the narratives in a direct and undeveloped manner. However, Lydgate does exceptionally use the envoys to the accounts of Agathocles (IV. ch. 13), the third-century tyrant of Syracuse, and the laundress Philippa of Catania (IX. ch. 26) to voice his disapproval (also found in the narrative of the Indian emperor Sandrocottus, IV. ch. 14) of the ignobly born who ascend

---

[39] Of the remaining envoys, three are directed to Lydgate's patron, one (that to II. ch. 11) to widows, another (IV. ch. 12) to princesses, and one to the book itself (at IX. 3589–604).

to rule: a large-scale addition to the narrative of Agathocles venomously allegorizes the social distinctions between princes and commoners (as gold and copper, lions and asses, roses and thistles), warning that 'thestat of politik puissaunce | Is lost wher-euer knaues haue gouernaunce'.[40] Moreover, the problem with Lydgate's envoys is not just that they are unsystematic, but that there are genuine inconsistencies in his advice. Lydgate's exhortations to princes to regulate their moral behaviour frequently clash with his pathos-arousing laments on the inconstancy of Fortune and the ephemerality of human power. The envoy to Book I, Chapter 5 expounds Saturn's malice, but then concludes with a warning to princes of the 'chaunge, the doubilnesse, | The gret onseurnesse, the variacioun' of this world (I. 1837–8); the narrative of Gideon, which celebrates the God-given victory of the Midianites, curiously concludes with an envoy on the mutability of 'ertheli blisse' (I. 3123). In a number of cases narratives which demonstrate the downfalls of the vicious, or which might be expected to articulate an ethic of moral accountability, support a fortunal *moralitas*. Examples of incoherence occur also: in Book V envoys to the consecutive chapters of Antiochus III and the Scipios are respectively made to voice the lessons of the power of human virtue to secure a long and prosperous reign (V. ch. 8) and the utter impotence of man in the face of Fortune's blind activity (V. ch. 9). The envoy to Mithridates (VI. ch. 5) declares that prudence and moral reformation will 'preserue your puissaunce | Geyn wordli chaung & Fortunys variaunce' (VI. 1756–7), and the envoy to Charles of Jerusalem (IX. ch. 19) preaches an ethic of strict desert ('Lik desertis men haue ther guerdonyng') (IX. 2033), yet Lydgate's envoy to Fortune in the closing stages of the poem affirms a straightforwardly fortunal reading of the work:

> And for to sette a short conclusioun,
> In a breeff somme this book to comprehende:
> Fortunis wheel bi reuolucioun
> Doth oon clymbe up, another to discende.[41]

---

[40] Ibid. IV. 2673–4: the material original to Lydgate comprises ll. 2654–723.

[41] Ibid. IX. 3299–302: for examples of fortunal envoys see III. ch. 12 (Alcibiades); IV. chs. 9 (Darius), 15 (Arsinoe), 16 (Brennus); VI. chs. 5 (Mithridates) and 11 (Caesar); VIII. ch. 19 (Arthur). The role of Fortune in the poem is discussed in Ch. 5.

Interestingly, Catherine Reynolds has suggested that one implication
of Lydgate's inclusion of the envoys may be the striking dearth of
illustrated manuscript copies of the *Fall*:

Le elaborazioni del Lydgate sulle implicazioni morali delle storie, che
sembrano essere state le sezioni più interessanti per il pubblico inglese,
erano invece meno adatte alla traduzione visuale . . . L'apparentemente
limitata richiesta di copie illustrate del *Fall of Princes* riflette forse l'ap-
prezzamento degli Inglesi per lo spirito moralistico del Lydgate a spese del
taglio più esplicitamente narrativo del Boccaccio.

(Lydgate's elaborations on the moral implications of the narratives, which
seem to have been the most interesting sections for the English public,
were however less suited to visual rendering . . . The apparently limited
demand for illustrated copies of the *Fall of Princes* perhaps reflects the
value the English placed on Lydgate's moralizing spirit at the expense of
Boccaccio's more explicitly narrative style.)[42]

While it would be misguided to expect the *Fall* to present
regiminal advice with the textbook clarity of more explicitly
advisory texts, it is plain that the work was valued by its patron
partly for its embodiment of ethical and political wisdom.
Aside from his request for summary and moralizing envoys,
Humphrey's most specific involvements with Lydgate's poem are
linked by an interest in aspects of the history of the Roman
empire: the most substantial intrusion into the composition of the
Fall comes in the form of a request that the poet should offer a
version of one particularly potent Roman legend, that of the rape
of Lucretia.

LYDGATE'S DEPOLITICIZED LUCRETIA

Although Lydgate, having praised the 'legende souerayne' of
Lucretia which he finds in the work of Chaucer, modestly
claims that it would be 'presumpcioun & veynglorie' on his
part to attempt to treat a narrative already told by the 'cheeff
poete off Bretayne', he nonetheless resolves that he will supply a
version of the story, partly because 'it were pite hir story for to

[42] 'I codici del Boccaccio illustrati in Inghilterra', (Reynolds 1999: iii. 268–9);
on the relatively modest formats of the surviving *Fall* manuscripts see Edwards
and Pearsall (1989: 270).

hide', but chiefly because he has been commanded to do so by his patron:

> Also my lord bad I sholde abide,
> By good auys at leiser to translate
> The doolful processe off hir pitous fate.[43]

A patronal request would suggest that the story of Lucretia's rape exerted a powerful attraction on Humphrey, but the decision to include the narrative in Book II has unfortunate consequences. Most important is the awkward repetition when Lydgate comes to deal with the fall of Tarquin in his next book (III. 932–1148), but the insertion of an extended *planctus* here, with its emphasis on human drama and moral debate, also distracts from the theme of the downfalls of proud kings which had united the stories of Rehoboam, Mucius Scaevola, and Tarquinius Superbus in the French source. In this section I shall examine some of the traditional interpretations of the Lucretia legend and, by discussing Lydgate's alterations to his sources, attempt to sketch some of the possible reasons for its appeal for his patron.

Premierfait's handling of Lucretia (II. ch. 5: 'In fastosam regum superbiam'), sandwiched between the accounts of Mucius Scaevola and of Virginia and Appius in his second book, makes, as did Boccaccio's, only a brief reference to the political consequences of her rape by Sextus Tarquinius:

En chascun estat ont este aucuns qui ont ose entreprendre 7 acomplir tresgrans choses | car Iunius brutus vng citoyen de Romme 7 cousin de la treschaste Lucresse tourna a sa partie tout le peuple de Romme contre Tarquin lorgueilleux roy des rommains pource que son filz Sexte tarquin auoit par malice 7 par force charnellement congneue ladicte Lucresse tandis que son mary Collatin tarquinian noble citoyen de Romme estoit en puille auec le roy Tarquin | comme plus a plain est racompte en son hystoire.

(There have been folk of every social degree who have dared to undertake, and have achieved, the greatest of things. Junius Brutus, a Roman citizen and cousin of the chaste Lucretia, rallied the people of Rome to his cause against Tarquin the Proud, king of Rome, because his son Sextus Tarquinius had wickedly raped Lucretia while her husband

---

[43] *Fall* II. 1006–8; Lydgate had likened Humphrey's first wife, Jacqueline of Hainault, to Lucretia before their wedding in 1423 ('On Gloucester's Approaching Marriage', in *MP* ii. 604).

(the noble Roman Collatinus Tarquinius) was away on campaign with King Tarquin, as is set forth more fully in his later narrative.)[44] The rape is not described, nor is Lucretia's suicide. Indeed, as the title to the chapter indicates, the interest of the Latin and French narratives here is not Lucretia at all, but, rather, Brutus and (more narrowly) the principle that great things have been achieved by men of every social degree. Premierfait's interest in Lucretia is cursory and political, limited to the role she plays in the overthrow of a proud king.[45]

The story of the rape of Lucretia by Sextus Tarquinius (youngest son of Tarquinius Superbus, the last of the Roman kings) is one of the most frequently discussed episodes in Roman history; such is the power of the story that not only are there eight surviving classical authorities for the narrative, but it has also attracted the appeal of artists, poets, and musicians ever since the fall of the Roman culture for which it was a legend of such foundational significance. Classical and patristic responses to the tragedy of Lucretia neatly define the challenges the legend presented to its medieval reader, with different writers often emphasizing different aspects of the story. An influential 'political' reading of the legend finds its clearest classical proponent in the account of the rape given in Livy's *Historia*, in which the story of the private sexual crime of the younger Tarquin is firmly placed within the context of the larger public acts of his family. Tarquin's duplicitous military triumph over the city of Gabii (i. liv) is described in detail and prepares for the later rape not only by demonstrating the moral nature of the prince but also by presenting him primarily as an invader, an intruder into space that rightly belongs to others. Indeed, so insistent is Livy in his emphasis on the larger significance of Lucretia's personal tragedy that he recalls Tarquin's military successes at the

---

[44] *Des Cas* fo. 28ʳ. For Boccaccio, Lucretia seems to be the typical pure woman (see Messalina's words in vii. ch. 3 ('Tristes quidam . . .') (*De casibus* fo. 83ʳ (p.171)), and Boccaccio's ironic comment at the end of 'In mulieres' (I. ch. 18) (*De casibus* fo. 12ᵛ (p. 48)). An important study of the literary traditions of Lucretia is given in Galinsky (1932), although no reference is made to the *De casibus*, *Des Cas*, or *Fall* versions.

[45] The reader of the *De casibus* and the *Des Cas* must wait until Book III for a treatment of the rape legend (iii. ch. 3: 'De Tarquinio Superbo Romanorum rege novissimo'), although even there the emotional force of the rape is undermined.

moment of the rape itself in his use of the terminology of military campaign.[46]

Similarly, the Livian account provides a full exploration of the establishment of the Republic. On seizing the knife from Lucretia's body, Lucius Junius Brutus, her husband's distant cousin, vows to pursue the Tarquins and to eradicate the principle of regal government from Rome altogether:[47] the assault on Lucretia is seen not as sexual violence, but as violence that is by its very nature specifically regal ('regiam iniuriam'). As a consequence, revenge is to be exacted not simply on the perpetrator of the rape, but also on the entire royal family—beginning with the king himself—and on the political system that springs from his whole dynasty. After an account of Brutus' march on Rome, his address in the Forum, and the success of his coup, Livy concludes with a careful explanation of the new consular form of government.[48]

Given the nature of the *History*, it is not surprising that Livy's account of the rape sees Lucretia's tragedy in terms of its political consequences: the *planctus* of the distressed woman is comparatively brief (I. lviii. 7–8) and amounts to little more than a plea for revenge on her assailant—a request which Brutus chooses to reinterpret anyway. In contrast to this 'political' reading of the legend, however, a separate classical tradition turns attention back to the victim of the rape. Ovid's *Fasti* typifies this kind of reading: Lucretia is seen as a tragic figure, the interest of the account lying in its pathos. Lucretia is discovered working her wools with her woman servants, as in Livy, but the wool is softened ('lanaque mollis')[49] to suggest the character of the woman who spins it. In a dimly lit room Lucretia delivers a tender monologue of conjugal concern and breaks into tears;[50] at the moment of the rape she is likened to a trembling lamb finding itself before a wolf.[51] The political agenda of the Livian narrative is consistently marginalized, and at every

---

[46] Livy, *History (Ab urbe condita)* I. lviii.5: 'Quo terrore cum vicisset obstinatam pudicitiam velut vi victrix' ('At this dreadful prospect her resolute modesty was overcome, as if with force, by his victorious lust'; Loeb, 200–1).

[47] Ibid. I. lix. 1 (Loeb, 204–5).

[48] Ibid. I. lx. 1–4 (Loeb, 208–9). Ian Donaldson has, in another context, explored the symbolic significance of the rape for a political reading of the story (1982: 9).   [49] *Fasti* II. 742; see Livy, *History* I. lvii. 9.

[50] *Fasti* II. 745–58.

[51] Ibid. II. 799–800. This simile is reproduced in the English versions of the legend: Chaucer, *LGW* l. 1798; Gower, *Confessio* VII. 4983–5.

stage sentiment takes priority over any other concern: the only reference to the Gabii siege comes in a lurid and hyperbolic comparison between that campaign and the rape, while the republican consequences of the rape receive the slightest of attention.[52]

Patristic discussions of the legend diverge from both the Livian and Ovidian models. Tertullian, writing at the start of the third century, included Lucretia in his pantheon of noble pagans, opening with her name a list that includes Mucius Scaevola, Heraclitus, Empedocles, Dido, Marcus Attilius Regulus, and Cleopatra. He writes:

Longum est, si enumeram singulos, qui se gladio confecerit, animo suo ducti. De feminis ad manum est Lucretia, quae vim stupri passa, cultrum sibi adegit in conspectu propinquorum, ut gloriam castitati suae pareret . . . Si tanti vitrum, quanti margaritum? Quis ergo non libentissime tantum pro vero habeat erogare, quantum alii pro falso?

(It would take me too long to enumerate one by one the men who at their own self-impulse have put an end to themselves. As to women, there is a famous case at hand: the violated Lucretia, in the presence of her kinsfolk, plunged the knife into herself, that she might have glory for her chastity . . . If the bit of glass is so precious, what must the true pearl be worth? Are we not called on, then, most joyfully to lay out as much for the true as others do for the false?)[53]

Tertullian's list of the unpleasant deaths of pagans who sought glory in martyrdom offers a challenge to the commitment of Christians to their own religion.[54] Jerome, writing in the first book of his denunciation of the heretic Jovinian at the end of the following century, rather less sophisticatedly includes Lucretia in his list of women who have committed suicide rather than live a life of shame:

Ad Romanas feminas transeam; et primam ponam Lucretiam, quae violatae pudicitiae nolens supervivere, maculam corporis cruore delevit.

(I may pass on to Roman women; and the first that I shall mention is Lucretia, who would not survive her violated chastity, but blotted out the stain upon her person with her own blood.)[55]

---

[52] *Fasti* II. 852.
[53] *Ad martyres* IV, in *PL* i. 698C–699A, 700A; trans. *Ante-Nicene Library*, ix. 1 (1869: 5–6).   [54] Barnes (1971: 218–19).
[55] *Adversus Jovinianum* I. 46, 49, in *PL* xxiii. 287D, 294C; trans. Schaff and Wace, *Nicene and Post-Nicene Fathers*, vi (1893: 382, 386).

The most influential patristic appraisal of Lucretia's death comes, however, in the first book of Augustine's *De civitate Dei*. Writing in about 410 in the context of the sack of Rome by Alaric, Augustine famously responds to those critics of Christianity who had claimed that the many Christian nuns who were violated by invading barbarians should have followed the example of pagan virtue set by Lucretia and taken their own lives in preference to living in dishonour. With his unremittingly logical analysis and his refusal to give quarter (as Jerome had done) to the cult of the noble suicide, Augustine robustly upends the entire terms of the debate in order to disclose what he sees as its central significance—the primacy of the individual's freedom of will:

ita non amitti corporis sanctitatem, manente animi sanctitate, etiam corpore oppresso, sicut amittitur corporis sanctitas violata animi sanctitate, etiam corpore intacto . . . Quid dicemus? adultera haec, an casta judicanda est? . . . Sed ita haec causa ex utroque latere coarctatur [*sic*], ut si extenuatur homicidium, adulterium confirmetur; si purgatur adulterium, homicidium cumeletur: nec omnino invenitur exitus, ubi dicitur, Si adulterata, cur laudata? si pudica, cur occisa?

(just as bodily chastity is lost when mental chastity has been violated, so bodily chastity is not lost, even when the body has been ravished, while the mind's chastity endures . . . As for Lucretia, what are we to say of her? Is she to be judged adulterous or chaste? . . . Her defence is faced with a dilemma. If her homicide is extenuated, her adultery is established; if she is cleared of adultery, the murder is abundantly proved. There is no possible way out: 'If she is adulterous, why is she praised? If chaste, why was she put to death?')[56]

For Augustine the rape of Lucretia is not about the chastity of Christian religious at all, and still less does it raise for him questions of the introduction of republicanism to Rome. Instead, he sees the legend as a weak link in the belief of pagan shame-cultures that death is preferable to personal dishonour: in asserting that volition is a necessary condition of sin, Augustine deftly shows that an innocent Lucretia's chastity would be intact after her rape, and thereby questions the need for her self-punishment. In Augustine's reading of the legend there is no room for compromise between the pagan and the Christian ethic; an unnegotiable discontinuity has been affirmed between them.

---

[56] *De civitate Dei*, I. 18–19, in *PL* xli. 32–3; trans. Bettenson (1972: 28–30).

Lydgate's attempts to sway his reader's interpretation of the narrative are immediately noticeable in his introduction:

> Thei [men] sholde seen what pereil & what wo
> For comoun profit men haue vndirtake,
> As whilom Brutus for Lucrecis sake
> Chaced Tarquyn for his transgressioun
> And kynges alle out off Rome toun.[57]

In framing the narrative in this way, Lydgate seems to direct a reading of the tale that is primarily political in its emphasis: however, as his treatment of the story progresses it becomes apparent that Lydgate's focus is elsewhere. A vernacular precedent for this kind of weakly political Lucretia exists in the seventh book of the *Confessio Amantis*, where Gower initially signals the political consequences of the rape, only to suppress them later. Gower's version, in fact, concludes with a vague gesture to the republican significance of the legend:

> And al the toun began to crie,
> 'Awey, awey the tirannie
> Of lecherie and covoitise!'
> And ate laste in such a wise
> The fader in the same while
> Forth with his Sone thei exile,
> And taken betre governance.[58]

The fact that Gower excludes from this coda to the tale any specific reference either to the overthrown monarchy or to the emergent republic is surprising, for not only does his use of the name 'Arrons' for Sextus Tarquinius indicate his dependence on the Livian (or a Livy-derived) version of the story,[59] but he also includes it in his regiminal seventh book of the *Confessio Amantis*. Given the *speculum* theme of that book, Gower might have been expected to seize the opportunity for precise political comment which the Lucretia legend offers. However, the exact nature of the new political system is disguised by the blanket assurance that it resulted in 'betre governaunce'; even the

---

[59] Gower draws on Livy, too, for the narrative that follows, that of Virginia; see the claim of Chaucer's Physician that his source is Livy (*CT* VI. 1–2), when the *Roman de la Rose* ll. 5589–658 is in fact used.

reference to 'tirannie' is left unexpanded. Although the Latin side note to the text does detail the exile of the Tarquins, Gower seems deliberately to have sacrificed the more narrowly political possibilities of the verse narrative.[60] The whole concludes with a vague moral injunction, showing that the value of the narrative for Gower was as an opportunity to teach an ethical principle to a fledgling prince, rather than to capitalize on the potential of the narrative itself.[61]

Similarly, Chaucer begins his Lucretia narrative in the *Legend of Good Women* by gesturing to the political significance of the legend, only to reject it as an acceptable model later:

> Now mote I seyn the exilyng of kynges
> Of Rome, for here horible doinges,
> And of the laste kyng Tarquinius,
> As seyth Ovyde and Titus Lyvius.
> But for that cause telle I nat this storye,
> But for to preyse and drawe to memorye
> The verray wif, the verray trewe Lucresse.[62]

The reference to Ovid is significant: no sooner has Chaucer offered a recognizably political reading of the legend than he quickly turns back on himself and wrongfoots his reader with a reference to the more emotional model of the *Fasti*. As if this clash of possibilities were not sufficiently disorientating, he continues with a reference to 'grete Austyn [who] hath compassioun | Of this Lucresse'.[63] These signals to previous traditions are intended to puzzle; as elsewhere in his work, Chaucer 'over-interprets' his material, and, by erecting contradictory signposts, forces the issue of the narrator's role in fixing literary meaning. The improbable claim that Augustine's attitude towards Lucretia was one of 'gret compassioun' clearly alerts us to the playfulness of his approach.

---

[60] Gower ed. Macaulay (1901: 367–8). Scanlon notes that 'the transition from the old Roman kingdom to the Republic, which for Livy is the central meaning of this incident' is ignored, thus 'depriving it of any larger significance in the development of Rome' (1994: 293–5).

[61] *Confessio* VII. 5124–8. The Virginia narrative similarly concludes by instructing the reader to learn 'Hou it is good a king eschuie | The lust of vice and vertue suie' (VII. 5305–6). For the diminished importance of Lucretia in Gower's version, and the instructional focus on Brutus, see Bertolet (1991).

[62] *LGW* ll. 1680–6.   [63] Ibid. ll. 1690–1.

Chaucer's narrative proceeds firmly in the Ovidian tradition; and the political consequences of the rape are suppressed (as in the *Fasti*) until the final stages:

> Ne never was ther kyng in Rome toun
> Syn thilke day[64]

However, unlike Ovid's evocatively succinct half-line 'dies regnis illa suprema fuit',[65] which carries the weight of the end of his version of the tale, Chaucer busily sweeps on, supplying a further fifteen and a half lines of moralization. The effect is to efface the political impact of the narrative.

Lydgate's first version of the story is, as he explains, heavily dependent on the *Declamatio Lucretiae* of the Florentine humanist Coluccio Salutati.[66] A forceful prose presentation of the story of the rape in the form of a legal discussion, the *Declamatio* consists of two long monologues—in the first the joint voices of Lucretia's father and her husband Collatinus attempt to dissuade her from her proposed suicide, in the second the 'violata Lucretia' replies in thirty-nine lines, refuting their arguments and demanding that her honour be avenged. Lydgate's treatment of Salutati's text is of importance because, as one of the few large-scale departures from the *Des Cas* in the English poem, it demonstrates Lydgate's manipulation of his source texts in accordance with his own assumptions and concerns: in the case of the Lucretia narrative, furthermore, it seems probable that Lydgate would take care to ensure that these concerns matched those of his patron. The bipartite structure of Salutati's version results in a text that lacks the dramatic interest of the framing narratives found in Livy, Ovid, Chaucer, and Gower: Collatinus' boast of his wife's chastity, the discovery of Lucretia at her spinning, and the rape itself are either omitted altogether or seriously weakened by their presentation in the monologue form. Gone are the sentimental and lingering details of Lucretia's early-morning struggles with her own conscience. Instead, Salutati offers a spare and legal exchange, engaging directly with the terms of the Augustinian

---

[64] Ibid. ll. 1869–70; see Weiher (1976–7: 7–9).

[65] *Fasti* II. 852: 'That day was the last of kingly rule'.

[66] *Fall* II. 1009–11: 'Folwyng the tracis off Collucyus, | Which wrot off hir a declamacioun | Most lamentable, most doolful, most pitous . . .'; see III. 981–5 and Galinsky (1932: 44–6).

dilemma: Is Lucretia responsible for her own rape? Has her chastity in fact been lost? Does she deserve to live on as the wife of Collatinus?

Lydgate, by contrast, chooses to restore dramatic interest by supplying a framing narrative, and he prefaces his translation of the *Declamatio* with a version of the rape itself. The effect of these lines is to blacken the character of Tarquin ('this euel auised knyht, | This sclau*n*drid man, most hatful for his deede') and to stress the vulnerability of Lucretia ('Liggyng abedde ferr from hir folkes all'), thereby losing the emotional neutrality Salutati was presumably aiming for in his version.[67] Most importantly of all, Lydgate reintroduces in this inserted section an account of the threat of personal dishonour that Tarquin issues to his victim:

> He manacyng in his froward entent,
> On hir beholdyng with a furious cheer,
> That with his suerd[e], but she wolde assent,
> Hire and a boy he wolde prente ifeer,
> Such on as was most ougli off maner,
> Most onlikli off persone and off fame:
> Thus he thratte for to sclau*n*dre hir name.[68]

Furthermore, Lucretia's response is made to heighten the ethical significance of the threat, for the pressure of the pagan shame ethic here aligns the Lydgatean version of the story within the Augustinian tradition of the legend:

> In this mater this was hir fantasie: .
> Bet was to deie than to lyue in shame,
> And lasse wikke, to putte in iupartie
> Hir mortal bodi than hir good[e] fame.
> Whan hono*u*r deieth, farweel a manys name![69]

Lydgate follows this prologue with a largely accurate translation of the text of the *Declamatio*; however, he omits the details of the riotous royal wives[70] and the references to Tarquin's Gabii

---

[67] *Fall* II. 1023–57.   [68] Ibid. II. 1030–6.

[69] Ibid. II. 1044–8. The threat of dishonour is found in Livy (*History* I. lviii. 4), Ovid (*Fasti* II. 807–10), and Chaucer (*LGW* ll. 1806–11), although not in Gower.

[70] 'regis nurus et filias commessationibus occupatas invenimus' (Salutati ed. Menestò 1971: 35); trans. Jed (1989: 149): 'We discovered the daughters and daughters-in-law of the king busy reveling.' See Jed (1989: 133) for her editorial practice and decision to translate different readings from the ones she supplies in her printing of the Latin text.

campaign,[71] and (in keeping with the pattern of his interests we have already seen) introduces extended moralizations on the theme of personal reputation. Lydgate also radically alters the reasons given by Lucretia's menfolk in their attempt to persuade her to remain alive: in the *Declamatio* the men exhort her to delight in the death of Tarquin;[72] Lydgate's Romans less vindictively appeal to Lucretia to remain alive so that she may see that justice is done.[73] Unsurprisingly, Lydgate extends the sections of the Latin text that deal with Lucretia's guilt considerably—again pointing the harmartiological orthodoxy.[74]

In Lucretia's reply Lydgate elides the precise legality of Salutati's tract; in the *Declamatio* Lucretia's resolve to commit suicide is strengthened in part by her fear that if she were to live she might be seen by other women as having condoned adultery and be cited as a formal precedent:

vagabitur effrenis libido et ne dum viris absentibus sed in maritorum complexibus romane mulieres protervorum iuvenum violentia comprimentur. Et enim que mulier tuta erit, violata Lucretia?

(unrestrained lust will spread, and the Roman women, not only while their husbands are absent but even in the embraces of their husbands, will be pressed by the violence of shameless youth. For indeed, what woman will be safe if Lucretia has been raped?)[75]

Although Lydgate omits the references to Lucretia as the whore of Tarquin ('scortum Tarquini') and tactfully reduces discussion

---

[71] 'iste corruptor corporis tui quot cedes explevit in Gabios? quot ibi circumvenit innocentes?' (Salutati ed. Menestò 1971: 35–7); trans. Jed, (1989: 149): 'How much slaughter did he perform in Gabii, this corruptor of your body? How many innocents perished there?'

[72] 'si ipsum odis, si sibi ex animo supplicium optas, fac vivas, fac quod de te videat in suis penis exultare fac quod cum se viderit invisum et infamem periturum, te cuius corpus attigit, videat integro fame lumine superesse' (Salutati ed. Menestò, 1971: 37); trans. Jed (1989: 149): 'If you hate him, if you truly desire his punishment, make sure you live; let him see you exulting in his punishment. When he sees himself detested and disgraced and about to die, let him see you, whose body he assaulted, outlive him in the undiminished light of fame.'

[73] *Fall* II. 1121–7. Six stanzas from this section (II. 1058–99) are omitted in five manuscripts (*Fall* ed. Bergen vol. i. 229).

[74] As does the version in the *Roman de la Rose*, ll. 8608–51. My reading contests Pearsall's claim that Lydgate 'wearily' translated Salutati, and his likening of the poet to 'a driverless steamroller' (1992: 12). For a summary of the Lucretia story see Hammond (1927–8: 49–57).

[75] Salutati ed. Menestò (1971: 39); trans. Jed (1989: 150–1).

about whether she might become pregnant to one elliptic couplet,[76] we see his interest in the theological consequences of the rape assert themselves when he refuses to flinch from the possibility that Lucretia may have enjoyed the sexual violence she experienced. Salutati's heroine explains:

an putatis nullam esse violati corporis volutatem? . . . nichil muliere mobilius; egritudinem animique motus nedum mollit sed extinguit tempus. Si distulero incipiam mihi flagitiossa placere.

(Don't you think I will discover some pleasure in chastity of a corrupt body? . . . Nothing softens grief and emotions in a woman more quickly than time which extinguishes them; if I delay, perhaps shameful acts will begin to please me.)[77]

Lydgate alters the focus of these lines:

> Lust afforcid hath a fals appetit,
> Of freelte includid in Nature;
> Maugre the will, ther folweth a delit,
> As summe folk seyn, in eueri creature.
> Good fame lost, ful hard is to recure;
> And sith I may myn harmys nat redresse,
> To you in open my gilt I will confesse.
>
> Al-be I was ageyn my will oppressid,
> Ther was a maner constreyned lust in deede,
> Which for noun power myht nat be redressid[78]

The issue of Lucretia's sexual arousal during the rape is subtly different from Salutati's concern that she might survive to discover sexual pleasure in a polluted body. It is no sin to be raped (although it may be deeply shaming), yet Lydgate's Lucretia feels that she has offended: her will was 'oppressid' in the attack, but this does not fully address the issue of her accountability, for she is aware that her pleasure was aroused. Lucretia was not complicit in the rape (and therefore is not to be accused of adultery), but neither is she entirely free of guilt: Augustine's clear-cut logical

---

[76] *Fall* II. 1264–5; see Salutati: 'Quid si semen infaustum visceribus inhesit meis? An expectam donec ex adulterio mater fiam?' (Salutati ed. Menestò 1971: 41; trans. Jed (1989: 151): 'What if his unpropitious seed adhered in my womb? Or shall I wait until I become a mother from adultery?'

[77] Salutati ed. Menestò (1971: 41); trans. Jed (1989: 151). The first line of the text here is emended by Jed as 'Nan putatis ullam esse corrupti corporis castitatem voluptatem fatebor?' (ibid. 147).   [78] *Fall* II. 1275–84.

oppositions ('Si adulterat, cur laudata? si pudica, cur occisa?') seem to have been deliberately complicated. Lydgate's decision to discuss this 'constreyned lust' shows his engagement with patristic readings of the legend: consequently, literary models of the story of Lucretia's suicide which consider the political importance of the rape exercise little influence on the *Fall* narrative.

The version of the Lucretia story given in the third book of the *Des Cas* (III. ch. 3) is much fuller than the corresponding section in the *Fall*:[79] while Premierfait gives details of the deeds of Tarquinius Superbus (just as Gower chose to precede his version with an account of those of Sextus Tarquinius at Gabii), the boasting about the chastity of Roman wives, the subsequent chastity quest, and the men's discovery of Lucretia at her wools ('fillant de la laine')[80] as background to the rape story, Lydgate vaults over this prefatory material straight to Lucretia's *planctus* before her menfolk. The lament is then given in nineteen stanzas of close translation from Laurent and is followed by a single stanza in which the suicide itself is narrated.[81] Equally, the French version follows the suicide of Lucretia with an extended account of the subsequent careers of the Tarquins, the opposition they meet in Rome, their exiles, and final deaths; Lydgate instead breaks abruptly after the suicide and passes on to the next chapter (III. ch. 4: 'In portentosam principum libidinem'). In isolating the tragedy of Lucretia in these ways, Lydgate turns what is for Laurent and Boccaccio a narrative of the fall of Tarquinius Superbus into another version of Lucretia's lament.

This fundamental shift of emphasis may in part reflect Lydgate's inability to pass up an opportunity to explore the psychology of the suffering woman, but it also allows him once again to highlight certain aspects of the legend. Aside from small-scale alterations (e.g. Lydgate here follows Gower in dressing his Lucretia in black for her lament and suicide),[82] the only alteration to the foreshortened Book III narrative is Lydgate's exclusion of Laurent's detail (not found in Boccaccio's version) of Tarquin's threat to besmirch

---

[79] Laurent elaborates his Latin source narrative in adding the direct speech of Lucretia's lament which Lydgate gives at III. 1009–141. Laurent's version has been harshly received (see Smith 1934: 516).   [80] *Des Cas* fo. 48ᵛ.

[81] *Fall* III. 1009–48.

[82] Ibid. III. 995–1001; see *Confessio* VII. 5000–2. Livy, Ovid, and Chaucer do not include this detail.

Lucretia's reputation by killing a manservant next to her dead body. The French Lucretia relates this in her lament to her menfolk:

il me dist en menassant doccire qu*i*l mettroit vng scen varlet en ma chambre lequel il occiroit pareillement auecques moy 7 publieroit partout qu*i*l lauroit trouue couche auec moy et pource il nous auroit tous deux tue3

(he threatened to kill me, saying that he would place in my bedchamber a servant whom he would kill alongside me, and that he would announce to all that he had found this man lying in bed with me and, for that reason, he had killed us both)[83]

This threat is a common element in versions of the legend (including Lydgate's own narrative in Book II of the *Fall*), and sometimes the threat of dishonour is such that in certain versions Lucretia, concerned to preserve her good name, even yields to Tarquin's advances.[84] Its exclusion from the Book III account diminishes the influence of the pagan Roman public shame culture on the Lydgatean Lucretia's decision to take her own life. Lucretia still, of course, feels dishonoured, but the removal of Tarquin's threat simplifies the rape, somewhat reducing it to a straightforward physical assault: Lydgate thus again alters the circumstances of the legend in order to question the degree of Lucretia's guilt. In this he would appear to follow Laurent's own interest, for even though the French text introduces the threat to the narrative, Laurent goes on specifically to uphold Lucretia's innocence, saying that 'le iouue*n*ceau eut fait tout son desir ou corps de lucresse ce sa*n*s auoir corro*m*pu sa pe*n*see'.[85] Lydgate closely translates:

> Hir body corupt, she cleene off herte & thouht,
> Be force assailed was hir innocence,
> Oppressid hir beute, but hir sperit nouht,
> Hir chaast[e] will dede non offence;
> But entred is into hir conscience
> A gret remors, for al hir wifli trouthe[86]

Lydgate's engagement with the Lucretia legend, then, is not only particular, but is also remarkably systematic. The impact of both

---

[83] *Des Cas* fo. 49ʳ.
[84] Shakespeare hints that there may have been 'accessory yieldings' even as his Lucrece most violently protests that there were none (*The Rape of Lucrece*, ll. 1656–9); William Vaughan, in *The Golden-groue* (1608), attacked Lucretia for adultery. See Donaldson (1982: 24, 32).   [85] *Des Cas* fo. 48ᵛ.
[86] *Fall* III. 967–72.

Lydgatean versions differs from that of his sources: although he suggests that the chief significance of the legend in Book II will be political, Lydgate's treatment of Salutati's monologues advances a primarily moralized reading of the legend. In Book III Lydgate entirely disregards the historical and political detail of Laurent's account in order, again, to focus with greater clarity on the ethical dilemma of Lucretia's circumstances, yet doing so 'in a different manner' from his earlier, Salutati-based narrative.[87] It will never be possible to say whether Lydgate suppressed readings that would be unwelcome to his patron, but it is noticeable that 'republican' Lucretia has been sacrificed to theological enquiry. Given the fact of Humphrey's insistence on the inclusion of a Lucretia fall in Lydgate's translation (presumably not realizing that 'Boccace' provided such a narrative in his third book), it is highly probable that Lydgate was not solely motivated in his Lucretia legends by personal preference, but that he paid higher than usual regard to the expectations of his patron.

Evidence survives of the connections between Humphrey and Salutati. In 1415 Humphrey was given a copy of Cicero's letters by Zeno da Castiglione, bishop of Bayeux (later Henry VI's delegate to the Council of Basle), which had been copied from Salutati's own manuscript,[88] he donated an unidentified volume of 'Epistolae Collusii' to Oxford in 1439,[89] and owned at least two further manuscripts of Salutati's work: the *De laboribus Herculis* (now Vatican, BAV MS Urb. Lat. 694),[90] and a copy of the philosophical *De fato et fortuna* (now bound with the *De saeculo et religione* as Manchester, Chetham's Library MS 27929) into which the *Declamationes* (fos. 200ᵛ–205ᵛ) appear to have been

---

[87] As Thomas Gray noted (Gray ed. Gosse 1884: i. 401). For a suggestion of how Lucretia may have been a model for medieval political propaganda see Gransden (1992: 276–8).

[88] Humphrey donated his copy (now Paris, BN MS lat. 8537) to Oxford in 1439; Salutati's copy survives as Florence, Biblioteca Medicea Laurenziana MS. Plut. 49, 18: see Bodleian Library, *Duke Humfrey's Library* (1988: 28); Weiss (1957: 49–53); and Sammut (1980: 119).

[89] Anstey (1898: i. 183); Sammut (1980: 70); see Ullman, 'Manuscripts', in (1973: 346–9).

[90] Sammut (1980: 123–4); see Ullman (1963: 270–1, 280). For the suggestion that Lydgate may have been influenced by the *De laboribus* see Schibanoff (1974).

added by an English scribe.[91] It may well have been this volume, or a copy made from it, which lay behind the commission of a Lucretia story from Lydgate.

Each age has rewritten the Lucretia legend to reflect its own interests and needs, and Salutati's version of the story possesses a greater force than simple moral enquiry. Salutati was a humanist scholar with a formidably large library (he included Petrarch and Boccaccio among his correspondents and acted as mentor to a coterie that included Leonardo Bruni, Niccolò Niccoli, and Poggio Bracciolini),[92] yet he was also fully involved in public life. He was a lay papal secretary in 1368, became Chancellor of Todi in 1367, and was Chancellor of Florence from 1375 until his death in 1406.[93] Throughout his adult life he was closely involved with the affairs of high politics and, as Chancellor of Florence he was head of the civil service accountable to the Signoria and at one stage, as notary to the *Tratte*, was responsible for supervising public elections and for drawing up the lists of the *inborsati* (those Florentines eligible for public office)—one of the many subtle Florentine constitutional safeguards to prevent overlong or factional tenure of public office. Salutati had, then, more than an academic interest in the workings and limitations of despotic rule, and it comes as no surprise that such a man should own and produce works of political theory (a short tractate on the benefits of elective monarchy, the *Quod melius sit regnum successivum quam electivum*, and a longer work of 1400, the *De tyranno*).[94] One of his letters was said to be worth 'a thousand troop of horse'.

[91] Sammut (1980: 111–12). The *De saeculo*, originally separate, was bound at the front of the Manchester manuscript (fos. 1ʳ–89ᵛ) in the fifteenth century (see Bodleian Library, *Duke Humfrey and English Humanism* (1970: 9–10)).

[92] Salutati's library has been estimated as having contained over 800 volumes (Ullman 1963: 129). Although he was familiar with Boccaccio's Latin works, Salutati does not appear to have known or owned the *De casibus* (ibid. 201, 207, 209, 219–20). On his friendship with Petrarch and Boccaccio see Witt (1983: 62, 81 ff., 85). A sixteenth-century biographer reports that Salutati often visited the tomb of Boccaccio at Certaldo (see Emerton 1925: 46).

[93] Ullman (1963: 3–16).

[94] Salutati owned two copies of Giles of Rome's *De regimine principum* (Ullman 1963: 167–8, 180–1). The shorter of his two texts survives uniquely in an autograph manuscript in BAV MS Capponi 147, and has been published by Ullman (1964: 401–11). The *De tyranno* survives in five manuscripts and has been translated into English, with a discussion, by Ephraim Emerton (1925: 25–116); for careful criticism of some of Emerton's comments see Baron (1955ᵇ: ii. 503–4). See also Ullman (1963: 32–4).

Salutati's interest in the legend of Lucretia reflects his role in the government of Florence. Throughout the thirteenth century Florentines believed their city had been founded by Julius Caesar, and so took close interest in the sequence of political changes which the expulsion of the Tarquins inaugurated: in the early years of the sixteenth century Machiavelli, Salutati's successor as Chancellor, includes the political consequences of the assault on Lucretia in a list of historical examples of the role of women (and the rape of women) in bringing about the downfall of tyrants and political reform.[95] However, the later fourteenth century saw a revision of the Florentine founding myth: partly in response to the aggressive expansionist policies of the Milanese Visconti, support for the 'imperial' Caesar modulated as Florentines sought a figure to celebrate their own republicanism.[96] Salutati explicitly entered into this debate in a letter to the Ferrarese Chancellor Donato degli Albanzani in 1398, asking for help in locating sources which would lend support to a theory of Florentine descent from a pre-imperial Rome:

Ceterum alias tibi scripsi qualiter . . . nescio quid de civitatis huius origine sentiebas quare placeat non solum quid super hoc tibi videatur rescribere, sed an aliqua veterum opinione movearis plene quantum poteris indicare.

(I have written to you on another occasion . . . about how I do not know what you think about the origins of this city; please reply, not only saying how it seems to you in this matter, but also indicating as fully as you can whether you are influenced by some opinion of the ancients.)[97]

And yet, for all his involvement in the politics of Florence, Salutati seems to have been convinced of the merits of monarchy: his short tractate *Quod melius sit regnum* upholds monarchical government, while his *De tyranno* is essentially a vindication of Dante's decision to punish Caesar's assassins in the lowest circle of the *Inferno*.[98] In this Salutati was taking issue with his friend Bruni, who had attacked the tyranny of Caesar in his *Dialogi* and who went on to become the most forceful proponent of the theory of the pre-imperial foundation of Florence in his *Laudatio Florentinae urbis*

[95] *I Discorsi* III. 26 §2 (Machiavelli 1975: i. 539).
[96] For the Caesarian founding myth see Rubinstein (1942).
[97] 26 August 1398 (Salutati 1896: iii. 324–5).
[98] Emerton (1925: chs. iv–v, pp. 100–16); Baron (1955[b]: i. 121–39; ii, 500–2); Ullman (1963: 74–7); Witt (1976: 83–4).

(post-1402), where he claims that the city, having been founded by veterans of the general Cornelius Sulla, thereby had been nursed from the very beginning in the principles of republicanism:[99]

Florentini homines maxime omnium libertate gaudeant et tyrannorum valde sint inimici

(the Florentine people rejoice in every kind of liberty and stoutly show themselves the enemies of tyrants.)[100]

Salutati's belief that Caesar held power constitutionally and his condemnation of Brutus bespeaks an ambivalence towards republican government which re-emerges in the *Declamatio*, which, as we have seen, ignores the political implications of Lucretia's rape and focuses instead entirely on the moral debate.[101] Given the political upheavals in Florence at the opening of the fifteenth century, it is perhaps not surprising that Salutati should discuss the issue of tyranny so urgently, but neither is it surprising that he should shrink from a possibly contentious republican coda to what is otherwise an ethical work: the popularity of the *Declamatio Lucretiae* suggests that the ethical emphasis was welcome to his readers.[102] Furthermore, it is now possible to see why the version of the Lucretia legend given in Salutati's *Declamatio* disregards the traditional republican reading of the legend and produces a text which found such favour with Lydgate's patron. In asking that the Lucretia story be included in his latest commission, Humphrey ensured that the *Fall* became a mirror for the specific interests of its patron.[103]

---

[99] Baron (1955[b]: i. 49–63); Jed also considers the debate (1989: 18–50). Baron has revised the dating of this work (1968), and has called it 'the first Florentine work, and perhaps the first work in Humanism as a whole, to profit substantially from the knowledge of Greek' (ibid. 151). Baron also supplies the *editio princeps* of the *Laudatio* (1968: 232–63). See also Ullman (1946, repr. 1973). Bruni was invited to England by Humphrey in 1433, and translated the *Politics* for him (completed 1438) (Weiss 1957: 41, 46–9). Bruni's works were known to many in England, including Robert Flemmyng (an owner of the *De casibus*) and Abbot John Whethamstede (one of Lydgate's patrons) (Weiss 1957: 103–4, 36, 47).

[100] Baron (1955[a]: 100).

[101] Ultimately, Salutati's pro-Caesarean views lost the day in Florence and Bruni's ideology took hold: for the later development of the debate see Gordon (1957).

[102] It was 'the most popular of all his works', surviving in over fifty manuscripts (Ullman 1963: 34).

[103] Humphrey was not alone, it seems, in reading the *Declamatio* as a tragic narrative; a fifteenth-century manuscript of Salutati's text labels the work a 'tragedia' (see Cloetta 1890–2: i. 145).

THE SERPENT OF DIVISION

Much of the *Fall* (and in particular Books V, VI, and VIII) is devoted to figures from Roman history, yet this is not Lydgate's only extended treatment of the history of Rome: his prose treatise *The Serpent of Division* provides an account of the downfall of the Republic, the rise to power of Julius Caesar, and the civil wars with Pompey. Unlike the narrative of Lucretia, however, where the constraints of the *Fall* necessitate a focus on the tragic experience of an individual and compel him to marginalize the wider political significance of the story, Lydgate seems much more willing in this work to contextualize the actions of the characters he describes, illustrating the social dimension of individual error and the implications of personal immorality for the 'common profit'.

The *Serpent* is not, however, a straightforward work; it throws up several awkward problems of dating and of commission.[104] The text survives in four medieval manuscripts only: Cambridge, Fitzwilliam Museum MS McClean 182, fos. 1ʳ–9ʳ, the base text for Henry MacCracken's edition;[105] Cambridge, Magdalene College MS Pepys 2006, pp. 191–209;[106] London, British Library MS Additional 48031 (*olim* MS Yelverton 35, the 'C' (Calthorpe) manuscript), fos. 165ᵛ–75ᵛ;[107] and Harvard University, Houghton Library MS Eng. 530, fos. 49ʳ–57ᵛ.[108] An undated incomplete print appeared in the 1520s,[109] while the earliest full prints appeared in c. 1535,[110] 1559,[111] and, with Norton and Sackville's *Gorboduc*, in 1590.[112] The only evidence of dating internal to the

---

[104] MacCracken offers a summary of the problems complicating responses to the text (1911: 3–4).   [105] Ibid. 45.

[106] Ibid. 46: the Pepys MS attributes the treatise to 'j de b' on p. 209. The manuscript is a Chaucer anthology; see the facsimile (Chaucer ed. Edwards 1985).

[107] *Serpent*, 45–6.

[108] BL MS Addit. 38179 (formerly Ashburnham Appendix 128) is an eighteenth-century copy of the Pepys manuscript, see Hartung and Severs vi. (1980: 2154); Edwards (1985b: 451); Matheson in ed. Edwards (1986: 228–9, 243–4).

[109] Treverys's print: not in STC, but reprinted in Brydges ix (1809: 369–73).

[110] Robert Redman's print: STC 17027. 5—ignored by MacCracken (1911a), Hartung and Severs (1980), and Edwards (1985b).

[111] Rogers's/Stow's print: STC 17028; see Ringler (1961). Stow lists the *Serpent* in his bibliography of Lydgate in Speght's 1598 edition of Chaucer.

[112] Allde's print: STC 17029. Orwen (1941: 204) argues that Rogers had printed the work 'because the lesson it taught was thought necessary in Elizabeth's reign' and notes that the 1590 printing with *Gorboduc* coincides with Spenser's *The Ruines of Time*, the three works sharing an interest in the succession of authority; see Allde's preface urging comparison between England and ancient Rome (fo. Aiiᵛ).

text is found in two short sentences at the close of the London manuscript:

> The forseide division so to shewe I have remembred this forseid litill translacion. The moneth of Decembre the ffirste yere of oure souvereigne lorde that now ys king henry the vj^{te}.[113]

The dating of 1422–3 (1 Henry VI) which this sentence offers conflicts directly with the only manuscript inscription which supplies further evidence of dating, an authorial colophon (found uniquely in 'C') immediately following the note given above:

> Here endeth the cronycule of Julius Cesar Emperoure of Rome tyme [*possibly* 'toune'], specifying cause of the ruyne and destruccion of the same, and translated by me, Danne John Lidgate, Monke of Bury seint Edmund, the yere of our lord god MCCCC.[114]

The discrepancy between these two attestations receives close attention from MacCracken, who favours the later date of 1422–3: the fact that the colophon date of 1400 is solely given numerically inevitably makes it more vulnerable to scribal misrepresentation than the fuller, historically defined dating.[115] Furthermore, as MacCracken argued in a response to a review of his edition, 'C' is elsewhere unreliable on matters of numeration: the reviewer had claimed that the correct date for the work was that given in the colophon (1400) and suggested that the final sentence, unique to 'C', was added by Lydgate on the completion of a revised version of the text.[116] The evidence to support this position is scant. Moreover, the *Serpent* includes in its closing stages a reference to Chaucer which speaks of 'hym þat was flowre of poetis in owre englisshe tonge & þe firste þat euer enluminede owre langage with flowres of Rethorike' in the past tense:[117] if these words were written in 1400, it seems probable that Lydgate would refer to the death of the poet as a recent occurrence.

Schick followed Lucy Toulmin Smith in accepting 1400, even though he recognized that this would make 1400 'the first certain [*sic*] date' for any of Lydgate's writings,[118] while Schirmer and

---

[113] fo. 175^v; see *Serpent* 4.   [114] *Serpent* 3.
[115] Although the elision of *xxii* or *xxiii* from the date is rather more unusual than scribal omission of minims in lower-case datings.
[116] Atkins (1912), MacCracken (1913).   [117] *Serpent* 65.
[118] Norton and Sackville ed. Toulmin Smith (1883: xx–xxii); Lydgate ed. Schick (1891: xcix–c, cxii).

Scattergood accept MacCracken's dating of 1422; Eleanor Hammond cautiously expressed reservations on the later dating and Brie questioned Lydgate's authorship.[119] These uncertainties surrounding the dating of the *Serpent* have a wider significance, as is made clear by a sentence at the end of the text:

bi commaundemente of my moste worschipfull maistere & souereyne, I toke vpon me þis litill and þis compendious translacion, & of entente to don him plesaunce[120]

The identity of the 'maistere & souereyne' in this passage depends on the dating of the work: if the earlier dating is adopted, *The Serpent* is seen in the context of the earliest months of the reign of Henry IV. The first year of that reign was extremely troubled, for the usurpation of September 1399, while it has been described as an essentially aristocratic event arousing little popular opposition, met with the resistance of barons loyal to Richard II.[121] The first open attempt at insurrection was the baronial rebellion in January 1400: John de Montacute, third earl of Salisbury, and Thomas Holland, sixth earl of Kent, were killed by the mob at Cirencester, and Thomas Blunt (who had fled from Cirencester) was executed at Oxford. Holland's uncle, John Holland, first earl of Huntingdon and duke of Exeter, also one of Richard's favourites, fled through Essex, but was caught and executed at Pleshey.[122] The suppression of the barons' uprising by no means saw the end of Henry's troubles, for in September 1400 the English received the first of many skirmish attacks from the Welsh under Glendower. This conflict was to dog Henry for several years and was not settled by the battle of Shrewsbury in 1403, for after his refusal to ransom the captured Edmund de Mortimer in 1402 Henry lost the support of his most powerful allies, the Percys of Northumberland.

The early months of 1400, then, not only saw exactly the kind of civil division that Lydgate illustrates in *The Serpent*, but the disturbances also prompted highly topical literary comment and even, in the following year, a letter of advice on government to Henry

[119] Schirmer (1952, trans. 1961: 82); Scattergood (1971: 138–41); Hammond (1927: 177); Brie (1929: 281–3).

[120] *Serpent* 3, 66: the McClean MS is the only one to read '& souereyne'. For the possibility that the patron may be fictitious see Blake (1985: 286); for the semantic range of 'souereyne' see *MED* 'SM–SZ': 342–4.

[121] Scattergood (1971: 107).

[122] *An English Chronicle* ed. Davies (1856: 19–22, 169–70).

from Philip Repyndon the later bishop of Lincoln.[123] However, while the events of 1400 would seem in many ways an appropriate context for *The Serpent*, and while it is not impossible that a newly crowned monarch seeking a treatise on the historical consequences of civil division might turn to the Benedictine order to find one,[124] the choice of the later date seems in many ways far more convincing. Humphrey's political status in 1422 was sufficiently ambiguous for the term 'souereyne' to be applied to him, particularly by a writer who would have everything to gain from flattering his patron's sense of his own eminence. Furthermore, in 1400 Lydgate would have been unknown; by 1422, however, he was the author of the *Troy Book*, the result of a commission from the Prince of Wales in 1412.[125] While it is perhaps no more probable that Lydgate should receive his first royal commission from the heir to the throne than from the king himself, the commission from the Protector in the year following the death of Henry V does at least make sense. Humphrey's commission at this time could be a careful piece of self-advertisement, and the dating of 1422 would fit in with what is known of Lydgate's subsequent career: when Humphrey turns to Lydgate for a translation of the *Des Cas* in 1430–1 it is possible that he does so because he has already received work from the same monk his brother had entrusted with the *Troy* commission, and because he liked the product.

Several classical and medieval accounts of the career of Caesar may have been available to Lydgate. Lucan's *Civil Wars* (*Pharsalia*) may well have been the Lucan recorded by Mynors as having been known to the early fifteenth-century bibliographer John Boston of Bury,[126] although no record survives to suggest that the text was held at Bury. A Latin version of Plutarch's life of Caesar may have been available in Humphrey's library;[127]

---

[123] Bekynton (1872: i. 151–4; 4 May); Repyndon was Henry's chaplain in 1400. Other literary responses include *Richard the Redeless* and the verses of Bodleian MS Digby 102, which contain comment on the destructiveness of civil division: *Twenty-six Political and Other Poems* ed. Kail, EETS OS 124 (1904: 9–14).

[124] For the partisanship of the Benedictines see Horner (1990).

[125] Astronomical data permit so close a dating (see Schirmer 1952, trans. 1961: 42). [126] Mynors (1957: 209).

[127] Sammut (1980: 84); Humphrey owned translations of Mark Antony's life, and other Plutarch lives translated by Bruni and Antonio Pacini of Todi, surviving as BL MS Harley 3426 and Oxford, Magdalen College MS lat. 37; (ibid. 14, 80, 81, 116–17; Weiss 1957: 64); Bodleian Library (1988: 43–5).

Suetonius was known to Boston of Bury and was held at Bury in a copy datable as *s*.xii–xiii.[128] Humphrey donated a copy of Sallust's *Bellum Catilinae* to Oxford in 1444,[129] and the Bury library owned a twelfth-century Sallust (now Pembroke College, Cambridge MS 114).[130] Although Caesar's *De bello Gallico* was well known in the Middle Ages (Mynors notes that the text was known to Boston of Bury), many medieval readers, and among them the compiler of the *Li faits des Romains*, found Caesar's third-person narrative viewpoint confusing and believed that the text was written by a 'Julius Celsus'.[131] Influential versions of the life of Caesar include those by Vincent of Beauvais in his *Speculum historiale*, the French *Li faits*, which drew on Sallust and Suetonius and was the first complete medieval *vita* (*c.*1213), surviving in at least forty-seven manuscripts,[132] and the later thirteenth-century version of Lucan by Jean de Tuim, *Li Hystore de Julius Cesar*, which formed the basis for a fourteenth-century verse redaction, the *Roman de Julius Cesar*.

Of these medieval versions, that by Jean de Tuim seems to have influenced Lydgate most strongly; even here, though, he makes several interesting alterations to his text so as to illustrate the damaging effects of self-division for any state. In the initial stages of the treatise and after the account of the establishment of the dictatorship Lydgate announces that the 'noblesse' of Rome flowered only while the city was 'of oon herte': it was not until pride, personal ambition, and 'fals covitise' arose that the glory of Rome faded:

als sone als fals covitise broughte Inne pride and vayne ambicion, the contagious Serpent of Division eclipsed and appalled theire worthines; concluding sothely as in sentence that every kingdome be division is conveied to his distruccion.[133]

The effects of division, then, are not simply limited to the Roman republic, or other systems of republican government, but now, in a clear attempt to extend the topical relevance of the narrative, are shown also to threaten kingdoms. Similarly, throughout *The*

---

[128] Mynors (1957: 211); James (1926: 257).
[129] Anstey (1898: i. 236); Sammut (1980: 83).   [130] James (1926: 257).
[131] Beer (1976: 34).
[132] Flutre (1932: 27–87): Beer, however, gives the number as nearer 59 (1976: xiii).
[133] *Serpent* 49–50. The serpent imagery here is Lydgate's own: Jean de Tuim has a long passage on the wheel of Fortune (*Li Hystore de Julius Cesar* ed. Settegast (1881: 49–50)).

Serpent there is an emphasis on the danger of political ambition
that seeks to annex political power beyond its right. This, too,
is the aspect of the career of Caesar that Lydgate later stresses in
the envoy he supplies to the Pompey narrative in the *Fall of
Princes*:

> This tragedie of the duk Pompeie
> Declareth in gros þe cheef occasioun
> Whi he and Cesar gan first to werreie,
> Ech ageyn othir, thoruh veyn ambicioun
> To haue lordshipe and domynacioun
>
> .   .   .   .   .
>
> Swich dyuysioun made many man to deie,
> Brouhte the cite to desolacioun.
> With these too princis Fortune list to pleie,
> Til from hir wheel she cast hem bothe doun
>
> .   .   .   .   .
>
> Noble princis, remembreth what I seie,
> Peiseth this stori withyne in your resoun,
> Of fals surmountyng auarice berth þe keie,
>
> .   .   .   .   .
>
> No cleym is worth withoute title of riht.[134]

Although the early months of Henry's minority do not seem to have
been a time of civil disturbance, examination of the parliamentary
rolls for the Martinmas Parliament of 1422 reveals just how timely
Lydgate's discussion of the nature of civil order and the results of
excessive ambition among the nobles of republican Rome may have
been. The regiminal tone of the Parliament is set by the text chosen
for the opening sermon by the Archbishop of Canterbury, Henry
Chichele: 'principes populorum congregati sunt cum Deo'.[135] It was
during the course of this Parliament that the Protectorate of
Humphrey was defined (and subjected to the limitations which the
Duke found so offensive). Even five years later Humphrey was
to complain to Parliament in the Michaelmas session about the
limitations of his power; his demand for clarification of the extent
of his authority echoes the disputes of the early months of

---

[134] *Fall* VI. 2521–5, 2535–8, 2542–4, 2548.
[135] *RP* iv. 169, Ps. 46: 10 (Vulgate)/Ps. 47: 10 (BCP): 'The princes of the people
are gathered together with the God of Abraham' (Douai).

the minority, illustrating very clearly his desire to be free of the quasi-conciliar constraints imposed on him by the lords.[136] In a document held in the Public Records Office (first published in 1930) Humphrey's efforts to ensure a more authoritative title ('tutelam et defensionem principales') for himself are accompanied by an attempt to curtail the scope of the lords' own powers. Suggesting that the lords have acted without precedent, Gloucester implies that it is the will of the commons that he should be granted more than simply the Protectorate, and attempts to bargain:

he desireth that it shuld be enacted that like as he shall no grete thing do but by thavys of counseil except certain specialtes, so be it ordeined that the counseil do nothing but that longeth of cours and commune lawe without my lord is [sic] advis[137]

One of Lydgate's more explicitly regiminal passages in *The Serpent* takes the form of an exemplum derived from Valerius; the story of attempts to remove a tail from a horse demonstrates that whereas a strong man cannot remove the tail with a single pull, a far weaker man can easily remove it by extracting a single hair at a time.[138] Lydgate adds the story immediately after his account of Caesar's crossing of the Rubicon and enmity with Pompey, the conflict which 'began þe devision whiche neuer aftir myȝte perfitely be restorid nor reconsilid to vnyte', and moralizes the exemplum to illustrate the necessity of civil unity for 'all prudent prynces whiche haue gouernaunce in provynces and regions'.[139]

Humphrey was to fail in 1427–8, of course, just as he had failed in 1422. In the context of this very particular constitutional quarrel between his patron and Parliament, it is interesting to note not only the frequency with which Lydgate chooses to emphasize the conflicts between Caesar and the Senate (for these are unavoidable, given his subject), but, more precisely, the attention he gives to the Senate's power to sanction or veto the dictates of kings and consuls:

Tarquyne soone of Tarquyne the prowde, for his outragious offence doone vnto Lucresse . . . in pvnysshing of whiche trespace by the

---

[136] *RP* iv. 326: the lords reply that Gloucester's claim is 'nought caused nor grounded in precident, nor in ye lawe of ye land'.   [137] Chrimes (1930: 102).
[138] *Serpent* 29–30; MacCracken notes the existence of a Bury Valerius, now Cambridge, Pembroke College MS 105.   [139] *Serpent* 58.

manly pursuite of Collatyns kynrede *and ful assente of all the Senate* the name of kyngis ceased in the Citie of Rome for evur more (emphasis added).[140]

The power of the Senate is again shown when Pompey uses the death of his wife Julia, Caesar's daughter, as a pretext to summon Caesar back to Rome 'bi assente of all þe Senate'.[141] Again, Lydgate emphasizes references to the Senate whenever he *does* find them in his source: when Jean de Tuim claims that Pompey 'et li Senat' refused Caesar a triumphal entry to Rome, Lydgate writes that the refusal came 'with ful asente of all þe Senate'.

Lydgate, as would be expected, follows medieval tradition in his account of the refusal of the Senate to grant the triumph. The account in Suetonius is rather more balanced:

Pacataque provincia pari festinatione, non expecto successore ad triumphum simul consulatumque decessit. Sed cum edictis iam comitiis ratio eius haberi non posset nisi privatus introisset urbem . . . coactus est triumphum, ne consulatu excluderetur, dimittere.

(After restoring order in his province, he made off with equal haste, and without waiting for the arrival of his successor, to sue at the same time for a triumph and the consulship. But inasmuch as the day for the elections had already been announced and no account could be taken of Caesar's candidacy unless he entered the city as a private citizen . . . he was forced to forgo the triumph, to avoid losing the consulship.)[142]

In the classical accounts the point is clearly made that Caesar, realizing his dilemma, requested legal dispensation from the requirement to present himself at Rome as a civilian in person, and that it was this dispensation which the Senate refused to grant, rather than the request for the triumph per se. In both *The Serpent* and the highly influential *Li faits des Romains*, however, the Senate is depicted as mean-spiritedly refusing the triumph out of fear of Caesar's growing influence. The rationale for this would seem to be an attempt to justify Caesar's anger at what is shown as a deliberate snub. Compromising legal technicalities are elided and the decision is presented as an outrage to the honour of the man whom the Middle Ages counted among its

<hr />

[140] *Serpent* 49; the French *Hystore* does not mention Lucretia.
[141] Ibid. 52; see Jean de Tuim ed. Settegast (1881: 13), where Julia's death is briefly treated.   [142] Suetonius, *Lives* I. 18 § 2 (trans. Rolfe 1997–8: i. 22–3).

Nine Worthies:

> But towchynge þis honowre toforeseide whiche þat Iulius reqvired and
> askid of riȝte as for a guerdone whiche him þowȝt was meritorie and
> due vnto hym. Anonc [sic] þis foreseide Pompey with full assente of all
> þe Senate denyed all with o voyce his reqveste, and of one acorde
> answerde ageyne and seide him platly he schulde not be acceptid to no
> suche honoure, but pleynely bade hym knowe as for finall conclusion þat
> he had raþir deservid to be dede þan to haue eny suche worschipe,
> alleggynge ageyns him þat he was boþe a traitowre and a rebell to þe
> statutes of Rome. And whan þat Iulius clerely conceivid the schorte
> answere of þe Senat and of þis Pompye to foreseide, þer kyndlyd a full
> hote brennynge fire of envie in his herte of þe fretynge hate specially þat
> he bare in his breste to bene avenged vppon Pompey. And lyche as
> Lucan rehersith in his poeticall boke þat the denyenge of þis worschip to
> þis Iulius was chefe grownde and occasion of all þe werre þat began in
> Rome[143]

Jeanette Beer sums up the usual medieval emphasis:

> The political implications of Caesar's moves in the power struggle have
> become less important than Caesar's overall triumphal progression. For
> analogous reasons the actual triumphal procession acquires an over-
> whelming and unjustified importance in the medieval account of Caesar's
> motivation.[144]

This importance, unjustified though it may be, is found in Lydgate's
text, where it is emphasized that the triumph was not to be any
mere pageant of self-aggrandizement for Caesar, but was intended
rather 'for þe encresse and þe awmentacion of þe comyn profite of
þe Empire of Rome'.[145] The denial, then, is an affront to the whole
estate of the Republic, and the Senate is implicitly criticized for
placing its own petty self-interests and fears before the wider needs
of the 'comyn profite'. Lydgate embellishes the account of the usual
form taken by triumphal processions in ancient Rome by drawing
on details of the regalia and order of the procession found
in Isidore.[146] The care with which he revises his sources to

---

[143] *Serpent* 54.
[144] Beer (1976: 135); see the slighter importance given to the triumph in Lucan
I. 286–7, 338–42, and Tuim (Tuim ed. Settegast 1881: 20–2).   [145] *Serpent* 53.
[146] *De etymologiis* XVIII. 2 ('De triumphis') in *PL* lxxxii, 641B: Lydgate may have
had access to the copy of Isidore held at Bury (James 1926: 258); Humphrey donated
a partial copy to Oxford in 1439 (Anstey 1898: i. 181; Sammut 1980: 64).

incorporate these details is a clear indication of the importance of the triumph for him as an acceptable cause for Caesar's enmity with the Senate; the reader is made to feel exactly how great an honour, how splendid a ceremony, has been withheld. By following this section with an elaborated version of Lucan's account of the causes of the war, Lydgate implies that the denial of the triumph is to be understood as a fundamental cause of the civil dissension.

Although the character of Caesar is not the sole concern of *The Serpent*, Lydgate's reading of his denied military triumph fits with the typically favourable medieval view. In his account of the crossing of the Rubicon, for example, Lydgate attempts as far as possible to efface the criminality of Caesar's behaviour. For Lucan the crossing of the river was a highly aggressive act and a violation of Roman law; for Suetonius, and in the medieval tradition, the act is perceived rather as an attempt to preserve the privileges of the tribunes (who had vetoed a Senate decree to disband Caesar's army) and, as such, as a defence of the legal system of the state:

Ravennae substitit, bello vindicaturus si quid de tribunis plebis intercedentibus pro se gravius a senatum constitutum esset. Et praetextum quidem illi civilium armorum hoc fuit; causas autem alias fuisse opinantur.

([Caesar] . . . halted at Ravenna intending to resort to war if the senate took any drastic action against the tribunes of the commons who interposed vetoes in his behalf. Now this was his excuse for the civil war, but it is believed he had other motives.)[147]

Far from being a public enemy, Caesar is presented as a defender (if an opportunistic one) of the rights of the commons: in Lydgate's account, as in other medieval versions, the *pretext* becomes a *cause* and Caesar has no other motive than the one he himself professes.[148]

The critical response to *The Serpent* has been unremarkable; prior to MacCracken's edition the only published comments on the work were the brief remarks in Lucy Toulmin Smith's edition of *Gorboduc* and Schick's preface to the *Temple of Glas*. Although

---

[147] Suetonius, *Lives* I. 30 §§ 1–2 (trans. Rolfe 1997–8: i. 72–3).

[148] ' "Here I leve behynde all þe olde confideracions [*other MSS*: confederacies] made betwixte Rome and me . . . and of hole entente I begyn a riȝtfull werre, for cause onely þat bi mediacion of pees proferid on my side I may nat atteyne my title of riȝt" ' (*Serpent* 58). Lydgate seems to have added this, which is not found in the *Li faits*, from Lucan (I. 225–6) or from a Lucan-dependent intermediary, replacing the Latin Caesar's rejection of legality with a more favourable justification.

Margaret Schlauch suggestively analysed the characteristics of Lydgate's prose style in 1967, John Norton-Smith omitted *The Serpent* from his biographical survey of Lydgate's works, Alain Renoir summed the text up as 'an illustration of the catastrophic results of ambition', and Derck Pearsall relegated it to a single footnote reference; John Scattergood discusses the treatise briefly, intriguingly dismissing the possibility that Humphrey could have commissioned it 'in view of the theme of the tract'.[149] The six pages devoted to the text in Walter Schirmer's study constitute the most sustained critical attention the text has yet received.[150] Unfortunately, beyond introductory summary, a rather Procrustean analysis of *The Serpent* according to the sixfold *divisio textus* of the *ars praedicandi* tradition, and a (consequently rather puzzling) attack on the formlessness of the text, little is given in the way of textual commentary or discussion. However, Schirmer is interestingly explicit in his comments on the nature of the work:

> *The Serpent of Division* . . . is, however, not a chronicle, not a *vita* of Caesar, but a propagandist political tract, designed to show that discord has evil consequences for every community.[151]

Codicological analysis of the four extant manuscripts supports this view: if conclusions may be drawn from the nature of the texts with which early scribes and owners bound *The Serpent*, it would indeed seem that contemporary readers perceived the text to be primarily a moral work of advice for successful civil government, a *Fürstenspiegel* text rather than a piece of Roman history; it is found alongside Hoccleve's *Regement of Princes* (in MS McClean, 182 fos. 54ʳ–138ʳ),[152] Lydgate and Burgh's *Secrees* (in MS McClean, 182, fos. 12ʳ–49ʳ), a prose regiminal text (in the Harvard MS, fos. 38–48),[153] and, in MS Pepys 2006 (a Chaucer anthology), with the Parson's Tale, *Melibee*,[154] and Burgh's *Cato.*

[149] Lydgate ed. Norton-Smith (1966: xiii–xv); Renoir (1967: 105); Pearsall (1970: 158); Scattergood (1971: 138).

[150] Schirmer (1952, trans. 1961: 82–8).

[151] Ibid. 85; the preface to Allde's 1590 print suggests that some readers saw it exactly as a *vita*; however, see fo. Aiiʳ. [152] Seymour (1974: 285).

[153] See Robinson (1896: 181–6).

[154] Unexpectedly, the only one of the Canterbury Tales to appear in the manuscript—a testament to its moral intentions. Gerson claimed in a letter to the tutor of the dauphin Louis in June 1417 that Livy, Sallust, and Suetonius were among the twenty-two essential texts which should be in the library of every prince (Gerson 1960–73: ii. 213).

MS Additional 48031 is a collection of state papers, royal letters, chronicles (fos. 71ʳ–119ᵛ), oaths, and documents relating to the Privy Seal. Parliamentary rolls outlining Richard of York's claim to the throne in 1460 (fos. 130ᵛ–34ʳ) and accounts of Duke Humphrey's disputes with Bishop Beaufort (fo. 64ʳ) and of Jack Cade's 1450 rebellion (fos. 135ʳ–37ʳ) jostle with Fortescue's *Governaunce of England* (fos. 148ᵛ–64ʳ): that the *Serpent* finds itself in the company of official documents and works of political theory says much about how it was later read.[155] Furthermore, the three envoy octaves found in the Cambridge manuscripts read much like the advisory envoys added to the *Fall*, with warnings on 'fals diuision' and 'vayn ambicoun', thereby securing a reginal reading of the text.[156]

CAESAR, VIRTUOUS PAGANS, AND *SYNDERESIS*

Julius Caesar is the most ambiguous of the Nine Worthies. Classical and medieval commentators, historians, and poets are bewilderingly diverse in their assessments of the Roman leader: the 'myghty Cesar', whose 'wisedom, manhede, and . . . greet labour' are enthusiastically celebrated by Chaucer's Monk, is presented by Lucan as a wilful and coldly ambitious violator of Roman law. Petrarch's model of heroic clemency is also Cicero's tyrant and the illegitimate ruler of the schoolmen and canonists. Even ancient historians, as Ernest Schanzer has noted, show ambivalence:

Plutarch, Appian, Suetonius, are all far from single-minded in their attitude towards Caesar and his assassins, and Plutarch's wavering between opposing views repeatedly leads him into self-contradictions.[157]

These conflicting versions of Caesar's moral condition are perhaps nowhere more clearly seen than in Dante's *Comedy*, where Caesar, adorned with the symbols of his military prowess, is seen with Lucretia and Lucius Junius Brutus among the virtuous pagans in Limbo; however, while his murderers Marcus Brutus and Cassius are condemned with Judas Iscariot to suffer for their treachery in

---

[155] British Library, *The Yelverton Manuscripts: Additional 48000–48196* (1994: i. 118–26).   [156] MS Pepys 2006, p. 209.

[157] Schanzer (1955: 20); see Cicero, *De officiis* I. 26, III. 82.

the maw of Satan, Dante's position is muddled by the placing of
Gaius Curio (the counsellor who advised Caesar to cross the
Rubicon) among the instigators of schism, his tongue gruesomely
cut out. Alone of all the noble heathen, Marcus Cato, champion
of the Republic and Caesar's enduring enemy, is promoted from
Limbo to be the guardian of the shores of Purgatory.[158]

Lying behind the confusion of responses to Caesar among
medieval writers is the debate over the virtuous pagans, a theme
which surfaces in texts as diverse as the writings of the canonists
and the bizarre story of St Erkenwald and the pagan corpse, and
which finds its *locus classicus* in the story of Gregory the Great's
prayer for the soul of the Emperor Trajan.[159] At the heart of the
debate over the virtuous pagans lies the concept of natural law,
the eternal manifestation of the created will of God resting
(unalienably and regardless of national identity or civil allegiance)
in the heart of all human beings, prior both to the laws promul-
gated by societies to regulate their affairs (*ius positivum*) and also
to the dictates of canon law (*ius positivum canonicum*).[160]
Following St Paul, the canonists defined those who live without
the revelation of Christ as subsisting solely under natural law, with
a moral life—though it may follow the rules of the *ius positivum*
of a human society—which acts by a nature unaided by infused
grace (*ex puris naturalibus*).[161] Beryl Smalley and Alastair Minnis
have traced the impact of these legal ideas on the classicizing friars of the thirteenth and fourteenth centuries, and in particular
on the thought of Robert Holcot, the Oxford Dominican whose
commentaries on the sapiential books achieved considerable popularity in England and were known to Chaucer and Lydgate.[162]

[158] *Inferno* IV. 123–9; XXXIV. 61–7; XXVIII.94–102; *Purgatorio* I. 31 ff.

[159] *Policraticus* V. 8, Webb (1909: i. 315–18); see *Piers Plowman* B. XI. 140.
See Gradon (1983), Whatley (1984), Chambers (1923).

[160] The Isidorean definition was popular: 'ius naturale est commune omnium
nationum et quod ubique instinctu naturae, non constitutione aliqua habeatur'
(*De etymologiis* V. 1, in *PL* lxxxii. 199B).

[161] Rom. 2: 12–15; see Oberman (1963: 47–50, 103–8, 132–4, 235–48, 468);
Forerunners of the Reformation, trans. Nyhus (1967: 142 ff.); *DDC* vi. 966–90.
For discussion of the political implications of natural law see Barr (D. Phil. thesis,
1989: ch. 4) and (1992).

[162] For Chaucer see Spearing (1985: 44–6); Minnis (1988: 272 n. 19). Lydgate
refers to 'Holcot vpon sapience' in his *Isopes Fabules*, ll. 680–700 (*MP* ii. 589–90)
and Hoccleve cites the commentary in his *Male Regle*, ll.249 ff. See also Smalley
(1960: 133–202) and Minnis (1982: 57–60).

Against this background discussion of the virtues of the pagans,
then, Lydgate's accounts of Lucretia and Caesar, and his interest
in the political systems of pagan cultures may take on a new significance; issues of natural law have lain behind the two Roman
narratives we have examined—the violation of Lucretia and the
moral status of Caesar.

The envoy to Rome which Lydgate adds to the end of Book II
of the *Fall* concludes with an extended apostrophe to the Empire,
exhorting it to turn to the Christian God and to abandon its
pagan deities:

> Thouh Mars be myhti in his ascencioun,
>
> . . . . .
>
> And brihte Phebus yeueth consolacioun
>
> . . . . .
>
> Forsake ther rihtis and thi fals offryng,
>
> . . . . .
>
> Cast up off Venus the fals derisioun,
>
> . . . . .
>
> Off Iuno, Bachus, Proserpina, Lucyne:
> For non but Crist may saue the fro ruyne!
>
> Voide off Circes the bestiall poisoun,
> Off Cirenes the furious chauntyng;
> Lat nat Medusa do the no tresoun,
> And fro Gorgones turne thi lookyng;
> And lat Synderesis ha[ue] the in kepyng,
> That Crist Iesu may be thi medicyne
> Geyn such raskaile to saue the fro ruyne![163]

Lydgate's use of the term *synderesis* here signals his engagement
with the works of the canonists: *synderesis* was the scholastic term
for the inborn habit of knowing the precepts of moral conduct,
the natural tendency of the will towards good which is the 'guar-
antee of man's abiding attachment to the sovereign good . . . the

---

[163] *Fall* II. 4537, 4539, 4541, 4551, 4556–64: the Rome envoy seems to have
been popular, and is reproduced in MSS Ashmole 59, Trinity College Cambridge
R. 3. 19, Harley 367, Harley 2251, Harley 4011, Magdalene College Pepys 2011,
Balliol College 329, Pierpont Morgan Library M. 4. For Lydgate *contra paganos*
see II. 4208–11, Brie (1929: 278), and Dwyer (1978).

innate disposition by which man knows the first principles of the natural law'.[164] Peter Lombard defined *synderesis* as the spark of reason that Jerome believed had not been extinguished even in Cain.[165] In appealing to this legal concept, Lydgate seems to claim that the Romans' natural sparks of reason will inevitably lead them to Christ: the medieval dilemma of the virtuous pagans has been solved.

The problems of dating *The Serpent* mean that the picture is uncomfortably indistinct. We have already seen the inadvisability of drawing hard and fast historical correspondences for the events narrated in literary texts without evidence of the most explicit kind; all too often Lydgate criticism has been bedevilled by loose suggestion of topical reference or historical relationship which has lacked any kind of firm evidence, critical supposition being allowed to harden into a carapace of received wisdom, or of 'fact'. It is an unfortunate irony that Eleanor Hammond, whose article on the relationship between Lydgate and his patron opened up so significant a debate, herself exemplifies some of the excesses of this trend in a later article:

> It must have been there that Humphrey interfered . . . Not only was it Humphrey who put Coluccio's Latin into Lydgate's hands, but it was very probably he who gave Lydgate the hint about Dante, used in book IV, lines 134–40, of the *Fall of Princes*; it was from his library that Lydgate drew information about Petrarch; it was under his personal supervision that the carefully built rhythm of the Palladius translation was framed. And if it was also he who told Lydgate that Chaucer's *Troilus* was translated from the *Lombard tunge* and not from Latin, then Humphrey was no mean critic of letters.[166]

To date there has been little detailed analysis of the nature of the relationship between patron, poet, and text. However, analysis of *The Serpent* and of those sections of the *Fall* which result from Humphrey's intervention in the composition of that poem has revealed an unexpectedly rich seam of linking interests: we have

---

[164] *STh* I. q. 79 a. 12, Ia2ae q. 94 a. 1 ad. 2; see White (D. Phil. thesis, 1986: 3–4); O'Connor (1967: 42–4, 73); Brian Davies (1992: 244–9). Lydgate uses the term elsewhere in his work; three of the seven citations in the *MED* 'S–SL', 913, are by him.   [165] Peter Lombard, *Sententiae* II dist. 39, ch. 3 (1892: 391).
[166] Hammond (1927–8: 57).

found that it is in the context of disparate episodes from the history of ancient Rome that Lydgate repeatedly chooses to voice both ethical and political advice. Additionally, although we can not assume that his patron would explicitly have commissioned Lydgate's articulation of debates specific to natural law, Humphrey's interest elsewhere in classical political theory suggests that even the arcane topic of *synderesis* would not have been unwelcome to him.

4

Spiritual and Secular Authority in the *Fall*

Two of Lydgate's more immediately striking departures from the material he found in Premierfait's *Des Cas* are his additions of references to his Lancastrian patrons. At the opening of his version of Premierfait's narrative of the fall of Troy, Lydgate refers to his earlier *Troy Book* and to his patron for that work, Henry V, then Prince of Wales:

> For I hadde onys in comau*n*dement,
> Bi hym that was most noble & excellent
> Off kynges all[e], for to vndirtake
> It to translate and write it for his sake.

> And yiff ye list to wetyn whom I meene,
> Henry the Fiffte, most myhti off puissau*n*ce,
> Gaff me the charge off entent most cleene,
> Thyng off old tyme to putte in remembrau*n*ce,
> The same Henry, for knyhtli suffisau*n*ce,
> Worthi for manhod, reknyd kynges all,
> With nyne worthi for to haue a stall.

> To hooli chirch he was chieff defensour;
> In alle such causes Cristes chosen knyht.
> To stroie Lollardis he sette al his labour[1]

The terms Lydgate uses to frame his praise of Henry here are a curious blend of the familiar and the unexpected. Henry's 'knyhtli suffisaunce', his military and diplomatic achievements, are recognizably the material of encomium. However, these details are conscripted to frame an account of Henry's defence of Holy Church from the threat of Lollardy. Although this is not inappropriate in

[1] *Fall* I. 5954–67.

rhetorical terms, this praise *does* seem unusual when we consider the force of the narrative which this passage prefaces: the account of the fall of Priam's Troy is one in which issues of martial prowess rather than of religious orthodoxy would seem to be of more relevance. It would be misguided to seek to establish a coherence which is simply not here; the account of Henry's suppression of the Lollard threat is included in the sketch of the dead king for the simple reason that it is in this light that Lydgate feels that Henry *ought* to be remembered.

The description of Henry echoes that of his younger brother Humphrey which Lydgate appends to his translation of the second preface to Premierfait's B-version, the 'Prologue du Translateur'. Whereas Premierfait follows his discussion of the challenges of translation with a series of harsh and topical social criticisms, Lydgate chooses instead to honour those who have inspired his poem: Chaucer and Humphrey of Gloucester. Literary and political empowerment, then, have replaced polemic. Of Humphrey he writes:

> Eek in this land, I dar afferme a thyng:
> There is a prynce ful myhti of puissaunce,
> A kyngis sone and vncle to the kyng
> Henry the Sexte, which is now in Fraunce,
> And is lieftenant, and hath the gouernaunce
> Off our Breteyne, thoruh whos discrecioun
> He hath conserued in this regioun,
>
> .   .   .   .
>
> Duc off Gloucestre men this prynce calle,
> And natwithstandyng his staat & dignite,
> His corage neuer doth appalle
> To studie in bookis off antiquite,
> Therin he hath so gret felicite
> Vertuously hymsilff to ocupie,
> Off vicious slouthe to haue the maistrie.
>
> And with his prudence and with his manheed,
> Trouthe to susteene he fauour set a-side,
> And hooli chirch[e] meyntenyng in deed,
> That in this land no Lollard dar abide—
> As verray support, vpholdere and eek guide
> Sparith noon, but maketh hymsiluen strong
> To punysshe all tho that do the chirch[e] wrong.
>
> Thus is he bothe manli and eek wis,
> Chose off God to been his owyn knyht,

And off o thyng he hath a synguler pris,
That heretik dar noon come in his siht,
In Cristis feith he stant so hool vpriht,
Off hooli chirche diffence and champiou*n*,
To chastise alle that do therto tresou*n*.[2]

Again, Lydgate's portrait hinges on Gloucester's defence of the Church from the subversive attacks of heterodoxy: Humphrey's diplomatic and scholarly achievements meet in, and derive focus from, his activities in support of the sacred and (chiefly, for Lydgate) in his involvement in the suppression of the 1431 Midlands Lollard uprisings.[3] It is this relationship between the sacred and the secular which I will discuss in this chapter, looking first at narratives which outline models of support of the spiritual order by the secular arm, then at the more significant of the numerous accounts which dramatize the reverse (namely the *persecution* of the Church by those in positions of civil authority). Finally, by examining events and issues current in the Bury of the 1430s, I indicate some of the ways in which Lydgate's more outspoken manipulations of Premierfait's text engage with pressing contemporary Benedictine defences of the autonomy of ecclesiastical power from the menacing attentions of ambitious local magnates and diocesan authorities.

NARRATIVES OF EMPOWERMENT AND SUPPORT

Saul and Joas

Of all the biblical narratives Lydgate offers in the *Fall*, his versions of those of Saul[4] and of Joas (the biblical 'Joash') (in II. ch. 7: 'De Athalia')[5] demonstrate most clearly his emphasis on the authority

[2] *Fall* I. 372–8, 393–413.
[3] Gloucester's involvement in the suppression of these uprisings in the spring of 1431 is well attested, and Capgrave described him as a 'diligent extirpator of heresies' (see Humphrey's MS Oriel College 32, fo.3ʳ; Vickers 1907: 322–3; Griffiths 1981: 139–40). The Duke was praised by the University of Oxford for his persecution of heretics (Anstey 1898: i. 217), which has been described as an addiction (Griffiths 1981: 59). A Wycliffite New Testament now held in New York Public Library (MS 67) may have been owned by Humphrey (Sammut 1980: 131). Humphrey's enthusiasm for the suppression of heresy also appears to have been exploited in 1432 by an embassy led by Gerardo Landriani, bishop of Lodi, to seek English support for the Council of Basle, and we know that in 1433 Humphrey acquired a copy of the decrees of the Council of Constance (now BL MS Cotton Nero E. v) (Schofield 1961: 171, 175).   [4] *Fall* II. 162–532.
[5] Ibid. II. 1744–897.

of the spiritual order to legitimize and constitute secular rule. In both accounts Lydgate differs from Premierfait in his treatment of the coronation ritual of the monarch. The biblical account of Saul's investiture as king consists of a simple ceremony of unction at the hands of the prophet Samuel,[6] and both Boccaccio and Premierfait preserve this simplicity.[7] The French text runs:

Samuel par ladmonnestement de dieu respandit sur la teste de saul vne burette dhuylle consacree | et le oignit 7 ordonna pour estre roy des iuifz.

(Directed by God, Samuel poured a vial of holy oil on Saul's head, thus anointing and ordaining him king of the Jews)[8]

Lydgate's account is immediately more flamboyant:

> be precept & ordenaunce deuyne,
> Samuel made no prolongacioun,
> But shadde the hooli sacred vnccioun
> Vpon the hed off Saul, doun knelyng,
> And ful deuoutli off Israel made hym kyng,
>
> Off goddis peeple to ha[ue] the gouernaunce,
> With sceptre & crowne, and hool the regalie.
> And his noblesse mor myhtili tauaunce,
> With meek[e]nesse to reule his monarchie,
> God gaff to hym a sperit off prophecie,
> Which was gret glorie to his magnyficence,
> Off futur thynges to haue prescience.[9]

Saul's authority as king of the Israelites is enhanced by his powers of prophecy (which emphasize the divine origin of his princely rule); moreover, his investiture is also made to approximate to the drama of fifteenth-century coronation ritual by the inclusion of details such as Saul's posture and the regalia of power. Furthermore, Lydgate chooses to insert a brief comment on successful statecraft: monarchical power should properly be moderated by 'meekenesse'.

---

[6] 1 Kgs. 10: 1 (Douai): 'And Samuel took a little vial of oil; and poured it upon his head; and kissed him; and said: Behold, the Lord hath anointed thee to be a prince over his inheritance: and thou shalt deliver his people out of the hands of their enemies, that are round about them. And this shall be a sign unto thee, that God hath anointed thee to be a prince'; cf. 1 Sam. 10: 1 (AV).
[7] *De casibus* fo. 13ʳ (p. 49): '[Samuel] fusa super caput eius lenticula olei | Illum hebreorum vnxit in regem.'   [8] *Des Cas* fo. 24ᵛ (II. ch. 1).
[9] *Fall* II. 178–89: Lydgate's source for the detail of the prophetic powers of Saul is 1 Kgs. 10: 5–6 (Douai); cf. 1 Sam. 10: 5–6 (AV).

In this Lydgate is reflecting the distinctive nature of English coronation ritual in the later medieval period. The differences between French and English coronation ceremonial succinctly express the differing understandings of royal government in the two cultures; whereas French kings could claim authority by the sacredness of their blood, their English cousins were dependent on ritual oaths and unction to confirm their legitimacy of rule. In France a theocratic understanding of the principle of hereditary sucession led to a relative downplaying of the importance of the coronation rite; in England, however, kings were formally bound by their coronation oaths, as in a feudal contract, to their nobles.[10] So again Lydgate's later narrative of the coronation of the boy-king Joas places its emphasis far more fully on the sacramental function of Joiada (the biblical priest Jehoiada) in the confirmation of royal authority than is the case either in the Vulgate or in his French source. The biblical account devotes much attention to the precautions Joiada takes in order to ensure that the temple will be guarded adequately during the ritual as he surrounds it with soldiers; the coronation itself, however, is cursorily given:

And he brought forth the king's son, and put the diadem upon him, and the testimony. And they made him king and anointed him. And clapping their hands, they said: God save the king.[11]

Premierfait, following the spare account in Boccaccio,[12] omits the elaborate security arrangements of the Old Testament story and reduces the accession of Joas to:

Joyada lors evesque de hierusalem q*ui* secretement co*mme* dit est auoit prins 7 fait mourir ioas ado*nc* enfant filz du dit Ochozias de la lignee de David I cestuy Joyada euesque fist ledit Joas roy de hierusale*m* 7 fist ladicte Athalia gecter hors du royaulme.

(it is said that Joiada, bishop of Jerusalem, had secretly taken the boy Joas, son of the aforementioned Ahaziah of the house of David, and given out that he was dead; this bishop Joiada made Joas king of Jerusalem and caused Athalia to be banished from the realm.)[13]

---

[10] Lander (1989: 42–5); Wood (1976); Sir John Fortescue later vividly contrasts the unlimited royal dominion of the French throne with the comparative lack of coercive power of the English political monarchy (*De laudibus* §§ 34–6 and *Governance* §§ 3–4, in Fortescue ed. Lockwood (1997)).
[11] 4 Kgs. 11: 12 (Douai); cf. 2 Kgs. 11: 12 (AV).
[12] *De casibus* fo. 16ʳ (p.55): 'Ioa rege facto'.   [13] *Des Cas* fo. 29ᵛ.

Premierfait eliminates all sense of the coronation as a subversive assertion of the power of a priest to defy the tyranny of Athaliah, Joas's usurping mother, and of the ritual as a public (if secretive and heavily guarded) act of defiance; for him an assertion of Joas's lineage suffices. By contrast, Lydgate restores and enhances the drama of the *proclamation* of the boy-king seen in the biblical account; the centurions and soldiers, summoned merely as witnesses and guards by the Vulgate Joiada, are transformed into a gathering of princes, tribunes, Levites, and priests summoned not merely as spectators, but as 'a counseil':

> And in the seuente, the story doth deuise,
> Ioiada took on hym this emprise:
> Yonge Ioas withynne a certeyn day
> Be iuste[e] title to crowne hym yiff he may.

> His massageris he sendith out anon,
> Off pryncis, tribunes gan a counseil call,
> Off preestis eek, and leuytes euerichon.
> And whan he hadde discured to hem all
> Hool his entent, thus it is befall:
> Sworn and assentid, as it was sittyng,
> That yonge Ioas shal be crownyd kyng.

> 'For be promys, which that is dyuyne,'
> Quod Ioiada, 'yiff ye taken heede,
> God hath behestid to Dauid and his lyne,
> And assurid onto his kynreede,
> In Ierusalem how thei shal succeede;
> And thouh Ioas be yong & tendre off myht,
> He to the crowne hath neuer-the-lesse ryht.

> In this mateer I wil nat that ye slepe,
> But to shewe your trewe deligence,
> On foure parties the temple for to keepe,
> That no man entre be no violence;
> And in the myddis, be roial excellence,'
> Quod this bisshop, 'no man shal us lette,
> On Ioas hed a crowne for to sette.'

> And whan ech thyng was brouht onto the poynt,
> His hih estat tencrece and magnefie,
> The peeple anon, whan he was enoynt,
> '*Viuat rex!*' thei began to crie.[14]

---

[14] *Fall* II. 1810–38. Lydgate's account differs also from that of the Septuagint ('the seuente') (*The Septuagint Version of the Old Testamant, with an English Translation* (1879: 505)).

There emerges, then, in the English version a drama not so much of coronation (indeed the coronation is not described), but rather one of feudal *election*: the assembly is presented with the proposal that Joas should be crowned and seems empowered to grant or withhold assent. Explicitly judicial terminology ('Sworn and assentid') and the disputational character of Joiada's presentation of the boy's blood claims to the throne serve only to emphasize that the witnesses of the coronation are no arbitrary assembly of onlookers, but rather form a legally constituted body who will legitimize the transfer of rightful authority which the ritual is to enact. In its intriguingly suggestive echoes of the recent Westminster and Paris coronations (in 1429 and 1431 respectively) of the boy-king Henry VI, the whole drama recalls the conciliarist wrangles in Parliament after the death of Henry V about the disposition of power in England and France during the minority—wrangles in which Lydgate's patron had played so prominent a role.[15]

The role of the spiritual order (even if, as in the narratives of Saul and Joas, it be a pre-Christian one) in authorizing kingly rule provides the framework for the *Fall* narratives which take the analysis of the Church–State relationship several steps further. There are six narratives which illustrate the grateful response of an earthly prince to the Church that secures his authority: those of Hostilius, the two Philips, Theodosius, Constantine, Constantine IV, and of Henry of Hohenstaufen (son of the Holy Roman Emperor Frederick II).[16]

Hostilius

Of these, the first—the narrative of the Roman king Tullus Hostilius—is complicated by the pre-Christian context of the story. In Laurent's French account Hostilius is cured of his illness by a simple act of subjection to the gods ('le seul remede estoit crier mercy aux dieux et impetrer leur grace').[17] Lydgate alters the story by imbuing it with a contemporary colour: Hostilius is cured not

---

[15] It is suggestive to read the anaphoric one-stanza *moralitas* with which Lydgate concludes and points the political significance of the narrative (II. 1856–62) in the context of his involvement in assaults on dauphinist denials of Henry VI's legitimate succession to the French throne.

[16] *Fall* III. 708–91; VIII. 365–78; VIII. 1800–2107; VIII. 1170–463; IX. 621–51; IX. 1667–743.   [17] *Des Cas* (III. ch. 2) fo. 48ᵛ.

after a prayer but after the more apparently fifteenth-century discipline of a pilgrimage. On his recovery, Hostilius devotes himself more fully, Lydgate assures us, to 'comou*n* proffit':[18] successful and unselfish statecraft is again shown as the natural result of a proper awareness of spiritual imperatives.

The account of Hostilius' downfall, however, sits awkwardly in the narrative of piety-rewarded which Lydgate has fashioned from his French source. While Premierfait's Hostilius is punished by the gods for the presumption of offering inadequate sacrifice, Lydgate (having to some extent compromised the *de casibus* potential of the narrative in his sympathetic description of the priorities of Hostilius' regenerated rule) transforms the thrust of the downfall into a sermon on the folly of pagan worship:

> His false goddis myhte hym nat auaile,
> Iubiter, Saturnus nor Venus.
> Lat al *Christ*ene defie such rascaile;
> For to our feith thei be contrarious.
> And among goddis, a thyng most outraious,
> Ys, whan that pryncis, blent in ther folie,
> List ertheli thynges falsli deifie.[19]

The whole nature of the relation between king and deity has been altered in the English text: the cause of the death of Hostilius is not that he offers the ritual sacrifice unceremonially (in fact, Lydgate obviously regards the 'riche sacrifice' as evidence of the king's dutiful gratitude), but that he offers it to the wrong gods in the first place. The blurred logic of this narrative is evident (Does the lightning bolt come from outraged Olympians or from an omnipotent Christian deity?) and it is a muddle into which Lydgate has fallen precisely because of his decision to strengthen the sense of the dependence of the earthly ruler on heavenly aid. This apart, the story of Hostilius is in other respects atypical of those *Fall* narratives which deal with the ways in which secular rulers repay their debts to the spiritual: the remaining narratives turn more clearly on the relations between the Christian Church and imperial authority. These themes find their most cogent articulation in the narratives of St Ambrose's rebuke of Theodosius and of the Donation of Constantine.

---

[18] *Fall* III. 756.   [19] Ibid. III. 778–84.

Theodosius

Lydgate's version of the narrative of the career of the Emperor Theodosius falls into three distinct sections: the conflict with Maximus, the governor of Britain; the Emperor's piety in the face of his battle with the Frankish general Arbogastes; and the clash between Theodosius and St Ambrose after the Emperor's intemperate revenge (in the form of a widespread massacre) on the commons of Thessalonika. Lydgate prefaces the whole with a clear and original statement of the emphasis he intends to place on the narrative:

> Theodosie and Gracian of assent
> Destroied templis as in that partie
> Of false goddis; thei haue also dou*n* rent
> The grete idoles & al suich maumetrye,
> And ful deuoutli ga*n* chirchis edefye.[20]

Theodosius is presented here primarily in his role as upholder of the Christian faith. *Imperial* authority works here to strengthen the Church, both by the destruction of the temples of rival religions and also by the erection of churches. That Lydgate should add this detail is not unusual; patristic readings of the career of Theodosius emphasize the Emperor's role as a supporter of a vulnerable Church. Augustine, who concludes the argument of the fifth book of his *De civitate Dei* with a chapter on the Emperor, writes of Theodosius in exactly this capacity:

Inter haec omnia ex ipso initio imperii sui non quievit iustissimus et misericordissimus legibus adversus impios laboranti Ecclesie subvenire quam Valens haereticus favens Arianis vehementur afflixerat: cuius Ecclesie se membrum esse magis quam in terris regnare gaudebat.

(Among all these anxieties Theodosius, from the beginning of his reign, never relaxed his endeavours to help the Church against the ungodly by just and compassionate legislation; and the Church at the time was in difficulties, for the heretic Valens had dealt her heavy blows in his support of the Arians. Theodosius was more glad to be a member of that Church than to be ruler of the world.)[21]

---

[20] Ibid. VIII. 1807–11. For an account of the historical events, see McLynn (1994: 315–30).

[21] *De civitate Dei*, v. 26 in *PL* xli. 173–4; trans. Bettenson (Augustine 1972: 223). The impact of the chapter for Augustine seems to lie in the contrast Theodosius forms with most earthly rulers who fail to acknowledge the frailty of their authority

Lydgate's portrayal of Theodosius is developed still further in his reworking of the Emperor's night-long prayer before his battle with the army of Arbogastes.[22] Alongside those additions that serve to heighten the pathos of Theodosius' situation (the graphic specification of the nature of his dilemma and the danger he faces at VIII. 1932 and 1947, the use of rhetorical devices to dramatize the act of prayer itself at line 916, and the heightened diction to enhance the sense of crisis at line 1918), Lydgate makes two significant alterations to his source. First, it is noticeable that Theodosius takes on to himself the imperfections of character which Premierfait had deployed to describe the state of sinful man prone to social disorder and misgovernment; the 'aueuglesse de pensee | 7 . . . fragilite de chair' that incline men to sin and which caused God to establish the principles of kingly government and dominion ('royaulmes et seigneuries') are confessed by Lydgate's emperor as personal failings:

> Considre & see how that I am thi kniht,
> Which ofte sithe thoruh my fragilite,
> With flesshli lustis bleendid in my siht,
> A thousand tymes haue trespasid onto the[23]

Whereas, then, in Premierfait's version Theodosius offers an objectively held theoretical statement of the divine origins of polity, Lydgate's Theodosius implicates himself in the fallenness that makes civil government necessary. Premierfait's vague profession of personal inadequacy ('moy indigne') has been reworked by Lydgate in order to reinforce the dependence of the secular order on the spiritual, an emphasis we have seen in his Joas narrative. Furthermore, the personal insufficiency of Theodosius is neatly secured by the introduction of feudal terminology: rather than the unworthy *king* of the French text, Lydgate presents an unworthy *servant* ('I am thi kniht').

Secondly, Lydgate adds Susannah to the list of Old Testament exempla of those delivered from danger by God which he finds in Premierfait's version of the prayer. Initially this addition seems

---

and their consequent dependence on God (e.g. 'haec ille secum, et si qua similia, quae commemorare longum est, bona opera tulit, ex isto temporali vapore cuiuslibet culminis et sublimitatis humana . . . ista temporalia, quae sola stulti habere concupiscunt').

[22] See Appendix I to this chapter.   [23] *Fall* VIII. 1919–22; cf. *Des Cas* fo. 184[v].

perplexing: the references to the delivery of Israel from Egypt in the Mosaic exodus and to the rescue of Daniel from the den of lions reflect more closely the kind of military and physical danger Theodosius himself is confronting. Regarded, however, as a sequence, the three allusions form a powerful triptych of biblical evidence for God's loyalty to His covenant with the Israelites: whether leading the whole nation into the promised land or intervening to rescue the wronged Susannah ('in hir mortal greuau*n*ce'),[24] God is shown in these *exempla* to be faithful to His own promises and so, in a prayer devoted to a discussion of the need for princes to fulfil their duty of service to God, these three references are highly apt. That Lydgate's addition fits neatly into (and to a degree clarifies) this sequence testifies to his active involvement with the verbal detail of his French source: where he feels an association of ideas could be made more secure, he intervenes in order to achieve the effect he desires. It is also noticeable that Lydgate's addition characteristically heightens the pathos of the larger speech.

Nowhere, however, in the Theodosius narrative do Lydgate's concerns with the proper subservience of the temporal order to the authority of the Church emerge more clearly than in the account of the legend of St Ambrose's rebuke of Theodosius for the Thessalonikan massacre (which he chooses to add to the chapter he found in Premierfait). The dramatic confrontation between bishop and emperor at Milan is a graphic demonstration of the superiority of spiritual authority to that of civil government. Denied entry to the cathedral and excommunicated by the bishop, Theodosius' distress and subsequent penance are clear:

> That to behold the gret humylite
> Of themperou*r*, considred euerideel,
> It wolde haue perced an herte maad of steel.

> With hed enclyned he spak no woord agey*n*,
> Brast on weepyng with sobbyng v*n*stau*n*chabl*e*,
> His purpil weede bedewed as with rey*n*,
> Returnyng hom with cheer most lame*n*tabl*e*,

> .   .   .   .   .   .

> To the cherche he meekli did obeye,
> [Lik] Goddis kniht did lowli his penau*n*ce[25]

24 Ibid. VIII. 1936.   25 *Fall* VIII. 2063–9, 2080–1.

It is again noticeable that Lydgate chooses to articulate Theodosius' penitence in terms of the chivalric relationship he has already established between the Emperor and God: the very sin which Theodosius had ordered to be carried out by his own 'knihtis' is now atoned for by his own assumption of the role of knight (of God) rather than of commander (of other knights). In this respect the description of his tears of regret and anguish soaking the purple grandeur of his imperial regalia takes on a moving symbolic resonance.

Verbal echoes and symbolic colour heighten the impact of Lydgate's episode; yet omission is here as significant as addition. The Augustinian account of the massacre (which may have influenced Lydgate's version) compromises the clarity of the confrontation between episcopal and imperial authority which, for him, lies at the heart of the story. Augustine states that Theodosius has previously promised the Church that he would *not* avenge the deaths of the Thessalonikan judges:

Quid autem fuit eius religiosa humilitate mirabilius quando in Thessalonicensium gravissimum scelus, cui iam, *episcopis intercedentibus, promiserat indulgentiam,* tumultu quorundam, qui ei cohaerebant, vindicare compulsis est, et ecclesiastica coercitus disciplina, sic egit poenitentiam, ut imperatoriam celsitudinem pro illo populus orans magis fleret videndo prostratam, quam peccando timeret iratam?

(But nothing could be more wonderful than the religious humility he showed after the grievous crime committed by the people of Thessalonica. *On the intercession of the bishops he had promised a pardon*; but then the clamour of certain of his close supporters drove him to avenge the crime. But he was constrained by the discipline of the Church to do penance in such a fashion that the people of Thessalonica, as they prayed for him, wept at seeing the imperial highness thus prostrate, with an emotion stronger than their fears of the emperor's wrath at their offence.)[26]

Lydgate, then, gives nuance and depth to what is for Augustine an account of the sinful breaking of a vow made by an emperor to the Church. Although the version of the story in the *De civitate* dramatizes clearly enough the Emperor's willingness to bow to the power of the spiritual order, the issue of Theodosius' repentance is actually straightforward for Augustine: Theodosius repents because

---

[26] *De civitate Dei*, v. 26 in *PL* xli. 173; trans. Bettenson (Augustine 1972: 223) (emphases added).

he has broken his word. In a sense, Augustine's Theodosius has betrayed *himself* as much as he has the bishops. Lydgate's narrative is, by contrast, much more complex—and it is made so because it has been 'irrationalized': his Theodosius has broken no prior understanding. (In fact, the massacre as Lydgate describes it is shown to have been ordered as a result of an infamous act of revolt against judges appointed to uphold the law.) Therefore the rebuke of the Bishop is no longer a simple expression of disappointment at an act of perjury, but is instead a condemnation of Theodosius' moral behaviour in ordering the attack per se. In submitting to the judgement and penalty of the Church, Lydgate's Theodosius in fact concedes a larger principle than does his patristic model: that there is no broken contractual commitment in no way diminishes the authority of the spiritual order to chasten the temporal. An ecclesiological, and not merely a legal, point is made.

Ambrose of Milan's fearless assertions of the subordination of the imperial power to the authority of the Church survive in his letters, a manuscript copy of which was given by Humphrey to Oxford University.[27] That Lydgate should select the story of the Bishop's challenge to imperial authority as one of his two longest original additions to the *Fall of Princes* gains in significance when we turn to consider the other—the narrative of the Donation of Constantine. Once again, when Lydgate chooses to diverge from the plan of his source text in any sizeable way, it is in order to introduce a narrative which focuses on the themes we have seen to emerge in the story of Theodosius: the role of the Church in authorizing the power structures of the temporal order and the conflicts of authority that can arise from misunderstandings of the nature of Church–State relationships. Further evidence of the importance Lydgate attached to the Theodosius and Constantine

---

[27] Ambrose's Epistle XX (to his sister Marcellina) on his defence of ecclesiastical immunity from imperial authority when asked by Valentinian II to surrender his basilica for use by the Arians: 'Do not, O Emperor, lay on yourself the burden of such a thought as that you have any imperial power over those things which belong to God. Exalt not yourself, but if you desire to reign long, submit yourself to God. It is written: "The things which are God's to God, those which are Caesar's to Caesar". The palaces belong to the Emperor, the churches belong to the bishop. Authority is committed to you over public, not over sacred, buildings', *PL* xvi. 1042A; trans. Schaff and Wace, in *Nicene and Post-Nicene Fathers* x. 425; cf. Meyendorff (1989: 37). A Bury Ambrose is now Pembroke College Cambridge MS 42 (fos. 19ʳ–172ᵛ); Humphrey's donation is recorded in Anstey (1898: i. 180) and Sammut (1980: 62).

episodes can be seen when we consider that he was prepared to
fracture the unity of the entire *Fall* in order to accommodate them:
these two narratives are not *casus* narratives, not actually *falls*
at all. Though each contains a turning point that might lead to
downfall, neither pursues a tragic trajectory: in formal generic
terms each is more appropriately considered a *comedy*.

Constantine

Issues of ecclesiastical and secular authority in the *Fall* find their
clearest theoretical expression in the story of the conversion and
Donation of Constantine. Though the document of the Donation
was demonstrated to have been a forgery at various stages in the
fifteenth century,[28] the power of the account of the voluntary
endowment of the Church by the head of the Empire (a tradition
originating in eighth-century France) was unweakened in popular
imagination: certainly, Lydgate's treatment offers no evidence that
he regarded the story in any other light than that of historical fact.

Early patristic accounts of the legend of Constantine's conversion provide a telling contrast to the emphases traced by medieval
versions. In the chapter immediately preceding his account of
Theodosius, Augustine manipulates his reading of the legend in
order to serve the larger argument of the *De civitate*; refuting the
accusation that the abandonment of pagan deities by the Christian
Empire was responsible for the sack of Rome, Augustine argues
that the conversion of Constantine illustrates that God safeguards
those who honour Him.[29] The patristic account, working centuries
before the emergence of the legend of the material endowment of
the Church, finds its focus on the successful expansion of the
Empire under the devout Constantine. Political safety, rather than
material enrichment, answers more exactly the charges of late
classical opponents to Christianity: Rome may have fallen, but
God-fearing Constantinople still flourishes.[30]

[28] Namely *c.*1433 by Nicholas of Cusa, *De concordantia catholica* III. ch. 2
§§ 294–312, trans. Sigmund (Cusa 1991: 216–22); by Lorenzo Valla, *Declamatio
de falso credita et ementia donatione Constantini* (1440); and by Reginald Pecock
(see Valla, trans. Coleman 1922). Hus was examined at Constance in 1415 over
the Donation.
[29] *De civitate Dei*, v. 25 in *PL* xli. 171; trans. Bettenson (Augustine 1972: 220–1).
[30] Ibid.: 'To him also He granted the honour of founding a city, a companion
to the Roman Empire, the daughter, as it were, of Rome itself, but without any
temple or image of the demons.'

The fullest English verse account of Constantine's career before that in the *Fall* is the version—based on the *Golden Legend*—at the close of the second book of Gower's *Confessio Amantis*.[31] The narrative found there is intended by Genius to be a counterpoint to the exempla of envy set forth in that book: the story of Constantine, Genius claims, will illustrate the efficacy of pity as a remedy for envy.[32] When Constantine is afflicted in his prime by leprosy the remedy his councillors advise is that he should bathe in the blood of children. It is the pity he feels for the innocent victims that causes Constantine to reject this cure and to choose to continue in his illness.

> The yonge babes criden alle:
> This noyse aros, the lord it herde,
> And loked out, and how it ferde
> He sih . . .
>
> .   .   .   .   .   .
>
> And with himself stod in debat,
> And thoghte hou that it was noght good
> To se so muchel mannes blod
> Be spilt for cause of him alone   (II. 3238–41, 3282–5)

Pity, however, plays only a small part in the Emperor's decision to spare the children; emotive as these comments are, the deliberation they frame hinges on a careful and theoretical consideration of the nature of imperial authority. Gower argues that the force of 'kynde . . . preferreth no degre' of man, even though the structures of society clearly do demarcate individuals:

> The povere child is bore als able
> To vertu as the kinges Sone;
> For every man his oghne wone
> After the lust of his assay
> The vice or vertue chese may.   (II. 3258–62)

The disposition of temporal authority, then, is shown as illusory; though the orders of society are fixed ('in astat thei ben divised . . . On lordeth and an other serveth', II. 3264, 3267), Constantine decides that it is incumbent on those in authority to surrender the right society spuriously grants them to exercise

---

[31] *Confessio* II. 3187–496. Larry Scanlon discusses the Constantine section of the poem (Ph. D. thesis, 1986: 131–6) and (1994: 263–7).
[32] *Confessio* II. 3105–86.

power over others. Those who are in 'subjeccioun' to an earthly
ruler may be his social inferiors, but they are nonetheless 'of his
semblance' (II. 3272, 3273). In order to act justly Constantine
must destabilize the social fixity he embodies; he articulates his
'pity' in terms of the reversal of social roles:

> Who that woll maister be,
> He mot be servant to pite.   (II. 3299–300)

There is, of course, no revolutionary egalitarianism here:
Constantine's act of pity will, after all, preserve his 'maistrie'. By
electing to limit the extent of his power, Constantine may well
jeopardize his physical well-being, but he demonstrates that he is
aware that his moral supremacy will thereby be confirmed. His
decision to curb his own potential for tyranny serves to inscribe
his power at a less visible level.

A careful sequence of reversals emerges as the chief structural
principle of the narrative; the social inversions Constantine deliberately embraces are tellingly echoed in the gospel Pope Silvester
preaches. On Doomsday, the Pope says, God will judge impartially:

> Als wel the plowman as the kniht:
> The lewed man, the grete clerk
> Schal stonde upon his oghne werk.   (II. 3422–4)

The social categories Constantine learned to distrust will indeed
be levelled and, furthermore, Silvester predicates the drama of the
Incarnation on exactly the kind of voluntary self-limitation the
Emperor himself demonstrated:

> the hihe god therfore
> His Sone sende from above,
> Which bore was for mannes love,
> And after of his oghne chois
> He tok his deth upon the crois.   (II. 3388–92)

The sermon here initially seems to support the arguments of self-
denial: the example of Christ's kenosis and the levelling of social
differences are reminiscent of the Emperor's decision to reject the
privileges available to him by virtue of his temporal authority.
Indeed, in Gower's version, the vessel intended for the bloodbath
is co-opted to become the font for Constantine's baptismal regeneration, again illustrating the tight parallels and reversals Gower
uses to unify his narrative (II. 3445–6).

There is, however, a significantly unexpected emphasis in
Silvester's sermon. Unlike the tight and self-inverting logic of
Constantine's earlier debate, the sermon does not permit any
imperial sleight of hand: whereas Constantine fragmented the social
distinctions defined by his power only to reinstate them ethically,
Silvester insists that such temporal social distinctions must *remain*
broken down. The seeming egalitarianism of Constantine is actual-
ized in the preacher's eschatological debate. This conundrum having
been exposed, Constantine is compelled to surrender his last vestige
of authority: it is not enough for temporal power merely to efface
its own excesses—it must surrender power altogether to the authority of the Church.

In the light of Gower's absolute insistence on the incommensurability of sacred and secular authority, it is not surprising that
Constantine's donation of temporalities to the Church, treated
at such length in the *Golden Legend*, is relegated to a brief coda
in the *Confessio*, nor that Gower includes the later medieval
legend that the Donation was accompanied by a warning from
heaven:

> Bot how so that his will was good
> Toward the Pope and his Franchise,
> Yit hath it proved other wise
>
> . . . . . .
>
> Anon as he hath mad the yifte,
> A vois was herd on hih the lifte,
> Of which al Rome was adrad,
> And seith: 'Today is venym schad
> In holi cherche of temporal,
> Which medleth with the spirital.' (II. 3482–4, 3487–92)

The legend of divine disapproval of the Donation has, of course,
a long pedigree: as the writings of many (including the classicizing friar Robert Holcot, Wyclif, the Lollards, and Jean Gerson)
show,[33] the temporal endowment of the Church was seen as a
departure from the model of apostolic poverty of the primitive
Church. The acquisition of material possessions and jurisdiction
was held to have confused the otherwise sharp disjunction
between secular and spiritual leadership: in Wycliffite terms, the

[33] For the spread of this addition to the legend, see Smalley (1960: 195 n. 5);
Jochums (1964); Pascoe (1974: 476 n. 29); Hudson (1988: 330, 335 n. 115, 405
n. 60).

Church had become 'Cesarean'. This contamination of the purity of the Church quickly became a commonplace of satire on the venality and (interestingly) litigiousness of the later medieval Church.[34]

Lydgate's version of the Constantine narrative differs in important respects both from Gower's highly wrought narrative (its nearest vernacular antecedent) and also from the Latin *Golden Legend* which it takes as its immediate source. Whereas Gower, like Augustine before him, stresses the disjunction between Church and Empire and the incommensurability of sacred and secular authority, the *Legend* and Lydgate's accounts narrate the Donation not simply with regard to the material endowment of the Church, but, rather more significantly, with an emphasis on the concomitant endowment of the Church with civil authority. This endowment is figured in both the *Fall* and the *Legend* as an eight-day drama of regeneration: on seven successive days Constantine makes grants to the Church of wealth and legal privilege. Only one of these (the seventh and last) actually grants the Church material possessions:

hanc legem dedit . . . ut aedificationem ecclesiarum decimae possessionum regalium tribuantur.

(Constantine proclaimed as law . . . that the tenth part of the royal income was allotted to the building of churches.)[35]

> The seuenthe day, this lawe he did eek make:
> Of all pocessiouns which that be roiall,
> The tenthe part [y]eerli shal be take
> Be iugis handis, in parti & in all,
> Which[e] tresour thei delyuere shall,
> As the statut doth pleynli specefie,
> Hool & enteer cherchis to edefie.[36]

In both versions this muted treatment of the material donation naturally allows a stronger emphasis to fall on the issue of ecclesiastical

---

[34] See Dante, *Paradiso* xx. 55–60; Langland, *Piers Plowman*, B. xv. 500 ff./C. xviii. 199. ff.; note also B. xv. 239; Wyclif, *De civile dominio* ii. 195/30 (Wyclif ed. Poole 1885–1904); *De ecclesia* 359/7 (Wyclif ed. Loserth 1886); *Dialogus* 66/10–17 (Wyclif ed. Pollard 1886); Hus, *De ecclesia*, trans. Schaff (Hus 1915: 150–1). See also Pascoe (1973: 49–58, 208, 214).

[35] Jacobus de Voragine, *Legend* xii. 2 'De sancto Silvestro', ed. Graesse (1850: 73); (trans. Ryan 1993: i. 65).   [36] *Fall* viii. 1331–7.

dominion. The grants of the fourth and fifth days strike at the heart of the debate:

hanc legem dedit . . . ut sicut imperator Romae sic Romanus pontifex capit ab universis episcopis habeatur. Quinta ut quicunque in ecclesias confugerit, ab omnibus servetur injuris immunis.

(Constantine proclaimed as law . . . that just as the Roman emperor was supreme in the world, so the bishop of Rome would be the head of all the world's bishops; on the fifth, that anyone taking refuge in a church was to be held immune from all injury.)[37]

> The fourthe day among[es] Romeyns all
> This pryuylege pronouncid in the toun,
> Youe to the pope sittyng in Petris stall,
> As souereyn hed in euery regioun
> To haue the reule and iurediccioun
> Of preestis alle, allone in alle thyng,
> Of temporal lordis lich as hath the kyng.
>
> To the cherche he granted gret franchise
> The fifte day & special liberte:
> Yif a feloun in any maner wise
> To fynde socour thider dide flee,
> Withynne the boundis fro daunger to go fre,
> To been assurid & haue ther ful refuge
> From execucioun of any temporal iuge.[38]

Furthermore, Lydgate does not passively absorb the Latin account of the narrative he finds in the *Legend* (which is primarily focused on St Silvester rather than on Constantine), but he instead subtly retunes that account so as to shift the emphasis away from the Pope and towards the figure of the Emperor. In his departures from the story he found in the *Legend* Lydgate strengthens the focus on the voluntary secession of imperial authority and condenses considerably the lengthy Latin account. The Council of St Helena's twelve Jewish masters and the miracles of the bull and the dragon are omitted entirely—as are two further small, but significant, details. First, in the Latin account it is clear that Silvester's retreat to Mount Serapti is not the quasi-monastic retreat it is made to be in Lydgate's version. Instead, we are told

---

[37] *Legend* XII. 2, ed. Graesse, 72 (trans. Ryan 1993: i. 65).
[38] *Fall* VIII. 1310–23.

that Silvester has fled to the mountain to evade the persecutions of Constantine:

Persequente autem Constantino christianos, Silvester de urbe exiit et in quodam monte cum suis clericis mansit. Ipse autem Constantinus merito persecutionis tyrannicae in incurabilem cecedit plagam leprae.

(Constantine continued to persecute the Christians, and Silvester left the city and settled in the mountains with his clerics. The emperor himself, in punishment for his tyrannical persecution, fell victim to the incurable disease of leprosy.)[39]

Not only, then, is Constantine shown to be a 'tyrannical' oppressor of the Church, but his leprosy is described as a punishment for his persecutions of the people of God. Secondly, in the *Legend* the Emperor is told in a dream by Saints Peter and Paul to offer thanks for his cure by destroying pagan temples and erecting Christian churches in their stead:

Tu vero Christo hanc vicissitudinem reddas, ut ydolorum templa diruas, Christi restaures ecclesias et ejus deinceps cultor has.

(In exchange you are to do something for Christ: demolish the temples of the idols, restore the Christian churches, and become a worshipper of Christ henceforth!)[40]

In Lydgate's poem no mention is made of this apostolic command: far from being the obedient performance of a condition of his recovery of health, the destruction of Roman temples and idols by the Lydgatean Constantine is adduced as further evidence of the Emperor's virtue.[41]

In this alteration, as in his suppression of any suggestion that Constantine was himself an enemy to the Church, Lydgate lays greater emphasis on the Emperor's voluntary submission to the Church and on his safeguarding of its interests. Indeed, in the encomiastic coda which he appends to the episode, Lydgate specifically shows Constantine, as he did Theodosius, fulfilling chivalric duties in loyal service of the spiritual order. He tells us that Constantine was,

> Duryng his tyme holde the beste kniht
> That owher was in any regioun,

[39] *Legend* XII. 2, ed. Graesse, 71 (trans. Ryan 1993: i. 64).
[40] Ibid. XII. 2, ed. Graesse, 72 (trans. Ryan 1993: i. 64).
[41] *Fall* VIII. 1275–81.

> Of Cristes feith thymperial champiou*n*,
> Thoruh his noble knihtli magnificence
> To alle Cristene protecto*ur* & diffence.[42]

Whereas, then, the traditions of the careers of Theodosius and Constantine seem to point towards different conclusions in Lydgate's sources (in that Theodosius' encounter with Ambrose illustrated the superior authority of the Church and its autonomy from the secular order, while the Constantine and Silvester *exemplum* instead showed that the State in some way empowers, and even compromises, that autonomy), Lydgate's own narratives deliver a unified message. Constantine's donation is figured, not as the act of a powerful (if grateful) man, but rather as the loyal duty of a servant. The autonomy of the ecclesiastical sphere is heightened even further when Lydgate inserts into his narrative a drama of submission in which the Emperor lays aside his regalia of imperial authority:

> This exau*m*ple in open he hath shewed,
> His staat imperial of meeknesse leid aside,
> His purpil garneme*nt* with teres al bedewed;
> Suerd nor sceptre nor hors upon to ride
> Ther was non seyn, nor baners splaied wide;
> Of marcial tryu*m*phes ther was no tokne fou*n*de,
> But criyng m*er*ci, themp*er*our lay plat to grounde.
>
> The peeplis gladnesse was medlid w*ith* wepy*n*g,
> And ther weepyng was medlid w*ith* gladnesse,
> To seen an empero*ur* and so notable a kyng
> Of his free chois shewe so gret meeknesse.[43]

These narratives of the support and endowment of the spiritual order by the temporal are, however, considerably outnumbered in the *Fall of Princes* by the many narratives of official heterodoxy and persecution, narratives in which Lydgate clearly develops his characteristic assumptions about the proper relations between the two orders. It is to these narratives that we now turn.

---

[42] Ibid. VIII. 1438–42. Hoccleve likened Henry V to Constantine in the context of his defence of the Church from Lollardy ('Balade au tresnoble Roy H[enry] le quint', 1.10 (*IMEV* 3788), Hoccleve ed. Furnivall (1892: 41–2), and Scanlon has seen the emperor as 'the most heroic figure' in the *Fall* (1994: 329).

[43] *Fall* VIII. 1366–76.

NARRATIVES OF PERSECUTION AND HETERODOXY

The narratives discussed thus far have all shown how it is that, by a series of careful additions to or adaptations of the material he found in his French source, Lydgate dramatizes a cooperation between Church and Empire which enhances the dependence of the secular order on the spiritual (in the kingship rituals by which it authorizes its own power, in its acceptance of limitations of its right to political action and decision in otherwise entirely secular fields, and in its voluntary participation in public demonstrations of self-abasement and self-denial). However, narratives illustrating the *support* of the Church by secular authority are considerably outnumbered in Premierfait's *Des Cas* by accounts of persecution of the Church by secular rulers and, more interestingly still, by the account of the Emperor Julian, whose apostasy forms a neat counterbalance to Constantine's movement away from pagan self-reliance towards Christian obedience. These twenty-one narratives of 'persecution and heterodoxy' can be grouped into six categories which illustrate the common themes and assumptions implicit in Lydgate's reworkings of Premierfait's material. These are narratives of persecution of individual Christians (those of Diocletian, Maximian, Galerius, and Valence);[44] of persecution of the faith (Maximus, Valerian, and Maxentius);[45] of desecration of Church property or ritual ('Iosias' and 'Ozias', Belshazzar, Xerxes, Dionysius, Brennus, Antiochus, Azariah, and Vitellius);[46] of idolatry and iconoclasm (Domitian and Philippicus),[47] and of apostasy (Julian).[48] Finally, the narratives of Odoacer and Anastasius, with their explicit discussions of the necessity that temporal rulers be subservient to the Church and for the Church to remain vigilant against the corruption of being too greatly influenced by its own temporalities, seem in many ways to summarize the significant points of the argument that emerges from Lydgate's intervention in these accounts of tension and persecution between the spiritual and the secular. I am able here only to give close analysis of a representative selection of these narratives.

[44] *Fall* VIII. 743–854, 855–903, 981–1022, 1709–92.
[45] Ibid. VIII. 337–50, 428–560, 1023–36.
[46] Ibid. II. 2668–779, 3494–556; III. 2206–639; IV. 799–938, 3591–744; V. 1471–621, 2299–312; VII. 929–1103; VIII. 302–15.
[47] Ibid. VIII. 204–52; IX. 771–91.   [48] Ibid. VIII. 1464–708.

Persecution of Individual Christians—Diocletian, Maximian, and Valence

The account of the fall of the low-born Emperor Diocletian in Premierfait is a characteristically lengthened version of the brief (twenty-two line) chapter in Boccaccio's eighth book (VIII. ch. 7): 'Pauca de Diocletiano . . .'. Lydgate abridges the five columns he finds in Premierfait, omitting the accounts of Diocletian's complex military and political campaigns, the uprisings of Achilleus in Egypt, the Gencian attacks in Africa, and Narseus' oriental campaign. Instead, his focus rests on Diocletian's rise from obscurity, his marriage to Theodora, and the persecutions of the Christians. The effect of Lydgate's elimination of Diocletian's considerable military successes (signalled when he writes 'I will passe ouer breeffli as I can, | Set aside al foreyn incidentis')[49] is to simplify the complicated personal response towards Diocletian felt by the reader of the French text. Lydgate is not interested in the competing claims Diocletian makes on our admiration and our disapproval: the ambivalence is removed and Diocletian slips into the role of a two-dimensional pagan tyrant. (Lydgate actually introducing the terms 'tirannye' and 'tirauntis' at VIII. 828 and 831.)

At the heart of this narrative lies a five-line section that has no counterpart in the French text. Having introduced Diocletian and Maximian as persecutors under 'whos swerd many a martire deies', Lydgate supplies details of victims of the persecution, saying that the Theban legion at Octoduram was killed by Maximian, and that

> At Verolamye, a famous old cite,
> Seynt Albon slayn; his legende doth so telle.
> And in Roome be furious cruelte
> The pope slayn, which callid was Marcelle.[50]

Lydgate could have derived the detail of the martyrdom of St Alban from many sources. Bede devotes a chapter to the legend in the *Historia* and Geoffrey of Monmouth refers to the martyrdom: both of these authorities were available in the libraries of Bury and of Humphrey of Gloucester, as surviving records show.[51]

---

[49] Ibid. VIII. 820–1.   [50] Ibid. VIII. 834–7.
[51] Bede, *Historia* I. 7; Geoffrey of Monmouth, *Historia regum Britanniae*, V. 5. Bede's history was held at Bury in a fifteenth-century manuscript, extant as Cambridge, Sidney Sussex College MS 102; many other works by Bede survive from the Bury library, and it is highly probable that earlier copies of the *Historia*

On completing the *Fall* Lydgate himself, of course, went on to produce for Whethamstede the rhyme royal *Life of SS Albon and Amphibel*, based on two short Latin prose lives.[52] Not only does Lydgate enhance the force of Diocletian's persecutions by inserting names of specific victims in this way (the far more anonymous details of burned churches and martyrs follow at VIII. 839–42), but he also chooses to omit the coda Premierfait adds after the account of Diocletian's suicide:

Mais toutesfoys ie croy q*ue* Diocletien porta la peine du peche quil auoit desseruy en desrochant eglises | en bannissant et occisant les sainctz hommes chrestiens.[53]

(However, I believe that Diocletian suffered the punishment that was due to him for destroying churches and for banishing and killing holy Christians.)

Given the fact that Lydgate usually draws the *moralitas* from a narrative wherever this is possible (if only to fulfil Humphrey's request for envoys in the *Fall*) and makes explicit the connections and causal relationships his sources leave tacit and implicit, it is interesting that Diocletian's suicide is left unmoralized. The effect, however, of removing the accounts of desecration and persecution as the sins for which Diocletian suffers deservedly is to predicate the account of the frenzied suicide on the opening words of the stanza: 'Froward enmy he was to Cristes lawe.'[54] Lydgate's emperor suffers, then, not so much for the individual atrocities he perpetrates as a result of his opposition to the Church (although, as we have seen, Lydgate does enhance the portrayal of these), but rather for his obstinate opposition to the authority of Christ (here figured as a 'lawe') per se.

The account of Maximian in the French (VIII. ch. 8) makes no mention of the Emperor's persecution of Christians: Lydgate, however, adds this detail in his version.[55] The narrative of the persecutions of 'Valence' (the fourth-century Emperor Flavius Valens) is similarly heightened by Lydgate. Abridging the detailed description of the Emperor's military achievements given in the French text, Lydgate opens with a stirring account of the 'parfit hoolynesse'

may have been held alongside these exegetical texts. The twelfth-century manuscript of Geoffrey held at Bury (now Oxford, Magdalen College MS 172) has been challenged by Ker (1964: 22); cf. James (1926: 254). Humphrey donated an unidentified volume of Eusebius and Bede to the University of Oxford in 1439, see Anstey 1898: i. 180, and Sammut (1980: 61).

[52] McLeod (1980: 420–1).   [53] *Des Cas* fo. 177ᵛ.   [54] *Fall* VIII. 841.
[55] Ibid. VIII. 857–8; cf. *Des Cas* fos. 177ᵛ–78ʳ.

which he claims to have found in 'Bochas':

> Bochas in hast[e] doth his stile dresse
> Next to them*perour* þ*at* callid was Valence,
> Rehersi*n*g first the parfit hoolynesse
> Of hermytis, that dide ther dilligence
> To lyue in penau*n*ce & in abstynence;
> Forsook the world[e], & for Cristes sake
> Into the desert thei haue the weye take.
>
> In this world heer thei list no lenger tarye,
> Dyuers & double, of trust nou*n* certeyn;
> Ferr in Egipt to lyue solitarye,
> Deepe in desertis, of folk nat to be seyn.
> The soil was drye; of vitaille ful bareyn;
> The frutles treen up sered to the roote:
> For Cristes loue thei thouhte that lyff most soote.[56]

'Bochas', however, reads entirely differently; the French account of the desert hermits is preceded by (and made to seem resultant on) a description of Valence's legislation that the 'moynes' should enter the army:

[Valens] donna vne loy contenant q*ue* tous chrestiens, q*ue* lors on appelloit moynes fussent contrainctz soy employer en cheualerie | cest a dire en faict de guerre.

([Valens] passed a law that all Christians (then known as 'monks') be forced to engage in military matters (that is to say, fight in battle))[57]

It is seemingly as a result of the dilemma of over-involvement in the temporal order (and, moreover, in its military affairs) that Premierfait's Christians embrace an eremitical life ('ilz delaissoient presque toutes besongnes seculieres | et tournoient leur courage a aco*m*plir la foy catholicque | qui contient vng seul ouurage. Cestassauoir acquerir le royaulme du ciel ['they abandoned nearly all worldly concerns and devoted themselves to the Catholic faith, pursuing one single end: gaining the kingdom of heaven']). It is noticeable that the language of kingship is used to point the contrast between commitment to temporal and to spiritual goals; Lydgate's elision of these details makes the reclusive piety of the early Christians seem more disinterested, less reactive to topical event.

---

[56] *Fall* VIII. 1709–22.   [57] *Des Cas* fo. 183ʳ.

Valence's persecution (again presented in terms of tyrannical rule) is strengthened in Lydgate's version by his intriguing decision to ignore Premierfait's claim that a repentant Valence sought to atone for his errors:

Adonc Valens partit dantioche | 7 pource quil vouloit esprouuer la derniere fortune de sa malheureuse bataille il fut aguillonne dune tardiue repentance de son tresgrant peche si commanda que les euesques | 7 les autres sainctz chrestiens fussent rappellez de leurs exilz | et retournassent en leurs lieux | dont il les auoit bannis et dechassez.

(And so Valens left Antioch and, distressed by his recent misfortune in battle, he was pierced by belated penitence for his grievous sins; he ordered that the bishops and other Christian saints be recalled from their exile and be restored to those places from which they had been banished and chased out.)[58]

Lydgate's Valence, in contrast, continues the persecution of hermit Christians with fervour (VIII. 1776–8) and his fall, when it comes, is thereby open to moralization as a punishment for the persecution of the Church:

> Loo, heer the fyn, ye pryncis taketh heede,
> Of tirauntis that seyntes blood do sheede![59]

Persecution of the Faith—Valerian, 'Maximus', and Maxentius

The decision to suppress details of individual Christian martyrdom or suffering in order to clarify the issues behind the persecution is one Lydgate takes in the three narratives of Valerian, 'Maximus', and Maxentius. Premierfait's lengthy version of the Valerian narrative (chapters 3 and 4 of Book VIII)[60] represents a conflation of two sections in Boccaccio's text: the first ('De Valeriano Augusto Romanorum imperatore') describes Valerian's rise to power, the second ('In Saporem Persarum regem & Valerianum Romanorum imperatorum') his subsequent defeat. The role of the Persian ruler

---

[58] *Des Cas* fo. 183ᵛ.

[59] *Fall* VIII. 1791–2. Premierfait also (at fo. 183ᵛ) offers Valence's fate as an exemplum ('Valens donnast exemple aux hommes de sa terrible pugnition | et de lindignation de dieu qui ainsi iustement pugnit les desloyaulx persecuteurs de leglise | et des sainctz hommes chrestiens'), but Lydgate's version, having blackened Valence more thoroughly, has far more graphic force. A further defamatory detail original to Lydgate comes at line 1784: Valence hides from the Goths 'lik a coward'.   [60] *Des Cas* fos. 172ʳ–174ᵛ.

Sapor in the downfall of Valerian, though essential and decisive, is one Lydgate abbreviates sharply; consequently the weight of the English narrative falls proportionally more heavily on the rebuke delivered by 'Bochas' to the fallen Emperor.[61] Depicting Valerian as a 'tyrant' (VIII. 485), Lydgate's rebuke shows concerns of its own, highlighting Valerian's persecutions as the cause of his downfall. Much of the material in the French version of the rebuke has been jettisoned as inessential. Furthermore, Lydgate's references to the persecutions (at VIII. 491–4, 543–6, 558–60) focus in slightly less detail on the sufferings of the martyrs than do the French versions ('O Valerian . . . tu meurtrissois les religieux chrestiens 7 deffendois les hommes sacrileges', fo. 174[r]) in order to focus instead on the opposition to the faith as a whole.[62] The short accounts of 'Maximus' (the third-century Emperor Maximinus) and Maxentius show Lydgate repeating this stratagem; in the latter, while Premierfait's text contains no suggestion of any persecution of the Church by the Emperor, Lydgate clearly presents Maxentius as the enemy of 'Cristes feith'.[63]

A clear pattern has emerged: accounts of persecutions of the Church by secular forces are characteristically either heightened (by Lydgate's inclusion of specific detail, by his omission of suggestions that the persecuting emperor atoned for his tyranny in acts of penitence, or by his presentation of the sufferings and downfall of the persecutor as a punishment for actions against the Church) or introduced wholesale into the poem. Where the focus of the French accounts is blurred by extraneous details, Lydgate omits these in order to clarify the importance of the persecution in the particular narrative in question. In a number of small-scale instances this clarification moves the weight of the persecution away from the suffering inflicted on adherents of the faith towards a presentation of the fundamental and irreducible antagonism between the 'law' of Christ and the tyranny of the secular order— an antagonism which Lydgate feels underscores these narratives.

---

[61] *Fall* VIII. 484–560.

[62] 'Thou wer . . . | Clad in purple withynne Roome toun, | To Crist contrarye in thyn imperial see' (*Fall* VIII. 491–4); 'sith Cristes feith began, | Which for mankynde starff' (VIII. 544–5); 'Cristene men thou madist falsli sterue, | Of whos lawe for thou dist nat rechche' (VIII. 558–9).

[63] Ibid. VIII. 1030. Premierfait is following his own source closely in his version of Maxentius' fall: there is no indication in Boccaccio that the emperor persecuted the Church; cf. *De casibus* fo. 94[v] (p. 196).

Desecration of Church Property or Ritual—'Iosias' and 'Ozias',
Belshazzar, and Xerxes

If the narratives we have discussed thus far begin to present a
characteristic Lydgatean concern with the institutional and ecclesiological impact of persecution rather than with the more narrowly
personal suffering and misfortune it causes, this is a concern which
also emerges emphatically in Lydgate's treatment of those narratives which turn on acts of sacrilege and desecration. Nowhere
is Lydgate's 'churchiness' more apparent than in narratives which
present persecution of the Church in the form of assaults on
its property, ritual, and autonomy, rather than on its individual
members.

As with the narrative of Hostilius, the downfalls of Kings
'Iosias' (II. 2668–779) and 'Ozias' (V. 2299–312) are shown to result
from the presumption of the temporal ruler in claiming the right
of participation in sacred ritual. Boccaccio's account outlines
Iosias's appropriation of priestly vestments and the leprosy with
which he was afflicted for this presumption:

Fatebatur quidem solenni die sacerdotalibus indutum se vestibus deo
sacrum in templo prohibentibus sacerdotibus volentez offerre. Primo terre
motu promonitum: confestim lepra cademque foedissima percussum.

(He admitted that he indeed dressed himself in priestly vestments on a
solemn feast day, intending to offer sacrifice to God in the temple, defying
the prohibition of the priests. Having first been warned by an earthquake,
he was suddenly struck down by a most loathsome leprosy.)[64]

Premierfait's lengthier account follows Boccaccio closely, but
emphasizes the transgressive aspect of the king's desire to offer a
sacrifice:

Le roy Ozias se attourna de vestemens de prebstre 7 voulut offrir sacrifice
a dieu ou temple de Salomon contre la deffense des prebstres et contre
ladmonnestement de dieu . . . que il ne se entremist des sacrifices diuins
qui seullement appartiennent aux prebstres.

(King Iosias clothed himself in priestly vestments and tried to offer
sacrifice to God in the Temple of Solomon, in defiance of the clergy and
despite God's own warning . . . that only members of the priesthood
should engage in holy sacrifice.)[65]

---

[64] *De casibus* fo. 18ʳ (p. 61).   [65] *Des Cas* fo. 36ʳ (II. ch. 14).

Lydgate brings the French account of Iosias's illness ('il
soubdainement fut feru de mesellerie') into line with the leprosy of
the Old Testament account from which Boccaccio drew his material:

> Beyng in purpos, on a solempne day,
> To take his way up to the hih auter,
> Falsli vsurpyng, who-euer seide nay,
> To sacrefie, holdyng the censer,
>
> .   .   .   .   .   .
>
> And sodenli among[es] al the pres,
> An erthequaue fill in the same place.
> And therwithal in the kynges face,
> Off the sonne ther smet a bem so briht,
> That al his visage was scorkid with the liht.
>
> He wex a lepre, ful foul and riht horible
> For his offence, as God list ordeyne[66]

Several details are noticeable in Lydgate's version, aside from the
expected medievalization (Lydgate's Iosias dresses in the robes
'off a bisshop' to offer the sacrifice, rather than in those of a
priest). Eliding the emphasis on *sacrifice* he found in Premierfait,
and reintroducing the thurible as the focus of Iosias's sacrilege,
Lydgate approximates the Jewish ritual to the eucharistic liturgy
with which his fifteenth-century readers would have been familiar—
thereby assimilating the confrontation between Israelite king and
Mosaic high priest into the pagan-secular | Christian conflict of the
later narratives about sacrilege and desecration. Iosias's affliction is
heightened by graphic detail; in a section borrowed from Josephus'
De antiquitatibus, the dramatic account of the generation of the
leprosy by the rays of the sun makes it clear that the disease is a
result of the king's opposition to the divine.[67] So significant does

[66] *Fall* II. 2717–20, 2733–9. The biblical version is at 2 Para. 26: 16–21
(Douai), 2 Chr. 26: 16–21 (AV): 'Going into the temple of the Lord he had a mind
to burn incense upon the altar of incense . . . And immediately Azarias the
priest . . . withstood the king and said: It doth not belong to thee, Ozias, to burn
incense to the Lord, but to the priests, that is to the sons of Aaron, who are con-
secrated for this ministry . . . Ozias was angry, and holding in his hand the censer
to burn incense, threatened the priests. And presently there rose a leprosy in his
forehead'; cf. 4 Kgs. 15: 1–7 (Douai); 2 Kgs. 15: 1–7 (AV).

[67] *De antiquitatibus*, IX. ch. 10 § 4, trans. Whiston, rev. Shilleto (1900–3:
189–90): 'A great earthquake shook the ground, and a rent was made in the
temple, and the bright rays of the sun shone through it, and fell upon the king's
face, insomuch that leprosy seized him immediately'. Lydgate goes on to
incorporate (at II. 2742–4) Josephus' account of the splitting of the mountain at
Eroge (cf. his abridgement of Josephus at II. 2605).

Lydgate find Iosias's refusal to recognize the autonomy of
the sacred that when he encounters the narrative of Joachim (the
biblical Alcimus) in the thirteenth chapter of Premierfait's Book V
he omits entirely that laboured account and retells (in two stanzas)
the fall of Iosias, whom he here renames 'Ozias' (the biblical
Azariah of 2 Kgs. 15).[68] While the story of Joachim deals with the
illegitimate claim to priestly status by one who is not 'of the seed
of Aaron',[69] Lydgate forgoes it in order to repeat a narrative that
hinges on the confrontation between a secular ruler (explicitly
introduced as a 'kyng' at v. 2299) and a high priest. Furthermore,
Ozias's downfall in this narrative is presented not simply as limited
to his physical afflictions (his loss of speech and his 'meselrie'),
but also as a loss of the symbols of his temporal authority:

> But or he passid he gretli was affraied,
>
> Lost his speche, [and] smet with meselrie
> Duryng his lyff: loo, heer a gret vengau*n*ce!—
> Off his crowne & his regalie
> Inpotent to vse the gouernau*n*ce,
> Parcel for pride & disobeissaunce;
> For he list nat meekli the lawe obeie[70]

The issue of usurpation of the office of the Mosaic high priest is
replaced by the clearer conflict between secular and sacred powers.
The *moralitas* seems clear: temporal rulers who encroach on the
spiritual order are guilty of disobedience (the Lydgatean emphasis
on 'lawe' we saw in Diocletian again appears) and lose their right
to wield even their secular authority.

This essential disjunction between the authority of Church and
of temporal rulers lies at the heart of Lydgate's treatment of the
narratives about sacrilege. For example, he omits nearly all of the
French narrative of Belshazzar in order to focus on the act of
blasphemy that underscores the ruler's feast; whereas Premierfait's

---

[68] *Des Cas* fo. 115ᵛ (v. ch. 13): 'le cas de Joachin jadis souuerain euesque du
temple de Hierusalem selon la loy des iuifz. Si est assauoir q*ue* selon la loy de
moyse escripte et prolongee par ordo*n*nance diuine aucun ho*m*me ne deuoit estre
institue en loffice deuesque ne de prestre ne de soy entremettre des sacrifices ne
des choses diuines'; cf. *De casibus* fo. 54ʳ (p. 133); *De antiquitatibus*, XII. ch. 9
§7; 1 Macc. 7: 5–25; 9: 54–7; *Encyclopaedia Judaica* (1972 ii. 550).

[69] 1 Macc. 7: 14. Josephus stresses this same principle: 'Alcimus . . . was not of
the stock of the high priests'.   [70] *Fall* v. 2305–11.

moralizing coda identifies the cause of Belshazzar's fall as his pride, Lydgate's envoy roundly blames his sacrilege:

> Which had mysusid ful falsli the treso*ur*
> And the vesseles brouht fro Ierusalem,
>
> .   .   .   .   .
>
> But God off riht took sodeynli vengau*n*ce
> On Balthasar for his transgressiou*n*s
>
> .   .   .   .   .
>
> Geyn hooli chirch[e] taketh no quarelis,
> But aduertisith in your inward siht;
> For Balthasar drank off tho vesselis
> Stole fro the temple off verrai force & myht[71]

Similarly, in his reworking of the French account of how the Emperor Xerxes pillaged the shrine of the Delian Apollo, Lydgate emphasizes the removal of the treasures from the shrine more than Laurent; the force of the envoy is enhanced by stressing Xerxes' attempts 'to robbe the goddis . . . | And spoile ther templis . . . | Take ther tresours ageyn al rihtwisnesse'.[72]

In the accounts of Dionysius, Brennus the Gaul, Vitellius, and Philippicus Lydgate again refocuses the French narratives so as to enhance the sin of sacrilege. The spoliation of sacred property dominates the envoys to Dionysius[73] and Brennus (in the latter, princes are advised that the 'Cheef preseruatiff of your magnificence, | Is first to God to do due reuerence'),[74] while Lydgate's account of the peculiar desecrations committed by Vitellius is sharper and more comic than the ponderous account in Premierfait: having appointed himself a 'bisshop', Vitellius interrupts his own sacrifices in order to have dinner on the altar.[75]

Idolatry and Iconoclasm—Philippicus and Domitian

In his narratives of Philippicus and Domitian, Lydgate's presentation of the persecution of Church property and privilege hinges on

---

[71] Ibid. II. 3498–9, 3545–6, 3550–3; cf. *Des Cas* fo. 42ʳ. Chaucer's Monk, too, emphasizes the sacrilege in his account (*CT* VII. 2183–246/3373–436).

[72] *Fall* III. 2621–3; cf. *Des Cas* fo. 58ʳ (III. ch. 7).

[73] *Fall* IV. 904–38; cf. *Des Cas* fo. 76ᵛ (IV. ch. 4).

[74] Ibid. IV. 3743–4: cf. *Des Cas* fos. 94ᵛ–95ʳ (IV. ch. 16).

[75] Ibid. VII. 985–1012: Lydgate describes Vitellius as 'a bisshop sacrid for Sathan'; cf. *Des Cas* fo. 162ᵛ (VII. ch. 6).

accounts of iconoclasm. Premierfait's version of Philippicus' destruction of devotional images of the saints is brief and factual:

> Philipique print guerre contre les secretz ymages de dieu le createur du monde et des sainctz | lesquelles auoient curieusement este painctes | 7 faictes par la religieuse deuotion daucuns chrestiens es [*sic*] eglises des terres subiectes a lempire.

(Philippicus joined battle against those skilfully painted images of the Creator God and of His saints that had secretly been made for religious devotion by Christians in churches throughout the territories of the empire.)[76]

Lydgate, however, specifically describes Philippicus' iconoclasm as the activity of a 'heretik cursid of lyuyng'.[77] Similarly, Lydgate introduces his Domitian narrative at the very start of Book VIII with the detail that Domitian ordered that images of himself should be erected in the Empire:

> Of al the world he sholde a god be callid.
>
> Thoruh hih presumpcioun, of hym it is eek told,
> Nouther of tymber koruen nor of ston,
> Set up images of siluer and of gold,
> In tokne ther was no god but he allon.[78]

The issue of veneration of images of the saints was, further-more, a pressing one in the early decades of the fifteenth century: one of the errors which the Bury chaplain Robert Bert was required to recant on 20 April 1430 in his ceremony of purgation in St James's parish church within the precincts of the Abbey was the Lollard belief that 'nullus honor est exhibendus ymaginibus crucifixi, Beate Marie aut alicuius sancti'.[79]

Apostasy—Julian

Lydgate's narrative about Julian the Apostate gains force from its discussion of the Emperor's other transgressive acts: in particular, Lydgate compounds the sin of apostasy with emphasis on Julian's

---

[76] *Des Cas* fo. 200ʳ (IX. ch. 4).   [77] *Fall* IX. 773.

[78] Ibid. VIII. 210–14: cf. Premierfait's claim that Domitian simply ordered that he should be 'ladorast comme dieu 7 seigneur de toutes choses' (*Des Cas* fo. 170ᵛ (VIII. ch. 2)).

[79] 'There is no honour in the display of images of the Crucified, of the Blessed Virgin Mary, or of any saint.' The details of this case are preserved in the register of Bishop William Alnwick of Norwich (now Westminster Cathedral MS B. 2. 8), fo. 68ʳ. ff; cf. *Heresy Trials in the Diocese of Norwich, 1428–31*, ed. Tanner (1977: 101).

apparent links with monastic orthodoxy. Claiming the authority of his source, Lydgate describes Julian as 'double Apostata . . . | First to his ordre & aftir to our feith'.[80] Omitting Premierfait's lengthy account of Julian's early commitment to monastic poverty (possibly because the whole burden of his interest in these narratives has been to stress the sacred autonomy of the possessions of the spiritual order),[81] Lydgate clearly regards the breaking of monastic vows as an apostasy of almost equal weight with that of abandonment of faith altogether. Throughout the narrative Lydgate blackens Julian's name by subtle changes to his text: he introduces (at VIII. 1497–505) the incident of Julian's necromantic trick with a laurel crown, but omits Premierfait's detail of the Emperor's striking of a bargain with demons to help him win military victory, thereby making Julian's later persecution of the Church seem less rational:

Iulien leur promist que les honneurs | les sacrifices | et les faulses anciennes cerimonies leurs fussent restituez qui par le treschrestien empereur constantin leur auoient este ostees.

(Julian promised them that the honours, sacrificial rites, and ancient false ceremonies abolished by the Christian Emperor Constantine would be restored.)[82]

Later Lydgate adds the detail that Julian 'trusted Sathan' and that he became an enemy 'to Cristes lawe',[83] and in his account of Julian's sending Christians to their martyrdom (at VIII. 1555 ff. and 1569–75) adds that he enjoyed doing so ('His lust was set & al his wordly ioye'). Noticeably, Lydgate omits Premierfait's details of Julian's blasphemy 'contre dieu le pere | et contre son seul filz et contre sa mere' (fo. 182r), but attributes the miraculous death of the apostate at the hands of an unknown 'angelik' knight to the intervention of the Virgin (VIII. 1600, 1699):

This tiraunt slouh, as cronicles don us lere,
Bi a myracle of Cristes mooder deere. (VIII. 1609–10)

[80] *Fall* VIII. 1483–4: despite Lydgate's claims, this detail is not to be found in the French text.
[81] *Des Cas* fos. 181r–2v (VIII. ch. 11); Premierfait talks of Julian's vocation 'par la sainct esperit . . . [il] donna soy voluntairement au seruice de dieu en conuersant comme humble et poure entre les aultres hommes religieux' (fo. 181r) and, later, of his abandonment of the rude garments of the cloister ('vestu de gros 7 aspres draps, chausse de rudes souliers'; fo. 181v) for the pampered lifestyle of a sybarite.
[82] *Des Cas* fo. 181r.
[83] *Fall* VIII. 1548. Premierfait simply says Julian 'seroit ennemy et aduersaire de Iesus le filz de dieu' (*Des Cas* fo. 181v).

In effect, Lydgate's version of Julian's fall simplifies Premierfait's complex (and prolix) account, offering a different logic for the Emperor's misfortune. Evaporating incidents and issues which he felt to be irrelevant or which might mitigate Julian's persecution of the Church, Lydgate even allows the apostasy itself to be over-shadowed by the initial, treacherous move from the cloister of spiritual discipline to the throne room of temporal authority. Attacking Julian's monastic piety as the ploy of a hypocrite ('Fih on al suich feyned parfitnesse! | For symulacioun ... | And fals[e] semblaunt with a sobre face'),[84] Lydgate establishes a telling continuity with the 'feignings' of Julian's later sorcery (the most melodramatic of which—the trick with the laurel crown—Julian stage-manages as a theatrical confirmation of his putative right to imperial power and which Lydgate has himself introduced to the narrative). Those who forsake their religious professions are, it would seem, inherently more likely to have a blurred under-standing of the distinction between legitimate and illegitimate spiritual authority.[85]

Apostolic Poverty Problematized—Anastasius and Odoacer

If Julian's career traces his move from ecclesiastical obedience to temporal ambition and supreme power, that of Anastasius II of Byzantium forms a neat contrast; deprived of his imperial power by usurpation, Anastasius enters holy orders and dies in humility:

> he was fayn thempire to forsake.
> For feer and dreed he did upon hym take
> The oordre of preest from the imperial see,
> Content with litil, lyued in pouertee.[86]

The contrast here between secular and sacred is one that explicitly structures the account of Anastasius in both the *Des Cas* and the *Fall*. For Premierfait, the whole thrust of the narrative (which he has elaborated from what is only a brief reference in Boccaccio,)[87]

---

[84] *Fall* VIII. 1474–6. The addition of the Marian detail in the narrative is typical of Lydgate's orthodox Benedictine piety and seems only to focus Julian's errors yet further.

[85] 'It cam by myracle, to chese hym emperour. | Which of trouthe ... | Was but collusioun & feyned apparence' (ibid. VIII. 1503–5). For an account of the apos-tasy of Julian see Wilken (1984: 164–96).   [86] *Fall* IX. 830–3.

[87] *De casibus* fo. 103[v] (p. 214).

is to offer an explanation of the Great Schism of the Church; he draws a series of contrasts between the apostolic purity of the primitive Church and the later post-Constantinian confusion of its mission and the loss of spiritual authority brought about by the corrupting influence of temporal endowments:

Adonc les bastons des clercz deuindrent orgueilleux palle frois I les hayres et aspres robes deuindrent robbes de pourpre I 7 chappes descarlate traynans parmy les boes I sobresse 7 chastete deuindrent gourmandie 7 bordelerie I les prestres des le plus hault iusques au plus bas en lieu de foy desperance I et de clarte prindrent heaulme dorgueil I haubergeon de luxure I et espee dauarice.

(And so the clergy's pilgrim staffs became elegant riding-horses; their rough hair shirts turned into purple robes and scarlet copes trailing in the mud; sobriety and chastity were forsaken for gluttony and lechery; priests from the most elevated down to the very lowest exchanged faith, hope, and charity for the helmet of pride, the mail shirt of lust, and the sword of avarice.[88]

Lydgate's Benedictine loyalties allow him only a certain amount of this; the contrast between horses, garments, and diet are preserved (IX. 799–812), while the charges of 'bordelerie' among priests of all degrees and the pseudo-Pauline imagery of the armour of moral delinquency (Laurent's helmet of pride, breast-plate of lust, sword of avarice) are ignored.[89] Premierfait's intro-ductory comments on the 'temporelle seigneurie' and 'la seigneurie espirituelle' are also elided. The fact that the Church has been endowed with temporalities does not in itself lead to corruption in Lydgate's view: for him, attitude is all ('richesse *brouht in pride,* ... I ... *coueitise and fals ambicioun* ... I Brouht in dis-cord and dyuysioun').[90] Finally, where Premierfait seems able to view the eastern rejection of the papacy (in that it is an eastern resistance to papal greed for Greek wealth) as a commendable step on the Church's path towards recovering its primitive purity, Lygdate has only criticism for the Greeks.[91] He sees no evidence

---

[88] *Des Cas* fo. 200ᵛ (IX. ch. 4).

[89] The implications of the Benedictine vows of stability, conversion, and obedi-ence, rather than explicitly to the evangelical counsels (of poverty, chastity, and obedience) are of interest here. See van Zeller (1959: 47–9), and McCann (1937: 142–66).   [90] *Fall* IX. 797, 820, 822 (emphases added).

[91] 'Le pape ... entreprint saouller son goufre de auarice I de richesses de Grece et de Asie ... par quoy leglise grecque se desserua de leglise Rommaine' (*Des Cas* fo. 200ᵛ).

of apostolic poverty in the schism; instead he claims it is mere avarice that leads the Greeks to break ecclesial unity, selfishly in order to protect their own local wealth:

> Fals auarice caused this offence,
> That the Grekis dide hemsilf deuide
> Fro the Romeyns for ther gret[e] pride.[92]

In the narrative of Odoacer the barbarian in Book VIII Lydgate lengthens to a whole stanza the French text's brief comment on the dependence of all kings on God for their authority,[93] and goes on to add a list of those kingdoms that have fallen as a result of the debauched behaviour of their leaders and their companions. Courtiers who 'drynke late, | Ly longe abedde . . . | And rekles folk that list nat heere masse'[94] are blamed for the falls of Belshazzar, Jerusalem, Darius of Persia, Alexander, Troy, Rome, Carthage, and—in an exhilarating moment—for the civil divisions of contemporary France:

> Rekne othir rewmys that been of latter date,
> As of dyuisiouns in France that fill but late.[95]

This unexpectedly topical reference not only allows Lydgate to make the point that secular authority that departs from the counsels he has just given (including the duties of piety and obedience to God, which have received a characteristically Lydgatean emphasis) is just as vulnerable to downfall and misfortune in the present as in the remote past, but it also enables him to score a victory in a contemporary political conflict (the factional 'dyuisiouns' among the French nobility being the source of the recent Lancastrian consolidation of power in France). It is to these contextual resonances of the *Fall* debate about the relationship between the spiritual and temporal orders that we now turn.

BENEDICTINE CONTEXT

Introductory

An examination of the narratives in the *Fall of Princes* that dramatize the relationship between spiritual and secular authority

---

[92] *Fall* IX. 817–19.
[93] Ibid. VIII. 2374–80; cf. *Des Cas* fos. 187ᵛ–188ʳ (VIII. ch. 16), *De casibus* fos. 92ᵛ–93ʳ (pp. 202–3).   [94] *Fall* VIII. 2432–3, 2435.
[95] Ibid. VIII. 2456–7.

has shown that Lydgate consistently elides and adapts these in significant ways. Furthermore, it has emerged that these alterations are by no means haphazard or adventitious, but, rather, are deliberate and programmatic: Lydgate's alterations systematically delineate models of cooperation between Church and Empire in which the latter is shown to be dependent on, and subservient to, the former. Far from finding the unreflective poet of conventional caricature, we have seen instead the remarkable degree to which Lydgate actively reprocesses his source materials in order to advance a tendentious and partisan argument: suppression or enhancement of textual detail are the careful means by which Lydgate advances a vigorous debate on the limits of secular power. It is not particularly unexpected that a Benedictine author should promote the concerns, teachings, and powers of the spiritual above those of the secular order: medieval monastic piety finds unambiguous sanction for this priority, if not in the gospels, then certainly throughout the writings of the Church Fathers. The observation of the author of the letter to the Hebrews that 'here we have no abiding city, but we look for the city which is to come'[96] gives rise to the tradition of the Christian as a *viator* 'to whom every foreign land is home and every homeland is foreign'.[97] Perhaps inevitably, the relationship between secular power and the pilgrim Church temporal quickly became aggressively adversarial. The second-century apologist Tatian, famous for his anti-Hellenist views, figured his own conversion in terms of a rejection of the sophistications and philosophical finesses of 'the Romans . . . and the Athenians' for a 'barbaric philosophy', thereby contrasting decadent pagan cultures with the rude simplicity of the early Church.[98] Tertullian is the most explosive advocate of the utter discontinuity between the sacred and the secular, devoting chapters of his *De idolatria*, his *Apologeticus*, and his *De praescriptionibus adversus haereticos* to a discussion of this very tension. It is in the last of these that he gives vent to his famously querulous outburst: 'quid ergo Athenis et Hierosolymis? quid academiae et ecclesiae?'[99]

---

[96] Heb. 13: 14.

[97] Letter to Diogenetus V. Cf. Jerome, Ep. 53. 11; Augustine, 'De peregrinatione hujus vitae'; Bernard of Clairvaux, seventh Lenten sermon ('In quadragesimo') in *PL* clxxxiii. 183, and 'Exposition of the Song of Songs' (Sermon 50 § 8).

[98] Tatian, *Oratio ad Graecos* § 35, trans. Pratten (Tatian 1867: 40).

[99] *De praescriptionibus adversus haereticorum* VII. § 9, in *PL* ii. 23B: 'What has Athens to do with Jerusalem, or the Academy with the Church?'

This patristic tradition of viewing the claims of the ecclesiastical and the secular orders as being intrinsically mutually exclusive evidently lies behind Lydgate's insistence on the priority of the spiritual over the temporal sphere. However, the fact that Lydgate was based in Bury St Edmunds throughout the period in which he wrote the *Fall of Princes* enables us also to examine the Benedictine community of the 1430s for events closer to home that must have exerted a more immediate influence on the poem's discussion about the relationship between spiritual and temporal authority.

So pronounced and energetic, indeed, does discussion of such issues appear to have been in the day-to-day affairs of the Bury Benedictines that the Abbey of Lydgate's day emerges as a lively and contentious community in which theoretical discussions of the limits and interaction of Church and civil power were by no means dry topics of disinterested enquiry, but were of pressing (and sometimes explosive) importance to the continued prosperity and independence of the Abbey. Whether one turns to the circumstances of the Abbey's foundation, to its legal privileges or—in the abbacy of William Curteys—to the seemingly daily confrontations with secular or (in the person of William Alnwick, bishop of Norwich) rival ecclesiastical authorities over such concerns as manorial income and inheritance, clerical-taxation assessment, or the investigation and trial of those suspected of Lollardy in the town, the Abbey typically frames its response to contemporary events in terms of its understanding of its inherited political privileges. International developments and movements for monastic reform (at, for example, the Council of Basle) similarly call forth from the community at Bury beleaguered redefinitions of its own anomalous historical position and are exploited to sharpen much wider debates over monastic authority.[100]

---

[100] For the nervousness of the English Benedictines over the proposed reforms of Basle see Whethamstede's letter to Curteys in 1435, urging that Curteys send a graduate from Bury to defend monastic privileges at the Council and 'crush the dog's tooth' ('dentem canem contundere'), adding that 'so loud is their slanderous barking growing that unless a quick and powerful counter-attack is made, it seems likely that our monastic order—which God forbid—will suffer permanent losses' (see *Memorials* ed. Arnold. iii (1896), 252–4). The importance of this letter for Curteys is seen in the fact that it is copied into his register twice, once in each volume (MSS Addit. 7096, fos. 161ʳ⁻ᵛ; Addit. 14848, fo. 140ʳ); for the correction of Arnold's dating of the letter, see Schofield (1966: 61–2; 1973: 114). Curteys

The Bury Exemption

The history of the jurisdictional exemption of Bury and of the succession of royal privileges bestowed upon the Abbey in the earlier period has been well documented:[101] the accuracy of our understanding of the pugnacious, and often wilfully provocative, autonomy of the community of the blessed king and martyr Edmund is made possible by the wealth of cartularies and registers from the Abbey which survived the depradations of the Reformation.[102] Despite the fact that the community itself was dissolved in 1539 (its abandoned buildings falling rapidly into ruin, its shrine desecrated, and its wealth appropriated), the preservation of the larger part of the community's considerable library collection and of much of its legal and administrative documentation enables us to reconstruct not only the preferred reading material of the later medieval community, but also the ways in which the members of the community chose to interpret the chronicle of events that had led to their establishment as an episcopal exemption.[103]

The community at Bury not only housed the mortal remains of a martyred king, but over the eight and a half centuries from the martyrdom of Edmund to the Reformation enjoyed a close and (for the community, at least) profitable relationship with successive English kings; indeed, the monks of the Abbey dated their foundation (somewhat precariously, as bishops of the see of Norwich were always quick to point out) back to the establishment of a monastic community at Bury by King Cnut. The martyrdom of Edmund of East Anglia by invading Danes in 869 was quickly interpreted

kept in touch with developments at the Council; in June 1435 he received a bleak report from Basle from the Norwich Benedictine John Forneste and he even seems to have been making arrangements to travel to the Council himself to defend abbatial exemptions (*Memorials* iii. 255–6); Schofield (1966: 61–2; 1971: 224–5; 1973: 55).

[101] General histories include those by Lobel (1935), Trenholme (1927), and Swanson (1989: 16–21).

[102] Abbot Samson, *The Kalendar of Abbot Samson of Bury St* Edmunds, ed. R. H. C. Davis (1954); *The Chronicle of Bury St Edmunds 1212–1301*, ed. Gransden (1964), pp. xiii–xvi; *The Customary of the Benedictine Abbey of Bury St Edmunds in Suffolk*, ed. Gransden (1973); *The Archives of the Abbey of Bury St Edmunds*, ed. Rodney M. Thomson (1980: 118–62). See G. R. C. Davis (1958: 13–17) and Fisher (1936–40: 268).

[103] See James (1926), Mynors (1957), Rodney M. Thomson (1972).

by early hagiographers not simply as the death of an outspoken Christian king at the hands of pagan barbarians (similarities with the martyrdom of St Sebastian in AD 286 struck early chroniclers forcibly), but as a primarily *political* event.[104] The kingship of Edmund is as important here as his status as a martyr. The refusal of Edmund to submit himself to the indignity of being under-king to the Danes led to a rapid association of the martyred king with political resistance: 'Edmund was the saint who resisted tyrants.'[105] The earliest surviving account of the passion of the martyred king, that of Abbo of Fleury, attributes not only qualities of good rule to Edmund, but also an interest in government when he claims that Edmund always kept in mind the precepts of Ecclesiasticus 32: 1 ('Principem te constituerunt? Noli extolli, sed esto in illis quasi unus ex illis').[106]

If later medieval French commentators seem to have found the cult ambiguous and incomprehensible, as the muddled comments of the chronicler Jean Juvenal des Ursins in 1444 suggest they did,[107] then no such misgivings affected Edmund's compatriots. Early legends report miraculous punishments of petty tyrants at the shrine (such as the lascivious sheriff Leofstan);[108] by the mid-twelfth century Edmund's political role is sufficiently commonplace that he is the natural choice for the political theorist John of Salisbury as an exemplum to support his thesis that 'omnium tyrannorum finem esse in miseriam' (VIII. ch. 21: 'All tyrants reach a miserable end') in his 1159 *Policraticus*:

In gente quoque Britanniarum, sicut quaedam nostratam restatur histori, ad compescendam et puniendam tirannidis rabiem gloriosissimi martiris et regis Eadmundi manum exercuit.

(In addition, among the nation of the Britons the hand of the most glorious martyr and king Edmund was employed for the suppression and

---

[104] Cf. Abbo of Fleury, *Passio Sancti Eadmundi*, § x (*Memorials* i. 15): 'sicque factum est ut spiculorum terebratis aculeis circumfossus palpitans horreret, velut asper hericius, aut spinis hirtus carduus, in passione similis Sebastiano egregio martyri'. Ælfric preserves this image in his English version of the passion: 'he eall wæs beset mid heora scotungum, swilce igles byrsta, swa swa Sebastianus wæs' (Mitchell and Robinson 2001: 200).   [105] R. H. C. Davis (1955: 228).
[106] 'Have they appointed you to be master? Don't lift yourself up, but be among others as one of the rest', *Passio* § iv (*Memorials* i. 8).
[107] Jean Juvenal des Ursins, *Traictie compendieux de la querelle de France contre les Anglois* (see P. S. Lewis 1964: 319–20).
[108] Davis (1955; 228); *Memorials* i. 23 (Abbo, *Passio* § xvii) and 30–2 (Hermannus, *De miraculis* § 2).

punishment of the savagery of tyranny, as is witnessed by certain of our histories.)[109]

In the eyes of the Black Monks, secular persecution had led directly to the foundation of their house. When King Sweyn attempted to levy the Danegeld on the early community in 1014, the saint punished him with instant death; Sweyn's repentant son Cnut atoned for his father's presumption (seen by John of Salisbury as the persecution of the Church by a hardened and rapacious tyrant)[110] by expelling the resident secular brothers and establishing fourteen regular clergy in their stead. As the anonymous account of MS Bodley 240 has it:

Rex autem . . . convocatoque consilio archiepiscoporum, episcoporum, abbatum, priorum, comitum, atque baronum totius Angliae, praecepit ut in praedicta basilica fierent monachi.

(The king, moreover . . . having assembled a council of the archbishops, bishops, abbots, priors, earls, and barons of the whole of England, declared that monks would be established in the aforementioned basilica.)[111]

From the very outset the notion of the king as a loyal servant of the Church, endowing *Ecclesia* with privileges and autonomy which may elsewhere have been regarded as either (at best) a remote ideal or (at worst) an unrealistic fantasy, was at Bury central to the community's sense of its own early history: the extent to which royal authority united with spiritual obedience in Cnut and the Abbey's subsequent royal patrons was an obvious consequence of the model provided by Edmund himself, and of the duality inherent in the very idea of the *rex sanctus*, the royal saint.

Cnut's endowment of the community included a conferment of the right to collect and keep the Danegeld tax in the Bury domains.[112] Alongside this valuable pragmatic privilege it was believed there had come also the political autonomy that was to become the distinctive (although not, of course, unique) privilege of the Bury peculiar—its exemption from episcopal jurisdiction:

Ipse quoque rex Canutus libertatem, quam rex Edmundus eidem sancto de clericis contulerat, monachis dedit et confirmavit, adjiciendo quod

---

[109] *Policraticus* VIII. 21 (1909: ii. 393–4); (trans. Nederman 1990: 212).
[110] Ibid. ii. 394.   [111] *Memorials* i. 359.
[112] Kemble (1839–48: no. 735); R. H. C. Davis (1955: 229).

monasterium S. Edmundi sit per omne aevum monachis deputatum ad inhabitandum, et ab omni dominatione omnium episcoporum liberum.

(King Cnut himself also gave to the monks and confirmed the liberty which King Edmund had conferred upon the clerks for the same saint, adding that the monastery of St Edmund for all time be assigned to the housing of monks and be free from the government of all bishops.)[113]

Although this charter is almost certainly spurious (the exemption in fact not being bestowed until a charter of Edward the Confessor),[114] the folklore beliefs current among fifteenth-century Bury monks about the history of their privileges are of greater significance than the veracity of those beliefs. The Bodley charter records the Edwardian donation in these terms:

ille locus nunquam sit locatus cum aliis personis quam cum monachis, nec aliquis episcopus habeat unquam potestatem in eodem monasterio nec infra fines eiusdem villae crucibus designatos.

(the place may never be contracted to persons other than the monks, nor may any bishop ever have power in that monastery nor within the boundaries of the same estate designated by the crosses.)[115]

Edward the Confessor's donation after his visitation to the house at Bury in 1044 certainly made him the most generous royal patron of the community: aside from the exemption, Edward granted the abbot the privilege of governing the eight and a half hundreds which surrounded the liberty of the town: a considerable tract of land corresponding approximately to the boundaries of modern west Suffolk. The hundreds had belonged to Edward's mother, the redoubtable Queen Emma, and his donation to the Abbey seems to have been motivated more by a desire to confiscate the lands from her in retaliation for her treason than to the other-worldly sanctity attributed to him by Bury historians.[116] Nonetheless, it is the hundredal donation which for the first time

[113] *Memorials* i. 360: the 'rex Edmundus' referred to here is Edmund I of Wessex (*regn.* 939–46). This exemption was confirmed by a charter of Hardecanute: 'Hardecanutus tamen S. Edmundo talem dedit libertatem, confirmando cartam patris sui Canuti, ut nullus archiepiscoporum vel episcoporum vel aliarum personarum eis adhaerentium praesumat quicquam consuetudinis sive dominationis amodo in eodem monasterio et villa super monachos clericos aut laicos proclamare, usurpare, justitiam aliquam facere, aut missas celebrare, nisi monitus fuerit ab ipsius loci abate' (ibid. i. 363, preserved in MS Bodley 240).
[114] Kemble (1839–48: nos. 735, 761).   [115] *Memorials* i. 363–4.
[116] Cf. R. H. C. Davis (1955: 229). Emma's disgrace is dated as 16 November 1043 (H. W. C. Davis 1909: 418).

unites in the person of the abbot a secular political authority with his own (not inconsiderable) spiritual authority. Within the hundreds the abbot of Bury (having been granted an impressively detailed list of forfeiture privileges, an exemption from every form of direct taxation, the right to collect taxes from the soke, and even the right to mint coinage) was in a sense both a bishop and a king. He was a bishop inasmuch as (in common with other mitred abbots) he exercised certain undeniably episcopal powers[117] 'in a kind of miniature, but highly-privileged, diocese of his own'.[118] He was a king in his personal enjoyment of ancient royal revenues and powers—including, within the limits of the boundary crosses of Bury town itself (the 'liberty of the four crosses' mentioned in the Edwardian charter), the power to exclude all royal officials and to appoint judges to sit in courts and dispense the powers of royal justices.[119] In the abbot of Bury, *imperium* and *sacerdotium* unite.

The history of the Bury exemption from the Conquest until the fifteenth century is famously turbulent. Successive bishops of Norwich were not only aggrieved that the abbot held powers considerably superior to their own, but also wanted Bury, and not Norwich, to be the cathedral town of their see.[120] Nevertheless, attempts to subordinate the Abbey to diocesan authority were successfully rebuffed by the community. It is not entirely surprising that (given its autonomous position with regard both to royal and ecclesiastical authority) Bury should have played so decisive a function in the baronial opposition to King John that culminated in the Runnymede Charter; it is appropriate that the initial oath

[117] Including, for example, the authority to issue letters dimissory of the Pope to authorize any bishop of his choice to ordain men to holy orders.

[118] Elston (Ph.D. thesis, 1979: 338). Abbot Anselm (*regn.* 1121–38) was the first to wear the mitre on licence; Curteys wore it to greet Henry VI at the south door of the Abbey Church in 1433, 'pontificalibus induti' (see Ord 1806: 68).

[119] Elston (Ph.D. thesis, 1979: 312). On 16 November 1281 Henry's 1102–3 charter ('ut nulla secularis persona aut minister regis in aliquo se intromittat de predicto burgo et hominibus manentibus in eo, nisi abbas at conventus et ministri eorum') was confirmed by Edward I—and witnessed not only by the bishops of London and Salisbury, but also by the Archbishop of Canterbury. For some of the administrative disadvantages of the abbatial judicial powers, see R. H. C. Davis (1955: 229–30). For details of the Edwardian donation, see H. W. C. Davis (1909: 417–20) and the pertinent documents in Kemble (1839–48); namely, nos. 875, 895, 915, 1342, 1346.

[120] These claims have been shown to be based on undeniable precedent (Galbraith 1925).

to force a charter of liberties from John, a tyrant, was taken (in November 1214) on the high altar of an abbey that housed the shrine of a king who had become regarded as a scourge of tyranny. Again, the community found itself the focus of resistance to Henry III in 1263–7, even to the point that the monks lent support to the rebel barons and Simon de Montfort,[121] and a century later was violently caught up in the 1381 Uprisings.[122]

It seems equally appropriate that devotion to one of the most contentious occupants of the Chair of St Augustine should have been vibrant at Bury: in Thomas Becket the Bury monks found a man who had striven as strenuously to define and defend his privileges (both secular and ecclesiastical) as successive abbots had been forced to protect those of their community. Jocelin of Brakelonde tells that Abbot Hugh met his fatal horse-riding accident at Rochester on 9 September 1180 as he was journeying to pray at the shrine of St Thomas; Abbot Samson, the subject of Jocelin's chronicle of the Abbey community, was to die at dusk on the feast of the martyr in 1211, as is recorded in the anonymous *Cronica de electione Hugonis Abbatis*.[123] Furthermore, Robert Dinn's research into the contexts of popular devotion in later medieval Bury has not only revealed that Becket was the patron of two local gilds (at Ixworth and Hopton), and that the two parish churches at the boundary wall of the Abbey precincts each had an altar devoted to the saint at which mass was offered daily,[124] but has also shown that testamentary evidence among Bury laity from 1380–99 and 1439–1530 indicates that the Thomas altar in the parish church of St James was 'one of the most popular locations for chantries to be celebrated in the town'.[125] Moreover, revered among the many relics held in the abbey church of the community were the boots and 'penneknyf' of St Thomas.[126]

---

[121] Elston (Ph.D. thesis, 1979: 9).   [122] *Memorials* iii. 126–9, 137–8.
[123] *Memorials* ii. 29 (ll. 214–15); trans. Rodney M. Thomson (1974: 2–3).
[124] Dinn (Ph.D. thesis, 1990; 238); cf. Suffolk Archaeological Society (1904: 75–6).   [125] Dinn (Ph.D. thesis, 1990: 138, 229–30).
[126] Duffy (1992: 384). If William Fitzstephen's account of Becket's assassination is to be believed, Becket himself acutely manipulated the tension between secular and spiritual authority in his final hours, replying to his accusers that he was no traitor, but a Christian priest with higher loyalties than the local secular order (*Vita* § 139, in Becket (1875–85): iii. 140). Throughout the Middle Ages Becket was cited as an exemplary defender of the liberties of the Church (see Giraldus Cambrensis, *De regimine principum* I. § 3): Phyllis B. Roberts (1992) has identified

The Abbacy of William Curteys (regn. 1429–46)

The early history of the Abbey at Bury illustrates how far issues of the autonomy and interdependence of sacred and civil authority lay at the heart of the community. These issues were made particularly complex by the ways in which successive kings confirmed and enhanced the abbatial exemption, voluntarily divesting themselves of their own *imperium* in ways which provide a clear model of the empowerment of the Church we have seen in Lydgate's narrative of, in particular, the Donation of Constantine in the *Fall of Princes*. Within the eight and a half hundreds of the Bury exemption and, even more manifestly, within the liberty of the town's four crosses, the abbot of Bury occupied an anomalous legal and ecclesiastical position which derives its powers solely from a renunciation of these same powers by officials who would elsewhere occupy positions of authority over the abbot. It has become apparent that these issues of rival authority are heightened and receive sharp definition in the abbacy of the man who presided over Bury during the period in which Lydgate composed not only the *Fall*, but also (at the request of Curteys) his own paean to the martyred St Edmund.[127]

Much of our knowledge of the day-to-day business, conflicts, and gossip of Curteys's abbacy is derived from the two volumes of his personal register (now British Library MSS Additional 7096 and 14848), lengthy documents which strongly attest to Curteys's businesslike and occasionally devious mind. In these manuscripts we find a self-conscious archive of the concerns of the mid-fifteenth-century community as Curteys records, reorders, and interprets detail in such a way as to make its significance apparent. The provision of a critical apparatus (including explanatory prefaces and commentary) and a consistent emphasis on the need to verify the authenticity of various charters, accounts, and deeds (as well as of local hearsay and scandal) in the register all reveal a shrewd and competent administrator who recognized the

---

fifty-three medieval Latin sermons which present Becket in this way. Walsingham records that Richard II kept an ampulla of Becket's holy oil on his person at the end of his reign which Archbishop Thomas Arundel used at the coronation of Henry IV (1863–4: ii. 239–40).

[127] Curteys commissioned the lives of Saints Edmund and Fremund from Lydgate to commemorate the 1433–4 visit of the boy-king Henry VI to the Abbey.

importance of establishing truth by scrupulous documentary analysis.[128] With good cause has this register been described as 'a carefully-planned encyclopedia'.[129]

On his election to the abbacy of Bury, Curteys assumed, as had his predecessors, a significant role in the government of the country on a variety of levels. His influence was not confined to the considerable tracts of land under his exempt jurisdiction, for he was also one of the twenty-seven abbots and priors who could be summoned by private writ to Parliament and sessions of the Great Council.[130] His attendance at Parliament is recorded several times (in 1429, 1431, 1432, and 1437); he was at the Great Council at Sheen in November 1437 and on at least three occasions he was trier of petitions at Parliament. As a colleague and fellow-conspirator of John Whethamstede (the early humanist abbot of the Benedictine House at St Albans, *regn.* 1420–40 and 1452–65, former prior of the Black Monks' College at Oxford during the years when Lydgate may himself have studied at the university, and patron of Lydgate's *Life of SS Albon and Amphibel*),[131] Curteys was close to the very centre of authority in the Benedictine order in England. The list of those Curteys admitted to the Confraternity of the Abbey during his reign reads as a catalogue of the Lancastrian and East Anglian ascendancy (and, interestingly, includes not only Lydgate's patron for the *Fall*—and his ill-fated second wife—but also Gloucester's chief rival, Cardinal Beaufort).[132]

---

[128] The contents of the two manuscripts are summarized by Rodney M. Thomson (*Archives*, ed. Thomson 1980: 135–9). Interesting preliminary work on the contents of the register was undertaken by John Elston in his unpublished 1979 Berkeley doctoral thesis.

[129] Elston (Ph.D. thesis, 1979: 31): translations from the register volumes given here are Elston's. While he was still Prior of the Abbey (a position he held from 1425 until his election as abbot) Curteys completed the 'Registrum rubeum' of Cratfield's abbacy, now preserved as CUL MS Ff. ii. 29. The period of Curteys's abbacy generated fifteen extant archival books and has been described as 'the high-point of archival activity and expertise at Bury' (*Archives*, ed. Thomson 1980: 34).

[130] Elston (Ph.D. thesis, 1979: 55).

[131] Howlett, 'Studies in the Works of John Whethamstede' (D. Phil. thesis, 1975: 205–7). Whethamstede was a close ally of Duke Humphrey and gave him at least two books, one of which (Oxford, Corpus Christi College MS 243) contained a work on Fate (Sammut, 1980: 106, 115–16). In turn Humphrey donated works by the Abbot to Oxford, Anstey (1898: i. 235); Weiss (1957: 30–8, 463–5); Sammut (1980: 78); Howlett (1975: 215–20).

[132] Those admitted include: William Paston (4 April 1429, MS Addit. 14848, fo. 39ʳ); Richard Beauchamp, earl of Warwick, Isabella (his wife), and his children (3 March 1434, fo. 121ᵛ); Henry VI and Humphrey, duke of Gloucester (23 April

Key events of the earlier years of Curteys's abbacy are illustrative of exactly how urgent and pervasive the conflict between secular and episcopal authority was in the decade during which Lydgate was composing the *Fall*: fascinatingly, local threats of Lollardy (which bring about further refinement in understandings of abbatial authority in Bury) influenced Lydgate in works other than the *Fall of Princes*.

Manorial Authority

When, just a few days after his election to the abbacy, Curteys was in London in 1429 in order to take his oath of fealty to the boy-king, he found himself involved in exactly the kind of dispute which was to dog him throughout his period of office. The Earl Marshal, John Mowbray, duke of Norfolk, demanded £10 of the new abbot in a writ dated 24 February.[133] The basis of the Norfolk claim was a highly contentious one, resting on the assertion that the abbot held certain lands not by free alms, but rather by barony to the dukes of Norfolk: as such the Norfolk case, which might otherwise seem of small significance, strikes at the heart of Curteys's awareness of his own legal exemptions. As John Elston has shown, Curteys's predecessors *did* in fact hold lands by barony as well as by free alms: Abbot Baldwin held his barony of William I for the service of forty knights and Abbot Samson had met his military obligations by leading knights personally to the siege of Windsor in 1193.[134] Similarly, in June 1385 the Abbey had contributed to the defence of coastal Suffolk in response to feudal requirements.[135] By 1401, however, the Abbey was beginning to contest these exactions and forced an inquest into the status of its landholdings; this enquiry returned a verdict that the abbot did indeed hold his lands in pure alms, save for 'a strip of land' in Hertfordshire which was held 'from the king for the service of one knight's fee'.[136] The Norwich challenge in 1429

1434, fo. 128ᵛ); Cardinal Beaufort (12 October 1436, fo. 175ʳ); Elizabeth de Vere, countess of Oxford (11 March 1440, fo. 344ᵛ); William de la Pole, first duke of Suffolk (2 April 1440, fo. 346ʳ); Eleanor Cobham, duchess of Gloucester (5 June 1440, fos. 339ʳ⁻ᵛ); Humphrey Stafford, later first duke of Buckingham, and thirteen members of his family (6 March 1440, MS Addit. 7096, fo. 138ᵛ).

[133] MS Addit. 14848, fo. 26ʳ: Curteys had been elected abbot on 18 February.
[134] Elston (Ph.D. thesis, 1979: 12, 223–5; cf. *Memorials* i. 287–9 (Jocelin, *Cronica* § 63).   [135] See N. B. Lewis (1958).
[136] Elston (Ph.D. thesis, 1979: 224).

went badly for the new abbot and it is typical of Curteys that he should have sold the compromising landholding in November 1435,[137] warning the community at his 1441 synod that the monks should exercise considerable vigilance in accepting gifts of land which might carry hidden feudal obligations which would threaten the legal immunity of the whole Abbey:

> Lest our church, which is now free, should be reduced to servitude, and thus fall, like one enslaved, under tribute, as a result of paying homage or services for such lands to any lords, spiritual or temporal, other than the king.[138]

Clerical Taxation and the Archdeacon of Sudbury

The year 1429 saw not only the election of William Curteys as the abbot of Bury, but also of Clement Denston as the archdeacon for the deanery within which the liberty of Bury fell. In the same year Convocation votes for new graduated income taxation of stipendiary clergy generated conflicts between Curteys and William Alnwick, the bishop of Norwich, which hinged on the abbatial exemption from diocesan authority. As these were new forms of clerical taxation, new assessments of the wealth of the clergy were necessary.[139] When, after the king's order on 20 February 1430 that diocesan bishops should supervise the collection of the tax, Alnwick sent the recently preferred Archdeacon on 15 March to conduct the Bury assessment, Curteys prevented Denston from carrying out the assessment, regarding this as an infringement of his own privileges:

> It was the Abbot's opinion that if such an inquest were held within his exempt jurisdiction by virtue of the bishop's orders it would result in serious damage to the privileges which had been granted to the monastery by papal authority.[140]

Similarly, when Denston returned with a copy of the king's writ to the bishops, Curteys again refused the Archdeacon permission to conduct the assessment, but compromised by examining the income of his clergy himself. By 1436 the situation had worsened: by this stage Curteys (smarting from certain physical assaults

---

[137] MS Addit. 7096, fo. 174ᵛ.
[138] Ibid., fo. 206ʳ, trans. Elston (Ph.D. thesis, 1979: 224–5).
[139] Elston: (Ph.D. thesis, 1979: 355); cf. McHardy (1984: 185–6).
[140] MS Addit. 14848, fo. 87ʳ.

made on his bailiffs in Sudbury in 1434 and his own lengthy
campaign against the person of the Archdeacon) was even less dis-
posed to admit Denston's authority as the deputy of the diocesan
bishop within the abbatial liberty than he had been in 1430. He
again collected the tax himself from his clergy:

Bishop Alnwick, who still had not buried the hateful grudge which he
bore against the church of St Edmund, though he could not directly
oppose or undermine the privileges of this house, subject as it is only to
the apostolic see; yet he pleased, though in vain, to injure them by subtle
and indirect means, by addressing his commission to master Clement
Denston, the archdeacon of Sudbury.[141]

The 1430 conflict between Denston and Curteys over the diocesan claims to examine Bury clergy for the taxation soon exploded
into bitter hostility. The incident which led to their feud seems in
itself to be of trivial significance: on the evening of the annual
Abbey banquet on the vigil of the feast of the martyr Edmund
(20 November 1434) Denston left the meal suddenly and without
explanation, his food untouched. Although Curteys also records
that the Archdeacon had raised his voice to the Abbot on the previous evening and that he had deliberately disobeyed the Abbot's
prohibition that he should join in the procession of St Edmund's
relics at the festal High Mass, it seems to have been the affront
to the Abbot's hospitality that initially caused Curteys's displeas-
ure. When Curteys learned that Denston's departure was caused
by news that his pregnant mistress, Alice Cayle, had successfully
escaped from Bury (disguised, as Curteys notes, as a nun 'who
had taken vows to God'[142]) to the Archdeacon's manor at West
Stow, the Abbot's fury seems to have needed only one further
spark to ignite. After a complex sequence of events relating to
Denston's unlawful examination of a matrimonial case which fell
under the Abbot's jurisdiction and his failure to present himself
at a session of the Abbey Sacrist's court on 16 January 1435
(when he had been charged with fornication),[143] Curteys indicted
Denston of rape on 31 March;[144] on 22 April the Archdeacon was

[141] Ibid. fo. 193ʳ, trans. Elston (Ph.D. thesis, 1979: ch. 11 n. 38).
[142] Ibid. fo. 286ᵛ.
[143] Ibid. fos. 217ʳ⁻ᵛ: just as episcopal consistory courts were held in Bury not
by the diocesan bishop but by the abbot, so too archdiaconal jurisdiction within
the liberty fell to the abbot's 'archdeacon', the sacrist of the Abbey (Dinn Ph.D.
thesis, 1990: 46). [144] MS Addit. 14848, fo. 277ᵛ.

arrested at West Stow and led on foot to Bury gaol where Curteys held him for eleven days.[145] Of the arrest the register records that all had been accomplished 'with the aid of St Edmund, against whose monastery and monks the Archdeacon had long laboured'. Four days *before* Denston's release (on 2 May) Curteys found him guilty of failure to present himself at his court and excommunicated him accordingly.[146] The date of this act was symbolic: 28 April is the eve of the feast of the translation of the relics of the martyr Edmund, and was the day on which the Abbey commemorated its historical liberation from episcopal authority. The irony may even have amused Curteys:

The glorious martyr cast down and humbled the archdeacon and kept him in prison on the day of his translation . . . he who in his pride offended the glorious martyr on the vigil of his passion[147]

Releasing Denston for a bond of 1,000 marks and staging a public act of submission from his defeated enemy in a crowded Abbey nave (9 June 1435),[148] Curteys must have felt that his exempt jurisdiction had at last been vindicated by an overwhelming demonstration of abbatial power. The sheer energy he devoted to crushing Denston attests to Curteys's single-minded and unnerving steeliness of will: Elston has calculated that thirty-four folios (14 per cent) of the first volume of the register are devoted to relating the Sudbury feud, several of which show that Curteys systematically collected bills of complaint against Denston for previous misdemeanours from disaffected Bury residents in order to strengthen his own actions with accusations of theft, extortion, simony, and other improprieties.[149]

Episcopal Spiritual Authority: Letters Dimissory
In hounding and attacking the archdeacon of Sudbury in this way, Curteys may have intended to send warning shots to other, more intimidating, enemies: the Court of Arches, Henry Chichele, the archbishop of Canterbury, and the bishop of Norwich seem to have been his actual opponents during these months rather than the hapless cleric who bore the brunt of the Abbot's anger.

---

[145] MS Addit. 14848, fos. 284ᵛ–5ʳ.   [146] Ibid. fo. 220ʳ.
[147] Ibid. fo. 286ᵛ: Curteys here refers to Denston's early departure from the banquet six months previously.   [148] Ibid. fo. 223ʳ⁻ᵛ.
[149] Elston (Ph.D. thesis, 1979: 381–6).

In particular, a rather more long-standing feud with Bishop Alnwick turned on documents known as 'letters dimissory'. In the Middle Ages, as today, *litterae dimissoriales* were the official response of the Church to conflicts of spiritual authority between rival prelates. Issued by cardinal or bishop, the letters empower a delegate to perform episcopal functions (usually ordination) on territory or in contexts where he would otherwise lack ecclesiastical authority. In issuing such letters, bishops permit a fellow-bishop, for example, to ordain in his own diocese someone under the jurisdiction of the authorizing bishop or to enter his episcopal colleague's diocese in order to perform ordinations there. In that they are a means by which a bishop voluntarily cedes part of his spiritual authority, the *litterae* are a jealously guarded privilege.[150]

The right of successive abbots of Bury to issue letters dimissory of the Pope (bypassing both diocesan and provincial ecclesiastical superiors) was, unsurprisingly, a source of considerable contention between the bishop of Norwich and the head of the Bury community. In October 1430 William Alnwick suspended John Benet for having been ordained to the subdiaconate in Bury without Alnwick's licence;[151] in 1433 he went still further and sought to invalidate all the ordinations in Bury licensed by abbatial *litterae* since the beginning of the abbacy of William Excetre, Curteys's predecessor, in 1415.[152] This attempt to undermine Curteys's powers would have been especially pointed after snubs Alnwick had received from the Abbot over the collection of clerical taxation. Curteys's decision to greet the royal party on its arrival in Bury in December of the same year by wearing (as was his right) the mitre in Alnwick's presence may well have been calculated to be a (typically stage-managed) affront to the bishop after their quarrel over Curteys's power to license ordinations. Curteys's register records their enmity in extraordinarily intemperate terms:

the monastery . . . has always been exempt since the first introduction of monks in the time of King Cnut . . . But various satellites of Satan, inspired by the spirit of the devil, have often tried to violate the privileges of the monastery . . . a certain William Alnwick, who was bishop of

---

[150] *Catholic Encyclopedia* (1907–14: iv. 797); see also the entry 'Excardination' (Swanson 1989: 19).

[151] MS Addit. 14848, fo. 52ᵛ (see Elston Ph.D. thesis, 1979: 353).

[152] Ibid. fos. 109ᵛ–10ʳ: Curteys says of Alnwick that he 'had ever been an enemy of our exemption'.

Norwich in the time of Abbot William Curteys, blew up a great north wind, uttering the most hideous words against the privileges and exemption of the monastery.[153]

It is natural to ask the origin of so virulent a personal vendetta: tensions over the Abbey's historical privileges cannot of themselves have been sufficient to unleash such hatred. The flashpoint in question came in heavy-handed attempts by Alnwick in 1429 to intervene in an affair which raised into sharp profile not simply the nature of abbatial exemption from other ecclesiastical authority, but also the much larger issue of the validity of ecclesiastical authority itself in the face of secular power: namely, in the trial of adherents to the Lollard heresy in the Norwich diocese.

The Examination of Lollards

William Alnwick was no friend of the Lollard heresy; he seems, indeed, to have shared his patron Humphrey of Gloucester's energy in his pursuit of heretics.[154] In September 1428 (the year in which the supposed bones of Wyclif were burned) he had three priests burned in Norwich for their heterodox views and turned his attentions to Bury, where he announced that he would hold an investigation on 4 October in St James's Church, one of the two parish churches on the west boundary of the Abbey precincts.[155] Episcopal examinations of Lollards (possibly because they were a new phenomenon) seem not to have been adequately covered by the Abbey's historical privileges, and Curteys, though as yet only Prior of the Abbey, played a pivotal role in the Black Monks' response to this new infringement of their spiritual exemption; he was appointed by the ageing Abbot Excetre to head an Abbey investigation, timed to take place on the same day, in the same venue, and at the same time as the unlawful

---

[153] Ibid. fo. 243ʳ: 'cum monasterium gloriosi Regio 7 martirio Sancti Edmundi . . . a prima introductione monachorum usque a tempore Regio Canuti . . . nonnulli tum sathane satellites spiritu ducti satannico sed monasterii infringere privilegia prosepe attemptarunt . . . Quidam eiundam W. Alwyk [sic] Norwice Episcopus tempore praefat`o´ W. Curteys Abbis [sic] contra privilegia 7 exempt comunem monasterii veces emisit teternissimas ventisque aquilonarem fortit`o´ exsufflauit' (trans. Elston, Ph.D. thesis, 1979: 439–40).

[154] See Griffiths (1981: 104); Tanner (1977: 7–10).

[155] Welch (1962–4: 154); J. A. F. Thomson (1965: 120–32); Aston (1982); Hudson (1988: 33–4); Swanson (1989: 335–6).

episcopal enquiry. At best this was a messy and barely face-saving compromise.

On his election Curteys moved understandably swiftly to prevent a repetition of these events: he petitioned Martin V to rule against further episcopal activities of this kind in the Bury liberty, and Whethamstede (the papal deputy) decided in the Abbey's favour in February 1430. Less than a fortnight later there arose the most famous Lollard case Bury was to experience. A Bury chaplain, Robert Bert, who the trial records claim was 'known for heretical deformity',[156] was examined before Alnwick in the chapel of the episcopal palace in Norwich. The first part of the trial interestingly hinged on Bert's past ownership of the vernacular text *Dives and Pauper*, which Alnwick claimed contained 'plures errores et hereses quamplures'.[157] Regardless of Bert's various defences (in which he claimed that the errors must have been added to the book after he had passed it on to another man whose name he could not remember, and that when he himself owned it he never knew it to be heterodox),[158] he was challenged for heretical views on tithes, on images of the Crucified, of the Virgin and of the saints, and on the efficacy of pilgrimages,[159] and was charged to present himself for public purgation: this ceremony took place in St James's Church in Bury on 20 April.[160]

This decision caused Curteys concern, and a long entry in his register shows that he was advised that legal technicalities made him unable to use the papal exemption of the previous month: the entry self-defensively concludes that, instead of murmuring against him for failure to defeat the Bishop, 'every right-thinking person ought to give him thanks for the sincere intentions with which he acted'.[161] Nonetheless, the saga shows not just that Bury was not shielded from the heretical activity of the opening decades

---

[156] 'de heretica pravitate notatus' (Tanner 1977: 98).

[157] *Dives* is not a heretical text: Anne Hudson several times notes that Whethamstede paid for a copy to be made for St Albans (1973: 145; 1981, repr. 1985: 173–4; 1988: 418–20). In 1464, however, even the *Canterbury Tales* were cited in a heresy trial (see Hudson 1982: 262).

[158] Tanner (1977: 90): 'dixit ... Robertus quod tempore quo ipse habuit dictum librum in custodia sua ipse nunquam scivit fuisse nec esse errores vel hereses in eodem'.   [159] Ibid. 101.

[160] Ibid. 100–2; cf. Welch (1962–4: 160–1).

[161] MS Addit. 14848, fo. 109ᵛ, trans. Elston (Ph.D. thesis, 1979: 352–3).

of the fifteenth century, but also that heresy was another context in which the community at this time defined its awareness of its own fragile spiritual independence.[162]

It is not just in the *Fall* narratives that Lydgate advances the position that temporal rulers should protect ecclesiastical interests and spiritual authority. In his 'Ballade to King Henry VI upon his Coronation' (a sixteen-stanza poem surviving in four manuscripts) and his 'Defence of Holy Church' Lydgate cites figures we have seen in the *Fall* narratives. The eight-year-old Henry VI is counselled to pursue the qualities of certain classical and biblical models (including being told to cherish the Church 'lyke to Constantine'), and the boy is offered two modern models—the Emperor Sigismund, and his own father, Henry V:

> And þat þou mayst beo resemblable founde
> Heretykes and Lollardes for to oppresse,
> Lych þemperour, worthy Sygesmound,
> And as þy fader, floure of hye prowesse,
> At þe gynnyng of his royal noblesse
> Woyded al Cokil fer oute of Syon,
> Crystes spouse sette in stabulnesse,
> Outraying foreyns þat came frome Babylon.[163]

The discussion here is of Sigismund's moves against the Hussites and Henry V's action against the Oldcastle Lollard plot of 1413: both are mentioned in the 'Sotelties' at Henry's coronation banquet,[164] and the second of these is also the subject of the 'Defence',

---

[162] The purchase of a 1403 Oxford copy of Wycliffite *postilla* on the New Testament (now MS Bodley 716) by the Abbey sacrist John Cranewys shows that the Abbey library was not ignorant of Wycliffite thought, see Smalley (1953: 187–9); Hudson (1975, repr. 1985: 77; 1988: 86n.); Heale (D. Phil. thesis, 1994: 145–6). An entry (fo. 109ʳ) indicates that Curteys had been aware of the presence of heresy in Bury towards the end of Excetre's abbacy, while 1438 royal writs concerning Lollard disorders in the register suggest that the Abbey remained alive to the dangers of heresy throughout the decade (MS Addit. 14848, fos. 84ʳ, 301ʳ; see Gage (1831) and J. A. F. Thomson (1964)).

[163] 'Ballade' ll. 81–8, in *MP* ii. 624–30.

[164] 'Sotelties' ll.9–16, in *MP* ii. 623–4. On Lydgate's attitude towards heretics see Brie (1929: 275), but note that Lydgate does exclude Laurent's more narrowly

a short and undated address to a royal prince, which celebrates its addressee's role as defender of 'Cristus spouse douhtir of Syoun'.[165] Among Lydgate's religious lyrics, his prayers to St Edmund and St Thomas Becket are also of interest here: Thomas is typically depicted in his role as a defender of ecclesiastical authority ('Stood as a peeler for hooly chirchis right') and as an opponent of tyrannical secular power; Edmund, too, is presented as an opponent of tyranny.[166]

Surviving in Curteys's register (MS Addit. 14848) is a lengthy versified charter of the liberties of the Abbey of Bury (fos. 243^r-254^r) which a prefatory statement claims was written at the request of Curteys in order to document (and, presumably, render in an accessible vernacular form) the community's historical claims.[167] No details are given of the authorship of this text, but the evidence of idiom and style (especially when the poem introduces maxims on the mutability of worldly affairs and imagery of the unstable, ever-moving wheel) are sufficient for Lydgate's authorship to be highly probable, even if final certainty cannot be reached. The *Cartae versificatae* consist of four sections: the charters of Cnut, Hardecanute, Edward the Confessor, and William I are given in order, the second and third being followed by an envoy section by the translator. Unsurprisingly, the work places repeated emphasis on the unalienable nature of the privileges whose origins it traces:

> I make by them a confirmacioun
> to stonde stable, the monkys there tassure,

historical account of the Sabellian heresy from the *Fall* in his version of the narrative of the Roman Emperor Aurelius 'Caracalla' (VIII. 302–15).

[165] 'Defence' ll. 5–14, in *MP* i. 30–5. The poem survives in two manuscripts (BL MSS Sloane 1212 and Harley 1245—where it follows the *Fall* in the same hand), but is dated in neither: Schirmer dates it as *c*. 1431, presumably reading the discussion of opponents of the Church as references to the Midland Lollards whose uprising Humphrey was so instrumental in suppressing (Schirmer 1952, trans. 1961: 134). However, this reading falters on Lydgate's claim that the Church was oppressed in 'thy rewme', a phrase that it is unlikely would have been appropriate for the embattled Gloucester in 1431. Again, the later sections of the poem slide into an advisory idiom that might seem more appropriate for a young king at the outset of his reign.

[166] *MP* i. 124–7, 139–43: at *Fall* IX. 2416–19 Lydgate adds four lines in praise of St Edmund to Laurent's list of martyrs who opposed 'tirauntes'.

[167] Printed in *Memorials* (iii. 215–35). See MacCracken on the Lydgate canon (*MP* i. p. xiii) and in *Archives* ed. Rodney M. Thomson (1980: 137).

in ther fraunchyse perpetuelly tendure

. . . . . .

that monkys first ha ful posessioun
there for tabyde evere in ther fraunchyse

. . . . . .

Fre from al daunger and jurediccioun,
to have ther lordshipppes and ther liberte,
and that no bysshop by none occasioun
have interesse in no maner degre,
to interupte ther tranquyllyte

. . . . . .

that nouther bysshop, duk, erle nor baroun in no thyng
shal ha no power myn ordynaunce to lette[168]

Although the *Cartae* have received little discussion (Pearsall notes their existence, Schirmer dismisses them as yielding 'little pleasure'), they testify to a keen interest in the protection of spiritual authority: the author's collusion with Curteys to produce so precisely legal a statement of the Abbey's privileges may well be the most striking statement we have of Lydgate's involvement in the minutiae of ecclesiastical politics.[169]

A significant number of ecclesiastical historians turned their attentions to Lydgate in the 1990s: Miri Rubin, Eamon Duffy, and Nicholas Heale variously considered Lydgate's religious poems as examples of a kind of vernacular pastoral manual aimed at a literate lay readership, designed to focus orthodox private spirituality or public devotion at the Mass.[170] Lydgate's eucharistic poems, his Marian antiphons, his indulgenced hymns of the Fifteen Joys of the Virgin, and his numerous hagiographical writings have been seen as attempts both to help 'lewed' men and women to a working understanding of the liturgies they saw enacted from their naves, and also to edify the 'aristocratic lay-clientele of his monastery at Bury and around the Lancastrian court'.[171] However, these welcome revaluations of Lydgate's

---

[168] MS Addit. 14848, fos. 244[r], 248[r].

[169] Pearsall (1970: 25–6, 46 n. 14, 219); Schirmer (1952, trans. 1961: 236, 268).

[170] Rubin (1991: 28, 100, 103, 106, and *passim*); Duffy (1992: 173, 178, 223, 253, 304); Heale (D. Phil. thesis, 1994).

[171] Duffy (1992: 223). Lydgate's *Virtues of the Mass* (*MP* i. 87–115), for example, was written for Alice, countess of Suffolk.

religious writings could usefully be contextualized: it will by now be clear not only that Lydgate's treatment of those narratives in the *Fall* dealing with the relationship between secular and ecclesiastical authority shows that his interest in these issues was active and partisan, but also that the context of Benedictine Bury St Edmunds was one in which such questions were not disinterested topics of theoretical enquiry, but were instead highly contentious and of current importance. This topicality is not confined to local ecclesiastical jockeyings for power: we know international conciliar discussion at Basle about the autonomy of monastic communities was making its influence felt at Bury in the 1430s, the decade throughout which Lydgate was producing the *Fall*. We should be careful to remember that even his major hagiographical poems were produced for powerful political figures; Lydgate is often at his most politically engaged when the subject matter of his work seems most remote from contemporary or secular concerns.[172]

APPENDIX: THE PRAYER OF THEODOSIUS

[*Des Cas* fo. 184ᵛ] Trespuissant dieu createur 7 pere de toutes choses celestes 7 terriennes | qui pour refraindre 7 pugnir les mesfaictz 7 oultrages des hommes plus enclins par aueuglesse de pensee | 7 par fragilite de chair a pechez que a vertus | ordonnas royaulmes 7 seigneuries entre les hommes | affin de les deffendre de iustes [*sic*] ennemys | et de les maintenir en delectable paix. Tresbegnin Iesus qui comme vray dieu et homme approuuas lempire Rommaine quant tu respondis aux fallacieux iuifz que len rendist a cesar ce qui estoit de son droict | et a dieu pareillement le droict qui luy affiert | ie te adore bon roy Iesus | ie te prie et requiers que non mye pour le salut de moy | ne pour le singulier prouffit du royaulme terrien | au gouuernement duquel tu as daigne appeller moy indigne | mais pour lexaulcement 7 accrois de ta saincte foy 7 de leglise catholicque tamye et espouse que tu par le don de ta singuliere grace et benigne faueur me vueilles donner conseil et ayde | parquoy a la gloire de ton nom ie puisse auoir victoire des ennemys de ta foy | 7 des aduersaires du sainct peuple chrestien. Sire dieu ainsi comme tu deliuras de

---

[172] *SS Edmund and Fremund* was composed to commemorate the extended visit of the young Henry VI to Bury in 1433–4 and Lydgate received £3 6s. 8d. for writing *SS Albon and Amphibal* for Whethamstede (Amundesham ed. Riley 1870–1: ii. 256).

seruage de Egypte le peuple de Israel par ta puyssance | 7 sauuas 7
deffendis le sai*n*ct prophete Daniel de la cruaulte des lyo*n*s vueilles moy
secourir | deliurer 7 sauluer des mains et de la puissance des cruelz
ennemys de ta foy | affin que ilz co*n*gnoissent que tu es vng seul dieu |
grant | terrible 7 puissant | qui faiz vainqueurs ceulx qui mettent leur
esperance en toy & non pas en faulx dieux | ne en hommes.

(Most powerful God, Creator and Father of all things in Heaven and
on earth, in order to restrain and punish the misdeeds and offences of
men more inclined, by blindness of thought and by weakness of the flesh,
towards sin than to virtue, you have ordained kingdoms and dominions
among men in order to defend them from unjust enemies and to main-
tain them in the delights of peace. Most benign Jesu, as true God and
man, you supported the Roman Empire when you replied to the false
Jews that we should render to Caesar that which is his by right and,
likewise, to God the rights that belong to him,[173] I adore you good
king Jesu: I beseech you not for my own safety, nor only for the profit
of the earthly kingdom which you have deigned to call me to govern,
unworthy though I am; rather, I pray for the exaltation and increase of
your holy faith and of the Catholic Church—your lover and bride—I ask
that, by the gift of your singular grace and blessed favour, you may be
pleased to give me counsel and aid so that, to the glory of your name,
I may have the victory over the enemies of your faith and [the] adversaries
of all Christ's blessed people. Lord God, just as you delivered by your
power the people of Israel from the bondage of Egypt and saved and
defended the holy prophet Daniel from the cruelty of lions, be pleased to
succour, deliver, and save me from the hands and the power of the cruel
enemies of your faith, so that they may know that you are the one God—
great, terrible, and powerful—who makes conquerors of those who put
their hope in you rather than in false gods or in men.)

---

[173] Matt. 22: 21; cf. Rom. 13: 7.

5

'When the Good Bleeds': Tragedy in the *Fall of Princes*

One of Lydgate's most important additions to his reworking of the *Des Cas* is his use of the word 'tragedye': the term appears eighty-five times in the poem, a large proportion of these instances (fifty-seven) occurring in the post-narrative envoy sections which Lydgate claims he added to the poem at the request of his patron.[1] In so far as the importance of Lydgate's *Fall of Princes* has been acknowledged at all, it has been agreed that the poem occupies a significant (if rather unclear) position in the emergence of tragedy in English.[2] This critical response has a long pedigree: towards the end of the eighteenth century the poet Gray (whose interest in the *Fall* is focused on what he saw as Lydgate's metrical, satirical, and pathetic accomplishments) states in his 'Some Remarks' that the sixteenth-century *Mirror* tragedies illustrate the 'esteem' in which the poem was held.[3] Thomas Warton, writing shortly after Gray's death in 1771, similarly made this connection, but went further, claiming that the *Fall* might 'not improperly [be] styled a set of tragedies'.[4] Early in his 1885 Munich thesis Emil Koeppel noted Lydgate's role in mediating the tragic vision of Chaucer to the writers of the later sixteenth century:

Lydgates großem Reimwerk *The Falls of Princes* [*sic*] . . . welches das Bindeglied zwischen Chaucers *Monkes Tale* und der Schöpfung der elisabethanischen Dichter ist

---

[1] The uses of the term 'tragedy' in the poem are listed in an appendix to this chapter (App. II).

[2] e.g. Norton-Smith's introduction to his 1966 edition of the poems (Lydgate 1966: xi); Kelly (1993: 175).   [3] Gray (1884: i. 409).

[4] Warton (1774–81: sect. xxii, p. 356): I quote from the London reprint of 1875. It is notable that Gray at no point identifies the narratives of the poem (which he terms 'histories') as tragedies (or even as specifically tragic in effect).

(Lydgate's long poem *Fall of Princes* . . . which forms the link between Chaucer's *Monk's Tale* and the work of Elizabethan writers)[5]

This view is echoed by Wilhelm Cloetta in 1890:

in besagter metrischer Bearbeitung dieses letzteren Werkes nennt Lydgate denn auch die einzelnen Erzählungen ebenfalls Tragödien und diese Bezeichnung lebt noch im Myrrour for Magistrates [*sic*] für die daselbst berichteten Geschichten fort

(likewise, in the aforementioned metrical version of this latter work Lydgate also calls some accounts 'tragedies', and this term lives on for narrated histories of the same type in the *Mirror for Magistrates*)[6]

Of course, to make the connection between Lydgate's *Fall* and the later *Mirror* texts is not to say anything new, as a comment in Elizabeth Barrett Browning's posthumously published essay 'The Book of the Poets' drily made clear: any glance at Baldwin's dedication to the 1559 edition of the *Mirror* would show that this debt had been freely acknowledged by the sixteenth-century Lydgateans.[7] The *Fall* had already demonstrated the punishments visited by God on 'euill rulers from time to time, in other nacions', so the *Mirror* continuation was intended to show 'how he hath delt with sum of our countreumen your auncestors, for sundrye vices not yet left [abandoned]'.[8] In my final chapter I examine the nature of Lydgate's influence on subsequent English writers: the present chapter explores the commonly encountered claim that Lydgate's function in the development of English tragic writings was simply to hand on to his successors the achievement (possibly consolidated, certainly exhaustively expanded) of his master Chaucer's 'Monk's Tale'. This is an assumption which has been strengthened both unintentionally (by, for example, likenings of the fictitious monk Daun Piers to the Monk of

[5] Koeppel (Ph.D. thesis, 1885: 3). Here, as elsewhere, I have normalized Koeppel's spelling according to the conventions of modern German.
[6] Cloetta (1890–2: 43). I have found no evidence that Cloetta knew Koeppel's work.   [7] Browning (1863: 133).
[8] *Mirror* ed. Campbell (1938: 65). The preface to this edition clearly states its plan to 'followe where *Lidgate* left' (ibid. 68–70). Cf. also Wayland's projected (but abortive) supplement to the narratives in his undated (*c*.1555) edition of the *Fall* as it appears on the unique (unprinted) title page held at the Victoria and Albert Museum (ibid. 5–6).

Bury)[9] and by explicit assertion:

The poet's insights into the concept of Fortune and human motivation are inconsistent and eclectic. They are scarcely combined into an intelligible pattern . . . Whatever Lydgate's additions and abridgements, the *Fall* lacks formal shape. It is Chaucer's Monk's collection of tragedies considerably filled out.[10]

Although rarely burdened by supportive argument or textual study, such claims as these quickly harden into critical dicta.[11] While it is quite clearly the case that Lydgate *was* influenced by the 'Monk's Tale' (indeed, he acknowledges as much in the prologue to the first book of the *Fall*[12]), it remains to be shown how far the versions of the misfortunes of the poem reflect Lydgate's personal insight (if, indeed, anything as coherent as 'insight' can be discerned) and how far they instead witness to the influence either of Chaucer or of Premierfait's 'Bocace'. The issue, too, of the status of the narratives as 'tragic' at all is one that demands delicate examination: how appropriate is such a term for those narratives in which morally inadequate princes deservedly bring about their own suffering? The interplay between the forces of deliberate vice, unintentional failing, innocent victimization, just retribution of an outraged deity (Christian or pagan), malicious caprice of hostile Fortune, and the straightforward inevitability of a fixed destiny or stellar influence is a complex and daunting one.[13]

The word 'tragedy' was used rarely in European vernaculars in the Middle Ages, and those writers who do use it follow Latin

---

[9] This gambit is encouraged, of course, by Lydgate's witty inclusion of himself as a monk among the Canterbury pilgrims in his *Siege of Thebes* (see Schirmer 1952, trans. 1961: 225–6; Pearsall 1970: 43).

[10] Lydgate ed. Norton-Smith (1966: 127).

[11] It is, for example, striking that such assertions do not offer comparison of Lydgate's text with that of his source: the name 'Premierfait' is rarely found.

[12] *Fall* I. 246–9, 349–50.

[13] In such uncharted territory neat formulations are inadvisable. Henry Ansgar Kelly's claim that 'Lydgate . . . combined Boccaccio's stress on retribution with Premierfait's stress on Fortune to match Chaucer's emphases both on lack of caution and on the unexpectedness of misfortune' (1993: 175) may be one such. Since I wrote this chapter Kelly has added a study *Chaucerian Tragedy* (1997) to his many articles on the evolution of understanding of tragedy in the medieval period: his discussion of Lydgate's *Fall* narratives does not significantly overlap with my findings here inasmuch as no sustained analysis of Lydgate's immediate source text, the *Des Cas*, is offered.

authors in varying considerably in the meanings they attach to the term.[14] Henry Ansgar Kelly has forcefully attacked the mistaken belief that '*tragedy* was a common word and idea in the Middle Ages' as a 'fundamental error' which has given rise to numerous misreadings and misplaced emphases in modern assessments of medieval texts.[15] In fact, Kelly claims, only four English authors of the fourteenth century use the word at all: Chaucer, John Arderne (*c.*1379), John Trevisa (*c.*1387), and the Benedictine chronicler Thomas Walsingham (*c.*1388). Of these, the only writer whose use is sufficiently extensive to demonstrate that he has a sophisticated understanding of the semantic range of the possible meanings of the term is Chaucer.[16] While Walsingham uses the word in his *Chronicon Anglie* to describe events that are suitably grave (the bloody events at Westminster Abbey in 1378 and those in London and St Albans as part of the 1381 uprisings), the term 'tragic' here is vague and undeveloped.[17] Trevisa's use simply occurs in his translation of Higden's list of Seneca's works; Arderne's preface to his *Treatises of Fistula in Ano* shows the confusion current at the time, for he recommends the Bible and 'other tragedieȝ' as useful sources for amusing stories to cheer up anxious patients.[18]

Although he does use the word in his *De casibus*, Boccaccio famously does not describe the narratives of that work as tragedies,[19] despite (or perhaps because of) his sensitivity to the

---

[14] Kelly (1993: xiii).   [15] Kelly (1986: 93).

[16] Chaucer uses the term 'tragedie(s)' on ten occasions and 'tragedien' once; for other usages see the *MED* entry, which gives Chaucer as the only fourteenth-century user.

[17] *Chronicon Angliae*, ed. E. M. Thompson (1874: 206, 301, 312).

[18] Trevisa (1865–86: vol. iv, ch. 9, pp. 402–3). Kelly elsewhere shows that Trevisa is cautious with regard to the term, translating it as *geste* when he encounters it at *Polychronicon* VII. ch. 16 (vii. 461) (Kelly 1993: 170); Arderne ed. Power (1910: 8); Kelly (1986: 93–4).

[19] See H. A. Kelly (1986: 94; 1989*a*: 45; 1989*b*: 192; 1993: xiv, 171). Kelly sails rather close to the wind in some of these assertions, as too does Helen Cooper in her claim that 'the term *tragedia* never appears in the work' (1996: 327). In fact, Boccaccio uses the term in I. ch. 11 ('Adversus nimiam credulitatem'): 'clamitant tragoediae' (fo. 7ᵛ (p. 38)); in his narratives of Astyages (II. ch. 17): 'sic nec euripides nec demosthenes . . . tragoediarum clamores ingentes & eloquentiae mellifluas suauitates . . .' (fo. 19ᵛ (p. 64)); and Nero (VII. ch. 4): 'aurigauit & sepius ac Herou*m* tragoedias finge*n*s Mimoru*m* more saltauit i*n* scena' (fo. 85ᵛ (p. 176)). The point to be made is that none of these instances refers to the text of the *De casibus*.

significance of generic categories.²⁰ Chaucer, however, repeatedly uses the term with reference to his own work: *Troilus and Criseyde* is saluted as 'litel myn tragedye' and the word threads itself throughout his 'Monk's Tale', both in the Monk's own elaborate definitions of the genre and in his accounts of the tribulations of Hugelyn and Cresus.²¹ Kelly has repeatedly argued that this confident application of the term 'tragedy' to modern (non-dramatic) literature is one of Chaucer's greatest achievements. Boccaccio regarded the tragic as an obsolete category of staged performance; it was Chaucer who revived this archaic genre and who should be seen as 'the real inventor of the *de casibus* tragedies':²²

Apart from Dante . . . Chaucer was the first vernacular author anywhere in Europe who not only considered tragedy to be a living genre but also thought of himself as a writer of tragedies.²³

The use of the phrase *de casibus* (or *falle of princis*) as an incipit or explicit to the 'Monk's Tale' in fifteen manuscripts, including Ellesmere, shows how quickly tragedy and the separate *de casibus* tradition coalesce: the terms very quickly became synonymous in English.²⁴

---

²⁰ Boccaccio's 1373–4 lectures on Dante contain a discussion of the reasons for Dante's classification of his *Divine Comedy* as comedy (*Esposizioni sopra la Comedia di Dante*, prologue §§ 17–26, repr. in Minnis and Scott 1988, rev. 1991: 507–9); see Kelly (1989*a*: 47).

²¹ *TC* v. 1786; *CT* VII. 1971/3161, 1973/3163, 1991/3181, 2458/3648, 2761/3951; also VII. 2783/3973. Following convention, I give line references to both group B² and fragment VII of the *Tales*.

²² Kelly (1989*a*: 45; 1989*b*: 192; 1993: 171).

²³ Kelly (1986: 94). Dante considered tragedy to be a living literary genre (the highest style suited to the highest topics, preferably in hendecasyllables) and describes his own lyrics as tragedies (*De vulgari eloquentia* II. 4. 5–8, 8. 8, 12. 3). A discussion of tragedy was to be the subject of the unwritten fourth book of this treatise (see H. A. Kelly 1989*a*: 1–3; 1993: 145–6). Dante's description of the *Aeneid* as a tragedy (*Inferno* XX. 112–13) and his own poem as a comedy (*Inferno* XVI. 127–8, XXI. 1–3, *Paradiso* XXX. 22–4) further illustrates that he regarded neither tragedy nor comedy as necessarily dramatic categories.

²⁴ Root (1941, repr. 1958: 615–16). As incipit in Corpus* (McCormick 1933: 92), Devonshire (ibid. 116), Ellesmere* (152), 'Glasgow' (181), Huntington 144 (543–4), Lansdowne MS 851* (281), and CUL MSS Ii.iii.26 (267) and Mm.ii.5 (337); as explicit in Cardigan (51), Egerton 2864 (143), and 'Manchester' (324); as both in Egerton 2726 (124), Hatton (230), Lincoln (317), and CUL MS Dd.iv.24* (100). This list includes four of the six earliest (pre-1420) manuscripts of the *Tales* (here designated by *): the fact that Hengwrt does not describe the tale as a *de casibus* collection may be taken as evidence against the designation being authorial (see Cooper 1996: 326).

PATRISTIC AND MEDIEVAL UNDERSTANDINGS
OF TRAGEDY

The loss of the ability to read Greek in the later classical period
meant that the formulation of tragedy which has come to be
regarded as the seminal account, namely that of chapters 6, 13,
and 14 of Aristotle's *Poetics*, was unknown in the Latin Middle
Ages and (even though translated twice into Latin in the thirteenth
century) had little influence in the fourteenth and fifteenth
centuries. The popular version of 1256 by Hermannus
Alemannus, bishop of Astorga, which survives in twenty-three
manuscripts and was known to Aquinas, was in fact a translation
of the Arabic commentary on the *Poetics* by Averroes which
represents tragedy and comedy as the 'praise' and 'blame' of
(respectively) good and evil men.[25] Kelly has suggested that the
Averroistic presentation of tragedy as the praise of suffering virtue
would have commanded greater influence in the Latin west if only
the word *tragedy* had been explicitly used in the commentary. As
it was, although popular, the commentary had 'almost no influence'
on the development of understandings of the genre: its readers seem
simply to have failed to connect the subject of the treatise with
the traditions of tragedy which they had inherited from the Latin
fathers.[26]

Although the thirteenth century did yield a Latin translation
taken directly from the Aristotelian text, that of William of
Moerbeke, bishop of Corinth (1278), this survives in only
two manuscripts and was largely unknown: the only person in the
Middle Ages who can certainly be said to have known this version
of the text (and thus to have known Aristotle's formulations at

---

[25] Hardison (1970); Minnis and Scott (1988, rev. 1991: 277–313); cf. Kelly
(1979). Kelly differs from Hardison and Minnis and Scott in his claim that twenty-
four manuscripts of Herman's translation survive (1993: 118). A powerful fictional
attempt to represent the incomprehension of Averroes when confronted by the
concept of dramatic tragedy in Aristotle's text is Jorge Luis Borges's short story
'Averroes's Search'.

[26] Kelly (1993: 118). Interestingly, the moralistic bias of the Averroistic middle
commentary has been credited by Hardison for making the *Poetics* attractive and
assimilable to a medieval audience: 'In effect, it enlisted Aristotle in support of the
most characteristic (and most un-Aristotelian) features of medieval poetic theory'
(Hardison et al. 1974: 83). For the increasing concern of the poet with matters of
ethics, see Minnis and Scott (1988, rev. 1991: 281 and *passim*).

all) is the Paduan Albertino Mussato who in 1314–15 produced his own Senecan drama, *Ecerinis*.[27]

The Latin transmission of understanding of what is meant by the term 'tragedy', then, takes a separate course. Aristotle's definition of tragedy had been that it dealt with an action that was of a certain seriousness (*spoudaion*, variously translated as 'high' or 'worth serious attention').[28] Although he goes on in his thirteenth chapter to advocate a specific plot movement as particularly suitable to tragedy (the fall through error, rather than vice, of a man neither spotlessly virtuous nor straightforwardly evil), the character essential to the tragic in the *Poetics* is primarily a qualitative one— an issue, as it were, of register or timbre.[29] In the first century BC this emphasis on style, rather than content or any prescriptive plot structure, also becomes the keynote of Horace's formulation, who, even though he permits occasional variation from the pattern he recommends, prefers that poets observe a generic decorum: 'swelling eloquence' and an appropriate metre suit tragedies best.[30]

Patristic and later Latin attitudes towards tragedy depart from this 'stylistic' definition of the genre and, as stage drama gradually disappeared, knowledge of classical dramatic forms became increasingly dependent on the definitions supplied in florilegia and by encyclopedists.[31] In his essay *De fabula* (which the Middle Ages believed to have been written by Donatus) the fourth-century grammarian Evanthius offers a definition of the genres of comedy and tragedy which specifies certain social criteria as appropriate for comic and tragic action:

In comedy the fortunes of men are middle-class, the dangers are slight, and the ends of the action are happy; but in tragedy everything is the opposite—the characters are great men, the fears are intense, and the ends

---

[27] H. A. Kelly (1993: 134–43); cf. Kelly (1979a: 161, 186–200). Salutati transcribed Mussato's play into his copy of Seneca's tragedies (Braden 1985: 101). *Ecerinis* survives alongside the *De casibus* in MS Harley 3565.

[28] *Poetics*, vi. I cite the translations of M. Hubbard in Russell and Winterbottom (1972: 97) and Dorsch (1965: 38–9).

[29] A serious play that ends happily is not, it would seem, therefore to be excluded from the category of the tragic: in chapter 14 Aristotle commends Euripides' *Iphigenia in Tauris* (a play that ends happily) as an example of the best kind of tragic action. That Aristotle here contradicts his earlier strictures on happy endings has troubled many critics (see Hubbard's summary (Russell and Winterbottom 1972: 109, n. 5)).

[30] Horace, *Ars poetica*, trans. Russell and Winterbottom (1972: 281–2).

[31] Hardison et al. (1974: 39).

disastrous. In comedy, the beginning is troubled, the end tranquil; in tragedy events follow the reverse order. And in tragedy the kind of life is shown that is to be shunned; while in comedy the kind is shown that is to be sought after.[32]

Although he, too, is more concerned to present the history, structure, and staging techniques of classical drama, Donatus himself also provides a (much briefer) contrast between the two genres in his essay *De comedia*:

Comedy is a form of drama dealing with the various qualities and conditions of civil and private persons. Through it one learns what is useful in life and what, on the contrary, is to be avoided ... by the acting out of the lives of men who live 'in the villages' because of the middle state of their fortunes, not in royal palaces like the characters of tragedy.[33]

In these two accounts new emphases emerge: tragedy differs from comedy in the quality of its characters, the subject matter and complications of the plot ('dangers . . . fears'), the moral lesson to be derived from the action, and the plot movement and final outcome (happy to sad). It is this stress on the miserable ending as the distinctive characteristic which, as Kelly has shown, comes to dominate the Latin tradition 'to the virtual exclusion of other kind of stories'.[34]

Alongside the handbook definitions of the subject matter or style most appropriate to tragedy, the plays of Seneca take a privileged place: for, although he nowhere categorizes his plays as tragedies, Seneca's dramas were highly influential in mediating an understanding of tragedy and in introducing certain key themes which dominate later (especially Boethian) discussions of the genre. Questions of the origin of unexpected suffering, and the appropriate attitude of the victim towards his own misfortune are raised throughout the plays. Seneca himself advocates a Stoic indifference to misfortune in his *De beneficiis*: Fortune cannot conquer the individual who weathers his adversity without

[32] Hardison et al. (1974: 45).
[33] Ibid. 45–6. Plautus defines his *Amphitruo* as a tragicomedy on the grounds of its mixture of social degrees of character ('Prologue' 50–63 (Loeb, 8–10)).
[34] Kelly (1993: 14, 132). Kelly notes that none of Seneca's ten plays in fact conforms to this model: none of them begins happily. Recent classical scholarship disputes the authorship of *Octavia* (see Rosenmeyer 1989: ix; Kelly 1979*b*: 21 n. 1).

allowing his spirit to be crushed.[35] Yet it is noticeable that, while the protagonists of Sophocles' and Euripides' tragedies die painfully, crushed by the intolerable weight of misery that has fallen to their lot, Seneca's heroes are predominantly defiant as their calamitous downfall or suffering closes around them and, thus, die triumphant: Astyanax freely leaps to his death rather than allow himself to be pushed ingloriously (*Troades*, ll. 1088–103). The contrast between Sophocles's Herakles and Seneca's Hercules is an illuminating one.[36]

The uncomfortable truth about Senecan tragedy, however, is that it offers contradictory possibilities, as Gordon Braden has noted: on the one hand his dramas illustrate the quietude and self-sufficient equanimity of the Stoic *sapiens*, while on the other hand this same independence of spirit provides the motivating energy for vaunting ambition, rapacious rivalry, and implacable revenge.[37] The self-control advocated in one of Seneca's most famous maxims ('imperare sibi maximum imperium est') can be used to sanction behaviour of the most violent and insatiable kind.[38] The whole question, then, of whether Seneca's dramas endorse Stoic attitudes of detachment and self-sufficiency at all is a problematic one and is still hotly contested.[39]

By contrast, patristic attitudes towards classical drama and to tragedy (whether staged or narrative) are famously hostile. Tertullian attacks the ancient theatres at length in his *De spectaculis*[40] and Augustine (though he himself once wept for the misfortunes of Dido)[41] denounces the depraved practices and obscenities of the Roman drama in his *De civitate* and finds the appeal of staged tragedy incomprehensible.[42] He asks: 'Why is it that a person should wish to experience suffering by watching

---

[35] Seneca, *De beneficiis*, v. 3. 1–4 (Seneca trans. Basore 1928–35: iii. 296–7).
[36] The poisoned Herakles in *Trachiniai* is broken and weak (' 'Tis I who play the woman now', l. 1076), while the hero of *Hercules Oetaeus* is deified ('I have conquered hell again', l. 1976) (see Herold, Ph.D. thesis, 1994: 184).
[37] Braden (1985: 5–27).
[38] Seneca, Epistle 113. 31 (Seneca trans. Basore 1928–35 iii. 298–9): 'Self-command is the greatest command of all'.
[39] See esp. Rosenmeyer (1989: 160–203). Extracts from Seneca's tragedies were originally in BL MS Royal 12 C. vi (a Bury manuscript, purchased by the Abbey in the fourteenth century), but these are now lost (see Heale Ph.D. thesis, 1994: 110).
[40] Esp. chs. x and xvii.   [41] *Confessiones*, I. 13.
[42] *De civitate Dei*, II. 13, II. 26; cf. *De symbolo*, 4–5, in *PL* xl. 639.

grievous and tragic events which he himself would not wish to endure?'[43] Jerome seems characteristically to have taken only as much from those tragedies he knew as accorded with his already fixed opinions: 'Whole tragedies of Euripides are censures on women.'[44] Although they may have been unsympathetic to the plays with which they were familiar, in their repeated concern with the origins of evil and its inexplicable relationship to the realities of human suffering the Fathers frequently discuss issues which strike at the heart of tragedy in its classical and medieval manifestations. Indeed, much of the urgency of the first book of the *De civitate* arises from Augustine's need to account for the seeming injustice of the adversities and sufferings which befell Christians during the sack of Rome.[45] Augustine's conclusions on the inscrutability of the divine will in permitting evil deeds and human misfortunes (XXII. 1–2) surface again in the work of Boethius: the force of tragedy subsists exactly on this tension between human freedom and inexorable necessity, between voluntary and constrained action.

It is in the *De consolatione Philosophiae* of Boethius (*ob.* 525 or 526) that these two major traditions unite: Christine Herold has argued that the achievement of Boethius is to integrate a revived Greek-idealist attitude towards suffering (born of his unrivalled familiarity with the works of Aristotle and Plato) with Senecan understandings of tragedy.[46] The Stoic influences on the *Consolation* have long been recognized: discussion of the origin of undeserved suffering and the ways in which one should react to adversity form the basis of Boethius' argument in the *Consolation* as he moves towards an understanding of the workings of divine providence and so acquires a philosophical framework in which to set his own imprisonment and impending

---

[43] *Confessiones* III. 2, Augustine trans. Chadwick (1991: 35).

[44] Jerome, *Adv. Jov.* I. 48, in *PL* xxiii. 292A; trans. Schaff and Wace (*Nicene and Post-Nicene Fathers* 1893: 385).

[45] *De civitate Dei*, I. 8–9. The *locus classicus* for the debate of undeserved suffering is, of course, the biblical account of Job. It is interesting that Jerome, whose *Commentarii in librum Job* profoundly influenced later patristic interpretations of the book, included Seneca among his *De viris illustribus*, xii (*PL* xxiii. 662A).

[46] As Chadwick observes (1981: xiii, 133–41), before Boethius the Latin west had access to almost none of the writings of Plato (just half of Cicero's version of the *Timaeus*) or Aristotle. An early fifteenth-century English copy of Boethius was kept at Bury, now in private hands (see Ker 1964: 22).

execution. Henry Chadwick has described the progress of Boethius' argument as a gradual ascent 'from a Stoic moralism to a Platonic metaphysical vision of the divine ordering of an apparently chaotic world'.[47] Certainly the early stages of the work articulate representative Stoic positions: the individual should learn to be self-sufficient ('Let men compose themselves and live at peace . . . And look unmoved on fortune good and bad')[48] and should not seek happiness in external circumstances. (II. pr. 4).The moral virtue of enduring innocent suffering in patient silence is advocated (I. m. 4. 3, II. pr. 7. 68–77), and adversity is declared to be better for one's ethical welfare than prosperity (II. pr. 8. 1–16: 'Good fortune deceives, but bad fortune enlightens'). The first half of the dialogue grants human freedom of will little importance. Boethius is cautioned not to exaggerate his personal misfortune: no one is free from anxiety in this life and, because he has himself previously enjoyed considerable happiness (II. pr. 3. 14–44), he should now quietly learn to be self-sufficient in his misery (II. pr. 4. 27–34). Things could, in fact, be yet worse for him (II. pr. 4. 10–27). The sensible course of action is to resign oneself to the inevitable chains of cause and effect which precipitate the changes in one's fortune.

The opening stages of the third book recap these Stoic arguments until the masterful poem 'O qui perpetua' (III. m. 9), which Chadwick describes as 'both the literary climax of the *Consolation* and a major turning-point in its argument . . . the nodal point in the work', introduces a new Platonic emphasis on the need to fix one's eyes on the divine being and shake off the 'clouds of earthly matter's cloying weight'.[49] The discussions of the third and fourth books consider the origins (and non-being) of evil and the problem of the apparent divine tolerance of suffering (IV. pr. 1. 9–12, et seq.) and introduce the topics which occupy the remainder of the text—namely those of destiny, fate, providence, Fortune, and the role of an uncompromised human

---

[47] Chadwick (1981: 228).
[48] *DCP* I m. 4. 1–3 (Boethius trans. Stewart et al. 1973: 144–5; Boethius trans. Watts 1969: 40).
[49] Chadwick (1981: 232, 234); Boethius, *DCP* III. m. 9. 25: 'dissice terrenae nebulas et pondera molis' (Boethius trans. Stewart et al. 1973: 274; Boethius trans. Watts 1969: 97). Philosophia signals her change of direction in her explicit reference to the *Timaeus* of her servant Plato at III. pr. 9. 100 (Boethius trans. Stewart et al. 1973: 270–1).

freedom of will in a world of apparent determined inevitability (especially v. pr. 3). In the final book it is explained that God's foreknowledge of future contingents does not predetermine their occurrence or undermine the free agency of the individual: the entire problem is short-circuited by the fact that God exists in an order that is not conditioned by time.[50] A belief in divine providence is affirmed as compatible with free will.

Writing after Boethius, Isidore, bishop of Seville (599–636), includes in his encyclopedic *Etymologiae* two definitions of tragedy. The first, in his eighth book, under the heading *De poetis*, asserts that while comedy deals with happy and domestic matters, tragedy treats sad affairs on a larger scale—the histories of kings and public concerns:

Sed comici privatorum hominum praedicant acta, Tragici vero res publicas, et regum historias; item tragicorum argumenta ex rebus luctuosis sunt, comicorum ex rebus laetis.

(If comedies make public the acts of private men, tragedies truly present public matters and the stories of kings; likewise, the arguments of tragedies spring from sorrowful affairs and those of comedies from joyful ones.)[51]

In the eighteenth book, however, he offers a subtly different definition:

De tragoedis. Tragoedi sunt qui antiqua gesta atque facinora sceleratorum regum luctuosa carmine, spectante populo, concinebant.

(*Tragedians.* Tragedians are those who sang in poetry of the ancient deeds and sorrowful crimes of wicked kings while the people looked on.)[52]

The two definitions part company precisely over the issues of blameless suffering which concerned Boethius and Augustine: the first proposes a view of tragic action in which the victims may not necessarily deserve the adversity which is visited upon them, while the second (in which Isidore is indebted to Lactantius) very

---

[50] Namely at v. pr. 4. 11–21 (Boethius trans. Stewart et al. 1973: 404–5), 53–62 (ibid. 408–9); v. pr. 5. 39–50 (ibid. 418–19); v. pr. 6. 59–94 (ibid. 426–9); v. pr. 6. 80–3 (ibid. 426–7): 'And therefore this divine foreknowledge does not alter the proper nature of things, but sees them present to him just such as in time they will at some future point come to be.' Philosophia describes this familiar debate as 'the old complaint' (v. pr. 4. 1 (ibid. 404–5)).

[51] Isidore, *Etymologiae*, VIII. 7 § 6, in *PL* lxxxii. 308C.

[52] Ibid., XVIII. 45, in *PL* lxxxii. 658B. See Kelly (1993: 49) for a discussion of the uncertainty of the text at this point.

clearly offers a view of tragedy in which deserved misfortunes meet the iniquities of evil men.[53] It is noticeable that the two Isidorean formulations define tragedy entirely by its content: the Horatian emphasis on high style is not mentioned. Furthermore, the insistence in the second definition on the blameworthiness of the protagonists of tragedy is (although neither Isidore nor Lactantius would have known it) strikingly un-Aristotelian: adversity as the deserved punishment of criminous behaviour was in the *Poetics* specifically censured for its unsuitability as a subject for tragedy.

CHAUCER: THE MODEL OF THE 'MONK'S TALE'

That Chaucer is a direct beneficiary of Boethius is clearly attested not only by his translation of the *Consolation*, but also by the marked influence of Boethian themes and passages in his other works; two of his more extensive additions to the material of *Il Filostrato* in *Troilus and Criseyde*, for example, are the Boethian 'Canticus Troili' in the closing stages of the third book[54] and Troilus' temple-soliloquy meditation on freedom of will and divine foreknowledge in Book IV.[55] Discussions of the role of Fortune in human affairs, of the countervailing possibilities of moral accountability on the one hand and of unyielding necessity on the other, thread their way throughout the poem as characters (or the narrator) consider their predicaments.[56] Similarly, Boethian elements are conspicuous in the 'Knight's Tale'.[57]

[53] Lactantius, *Divinae institutiones*, VI. 20. 27–30, in *PL* v. 710A: 'item tragicae historiae subjiciunt oculis parricidia, et incesta regum malorum, et cothurnata scelera demonstrant' ('the tragic histories put before the eyes the murders and incests of evil kings and present "elevated" crimes') (Lactantius trans. McDonald 1964: 435); see Kelly (1993: 47).

[54] *TC* III. 1744–71: the source of this song is *DCP* II. m. 8. The song Boccaccio had given Troiolo at *Il Filostrato* III. 74–9, itself derived from *DCP* II. m. 8, is moved by Chaucer to the proem of Book III, at III. 1–42 (see Chaucer ed. Windeatt 1984: 249, 338–9).

[55] *TC* IV. 958–1078: the source here is *DCP* V. pr. 3. For a conspectus of passages in which Chaucer is indebted to Boethius see Windeatt (1992: 99–100).

[56] *TC* II. 281–7; II. 621–32 (cf. *DCP* V. pr. 6. 163–7. Oxford, Bodleian Library, MS Arch. Selden B. 24 has a marginal note at this point reading 'fortuna Troily'); III. 617–20, 1625–8 (cf. *DCP* II. pr. 4. 5–9); IV. 1–14, 270–326.

[57] See Cooper (1996: 68–71).

Discussions of the 'Monk's Tale' and of Chaucer's understanding of tragedy characteristically take Chaucer's *Boece* as their starting point. Not always showing that they recognize Philosophia's ventriloquial irony in acting as the mouthpiece of Fortune, studies often cite the passage in Book II in which she asks: 'What other thyng bywaylen the cryinges of tragedyes but oonly the dedes of Fortune, that with an unwar strook overturneth the realmes of greet nobleye?'[58] There are considerable implications in taking this quotation as a rule of thumb for the kinds of action we might expect tragic narrative to encompass. The emphasis in this 'definition' is one that combines the customary socially elevated register ('greet nobelye') with the actions of a powerful, unpredictable, and hostile Fortuna. Not only does this account of the genre leave no room for discussion of human flaw or fault, but it seems unconcerned with tragedy on an *individual* scale at all; it takes as its subject the wider perspective of countries and societies. Disasters suffered by whole states, rather than just those visited on their leaders (whether iniquitous or innocent), are the adversities lamented here. Accordingly, the kinds of tragic action sketched out by Philosophia differ radically from the Lactantian/Isidorean crime- (and thus blame-) centred accounts. Tragedies need not, in this view, confine themselves to action in which blame is apportionable and in which sufferings and downfalls are thereby open to reasoned analysis or explanation: misfortune of any kind of shape (although still of only one *size*) is permissible, and the inexplicability of the ups and downs of human experience has assumed a central role. It need hardly be said that the privileged emphasis on Fortune's role in the world of human affairs which this 'definition' posits (possibly ironically) is not consonant with the tenor of Philosophia's consolation in the rest of the work.[59] Chaucer's own copy of the *Consolation* (which may be the text surviving as Cambridge, CUL MS Ii. iii. 21) contains an anonymous gloss at this point from Trevet's commentary on the text which reads 'tragedia est carmen de magnis iniquitatibus in prosperitate incipiens et in aduersitate terminans'. The fact that Chaucer's translated gloss at this point

---

[58] *Boece*, II. pr. 2. 67–70. See Boitani (1976: 51); Haas (1987: 45); Kelly (1979a: 192).

[59] Kaske (1957) has made a strong case for the Monk's inadequate Boethianism, but see Lepley's counter-argument (1977–8).

omits the blame-centred (and ultimately Isidorean Book XVIII) element of the Latin note ('de magnis iniquitatibus') to produce a definition from which the issue of guilt has been omitted ('tragedie is to seyn a dite of a prosperite for a tyme, that endeth in wrecchidnesse') suggests that his view of tragedy was closer to the Boethian model of the arbitrary and undeserved blows ('ictus indiscretus') of Fortune.[60] Although the Boethian model may seem eccentric in its view of what is appropriate material for tragedy, Philosophia's mocking reference to the genre in the *Consolation* was nonetheless influential: we know that Mussato and the early humanists were dependent on the Boethian formulation for their understandings of the genre.[61]

When we move from the *Boece* to the 'Monk's Tale' itself, a notoriously fuzzy picture emerges. It is by no means the case that the seventeen narratives supplied by 'daun Piers' conform to the view of tragedy encountered in the *Consolation*; even less do they provide evidence of a coherent understanding of the causes of the downfalls they chart, despite the unambiguous statement of intent with which the Monk opens the sequence:

> I wol biwaille in manere of tragedie
> The harm of hem that stoode in heigh degree,
> And fillen so that ther nas no remedie
> To brynge hem out of hir adversitee.
> For certein, whan that Fortune list to flee,
> Ther may no man the cours of hire withholde.
> Lat no man truste on blynde prosperitee;
> Be war by thise ensamples trewe and olde.[62]

It is noticeable that, although this 'definition' makes no mention of criminous activity, neither does it preclude it: Fortune can withdraw her favour from those who are innocent of any wrongdoing as well as (in a justly punitory way) from the blameworthy. Two figures fall through desert, with Fortune playing no role in their downfall: Lucifer ('for his synne') and Adam ('for mysgovernaunce').[63] Two further narratives unambiguously trace the falls

---

[60] See Kelly (1986: 95–6); (1989*b*: 193); Minnis (1981: 336–7). For Minnis's doubts that the gloss in CUL MS Ii. iii. 21 could furnish Chaucer with all he knew of Trevet's commentary (and for a severe attack on Kelly's misrepresentation of the situation) see *Chaucer's 'Boece'* (1993: 87–9). Scanlon (1994: 222) simplifies the situation unadvisedly.   [61] Haas (1987: 45 n. 5).

[62] *CT* VII. 1991–8/3181–8.   [63] Ibid. VII. 2002/3192; 2012/3202.

of those who have, equally, deserved the disaster that is visited upon them: in these instances, however, Fortune is the force that metes out a justly deserved punishment. Nero is guilty of 'vicius' pride[64] and so Fortune—formerly his friend—playfully exacts her revenge.[65] Holofernes, in a pointed parody of the violent treatment he receives at the hands of Judith, is kissed by a seductive Fortune as a reward for his pomposity and 'presumpcioun'.[66]

Deserved misfortune may not always be the result of a retributive Fortune. Nebuchadnezzar is described as being 'proude . . . and elaat' in the context of his own idolatry and is punished for these sins by God: this fall is then uniquely followed by a return to prosperity when God relents and restores the humbled king to his former dignity.[67] It is no surprise that there are no references to Fortune in a narrative which presents an account of vice justly punished and adversity mercifully alleviated: Nebuchadnezzar's tearful and pious thanksgiving would lack spiritual meaning if his restoration to prosperity had been no more than the caprice of arbitrary Fortune. The narratives of Belshazzar and Antiochus are more puzzling because Chaucer (or his unsophisticated narrator) renders the two kings (Belshazzar being guilty of pride and idolatry[68] and Antiochus of 'hye pride' and 'werkes venymus'[69]) subject equally to the forces of Fortune (who advances the condition of Antiochus) and to those of divine retribution.[70] Even if 'Fortune' here is no more than a shorthand term for the prevailing state of affairs that pertains in God's divine scheme, it is nonetheless unsettling that we find no awareness (or anticipation) of the possible confusion that may result from the conjunction of two terms which are usually perceived as being distinct and, even, antithetical.

Of the remaining ten figures of the Monk's abbreviated tale eight are the innocent victims of a malicious Fortune: Hercules is a 'sovereyn conquerour' and 'noble champioun' whose 'lemman' Dianira is used by Fortune as the agent of her

[64] *CT*, VII. 2463–4/3653–4; 2471–2/3661–2.
[65] Ibid. VII. 2478/3668; 2519–26/3709–16; 2550/3740.
[66] Ibid. VII. 2555–8/3745–8.   [67] Ibid. VII. 2167/3357; 2177–82/3367–72.
[68] Ibid. VII. 2186–90/3376–80; 2241–6/3431–6.   [69] Ibid. VII. 2577/3767.
[70] Ibid. VII. 2189–90/3379–80, 2225 ff./3415 ff. (Belshazzar); 2583/3773; 2599 ff./3789 ff. (Antiochus).

fickleness;[71] similarly, Zenobia, three of the four *moderni* (Peter of Spain, Peter I of Cyprus, and Ugolino della Gherardesca, count of Pisa), Alexander, Julius Caesar, and Croesus of Lydia are all blameless victims.[72] The two remaining cases (of Samson and Bernabò of Lombardy) awkwardly resist neat analysis altogether. Samson, although godly in his habits and a 'noble almyghty champioun', is plainly held responsible for his own downfall: his decision to trust women is his undoing.[73] The narrative of Bernabò Visconti consists of only one stanza, and attribution of vice contentiously rests on the line 'God of delit, and scourge of Lumbardye' (for *delit* is not necessarily sybaritic indulgence any more than a *scourge* is necessarily sinful). Historical evidence is less helpful in determining Chaucer's intent here than might be thought. Although Bernabò's infamous tyranny of Milan is now an established fact, his relations with the English court of the 1380s were good: he had married his niece Violante to Lionel, duke of Clarence, one daughter (Donnina) to the English mercenary Sir John Hawkwood, and had offered a second daughter (Katerina) to Richard II himself.[74] The picture is, indeed, hopelessly 'jumbled' and attempts to harmonize the dissonance usually only end up by distorting the tale yet further.[75]

It is because the understanding of tragedy and of the role of Fortune in generating tragic effect is so blurred in the 'Monk's

---

[71] Ibid. VII. 2095/3285; 2119/3309. The issue of whether Hercules is in fact at fault in trusting his wife is an interesting one: Chaucer, however, deliberately exculpates Dianira from any blame at 2129/3319 (following Ovid and Boccaccio) (see Root, 1941 repr. 1958: 630) and we are clearly not intended to regard her as the ultimate cause of his misfortune.

[72] Ibid. VII. 2367/3557 (Zenobia); 2376/3566 (Peter of Spain); 2397–8/3587–8 (Peter of Cyprus); 2413–14/3602–3, 2445–6/3635–6, 2457/3647 (Ugolino); 2658–62/3848–52, 2669/3859 (Alexander); 2678/3868, 2686/3876, 2694/3884, 2723/3913 (Caesar). The assertion of Croesus' innocence rests on the interpretation of the phrase 'amyddes al his pryde' at 2729/3919: 'pryde' here seems to me to mean no more than 'splendour' or 'prosperity', but cf. Ruggiers, who sees this pride as sinful (1973–4: 90). Equally, Alexander's love of wine and women (2644–6/3834–6) is not presented as causally bound up with his fall.

[73] Ibid. 2021–2/3211–12; 2052–4/3242–4; 2061–2/3251–2. The case of Samson is complicated by the fact that he is not punished with deserved misfortune for any viciousness of life; it is an error of judgement which leads to suffering being inflicted on him by his enemies. (see Grennen (1966) on the influence of the *Roman de la Rose*.)

[74] The date of the composition of the four modern instances is a crux in the dating of the whole tale (see Cooper 1996: 324–5).

[75] Ibid. 333; Socola (1950).

Tale' that it becomes important to examine the effect this muddle has on Lydgate's own treatment of the narratives held in common by the *Fall* and Chaucer's tale: how far is Lydgate's presentation of his *elati* and their downfalls predicated on issues of personal responsibility and how far on the workings of divine foreknowledge, necessitarian fate, or a capricious Fortune? Of Chaucer's seventeen narratives only eleven are treated in the *Fall*: that is, those of Adam, Samson, Hercules, Belshazzar, Zenobia, Ugolino, Nero, Holofernes, Alexander, Caesar, and Croesus. Lucifer, three of the four *moderni*, Nebuchadnezzar, and Antiochus have no counterparts in Lydgate's poem.[76]

Lydgate's narratives of Belshazzar, Nero, Holofernes, and Alexander all differ from their French predecessors in the *Des Cas* in their firmer ascription of blame to the protagonists for their miserable ends. Lydgate's independence of mind is illustrated by the fact that, while he may depart from his French source in these stories, he does not merely adopt wholesale the versions of his influential master: in each case his emphasis also represents a *divergence* from the Chaucerian model. For example, Lydgate's account of Belshazzar differs from that of Chaucer in its elaboration of Belshazzar's sacrilegious offences against Holy Church[77] and, again, the most striking modification of the Nero narratives in the *Des Cas* and the *Canterbury Tales* comes in his marginalization of the role of Fortune. We have seen that Fortune's caprice plays an important role in Chaucer's account: Laurent's text also contains a long excursus on Fortune.[78] In the version in the *Fall* Fortune is only mentioned once (at VII. 608), and in his envoy Lydgate fiercely lays the blame for Nero's deposition on the shoulders of the tyrant himself (as 'cheef merour of diffame').[79] Lydgate's brief account of Holofernes similarly resists the Chaucerian focus on the inscrutable will of Fortune.

---

[76] Nebuchadnezzar simply appears as the agent of divine retribution on the pride and faithlessness of Zedekiah (*Fall* II. 2871–940) and has no narrative of his own. Equally, the Chaucerian narrative of Antiochus provides no model for Lydgate's Antiochus (v. 99–245, from *Des Cas* V. ch. 1 and V. 1471–621, from V. ch. 8) because the two deal with different individuals: Chaucer's is Antiochus IV ('Epiphanes') whose grisly death is recorded in II Maccabees 9. Lydgate's Antiochus III ('the Great') and Seleucus III ('Ceraunus') are the father and uncle respectively to Chaucer's villain. I discuss Lydgate's Adam, Samson, and Hercules narratives in my analysis of the first book of the *Fall* below.   [77] *Fall* II. 3550.
[78] *CT* VII. 2519–26/3709–16.   [79] *Fall* VII. 784.

But if these narratives demonstrate Lydgate's firm attribution of blame in *Fall* narratives for which there are Chaucerian precedents (whether by the elimination of mitigating circumstances and outside forces—divine or fortunal—or by the insertion of censure and additionally damning evidence), they do so without reference to, or even significant dependence on, the 'Monk's Tale'. Four of the remaining narratives held in common by the two poets (those of Ugolino, Julius Caesar, Croesus, and Zenobia) present a slightly different picture, for each of these characters suffers misfortune undeservedly in Chaucer's accounts. This innocence is achieved at some cost in the case of Ugolino of Pisa, as Piero Boitani, Richard Neuse, and Helen Cooper have shown in their analyses of Chaucer's debts to Dante's account of his meeting with the evil and carnivorous count, in *Inferno* XXXIII.[80] Daring though Chaucer's transformation of the guilty and unrepentant Dantesque villain into his own victim-aristocrat may be, its influence on Lydgate is slight. The Hugolyn we find in the last book of the *Fall* is presented in just one stanza: we are told that he was the victim of insurrection and that he was killed in prison (rather than starving away, as did Chaucer's count)[81] and that this was 'cruel & vnky*n*de'.[82] Nothing is said of Ugolino's innocence (or otherwise) or of Fortune (who is strongly present in Chaucer's tale) and Lydgate dismissively concludes the stanza 'no mor of hy*m* I fynde'.[83] In all this Lydgate follows his French source fairly closely, for Laurent is similarly brief and similarly uninterested in Ugolino's innocence:

ie vy huguelin iadis noble conte de Pise qui a moy venoit affin q*ue* ie escripuisse son cas. Cestuy conte faisoit tresgra*n*s pleurs et tresprofons gemirs disa*n*t en brief q*ue* la cruaulte des Pisains ses citoyens fut enuers luy si gra*n*t q*ui*lz co*n*traignirent luy et ses enfans mourir cruelleme*n*t 7 par mesaise.

(I saw Ugolino, the former count of Pisa, coming to me in order that I write his fall. This nobleman, with much weeping and the profoundest of groans, said that the cruelty of the people of Pisa against him had

---

[80] See Boitani (1976); Neuse (1991: 151-9); Cooper (1999: 50-2). Neuse describes the encounter as the 'most elaborate, gruesome and enigmatic' episode in the *Inferno*. For the popularity of the Ugolino story see Wallace (1997: 314).
[81] CT VII. 2455/3645.   [82] *Fall* IX. 2054.   [83] Ibid. IX. 2055.

been so great that they had forced him and his children to suffer and die cruelly.)[84]

From this it seems unlikely that Lydgate had access to a version of the 'Monk's Tale' which included Ugolino's story: possibly his manuscript may not have contained any of the *moderni* (or, having been positioned, as in Ellesmere, at the end of the Monk's tale, these four narratives may have become detached before Lydgate encountered his codex). As eleven of the extant *Canterbury Tales* manuscripts have defective (or absent) texts of the 'Monk's Tale', but only two of these (MS Bodley 686 and the 'Paris' MS) can be dated among the ten earliest (pre-1440) witnesses, we have inadequate evidence to enable an identification of Lydgate's copy.[85] Lydgate's ignorance of the tale is especially irksome in that Ugolino's fall is the only one which is specifically labelled a 'tragedie' by the Monk in the course of its narration (at VII. 2458/3648): if this designation carried any particular weight for Chaucer it is doubly regrettable that Lydgate never seems to have seen it.

Lydgate's versions of the narratives of Caesar and Croesus of Lydia are equally independent of Chaucer. As we have seen, Lydgate's longest treatment of the life of Julius Caesar comes in *The Serpent of Division*, where his attitude towards Caesar is so consistently benign that he can even exert himself to efface the obvious criminality of Caesar's behaviour (the crossing of the Rubicon is a clear example of this): Lydgate's virtuous pagan

---

[84] *Des Cas* fo. 211ʳ (IX. ch. 20). Cf. Boccaccio's 'Infortunati quidam' (fo. 110ʳ (p. 227)). If Lydgate's highly abbreviated treatment of Laurent's description of the encounter between Dante and Boccaccio at IX. ch. 23 ('Numerosa querulorum turba') is of significance, then it may also be that Lydgate had only a vicarious knowledge of the poet. Certainly, Dante's Italian texts would have been beyond him. For the debate on Lydgate's poor knowledge of Italian see Koeppel (Ph.D. thesis, 1885: 76–83): 'er schöpfte nur aus den poetisch minderwertigen schriften Boccaccios und Petrarcas und kannte wohl Dantes Ruhm, nicht aber sein Werke' (p. 82).

[85] The 'Monk's Tale' is notoriously textually unstable in the positioning of the four *moderni*, with two-thirds of the manuscripts placing them after Zenobia, but the best (including Hengwrt and Ellesmere) placing them last. None of the extant manuscripts lacks the *moderni* only, although six do lack the 'Monk's Tale' completely (MSS Addit. 25718, Bodley 686, 'Holkham', Laud 739, Rawlinson poet. 223, and, together with the whole of the B² group, Harley 7335) and five have it only in part (MSS Egerton 2863, Laud 600, 'Lichfield', Rawlinson poet. 149, and Paris, BN MS *fonds anglais* 39) (see Tokunaga 2001: 223–35).

could not be further removed from Lucan's demonic dictator.[86]
The Caesar narrative in the *Fall*, following the bias of Laurent's
account in *Des Cas* VI. ch. 11, is similarly favourable: Laurent
had lamented the fact that Fortune had decided to assail the
'noble et victorieux Cesar' whom she had aided and advanced
for such a long time, particularly as the downfall, when it
comes, is dissembled under a veil of friendship ('vmbre de paix
et de amytie').[87] Caesar's only real vice is his naivety: he could
have avoided his fall had he only recognized the disloyalty of
Brutus and Cassius. Lydgate does not conceal his regard for
Caesar—indeed, he claims that this fall is the most sorrowful in
the collection:

> Thoruh al this booke rad ech tragedie,
> Afforn rehersid & put in remembrance,
> Is non mor woful to my fantasie,
> Than is the fall of Cesar in substaunce.[88]

Accordingly, Lydgate enhances the renown of Caesar by introducing
a catalogue of his military successes (at VI. 2822–8) and omits
Laurent's description of the tearful petitions of Brutus and Cassius
to Bocace (bewailing 'leurs dures fortunes'), thereby eliminating
the possibility that the reader might feel any degree of pity for the
murderers of his hero. As Bergen noticed, the 'boydekyns' of the
Capitol assassination and the conflation of the conspirators into
one 'Brutus Cassius' may result from a reading of the Chaucerian
version: indeed, the error is one Lydgate makes in *The Serpent*,
in his coronation ballad to Henry VI, and elsewhere in his minor
works.[89] However, these seem to be the only striking influences
Chaucer's poem wields over the Lydgatean version; although it is
true that Lydgate *does* introduce the forces of pagan deities and
adverse Fortune into his envoy on Caesar's fall, it is not necessary
to attribute this to the influence of Chaucer's insistent emphasis

---

[86] Given that Chaucer praises his Caesar so highly, the dedication of the story
to Lucan at VII. 2719/3909 is presumably ironic. Lydgate elsewhere praises Caesar,
in *MP* ii. 627 (ll. 62–4) and 783 (ll. 73–4), and laments his fall at II. 825 (ll. 89–95).

[87] *Des Cas*, fos. 142ʳ, 142ᵛ.

[88] *Fall* VI. 2871–4. For Boccaccio, Pompey—not Caesar—is the noblest example
of mortal misfortune (*De casibus* fo. 66ʳ (p. 157)): 'Neminem reor mortalium
ex tam sublimi vertice corruisse' (VI. ch. 10: 'Pauca auctoris verba').

[89] *Fall* VI. 2868 (*CT* VII. 2702/3892) and VI. 2877 ff. (*CT* VII. 2697/3887).
Cf. *Serpent* 65; *MP* ii. 627 (l. 65) and 824 (l. 92).

on the role of Fortune in the narrative. Laurent's account contains the lengthy tirade on the workings of fickle Fortune which I have already cited and this, as much as Chaucer's tale, may lie behind the one-line reference to Fortune in Lydgate's envoy.[90]

The influence of Chaucer on Lydgate's fall of Croesus of Lydia is similarly uncertain. Sources for accounts of the life of Croesus are plentiful and include not only the section Boethius devotes to him in the *Consolation*, but also the account provided by the Boethian section of the *Roman de la Rose*.[91] Certainly Lydgate's narrative is more clearly Boethian in tone than those of Chaucer and Laurent. Neither Laurent nor Lydgate includes the dream which marks the reversal of Croesus' fortunes in Chaucer's tale. However, whereas Laurent's king is specifically saved from being burned by a freak rainstorm sent by God ('le deux miracles que dieu auoit fait pour sauuer le roy cresus'),[92] Lydgate differs bewilderingly from both this and Chaucer's Fortune-led account: Jupiter, God, *and* Fortune are all accredited with the miraculous storm (even though he had opened his second book with an assurance that Fortune would play a less significant role in the narratives than she had in Book I).[93] This, however, is Lydgate's only reference to Fortune; whereas Chaucer's king is saved from death by Fortune and then killed by the agency of the gods, the downfall of Lydgate's (and Laurent's) Croesus merely takes the form of dispossession of his kingdom because Cyrus takes pity on his captive enemy.[94]

Chaucer's narrative of Zenobia, queen of Palmyra, is a mixture of two Boccaccian narratives—that of *De casibus* VIII. ch. 6 and of *De mulieribus claris* XCVIII—and it is, in Peter Godman's

[90] *Fall* VI. 2894.
[91] *Roman* ll. 6459 ff.; *DCP* II. pr. 2. 34–6. The account of Croesus' dream and his final hanging, which are found in both Chaucer and the *Roman* versions (but not in Lydgate or his predecessors) derives from William of Conches's Boethius commentary, which we know Jean de Meun to have used. (See Minnis (1981) and Dwyer (1976), esp. pp. 35–49, which contain a discussion of Lydgate's version.)
[92] *Des Cas* fo. 43[r].
[93] *Fall* II. 3711–17; *CT* VII. 2737–9/3927–9; cf. *Fall* II. 1–161. Possibly in response to his patron's request that moralizing envoys be included to enhance the didactic value of the collection, Lydgate voices a more retributive understanding of tragedy in the prologue to Book II, offering his accounts of deserved misfortune as a *speculum* for his readers: 'The fall off on is a cleer lanterne | To teche a-nother what he shal eschewe.'
[94] *CT* VII. 2751–6/3941–6; *Fall* II. 3718–24; cf. *CT* VII. 3138–40/4328–30.

words, the only instance 'in the *Canterbury Tales* as a whole where Chaucer relies upon the Latin works of Boccaccio'.[95] The two Boccaccian narratives are strikingly different in their emphases: the Zenobia of the *De mulieribus* is presented in a harshly political and military light as we are told that she overcomes her natural feminine weaknesses to become a warrior and wrestler. This Zenobia serves in armour in her husband's attack on Sapor of Persia, she assumes the royal purple after her husband's death, and drinks with her captains and with foreign princes as would any king. She is a hunter, able linguist, and—most importantly—practises strict sexual abstinence in her marriage after the birth of her two sons.[96] In this narrative characteristically feminine qualities are seen as debilitating weaknesses; Zenobia is ironically *mulier clara* precisely because she has abandoned the frailties of her sex. The *De casibus* narrative is significantly less strident: Zenobia is strong ('corporeo rubore') and experienced in the arts of war ('bellicis disciplinis instructa'), but there is no suggestion that to be so is in tension with her womanhood. The Sapor military campaign is not mentioned, and it is not until *after* Odenatus' death that she (endowed with a manly courage, 'vero virili . . . animo viro') abandons soft clothing (only *now* described as a feminine weakness) for severe and glittering armour: 'induta no*n* mollitie muliebris3 quada*m* militari austeritate refulgens'.[97] Her fatherless sons wear the imperial insignia, not she herself, and there is no mention of her barrack-room drinking, nor (as in *De mulieribus*) that she connived at the death of her stepson Herodes out of disgust at his effeminacy. The *De casibus* account also makes Zenobia a noble victim of Fortune and contains four references to the vagaries of Fortune and a long section on 'disharmonious change' ('dissonis mutationibus'): Fortune is not mentioned in the *De mulieribus*.[98] The woman who had been the equal of Dido and Semiramis is finally condemned by the Romans not only to obscurity, but to those very domestic and feminine chores which she had renounced on her husband's death.[99]

[95] Boitani (1976: 50–2); Godman (1983: 272). The text of the Zenobia narrative is in Boccaccio ed. Zaccaria (1967: 406–15) (there numbered 100 in the sequence); trans. Guarino (1963: 226–30).   [96] Boccaccio ed. Zaccaria (1967: 408).
[97] *De casibus* fo. 92ᵛ (p. 192).   [98] Ibid. fo. 93ʳ (p. 193).
[99] *De casibus* fo. 93ʳ (p. 193): 'nunc velata cogitur muliercularum audire fabellas'.

Chaucer's Zenobia (the subject of his Monk's longest narrative) introduces new elements to the story: his Zenobia has Persian (and not Ptolemaic) ancestry and the Monk cheerfully claims Petrarch as his source. Like the *De mulieribus* text, she is given to hunting and arms from her childhood, is studious and gifted in 'sondry tonges', and is sexually continent in marriage.[100] The Sapor account is given due prominence and the widowed Zenobia herself 'myghtily/The regnes heeld'.[101] Even though the slur that she caused the death of Herodes and the claims that Zenobia's masculine lifestyle specifically represents a defeat of feminine weakness (both distinctive *De mulieribus* positions) are omitted, and although Fortune is once mentioned and Zenobia's sons wear 'kynges habit' (as in the *De casibus* traditions), there is nothing to suggest that the *De casibus* account was of great influence.[102] Decorative details and exotic proper names provide an elevated style, but Zenobia's fall arouses less pathos and is less rhetorically lamented than is the case in the *De casibus*.

Laurent's account of the 'femme cheualeureuse' closely follows its source. While Zenobia is trained in 'disciplines darmes', she plays no part in the Sapor campaign and does not wear armour before her husband's death. She dresses her sons 'en la maniere des empereurs de Ro*mm*e' and follows them in procession; Fortune plays a central role and is the subject of several extended laments, while the whole concludes with a gnomic observation on 'le vent de fortune qui souffle les haultes choses . . . qui est trescertaine que nulz hommes ne leschappe'.[103] Lydgate's position is, therefore, extremely interesting: while his direct French source represents a redaction of the *De casibus* Zenobia, at the outset of his own narrative Lydgate reveals his indirect contact with the *De mulieribus* tradition when he salutes Chaucer's achievement in the 'Monk's Tale' version and (twice referring to the narrative as a 'tragedie') claims that it is his intention to abbreviate his own

---

[100] *CT* VII. 2307/3497, 2276–94/3466–84. The description of Odenake as sexually 'wilde or tame' (2291/3481) playfully echoes the earlier account of Zenobia's pursuit of 'wilde beestes' (2263/3453).

[101] Ibid. VII. 2327–8/3517–18.

[102] Ibid. VII. 2367/3557, 2343/3533; *pace* Wright (1957: 5); Godman (1983: 278).

[103] *Des Cas fos.* 175ᵛ and 176ᵛ. Laurent here translates Boccaccio's warning to respect the winds of Fortune or fall instead to certain death: 'ut aut omnem Fortunae spirantis auram timeatis; aut sopiti impulsu minimo in mortem certissimam corruatis' (fo. 93ʳ (p. 193)).

account in deference to the 'souereyn poete of Brutis Albioun'.[104] Examination of the *Fall* version shows a minor Chaucerian/*De mulieribus* influence (Zenobia is 'expert in al langage' and wears armour early),[105] but the Laurentian/*De casibus* influence is, as would be expected, stronger (for example, there is no mention of Zenobia's chastity). Although he omits Laurent's reference (from the *De casibus*) to Dido and Semiramis and his longer sections on the power of Fortune, Lydgate concludes with his own version of the 'wind of Fortune' adage.[106]

Any conclusions from this analysis of Lydgate's treatment of the Chaucerian narratives should be drawn with care, for in six of the eight narratives the evidence is too scanty for us to be certain that Lydgate was influenced by the 'Monk's Tale' versions. Even when, as with Zenobia and Caesar, the ground seems a little firmer, the influence of Chaucer is neither strong nor consistent: Lydgate inserts the influence of Fortune into his Croesus story and retains the fortunal element (if in an abbreviated manner) he found in Chaucer's stories of the innocent Caesar and Zenobia, suggesting that he is happy to place *undeserved* tragedies involving the intervention of Fortune alongside those falls which might be seen as the workings of justice.

Certain questions still remain unanswered: it is noticeable that three of the four narratives of the guilty turn on biblical subjects and that the fourth (that of Alexander), is given an envoy which explicitly discusses his tyranny as an expression of his opposition to God. In that the biblical context forms a more obvious link between these narratives than does the connection of guilt (which Lydgate has in any case enhanced), we should guard against allowing what may be a minor pattern of similarity to obscure a major one. Equally, the significance of human behaviour in the workings of Lydgate's tragic falls has yet to be examined: are falls

[104] *Fall* VIII. 674. Cf. Lydgate's similar profusions at the outset of his Lucretia narrative, at II. 974–80, and VI. 3627–33.
[105] *Fall* VIII. 684, 687. This last is a confusing detail, for Lydgate also includes the contrary Laurentian/*De casibus* claim that she donned her armour *after* the death of her husband: if this suggests (as would seem the only possibility) that Lydgate did not think that she wore armour for the first time when widowed, then he evidently did not absorb the full symbolic significance of the death of Odenate in the *De casibus*, for there it is only when her husband dies that Zenobia is fully released into masculine behaviour.
[106] *Fall* VIII. 740–2.

and suffering 'tragic' only when they are Fortune-generated? How far does the intention of the individual condition the intervention of Fortune (or other supernatural forces) in his or her downfall?

Narratives (such as those about Zenobia) in which innocent individuals are deprived of any power to control their own experiences or avert the suffering or misadventure that visits them are, of course, deeply affecting. However, the pathos these portraits generate should not blind us to the fact that such narratives are not in any philosophical sense different from those in which blameworthy and vicious characters are punished by the intervention of forces such as Fortune or Providence. Issues of guilt (and, concomitantly, of justice), while certainly shaping emotional responses to stories of misfortune, do not of themselves alter the fact that the principle of human freedom of will is suspended when chance intrudes into human affairs to determine the course of events (for good or ill, whether justly or unjustly) in such a way as to deprive human agents of their power to alter these predisposed occurrences. It is an unnegotiable tenet of medieval theology that without freedom of action there can be neither virtue nor vice, merit nor blame, innocence nor guilt. As Aquinas remarks:

> If there is nothing free in us, but the change which we desire comes about of necessity, then we lose deliberation, exhortation, command and punishment, and praise and blame, which are what moral philosophy is based on.[107]

> Man is free to make decisions. Otherwise counsels, precepts, prohibitions, rewards, and punishments would all be pointless.[108]

Or, as Herbert McCabe phrased it, human actions may indeed be *motivated*, but to remain free they cannot be *caused*.[109]

In any discussion of necessity and human freedom of will, however, it is important not to confuse modern freedom-centred assumptions with the orthodox theology which Lydgate would have known. It is not part of Thomistic teaching that the freedom of the individual (uncoerced though it is) is entirely undetermined: even contingent (unnecessitated) acts for him are not 'free' in the

---

[107] *Quaestiones disputatae de potentia*, 6, *STh* Ia. q.83 a.1 ('De libero arbitrio'). I quote from the translation given by Brian Davies (1992: 175).
[108] *STh* Ia. q.83 a.1, Blackfriars edn., vol. xi (Aquinas ed. 1970: 238–9).
[109] McCabe (1987: 13).

absolute and untrammelled, voluntarist sense of the term.[110] For Aquinas nothing can be done at all without God's will: even the free acts of men are willed by him. Whereas a modern outlook might assume that a God who is responsible for what the individual does (in any sense other than simply allowing it to happen) has prevented that individual from acting freely, this is not the medieval position. Theologically speaking, human actions can be caused by God without thereby ceasing to be free because this is exactly what grace involves (the alignment of the individual will with the divine).[111] God's foreknowledge of future contingent acts is affirmed as certain and infallible, not simply because God sees all contingent things as present from eternity (the Boethian argument), but because his will causes all things—even though some may be willed to be necessary and others only to be contingent (that is, to be variable and open to alternatives).[112] The Thomist position on the relationship between human freedom and the divine will is simply that nothing *created* acts on an individual to determine his or her behaviour and, because God is *creator* rather than *creature*, the divine will cannot properly be said to infringe our human freedom:

It does not of necessity belong to liberty that what is free should be the first cause of itself . . . God is the first cause . . . [and] by moving voluntary causes he does not deprive their actions of being voluntary.[113]

Debates about divine will and coercion are among the knottiest parts of medieval thought: the modern mind finds it hard to appreciate the distinction that human acts are 'free' not because they are independent of God's causal action, but because they are free of the determining influence of other *created* things. Any binary opposition between acts undertaken freely (and for

---

[110] Scotist and Occamist critiques of the Thomist view of contingency and the moral responsibility of created (human) wills are set out in Marilyn McCord Adams, ii (1987: 1115–50).   [111] Brain Davies (1992: 266–7, 144–9).
[112] *STh* Ia. q.19 a.8 ('Does God's will impose necessity on things?'), Blackfriars edn., vol. v. (1a 19–26), 34–9: see also Ia. q.22 a.4: Aquinas does use the Boethian argument elsewhere; namely, *In I Sent* d.38 q.1 a.5. Issues of necessity and contingency were among the theological positions defended by Etienne Tempier, bishop of Paris, in his condemnation of 219 erroneous propositions in 1277; namely, propositions 21, 38, 47, 60, 66, 142, 143, 160, 195, 196, 197, 198, 199, 206, 207 [renumbered and reordered by Mandonnet as 93–107], trans. Fortin and O'Neill in. Lerner and Mahdi (1963: 345–6).
[113] *STh* Ia. q.83 a.1 ad.3, trans. Brian Davies (1992: 177–8).

which one might expect to be held responsible) and those
predetermined by outside forces (of God, the gods, Fortune, fate,
or chance) in fact simplifies the medieval situation, where God's
providence and causal activity oversee all events, where even chance
effects must have causes, and where Fortune can function as the
obedient deputy (or 'bailiff') of God:[114] these are issues which come
to the fore in Lydgate's treatment of the figure Fortuna in the *Fall*.

BOCCACCIO, LAURENT, LYDGATE, AND FORTUNE

In his prologue to the first book of the *De casibus* Boccaccio sets
forth his reasons for collecting stories of those whose prosperity
has turned to misery:

Exquirenti mihi quid ex labore studiorum meorum possem forsan
reipublice vtilitatis adferre, mores hominum illustrium maxime obtulere
sese obuiam: quos dum illecebres turpique libidine foedos intuerer:
effrenesque non aliter quam si fortunam in sopnum [*sic*] perpetuum
soporassent haerbis aut cantato carmine . . . aduerterem: Nec ob id
solum caeteros pro viribus premere: quinimmo et in ipsum rerum omnium
opificem stulta quadam temeritate consurgere cernerem: obstupui.
Et dum damnarem dementiam: longam quepii patris patientiam
admirarer . . . Et quid deus siue (vt eorum more loquar) fortuna in elatos
possit describere . . . Set ex claris quosdam clarissimos excerpsisse sat
erit. vt dum senes fluxosque principes et dei iudicio quassatos in solum
reges viderint: dei potentiam: fragilitatem suam: & fortunae lubricum
noscant: & laetis modum ponere discant: Et sic aliorum periculo suae
possint vtilitati consulere.

(I was wondering how the labour of my studies could benefit the state
when I recalled the conduct of illustrious princes. These rulers are so
attracted to vice and debauchery, are so unrestrained, that it is as if they
had put Fortune perpetually to sleep either with drugs or with spells . . .
I realize how they not only oppress others with their power but also,
which is worse, with foolish temerity rise up against the Worker of all
good Himself. I was astounded. I condemned their folly and admired the
everlasting patience of our Father . . . Therefore I shall relate examples of
what God or (speaking their own language) Fortune can teach them
about those she raises up . . . From among the mighty I shall select the
most famous, so when our princes see these rulers, old and spent,

---

[114] Cf. *The Middle French 'Liber Fortunae'*, ed. Grigsby (1967: 15).

prostrated by the judgment of God, they will recognize God's power, the shiftiness of Fortune, and their own insecurity. They will learn the bounds of their merry-making, and by the misfortunes of others, they can take counsel for their own profit.)[115]

Though the princes of the present day are plainly castigated for their vicious living, Boccaccio is by no means insistent that the subjects of his narratives (the 'consternatos duces') are themselves always to be considered blameworthy. Indeed, the only hint that the princes might deserve their misfortunes comes in the claim that they have been 'prostrated by the judgment of God'. The contrast with Premierfait's translation of this prologue is striking:

Iay pense en mon cueur de demener mon present liure aulcunesfois par exemples, & de escrire quelle puissance ait dieu contre les orgueilleux qui appellent dieu fortune ... mais des nobles hommes & femmes Il me souffist prendre aulcuns des plus nobles affin que quant les hommes verront par escript les princes du monde estre febles & vains, & les roys ferus & quotis Iusques a [la] terre par le Iugement de dieu, Ilz ayent congnoissance de la puissance diuine & de la feblesse et muablete de lestat de fortune, & que Ilz ayent mesure & attemprance entre les bieneuretez mondaines.

(I intended to furnish my current book occasionally with examples, and write of the power of God against those proud folk who dub God 'fortune' ... but I only needed to select a few of the very greatest from among those noblemen and women for people to be able to see that the princes of this world are weak and shallow, and that kings have been shaken and struck to the ground by the judgement of God; in this way people will understand the power of God and the frailty and mutability of Fortune, and they will exercise moderation and temperance in their worldly prosperity.)[116]

There are several notable changes here. Boccaccio's graceful point that what misguidedly goes by the name of 'fortune' is no more than the power of God is twisted by Premierfait into an attack on the pride of those who call 'Fortune god, or God

---

[115] *De casibus* fo. 1ʳ (p. 25), repr. in *Fall* ed. Bergen vol. i, p. xlvii; trans. Brewer Hall (1965: 1–2).

[116] *Fall* ed. Bergen vol. i, p. lii. This is the first of Laurent's three prefatory passages; none is printed in Jean Petit's 1538 edition, nor is the long Berry preface (rewritten for the B-version) often found in the sixty-eight extant manuscripts of the *Des Cas* (see Gathercole 1968: 39).

fortune'. Furthermore, Laurent's tendentious (and over-specified) rendering of 'senes fluxosque principes' as 'les princes du monde estre febles & vains, & les roys ferus' suggests that his protagonists' misfortunes are deserved. Equally, Boccaccio's clear phrase pointing to the power of Fortune ('fortunae lubricum') is softened by Laurent a little and rendered as 'la *feblesse et* muablete de lestat de fortune'; the passage ends with a short moral on the inability of worldly goods to supply protection for those who are punished by God.

Premierfait's modifications to the role Fortune plays in the *Des Cas* are again seen in his dedicatory letter to Jean, duke of Berry: after its opening flatteries, the letter takes the form of a five-point exposition of the reasons for earthly matters being subject to Fortune, advice on how man may free himself from the power of Fortune, and analyses of the present condition of the three orders of the Church, of secular nobility, and of rural labourers. The first two of these discussions most clearly reflect what we will see to be Premierfait's habitual distrust of the category of Fortune: suffering enters the world entirely as a result of the primal sin of Adam and Eve and, while the human condition may seem to be subject to an arbitrary Fortune and her wheel, all in fact takes order from the will of God, whose chamberlain Fortune is:

Et celui qui obtient ce que il desiroit semble estre iuchiez ou hault degre de la roe de fortune, qui comme chamberiere de dieu pour la punicion de leurs pechies, vne foiz haulse et autre foiz abaisse hommes et femmes sans discreccion ne aduiz et non pas selon la quantite des merites des hommes. Maiz par vne confuse maniere dont les causes sont euidens a dieu. Maiz les hommes comme ignorans de lordrenance diuine ne peuent congnoistre telles causes . . . En la punicion des deulx premiers parens qui orguilleusement enfraingnirent la loy a eulx donnee, la iustice de dieu fut estroitement et droictement gardee parce que tous participent la mocquerie de fortune qui se Ioue en esleuant et en trebuchant les hommes.

(The person who gains whatever he desires seems to be perched at the very top of Fortune's wheel—she who (as the chamberlain of God) sometimes raises men up, and on other occasions brings them down in punishment for their sins. She acts without either showing discretion or taking advice and pays no regard to an individual's merits, but instead conducts herself in a confused fashion understood only by God Himself. Mankind, however, ignorant of divine ordinances, cannot know the causes of such things . . . In punishing our two first parents, who in their pride broke the law that had been given to them, the justice of God was strictly and directly exacted. We all suffer the mockery of Fortune who amuses herself by raising us up only to cast us down again.)[117]

Using the terminology that will reappear at the end of the Andalus section, Laurent says that Adam and Eve unfastened misfortune from its 'forte coulompne', but agrees with 'alain le poete' in that while it may seem to men that human affairs are random and that the evil are unjustly successful, this mistaken belief arises only from our limited perspective:[118] all is divinely sanctioned. Because there is no room for Fortune in so strictly voluntarist a position, Premierfait explicitly claims that it is possible to free oneself from its influence. The path of virtue, as Seneca teaches, places the wise man beyond the power of all misfortune:

Se donques homme veult soy affrancher et exempter de malheur Il lui conuient auoir la uertu de sapience qui en soy seule contient tous biens sans commixcion de mal. Le sage homme est en soy si parfait et si bienheureux que neiz pour bien viure Il na besoing Iamy. Le sage nest point subget a fortune, comme Seneque le preuue par vne exemple de demetrius ancien Roy de Surie

(So, if someone wishes to be free of unhappiness, it behoves him to acquire the virtue of wisdom, which contains in itself all that is good, with no hint of evil. He who is wise is self-sufficient and is so blessed that he has no need of any friend to help him live well; a wise man is by no means subject to Fortune, as Seneca demonstrates in his story of Demetrius, the king of ancient Syria)[119]

The emphases in this French preface exactly accord with the biases to be found at work in Laurent's treatment of the narratives of the *De casibus*: the category of Fortune is made redundant and concomitantly greater weight is placed on the freedom of the individual as a moral agent.

---

[117] *Fall* ed. Bergen vol. i, p. lvi.

[118] I have not been able to find this precise point in the work of Alan of Lille: the long oxymoronic description of the nature of Fortune in *Anticlaudianus* VIII. 1–3 may be the passage Laurent has in mind (especially if this Boethian maxim was supplied in the text or florilegium in which he read it by scribal addition or marginal annotation) (*PL* ccx. 559–62; Alan of Lille trans. Sheridan 1973: 189–91). Pembroke College Cambridge MS 119, a copy of the *Anticlaudianus*, may have been held at Bury.

[119] MS Royal 18 D. VII (fo. 3ʳ) and MS Bodley 265 (fo. 3ʳ) read 'damy' for 'Iamy' (see *Fall* ed. Bergen vol. i, p. lvii).

Whether Lydgate ever saw the Berry dedication is unclear, but his prologue to the first book of the *Fall* reinstates the character and power of Fortune, again reflecting his departure from Laurent's hardline position. We are told that the book is designed to illustrate 'Fortunys variaunce (*Fall* I. 54), and to show that there is no stability in wordly 'worshepe' (I. 56)—men of every social position are vulnerable to 'thawaityng & daunger of Fortune (I. 63). Fortune is blamed squarely for the falls of 'worldly pryncis in ther power roiall I Grete emperours, estatis and degrees' (I. 66–7):

> That thynges all, wher Fortune may atteyne,
> Be transitory of condicioun;
> For she off kynde is hasti & sodeyne,
> Contrarious hir cours for to restreyne,
> Off wilfulnesse she is so variable,
> Whan men most truste, than is she most chaungable.   (I. 107–12)

Lydgate continues by saying that 'Bochas' advised men to fix their affections not on the 'doubilnese' of Fortune, but on the unchanging realm of the divine (I. 113–19), and he introduces a strong statement of the power of Fortune over all princes:

> Off noble stories to make rehersaile,
> Shewyng a merour how al the world shal faile,
> And how Fortune, for al ther hih renoun,
> Hath vpon pryncis iurediccioun.   (I. 158–61)

Although he goes on to discuss the falls of proud princes (those, blinded with worldly prosperity and their own 'surquedie', who think—in the imagery of Boccaccio and Laurent—that they have successfully laid Fortune to sleep with their 'pociouns' and 'newe sorcery'), Lydgate quite plainly does not restrict the action of Fortune to the criminous. His Fortune is no mere executor for the just action of a righteous God, but is herself a wilful, capricious, and malevolent agent:

> And in this book bewepen and compleyne
> Thassaut off Fortune, froward and sodeyne,
> How she on pryncis hath kid her variaunce
> And off her malice the dedli mortal chaunce.   (I. 235–8)

Similarly, when 'Bocace' meets Fortune in the prologue to the sixth book of the *Des Cas*, the account carefully follows the version in the Latin text in providing a brief description of the tall and overwhelming figure. However, whereas Boccaccio is driven by Fortune's size and appearance to interject 'O Deus Bone, qua*m* gra*n*dis illi statura, quam admirabilis forma!',[120] the French author omits the mild outburst (together with the dramatically direct speech) and converts the moment into an opportunity for pious observation:

Je qui fuz esbahy de lymage de fortune me escriay a dieu qui est le donneur des vrays bie*n*s.
(I was so astounded by the appearance of Fortune that I cried out to God, the giver of all good things.)[121]

Lydgate's own treatment of the episode omits this Laurentian addition and extends the short French *effictio* of Fortuna into seventy-eight lines in which Fortune's duplicity and hideous appearance (greatly elaborating Laurent's reference to her 'face cruelle et horrible') are set forth in florid and rhetorical detail.[122] Interestingly, the 'chauntepleure' aspect of the operation of Fortune is made explicit in Lydgate's description, both explicitly (the word itself is used at vi. 8) and by symbolic detail—Fortune's right-hand side is 'ful of somer flou*r*s', while her left is 'oppressid with wyntris stormy shou*r*s' (vi. 20–1).

A comparison with the prologue to the second book of the *Fall* shows an apparently striking shift from this position, for in that prologue Lydgate offers—independently of Laurent—a strict ethic of desert:

> For fals Fortune, which turneth as a ball,
> Off vnwar chau*n*ges thouh men hir wheel atwite,
> It is nat she that pryncis gaff the fall,
> But vicious lyuyng, pleynli to endite
>
> .   .   .   .   .   .
>
> For ther weelfare and ther abidyng longe,
> Who aduertisith, dependith nat on chau*n*ce.
> Good liff and vertu maketh hem to be stronge,

[120] 'Oh God, how tall she was, what an extraordinary appearance!' (*De casibus* fo. 58ʳ (p. 141); trans. Brewer Hall (1965: 137).   [121] *Des Cas* fo. 123ʳ.
[122] *Fall* vi. 8–85. There is no suggestion that Fortune is ugly in the Latin text, merely that her hair is dishevelled ('capillitium multiplex per ora pendulum', fo. 58ʳ (p. 141)): lines vi. 3–29, 33, 40–2, 44–76, and 81–5 have no parallel in the French.

> And hem assureth in long perseueraunce;
> Vertu on Fortune maketh a diffiaunce,
> That Fortune hath no domynacioun
> Wher noble pryncis be gouerned be resoun.[123]

If tragedy here seems to be linked with an understanding of suffering that rests solely on personal merit or failing and which has little to do with injustice or chance, this is not a distinction that is sustained for long in the second book: though the first ruler (Saul) is an example of sinful pride (II. 218–24, 513), the stories of Lucretia and Dido in this book are explicitly tragedies of innocence. This (otherwise puzzling) shift becomes a little clearer when it is remembered that the prologue to Book II is the passage in which Lydgate explains his patron's intrusion into the composition of the *Fall*:

> Anon afftir, I off entencioun,
> With penne in hande faste gan me speede,
> As I koude, in my translacioun,
> In this labour ferthere to proceede,
> My lord cam forbi, and gan to taken heede;
> This myhti prynce, riht manli & riht wis,
> Gaff me charge in his prudent auys,

> That I sholde in eueri tragedie,
> Afftir the processe made mencioun,
> At the eende sette a remedie,
> With a lenvoie conueied be resoun,
> And afftir that, with humble affeccioun,
> To noble pryncis lowli it directe,
> Bi othres fallyng [thei myht] themsilff correcte.   (II. 141–54)

The bias of the prologue towards tragedies of guilt would seem to be something Lydgate feels required to add in order that Humphrey's request for regiminal and moralizing 'remedies' should make any kind of sense. Similarly, when in this second book he encounters a short reference to Euripides in the French, Lydgate does little to alter the retributive Laurentian emphasis on laments of justly punished and wicked princes he finds there, even though it is not representative of his own understanding of tragedy.

---

[123] *Fall* II. 43–6, 50–6. There is nothing of this in Laurent's preface; cf. fos. 24[r–v].

le poete euripedes qui fut tresnoble tragedien neust pas si subtillement
escript en vers les criz et les griefz complains quil fist contre les
mauluaises et horribles oeuures des roys et des gra*n*s seign*eur*s du
monde.

(The poet Euripides, a very great tragedian, wrote skilfully in verse of the
lamentable attacks and sufferings that requite the wicked and horrible
deeds of kings and other great lords of this world.)[124]

> The poete also callid Euripides,
>
> .   .   .   .   .   .
>
> Callid in his tyme a gret tragician,
> Because he wrot many tragedies,
> And wolde off trouthe spare no maner man,
> But hem rebuken in his poetries,
> Touchyng the vices off flesshli fantasies,
> Compleyne in pryncis ther deedis most horible,
> And ech thyng punshe that was to God odible.[125]

Once again this passage (which occurs in a long discussion of the
origins of regal nobility in the grace of God) demonstrates a clear
regiminal emphasis, and it would seem that Lydgate is happy to
follow Laurent closely in passages where his political readers
require an unambiguous advisory idiom: it is difficult to offer
ethical counsel to anyone who wishes to avoid downfall if you
have just provided an exemplum which attests to the irrational,
ineluctable workings of an amoral force.

In the remainder of this chapter I examine a larger field of
narratives (those of the first book of the *Fall*) to demonstrate

---

[124] *Des Cas* fo. 39[r]. This is one of the rare moments in the text where Lydgate
encounters the term 'tragedy' in his French source and translates it accordingly.
Premierfait's earlier comments (in I. ch. 11) on 'les paroles des poetes tragiques'
who tell of the destruction of cities caused by credulous princes is not rendered
by Lydgate—possibly, however, as a result of the reading in his own manuscript
of the *Des Cas*, for the Paris 1538 edition (*Des nobles maleureux*) reads 'des
poetes magicques' at this point (fo. 11[r]). However, Witart's 1578 Paris translation *Traité des mesaduentures de personnages signalez* has 'infinies tragedies
crient si hault' (p. 47), and the following manuscripts (A- and B-versions) have
'tragiques': MS Bodley 265 (fo. 23[r]); BL MSS Harley 621 (fo. 16[v]), Addit. 11696
(fo. 25[v]), 18750 (fo. 17[v]), 35321 (fo. 17[v]), Royal 14 E. v (fo. 37[r]), 18 D. vii (fo. 17[r]),
and 20 C. iv (fo. 24[r]). Gathercole's edition of Book I (based on six Bibliothèque
Nationale manuscripts) does not record 'magicques' as a variant reading,
(1968: 158). All this evidence suggests that 'magicques' is an infrequent reading.
[125] *Fall* ii. 3060, 3067–73.

Lydgate's characteristic attitude towards issues of culpable and undeserved misfortune in the poem. We must first turn to one of the clearest expressions in the text of the workings and power of Lady Fortuna: the story of the victory won by Poverty over her arch-rival Fortune after a heated debate and vicious bout of wrestling.

ANDALUS THE BLACK: THE *PAUPERTATIS ET FORTUNAE CERTAMEN*

The narrative of the Genoese Andalus the Black and the vivid fable he tells about the contest (*Certamen*) between Fortune and Poverty at the outset of the third book of the *Fall* is one of the most significant in the whole poem, in that it voices an explicit discussion of the forces which lie behind human misfortune. The competing possibilities of predetermined destiny, arbitrary Fortune, or the primacy of human choice (and consequent ethical accountability) are presented in subtly different ways in the Latin, French, and English texts; the three authors' varying emphases and exegeses not only offer intriguingly distinctive versions of this narrative in particular, but they also suggest the characteristic interpretations of the role of freedom of will in conditioning 'misfortune' that is to be found elsewhere in their texts.

Boccaccio's account of Andalus (Andalò del Negro) is preceded by an extended metaphor: those who undertake long and fatiguing journeys need to pause for rest, refreshment, and an opportunity to chart their progress.[126] So, too, the Andalus section and its enquiry into the causes of misfortune is to be regarded as a welcome break in the catalogue of the *infelices*:

Quae dum paululu3 mecumipse reuoluerem in profundissimam lapsus admirationem sigillatim coepi cuncta colligere: et potissimum quibus modis quibus viis quibus de causis hi quos deiectos adposui cecidere. Visum est (ni decipiar) eos in se sicuti plerique faciunt omnes aduersam prouocasse fortunam veramque probaui fabelle sententia3 quam olim ab adulescentia mea audire memineram. Et quoniam in contione presenti satis commode facere videtur: illam dum quieti indulgemus recitasse non erit inutile.

---

[126] 'sudores absergere, corpus leuare . . . et sitim poculis pellere: set etiam in tergum facie versa, iam acta metiri spatia' (*De casibus* fo. 22ᵛ (p. 70)).

(In the same way, after a little while I turned myself around, and with the most careful reflection I began to gather our personages together and wonder especially by what ways, by what powers, by what causes they were all overthrown. It seemed to me, if I am not deceived, that for the most part they called their adverse fortune down on themselves. I have found the essence of a fable I remember hearing as a young man to be true. And it doesn't seem inappropriate in the present assembly, while we are resting, to tell it.)[127]

For Boccaccio, then, the account that follows is a self-conscious interpolation, an excursus to prove a possibly doubtful thesis ('ni decipiar'), but one which the passage of his experience (since his youth) has tended to vindicate ('veramque probaui'). We are told that Andalus, Boccaccio's tutor in Naples, was a 'famous and respected master who taught us about the movements of the stars and of the planets':[128]

Inter legendum die vna verbu3 occurrit huiusmodi. Non incusanda sydera sunt. Quum sibi infortunium oppressus quaesierit.

(One day, reading to us, he came upon these words: 'The stars are not to be blamed when the victim himself has sought his own misfortune.')

Premierfait's version significantly differs from the Latin text of the *prohemium* and opening section of the *Certamen*. (A transcription and translation of the French is provided as Appendix I to this chapter.) Most noticeably, Premierfait introduces references to a personified Fortune and usages of the abstract term 'fortune' where no corresponding terms are to be found in the Latin: Premierfait specifies that he reconsiders, and marvels at, those who are overthrown *by Fortune*; for Boccaccio the enquiry is more neutral ('by what ways, by what powers, by what causes they were all overthrown').

Secondly, Premierfait emphasizes the suffering involved in a fall by means of an idiomatic tag ('cheuz du hault en bas', 'cheu du hault au bas') and by specifying that a fall may result in death

---

[127] Ibid; trans. Brewer Hall (1965: 67).
[128] Ibid. fo. 22ᵛ (p. 70): 'apud insignem adque venerabilem virum, . . . caelorum motus & syderum eo docente perciperem'. Boccaccio also includes Andalus and the proposition that misfortune is the result of desert in his *Genealogie deorum gentilium libri* (III. 22. 143 and XV. 6. 760). Boccaccio's slow composition of this work (from before 1350 to the mid-1370s) overlaps with the period in which he was working on the A-version of the *De casibus* (1356–60) (see Bergin 1981: 231).

('qui ont este tuez ius par fortune', 'on este tuez'); Boccaccio's
versions are less precise ('deiectos', 'infortunium oppressus'.)
Furthermore, the French account enlarges the areas of specialist
knowledge Boccaccio attributed to Andalus: Premierfait's Genoese
teaches not just abstract celestial movements, but also the ways
in which the stars exert 'influences', presumably on the affairs of
men. The fable which follows, then, is for Premierfait's Andalus
a fully professional concern: as one who has enquired into astral
influence, his Andalus tells the story of the *Certamen* to rebut a
position he finds indefensible. It is interesting in this respect that
the French Andalus, whom we are to regard as a spokesman for
the principle of ethical responsibility, is presented as 'gifted in
science and honourable in morals', rather than just as the 'famous
and respected' teacher we find in the Latin text. A further small
shift is that it is Premierfait's 'Bocace' who in his studies comes
across the proposition that the heavens are not to be held responsible for human misfortune and who presents this to his listening
master for clarification: Boccaccio's pupil persona was less closely
engaged in the debate, for him the *Certamen* was an ad hoc
exemplum Andalus spontaneously decided to relate in the course
of the lesson he was giving.

Finally, however, there is the crucial distinction between the
maxim 'Bocace' encounters and the one met by the Latin Andalus.
The Latin dictum cautions that 'the stars are not to be blamed
when the victim himself has sought his own misfortune'. The
French maxim, characteristically more verbose, instead proposes
that the heavens are never to blame for a fall 'puis que lhomme
qui est cheu du hault au bas ait procure 7 quis le cas de sa malle
fortune'. In this respect the two texts offer the story of Fortune
and Poverty as a demonstration of different principles: for
Boccaccio, that fortune (the stars) may at times be held responsible for a fall; for Premierfait, that it never is. The effects of this
shift in understanding of the *sententia* of the fable have already
been seen in the changes Premierfait makes to the introductory
sentences of his first chapter.

When we compare the two versions of the narrative of the
contest, then, it is apparent that Premierfait follows his Latin
source closely and seeks to develop his rereading of it by means
of nuanced modification and by the imposition of a different
conclusion, rather than by argued refutation. Both versions share

the same structure: a 'tennis match' of six exchanges (each initiated by Poverty) is followed by a short bout of wrestling, Poverty's victory, and her concluding speech. Asperity is the keynote to Premierfait's more dominant characterization of Poverty, as becomes evident from a study of the small changes made to the translated text.[129] Indeed, in her fifth speech Fortune is even brought to acknowledge the independence Poverty enjoys, a concession that does not appear in the Latin: 'Car puis que tu nas riens et ne veulx riens auoir tu es franche et exempte de toute loy.' Premierfait's emphasis on the power of Poverty to defeat Fortune emerges most clearly in Poverty's final speech: having overcome Fortune in the wrestle, the French Poverty imposes conditions on her enemy for different reasons from those of her Latin counterpart. She complains:

Car puis que il a semble a folle oppinion des poetes 7 philosophes anciens que les dieux ayent mis en ta franche voulente le bon heur 7 le malheur.

(That it seems to be the foolish opinion of poets and ancient philosophers that the gods have placed good and bad fortune absolutely in your hands.)[130]

In order to confound this false opinion, foolishly peddled by poets, Poverty demands that Fortune tie Misfortune up in a public

---

[129] *Des Cas* fos. 46ᵛ–48ʳ (but note the misnumbered foliation here, with fos. 47ʳ–48ᵛ being duplicated): Premierfait makes few substantive changes. His Fortune replies softly ('eut la chiere et la parolle doulce et assez souefue') to Poverty's first challenge; he lengthens Poverty's third speech in order to emphasize her physical frailty rather than her quietude of spirit ('mihi quidem, etsi vacua cutis et tacitus animi', fo. 23ʳ (p. 71), becomes 'combien que ie ay le cuir vuide de chair et de sang'). He also focuses more closely on the freedom Poverty has gained in her renunciation of worldly goods ('ie suis deuenue franche l ie suis hors de tes laz pourtant que iay delaisse tes dons 7 tes richesses', fos. 47ʳ⁻ᵛ), and, in order to emphasize the concomitant slavery of men in positions of affluence 'verum minas has tuas regibus inuce' (ibid.) becomes 'tu dois gecter tes menasses aux roys et princes qui quierent a grant douleur les biens transitoires que tu donnes et les gardent en paour l 7 si ont grant douleur a les prendre 7 laisser' (fo. 47ᵛ). Premierfait's view of regal authority in this narrative, thus, is one which is strongly compromised by earthly possessions. Elsewhere Premierfait omits biblical allusion, such as Fortune's reference to King Ahasuerus of Persia (cf. Esther 3–7; *Purgatorio* XVII. 28) in her sixth speech, and intervenes to explain geographical detail: the fabled Riphean mountains of Scythia ('ripheos montes') become 'les montaignes riphees qui sont a lentree dallemaigne'. Mythological colouring is added in the shape of the threat of 'le grant chien orchus' (seemingly a blend of the hound Cerberus and the infernal deity Orcus).   [130] Ibid. fo. 48ʳ.

place so that he may only ever enter a private household when he is untied and actually taken there by its inhabitant. Misfortune has therefore not simply been released from the power of Fortune, but has firmly been subordinated to the will of the individual, even to the extent of excluding other possibilities entertained by Boccaccio.[131]

The emphases in Lydgate's 'disputacion between fortune & glad pouert'[132] differ both from those of Boccaccio's slightly muddled and Premierfait's clarified and refocused accounts. Of course, in so far as Lydgate inherits the French text he also inherits Premierfait's bias; what is of interest is the way in which his version furthers the ethical impact of his source. From the outset of Lydgate's treatment of the Andalus excursus there is evidence of a consistent reinterpretation of the significance of the narrative: for Lydgate the Andalus fable articulates discussion of the workings of Fortune in a censorious regiminal idiom. In the stanzas following his version of Boccaccio's analogy of long-distance travel Lydgate seems to present the Andalus episode as an unambiguous demonstration of the principle that men often cause their own misfortunes; however, the situation is rather more nuanced than this. Lydgate's discussion of deserved misfortune is specifically linked to the ambition and avarice of 'wordli folk which so hih arise':[133]

> Ther clymbyng up the heuenes for to perce,
> In worldli richesse tencrecen and habounde,
> Ther gredi etik doth hemsilff confounde;
> And ther thrust off hauyng onstaunchable
> Causeth ther noblesse to be so variable. (III. 136–40)

Even before the material of Premierfait's first chapter is encountered, then, Lydgate has assimilated the fable to the wider regiminal concerns of his text: while the French text is directed at an unspecified audience, Lydgate's Andalus narrative is addressed to the wealthy and powerful.

---

[131] In interpreting the judgement in this way Premierfait omits Boccaccio's final reference to God ('Quam ego forsan adceptabilem arbitror, si velimus mentis acie mores hominum & dei iudicia intueri', fo. 23ᵛ (p. 72)) and instead inserts yet another statement to the effect that misfortune strikes only when it is deserved ('malheur attache a vng pieu pour ceulx seullement qui apres le deslyeroient', fo. 48ʳ), thereby eliminating Boccaccio's even-handed suggestion that divine providence should be borne in mind.
[132] John Rylands MS Crawford English 2, fo. 60ᵛ.   [133] *Fall* III. 148.

After the strongly focused prologue, Lydgate moves to a description of Andalus which further develops Premierfait's presentation. In the English version there is no question as to whether the principle of ethical self-sufficiency can firmly be attributed to Andalus:

> And heeld also in his opynyou*n*s,
> The fall off pryncis, the cause weel out souht,
> Cam of themsilff & off Fortune nouht.
>
> Nor the sterris wer nothyng to wite,
> Be ther meuyng nor by ther influence,
> Nor that men sholde off riht the heuene atwite
> For no froward wordli violence:
> For this clerk ther concluded in sentence,
> How men be vertu longe may contune
> From hurt off sterris outher off Fortune.
>
> Ther owne desert is cheef occasiou*n*
> Off the onhap, who-so taketh heede,
> And ther demeritis onwarli put hem dou*n*,
> Whan vicious liff doth ther bridil leede.
> Cours off Fortune nor off the sterris rede
> Hyndrith nothyng geyn ther felicite,
> Sithe off fre chois thei ha[ue] ful liberte.   (III. 173–89)

God, too, is introduced into the discussion as Lydgate further rationalizes the seemingly arbitrary fortunes which befall men. Evildoing brings about its own reward with the same inevitability as God visits punishment on the unjust: 'Syn*n*e ay requereth vengau*n*ce at his tail. | God off Fortune taketh no cou*n*sail' (III. 193–4). Lydgate's abbreviation of the Boccaccian frame narrative serves further to strengthen the attribution of this teaching to Andalus: the story the Genoese master rehearses is no longer an ad hoc response to a query, but is a consistent part of his own teaching. Even Lydgate's careful designation of Fortune's opponent as 'Glad' Poverty shows his concern that the principle of self-sufficient moral action, which is for him the burden of the tale, should be clearly understood. Poverty *willingly* embraced is the state which liberates men from the machinations of Fortune:

> Nor from hir meuyng no man is mor fre,
> As clerkis write, than is Glad Pouerte.   (III. 195–6)

Lydgate's version of the *Certamen* is strikingly more powerful than the French source narrative and is enlivened by a sense of drama as detail is added (and omitted) in order to enhance the adversarial nature of the combat. The account of the fight itself is considerably longer than the version in the French text (III. 526–602), chiefly so that Lydgate can allow himself the opportunity to moralize the action and to furnish an allegorical exegesis of the combat in terms both of self-government ('A mene is best with good[e] gouernau*n*ce . . . Gretter richesse is fou*n*de in suffisau*n*ce | Than in the flodis of superfluyte', III. 554, 556–7), and also as clarification (at III. 653–4, 657, 664–5) of the close association Lydgate sees between wealth and vulnerability to the vagaries of Fortune. In the concluding section of the fable, too, Lydgate adds a long homiletic passage which connects the terms of freedom, wealth, and power. (III. 645–707). A clear emphasis emerges from Lydgate's version of the fable: he evidently believes that unbinding 'onhappi aduenture' from her captivity and abandoning one's own ethical accountability typically leads to a life of avarice. Ambition *invites* misadventure.

It is clear from the study of these three narratives that each orientates the philosophical interest of Fortune and moral behaviour in the terms of a slightly different debate. For Boccaccio the fable fits rather oddly with the introduction before it; while the Latin prologue suggests that Fortune may have a remit, the fable's emphasis on freedom of will and its specification of Poverty as the force which binds Misfortune do seem to reduce the areas in which Fortune can be said to operate. For Premierfait Fortune is a non-category: his quarrel between a stronger Poverty and a less clearly delineated Fortune emphasizes the individual's role in fixing the limits of his moral freedom (so that while avarice clearly enslaves, this surrender of autonomy is one that he sees as unarguably self-imposed). Whereas Boccaccio has set out to teach discernment by questioning how far retribution can be distinguished from plain bad luck, Premierfait makes it his task to discredit Fortune altogether.

Lydgate's focus on the inadvisability of avarice produces the most consistent reading of the three—and also the most satisfactory in terms of the wider structure of the text. Lydgate realizes that a denial of the power of arbitrary Fortune would quite evidently be problematic in a poem in which some figures *do* fall through no fault of their own. So, while his assimilation of misfortune into the terms of greed, ambition, and covetousness may strike us as a dubious philosophical tactic (and even as an unwarranted simplification of a complex nexus of issues), it nonetheless yields a coherent attempt to formulate the relationship between Fortune and ethical accountability.

LYDGATE'S BOOK I

The Triumph of Fortune: Narcissus, Hercules, Isis, Samson, and Canace

The question of personal responsibility for actions, and the degree to which this may be compromised either by a voluntary surrender to the forces of sin (chiefly those of avarice or ambition) or by the intervention of an arbitrary Fortune is not just a concern which lies behind the presentation of the *Certamen* at the beginning of Book III. When the narratives of the first book of the *Fall* are considered it becomes apparent that Lydgate's characteristic (although not totally consistent) response in his treatment of his French source is to act as he did in his version of the Andalus narrative. Whereas Premierfait typically defends a voluntarist ethical position (in which the individual is held to be responsible for his own behaviour and downfall), Lydgate tends to complicate the moral certainties of the French text. Issues of personal responsibility, guilt, and punishment are regularly commuted in the English poem by means of the introduction of a *tertium quid* (whether it be the action of Fortune or of intervening deities) between the protagonist and his adversity.[134] The narratives which demonstrate Lydgate's careful introduction of exculpatory forces of Fortune in the first book are those of Narcissus, Althaea and Meleager, Hercules, Jocasta (and Oedipus),

[134] The first book of the poem is a profitable choice for an analysis of the forces at work in the downfalls of its protagonists. Small fields of samples tend to distort the results of any kind of survey, and so among its advantages are its length (with 7,070 lines it is Lydgate's longest, being nearly 2,000 lines longer than the next longest, Book III) and the range of narratives it offers: while certain books are arranged by content (for example, Book VI is Boccaccio's 'Roman book'), the first book contains a mixture of mythology, Trojan and Theban 'history', and biblical material. It is also usefully a book in which Lydgate exercises large-scale editorial power (as in, for example, his omission of chapters 13 and 15, and introduction of the story of Canace to the end of the book) and so one in which issues of his interpretative involvement are particularly heightened.

'Moides',[135] Ogyges, Ninus, the muddled 'Maia'-Isis story, Cadmus and his kin, the figures of Boccaccio's fourteenth chapter ('Contra superbos'), and the narrative of Canace and Macareus. A selection of these, including Lydgate's devious Samson narrative, will be discussed.

The narratives of Narcissus in Laurent's twelfth chapter and in the *Fall* are shaped in part by their use of differing literary authorities: Premierfait extends the brief reference to Narcissus in Boccaccio's twelfth chapter 'Conventus dolentium' ('e*um* seq*ue*ba*n*t*ur* narciss*us*, biblis, & myrrha'),[136] as he admits, drawing on his reading of the *Roman de la Rose* to produce a long and deliberate evocation of the indolent vanity of the languishing youth.[137] Lydgate's version, however, reverts to the account in the *Metamorphoses* and sees the narrative as much more than a story about self-enamoured beauty:[138] whereas the French narrative focuses solely on Narcissus (with only a brief reference to the nymph Echo), Lydgate repopulates the exemplum with the figures who determined Narcissus' fate in Ovid's account. At the outset of his version he introduces Tiresias, who foretells the newly born child's future 'be sperit off prophesie, | Touchyng his fate'.[139] The 'prophesie' is, in Lydgate's narrative, a curse: the gods have bestowed considerable beauty on Narcissus, but have also determined 'bi ordynau*n*ce off God and off Nature' that, once he sees a reflection of his own face, his pride will never allow Narcissus to return the love his 'natif fairnesse' inspires in others.[140] Narcissus' freedom of action is considerably reduced and it is apparent that the rest of his story is, for Lydgate, to be a playing out of a predetermined drama. Ovid's Tiresias is, by contrast, far more neutral in his prediction of the child's future,[141] while Premierfait, who makes no mention of the prophecy, firmly

---

[135] There is no corresponding character in the *Des Cas*: Lydgate has misread Premierfait's text, possibly as the result of a scribal conflation of the French in his manuscript: 'aussi a congnoissence des historians latins et pars especial de *moy, des* roys des Sodomes ne est aulculne chose venue' (see *Fall* ed. Bergen vol. iv. 144).

[136] *De casibus* fo. 8ʳ (p. 39).

[137] *Des Cas* fo. 14ʳ, 'vne fontaine telle et ainsi descripte comme le noble poete Jehan Clopinet [*sic*] de meun la figura par vers en son liure de la rose et pourtant plus nen parle'.   [138] Ovid, *Metamorphoses* III. 339–510.

[139] *Fall* I. 5564–5.   [140] Ibid. I. 5566–76.

[141] *Metamorphoses* III. 346–8: 'When asked whether this child would live to reach a ripe age, he replied: "Yes, provided that he does not come to know himself." '

blames the youth's own moral inadequacy for his behaviour towards those who love him:

Cestuy Narciscus [*sic*] *comme* fol 7 orgueilleux pour la beaulte de luy proposa en son cueur de non aymer quelconque femme.

(Narcissus, foolishly proud of his own beauty, determined never to love any woman.)[142]

Instead of the cursory treatment she receives in the *Des Cas*, Echo plays an integral part in the logic of the Lydgatean narrative; it is Narcissus' rejection of Echo's love which attracts the anger of the gods Venus and Cupid and leads to his punishment:

> And for Narcisus was nat merciable
> Toward Echcho, for his gret beute,
> But in port was foun*den* ontretable,
> Cupide thouhte he wolde auengid be.[143]

In the French version the hunter's gazing at his own reflection in the fountain of the *Rose* comes to dominate the narrative; this is the heart of the exemplum for Laurent.[144] Caught up in an enervating and solipsistic self-regard, his 'jouvenceaulx' eventually melts away, gradually becoming as insubstantial as the reflected image with which he has fallen in love:

il sans manger, tout seul et fort pensif considera fort longueme*nt* lumbre de son visage . . . il se coucha sur lherbe | 7 pour les causes cy par auant comptees auec grant douleur et desdaing qui griefuement le contraignirent il mourut

(in solitude and without eating, he gazed for a long time upon the reflection of his own face . . . he lay down on the grass and (for the reasons given above) he died, grievously afflicted by great pain and disdain)[145]

Whereas Laurent's Narcissus is blamed outright for his arrogance ('fol et orgueilleux pour la beaulte de lui') and dies slowly, the

---

[142] *Des Cas* fo. 14ʳ.
[143] *Fall* I. 5636–9. This alteration demonstrates, contrary to Koeppel's claims (Ph.D. thesis, 1885: 57), Lydgate's refining involvement with the narrative—in his Latin source it is not Echo, but simply one of the many admirers Narcissus had scorned, who calls to the heavens for Narcissus' downfall. In the Latin poem the avenging force is Nemesis (*Metamorphoses* III. 406), although in the *Roman de la Rose* Echo also lies behind the divine revenge.
[144] Cf. Guillaume de Lorris and Jean de Meun *Roman de la Rose*, ll. 1425–614, 20405–24, 20876–88 (trans. Dahlberg 1971, rev. 1983: 50–2, 334, 341).
[145] *Des Cas* fos. 14ʳ⁻ᵛ.

death of Lydgate's Narcissus again introduces the gods who, having punished the youth, now take pity and memorialize him as the medicinal water lily ('Thei turned hym into a fresshe flour').[146]

Though, then, the later stages of Lydgate's narrative do contain explicit criticism of Narcissus' vanity ('Presumptuous pride causid al to gon to wrak', 1. 5668), this has been predicated from the beginning of the story on the suspension of Narcissus' own freedom to act as a self-determining moral agent. Deprived of the ability to fashion his own behaviour, he cannot be held responsible for his treatment of Echo, nor be deserving of the gods' vengeance. By presenting Narcissus as the pawn of classical deities Lydgate subverts the version of the story he finds in his French source: Laurent selects his literary models to allow him to capitalize on the vanity of the youth and so present Narcissus' death as the deserved result of his personal failings.

Boccaccio's treatment of Hercules in his twelfth chapter is both brief and ambivalent. The brevity is, the author claims, intentional: to write more of Hercules, whom Boccaccio accuses of lust and effeminacy, would be to tarnish the reputation of a figure extolled beyond the stars by all the greatest poets.[147] Despite Laurent's retention of Boccaccio's accusations ('paoureux comme femme', 'fearful as a woman'),[148] there is throughout the French narrative a new emphasis both on Hercules' high personal worth and yet also on his self-aggrandizing desire to spread the glory of his own fame far afield.[149] The story of Hercules in the English text differs from that of Premierfait both in its clearer characterization and in the final exegesis imposed on to it. Lydgate's narrative of Hercules is much cagier and presents an account of Hercules in which he emerges, without the ambivalence of the French text, as an innocent hero: whereas, for example, the French Hercules is accredited with so great a desire for fame that it comes close to an ambitious overreaching, Lydgate simply omits these sections of his source.[150]

---

[146] *Fall* 1. 5675. The account of Narcissus' suicide (by jumping into the well and drowning), an incident which appealed to many illustrators of copies of the *Fall* (e.g. MS Bodley 263, fo. 4[r]; MS Harley 1766, fo. 74[v]), itself testifies to Lydgate's independence in his treatment of his sources.

[147] *De casibus* fo. 8[r] (p. 39).   [148] *Des Cas* fo. 12[v].

[149] Ibid. fo. 13[r]: 'Hercules espandit 7 sema son nom par tout le monde'.

[150] For example, where Laurent claims that Hercules travels to Africa in order to increase his glory ('Hercules pour accroistre la gloire de son nom autresfois vint

The most telling addition to the *Fall* narrative, however, comes in a speech Lydgate gives to Hercules which explains how the conflict between Jove and Juno shaped his destiny (Jove intending him to be 'most myhti off renou*n*, | Noblest off nobles both in werre and pes', while Juno sought to overturn 'The influence off his natyuyte, | . . . to reuerse his fame and eek his fate'.)[151] Lydgate further emphasizes his view of Hercules as an involuntary slave of larger forces by moralizing the untrustworthiness of Fame and her various trumpets, so that at his death (the protracted and gruesome details of which Lydgate omits) Hercules in the English version is more explicitly painted as a victim of the 'mutabilite', 'sleihte', and 'fraude' of woman as Lydgate's pen quakes and his ink mingles with his 'bittir teris salte' out of pity for his hero.[152]

The bizarre narrative of Isis, queen of the Argives, like that of Chaucer's Nebuchadnezzar, is one of downfall followed by restoration: Isis is made queen by her lover Jove and immediately declares war on the aged King Argus out of 'couetise'.[153] Defeated and imprisoned by Argus, Isis's career takes an upturn when she is miraculously released from her fetters by her own son, the god Mercury.[154] In the French, Premierfait represents this as an act of avarice and ambition (he speaks later of her 'malice') and so her defeat seems in part a deserved come-uppance. There is no mention of Fortune in the *Des Cas* account; in fact, it is not the downfall of Isis which forms Laurent's pitiable *casus* at all, but instead 'lhorrible mort du Apis' at the hands of his brother Typhon. In Lydgate's version, however, Isis is clearly the central figure and is defeated by her (much weaker) enemy when 'Fortune gan vpon hir

en affricque', *Des Cas* fo. 13ʳ), Lydgate instead claims that 'Afftir to Affrik he wente a ful gret pas, | Onli off purpos the gardyn for to see, | Which appertened to [the] kyng Athlas' (*Fall* 1. 5377–9).

[151] *Fall* 1. 5073–4, 5084–5.

[152] Ibid. 1. 5104–31, 5507, 5516, 5521, 5517–18. It has been argued that Lydgate must have been familiar with the account in Trevisa's translation of Higden's *Polychronicon* when writing the *Troy Book* (Dwyer 1967).

[153] Ibid. 1. 1684. Cf. the French 'de naturelle couuoitise' (*Des Cas* fo. 4ᵛ). Lydgate must take the blame for the considerable confusion in the *Fall* narrative between the Egyptian deity Isis (sister and wife of Osiris-Apis) and the Greek Maia (one of the Pleiades, mother of Mercury by Jove, and wife of Argus).

[154] Ibid. 1. 1695–1701.

frowne': by this means Lydgate removes the causal connection which in the French linked her defeat to the covetousness that led her to attack Argus. (I. 1688). Furthermore, in order to reinforce his interpretation of the narrative he finds in Premierfait's fifth chapter, Lydgate adds a four-stanza envoy in which he directs the attention of 'pryncis' and 'pryncessis' (I. 1835) to the principle which he feels is demonstrated by the stories in this chapter:

> Seeth off this world the chaung, the doubilnesse,
> The gret onseurnesse, the variacioun,
> And aduertisith, for al your hih renoun,
> Fortunes dewes, whan thei most suetli shoure,
> Than is she falsest, your glorie to deuoure. (I. 1837–41)

Again, Lydgate uses the opportunity of his original envoy passage to advance a reading of the *de casibus* exempla in which arbitrary Fortune assumes a greater significance than is the case in the source text (where it is never mentioned), and, again, it is the regiminal idiom of advice to princes which is used to articulate this new reading.

Boccaccio's narrative of the fall of Samson mentions Fortune twice, seeing the Old Testament hero as a victim of her 'slippery game' who is turned by her into a figure of fun.[155] The force of the Latin account is that Samson was an overreacher with too much self-confidence who had culpably allowed himself to be deceived by the wiles of women and, deprived of his manly strength, to be partly turned into one.[156] Boccaccio's next chapter ('In mulieres') is an extended misogynist rant which memorably concludes that, although there are some virtuous women around, the man who seeks a Lucretia is more likely to stumble over a Calpurnia or a Sempronia instead.[157] Similarly, Laurent praises Samson as a man of great courage, following Boccaccio in regretting the tendency men have of glorying in their own accomplishments rather than paying due heed to the

[155] 'Lubricum fortunae ludum ... verteretur in ludum' (*De casibus* fo. 11ʳ (p. 45)).
[156] 'Illum etiam fere effoeminatum in manibus hostium illudendum concessit' (ibid.).
[157] 'Ne dum lucretiam queris in calphurniam aut semproniam cadas' (ibid. fo. 12ᵛ (p. 48)).

inevitable time of judgement that awaits them,[158] and he finds Samson to be at fault for succumbing to Delilah's tears and female wiles:

Ceste dalida plouroit deuant San̄son . . . et finablement elle luy tira de la bouche par flateries et larmes

(Delilah wept in front of Samson . . . and eventually drew his secret from him with her wiles and her tears)

As we have seen, there is ambivalence too in Chaucer's narrative. Although the Canterbury Monk laments the downfall of a peerless champion, he (like Boccaccio and Laurent before him) refuses to shunt the blame on to Fortune; Samson triggered his own misfortune by foolishly trusting a woman with the secret of his strength.[159]

It is to be expected that, faced with so solid a tradition of culpable Samsons, Lydgate would follow suit: Fortune is not mentioned and the narrative appears straightforwardly retributive, charting a just punishment. Offering the story in his envoy as a regiminal 'tragedy', Lydgate assures us that Samson was wilfully negligent: other 'noble Pryncis' should take heed of his example and keep their 'conceitis vnder couerture' (I. 6504, 6508). In other words, Lydgate's Samson account seems to be entirely unremarkable. However, this bland treatment masks one of Lydgate's most devious manipulations of his source materials in the whole of the *Fall*.

The focus of Lydgate's interest is not Samson, but rather 'Dalida the double'; in the closing stages of the narrative he gives an extended description of her:

> She lich a serpent daring vnder floures,
> O lik a werm that wrotith on a tre,
> Or lich an addere off manyfold coloures,
> Riht fressh apperyng and fair vpon to see:
> For shrowdid was hir mutabilite
> With lowliheed[e] and a fair pretense
> Off trewe menyng vnder fals apparence.
>
> He mente trouthe, & she was variable,
> He was feithful, and she was ontrewe,

[158] 'la haultesse de gloire en quoy les folz hommes cuydent estre la bienheurete de leur vie l mais seullement il conuient regarder et attendre la fin des choses' (*Des Cas* fo. 20ᵛ).   [159] *CT* VII. 2021–2/3211–12; 2052–4/3242–4; 2061–2/3251–2.

> He was stedfast, and she was onstable,
> His trust ay oon; she loued thynges newe:
> She wered coloures off many dyuers hewe,
> In stede off bleu, which stedfast is and cleene;
> She loued chaunges off many dyuers greene.[160]

A catalogue of epithets conventionally used to characterize Fortuna (the simile of the hidden serpent, her dazzling colours, mutability, falsehood, layers of disguise, and wanton novelty) is applied to Delilah here in such a way as to alter the emphasis of the story. In effect, appearing to conform to the essentially retributive bias of the episode he found in his sources, Lydgate has in fact vigorously reinscribed the fortunal element (usually lacking in the European tradition of Samson narratives) in his portrayal of the duplicitous Delilah. Woman in this narrative is made to seem an embodiment of Fortune and the overall effect is to exculpate Samson from blame for his own ruin: as the Nun's Priest's Chauntecleer reminds the pilgrims, *mulier est hominis confusio*.[161]

Given that it is Lydgate's characteristic strategy in the opening book of the *Fall* to complicate Laurent's simple equation of misfortune with deserved suffering, often, as we have seen, by the introduction of other prevailing forces (Fortune's arbitrary fickleness or the action of jealous, avenging, or unprovoked deities), it seems appropriate that he should conclude the book with an elaborated narrative of the incest of Canace and Macareus.[162] It would seem, also, that Lydgate has prepared his ground carefully: his earlier abbreviation of Laurent's long account of Byblis in chapter XII suggests that Lydgate chose to sideline that story a little in order that it should not make the Canace story, his own lengthy incest narrative, seem repetitive.

Lydgate's sympathetic treatment of the misfortune of Canace is largely determined by Gower's version of the story, included in the third book of the *Confessio Amantis* in order to demonstrate the harmfulness of melancholic wrath, rather than the sinfulness

---

[160] *Fall* I. 6434–47. For a study of epithets used of Fortuna in the *Fall* see Kurose (1975).

[161] *CT* VII. 3164/4354. Cf. Chauntecleer's discussion of the acts of Fortune at ll.2999–3000/4189–90 and the Nun's Priest's own interpolation on 'symple necessitee' and freedom of will (as if in response to the Monk) at ll.3234–50/4424–40.

[162] *Des Cas*, fo. 23ᵛ. In this Laurent follows Boccaccio, who mentions 'macharei sacerdotis in templo apollinis delphici' (*De casibus* fo. 12ᵛ (p. 48)).

of incest.[163] Consequently, Lydgate's envoy claims that his own moral interest in the narrative is the hot-headed vengeance of the outraged king Æolus on his children:

> Kyng Eolus to rigerous was, parde,
> And to vengable in his entencioun
> Ageyn his childre Machaire & Canace,
> So inportable was his punycioun,
> Off haste procedyng to ther destruccioun.   (I. 7057–61)

The precedent set by Gower (a poet pre-eminently concerned with 'human actions as responsible, as part of a meaningful pattern'[164]) in dealing with the incest of the brother and sister in a tacitly sympathetic manner is made by Lydgate to fit his own interest in the ways in which individual responsibility and guilt for actions can be commuted by the intervention of other moral forces. Lydgate's expansion of Canace's letter (given just 27 lines in Gower's octosyllabics, but a doughty 136 lines in the *Fall* version) gives the lie to this professed interest; the embroidered rhetorical tour de force of the letter and the lurid pathos aroused when Canace's helpless infant falls from its mother's breast to bathe in the pool of blood from her corpse reveal Lydgate's enthusiasm in exploring the psychology of a woman in extreme emotional distress.[165] However, Lydgate's characteristic interest in Fortune asserts itself even after this distraction when, having recorded his disapproval of incest,[166] the authorial voice (and then Canace herself) uses the language of Fortune to mitigate any sense of absolute guilt:

> Fortune gan at hem so disdeyne,
> Hyndryng ther fate be woful auenture
> Touchyng ther loue . . .
>
>   .   .   .   .   .   .
>
> 'But loue and Fortune haue turned up-so-doun
> Our grace, alas, our welfare & our fame,
> Hard to recure, so sclaundrid is our name.'   (I. 6837–9, 6970–2)

---

[163] *Confessio* III. 143–360. See C. David Benson (1984), Hugh White (1989). Duke Humphrey owned a copy of the *Confessio*, now MS Bodley 294 (Sammut, 1980: 112–13) and Glasgow, MS Hunterian 7 may have been held at Bury (Heale, D.Phil. thesis, 1994: 109–10).   [164] Pearsall (1966b: 480).
[165] In Ovid's *Heroides* account (Gower's antecedent), the child dies *before* its mother at the teeth of Æolus' dogs, rather than afterwards (*Confessio* III. 310–15; *Fall* I. 7036–9).   [166] *Fall* I. 6839, 6845, 6855, 6858.

Gower, it should be noticed, makes no mention of Fortune in
his version of the story; furthermore, even his single reference to
outside agencies foreclosing the freedom of the two lovers (the
god Cupid, at III. 169) is seized upon by Lydgate and amplified
extensively:

> He is depeynt[e] lich a blynd archer,
> To marke ariht failyng discrecioun,
> Holdyng no meseur, nouther ferr nor neer;
> But lik Fortunys disposicioun,
> Al upon happ, void off al resoun,
> As a blynd archer with arwes sharp[e] grounde
> Off auenture yeueth many a mortal wounde.
>
> At the and me he wrongli dede marke,
> Felli to hyndre our fatal auentures,
>
> .   .   .   .   .
>
> Callid us tweyne onto the woful lures
> Off difame, which will departe neuere[167]

The Defeat of Fortune: Adam and Theseus

Lydgate's interest in presenting the action of Fortune, or similar
uncontrollable forces, on human affairs is not just to be found in
his introduction of such forces to narratives where Premierfait had
considered personal downfalls to be the result of blameworthy
behaviour: there are some countervailing examples. There are
seven exempla in which Lydgate manipulates his French source
in order to diminish the workings of an exculpatory Fortune,
thereby effectively strengthening the issues of guilt and deserved
suffering where these were downplayed in the *Des Cas*.[168]
The account of the Fall of Adam, which is of course the archetype
of all the subsequent falls in the *De casibus*, is one of these.
As would only be expected, Premierfait and Lydgate both
demonstrate the significance of the Fall of Man for Christian
theology, in that the Fall ushers in the world of moral choice and

---

[167] *Fall* I. 6987–95, 6998–9. Neither does Ovid's ingenuous Canace mention
either Cupid or Fortune, and the tone of her epistle is famously one of surprised
innocence.

[168] The narratives which illustrate Lydgate's suppression of the action of Fortune
are those of Adam, Nimrod, Byblis, Thyestes and Atreus, Theseus, Moses and
Pharaoh, and Sisera.

temptation to sin in which the careers of all the later protagonists subsist:

hoc tam detestandum facinus, malorum omnium radix: et humani generis
exitium fuit. per hoc, quasi reseratis postibus, victricia vitia orbem
intrauere terrarum . . . et (ut multa in vnum colligam) fortunae ludibrium

Ce peche, dinobedience . . . fut la racine de tous maulx . . . Par ce peche
entrerent au monde les vices a portes ouuertes

> And thus, allas, the seed was first isowe,
> The roote plantid off disobeissaunce,
> Which brouht our lynage to sorwe & myschaunce.
>
> Thus cam in first thoruh inobedience,
> As bi a gate, pouerte and neede[169]

It is not surprising, then, that each of the three different-language
versions of the story equates the ejection from Paradise with the
subjection of mankind to the forces of Fortune.[170] However, it is
noticeable that whereas Premierfait focuses on the disobedience of
our first parents and 'le mortel tresbuchet de fortune' in some
detail,[171] Lydgate is keen to reduce the emphasis on the introduction of Fortune into the fallen order; instead his focus rests on
the issues of Adam and Eve's freedom of will and the sacrifice of
'fraunchise' which their Fall represents. In essence, Lydgate shows
an awareness of the voluntary nature of the original sin and treats
the episode with an Augustinian clarity.[172] Furthermore, Lydgate
is also aware of the *good* that results from the Fall: his focus on
the issues of ethical freedom in the garden finds a balanced conclusion in the recognition that if the transgression ushered evil into
the world, it also ushered in the possibility to reject evil: the post-
lapsarian order may be one of failure and vice, but it is also (and
by the same token) one of virtue:

> For in this world is no thyng mor parfit,
> Nor taccomplisse thyng off mor plesance
> Than a man for to haue delit
> In litil good to hauen suffisance,

---

[169] *De casibus* fo. 1ᵛ (p. 26); *Des Cas* fo. 1ᵛ; *Fall* I. 684–8.
[170] e.g. *Fall* I. 687–93.
[171] Premierfait's Adam claims that 'nous auons premiers esprouue par
ladmonnestement du dyable le trebuchet de fortune'.
[172] See the envoy at *Fall* I. 974–87.

> And be content in his gouernance,
> Voide auarice and thynkyn euer a-mong,
> To his neihbour that he do no wrong
>
> .   .   .   .   .   .
>
> Fleen from his synne and hatyn for to lie,
> Off olde offencis a-mong ha[ue] repentance
>
> .   .   .   .   .   .
>
> There is no thyng mor fair nor agreable
> Than fynali his vicious liff to leue
>
> .   .   .   .   .   .
>
> Your haberioun most myhti off diffence,
> The feendis myht to venquysshe and oppresse
>   (I. 904–10, 918–19, 892–3, 955–6)

Although he does not use the phrase 'felix culpa', it is obvious that Lydgate has this doctrine in mind as he translates Premierfait's second chapter, where he points out the hope of the redemption of mankind and the divine action 'off grace and al vertu' which enable men to reclaim the joys of innocence 'And entre ageyn into Paradis | Fro when[ne]s whilom Adam hadde a fall' (I. 924, 962–3).

A concern for theological orthodoxy lies behind Lydgate's revision of the story of Adam. It is noticeable that other stories (those of Nimrod, Moses and Pharaoh, and Sisera) in which Lydgate treads warily, reducing Laurent's introduction of Fortune and restoring the primacy of human choice (and thus the possibility of blame), are also biblical. But we find the same response, too, in his treatment of the mythological figures of Byblis, of Atreus and Thyestes, and of Theseus: in each of these narratives Lydgate reverses Premierfait's relaxed attribution of the fall of the characters to arbitrary misfortune. In his concise treatment of Byblis (where he reduces Premierfait's long Ovidian account to just four stanzas) he focuses unflinchingly on the sinfulness of Byblis' unnatural desire for her twin brother and omits entirely Laurent's references to Fortune.[173] The difference between the French and English accounts of Thyestes and Atreus emerges in the focus on Fortune in the French, while Lydgate again makes it clear in his envoy that the story illustrates

---

[173] Ibid. I. 5678–705 ('She in her loue was nat vertuous, | For ageyn God and Kyndis ordynaunce').

the perils of transgressing the proprieties of natural law in behaviour that is 'Hatful to God and contrari onto kynde' (I. 4235).

Theseus, too, although a more complex case, is seen by Lydgate as a villainous figure: the harshness of Lydgate's attitude towards him is made clear by a comparison of the details of the French and English texts. While Premierfait follows Boccaccio in claiming that Ariadne was drunk when Theseus abandoned her on Naxos ('Adriana yvresse'), Lydgate suppresses the detail in order to cast her in the role of the innocent victim of Theseus' perfidy.[174] Similarly, Lydgate alone links the abandonment of Ariadne to the downfall that subsequently befalls Theseus, claiming that Theseus regards the death of Phaedra and Hippolytus as retribution for his broken vows to Ariadne:

> Of which[e] thyng, whan Theseus took heed,
> Thouhte it was vengaunce for his offencis olde;
> For he nat quit hym lik as he was holde
> To Ariadne, which sholde ha been his wiff.[175]

Although Lydgate does mention Fortune in his envoy to the Theseus chapter (there following a long concluding section on Fortune in Laurent), the role of Fortune is considerably diminished in this narrative too because Lydgate refuses to let Theseus off the hook of personal responsibility for his actions as a manipulative traitor. Neither biblical orthodoxy nor a Christian abhorrence of unnatural sins, however, lies behind his rereading of the French (as we have seen to be the case with the other narratives): it instead seems that the influence of Chaucer's depiction of Ariadne as a wronged innocent in *The Legend of Good Women* was simply too strong for Lydgate to resist.

There has been some scholarly confusion over the role of Fortune in the French and English texts in the muddled assessments of

---

[174] There is no mention of the drunkenness of Ariadne in Ovid's accounts (in the *Heroides* and *Metamorphoses* VIII. 175–6), in Chaucer's *LGW* ll. 2163–75, or in Gower's *Confessio Amantis* V. 5412–35. The phrase used in Boccaccio's version is 'Ariadnam apud Naxon insulam vinolentam' (*De casibus* fo. 6ᵛ (p. 36)), where it seems unlikely that the adjective could be qualifying 'insulam'; the translator of the 1983 edition of the *De casibus* supports Premierfait's reading, rendering the phrase 'Adriana, ubriaca'.

[175] Ibid. I. 4462–5. Again, Lydgate intrudes the word 'forswore' (I. 4444) into the account of Theseus' marriage to Phaedra, thereby alluding even at this point to the abandoned Ariadne.

Gathercole (who in 1954 claimed correctly that the French text warned 'the nobility of fifteenth century France [that] human wickedness results inevitably in tragedy', but who argued in 1967 that Lydgate changed his French source 'with a view to making sin more clearly the cause of human downfall') and Ebin (whose comments echo Gathercole).[176] While it is certainly the case that there are voluntarist and anti-fortunal comments in the *Fall* (Wright cites III. 193–4, VI. 283–7, VII. 403), it is rarely helpful to discuss such passages without a knowledge of how dependent they may be on the antecedent prose *Des Cas*.[177] In the majority of cases Lydgate's manipulations of his French source serve to highlight the haphazard and independent workings of Fortune, whether this be in the rise of the tyrant Agathocles to power (which Lydgate attributes to a stroke of plain good luck, whereas Laurent charts Agathocles' slow working of his way up through positions of increasing responsibility),[178] or in the insistently anti-Fortune chapters, 'In Hebraeos' (II. ch. 9) and 'In Dionysium & Fortunae excusationem' (IV. ch. 5), the first of which Lydgate ignores entirely,[179] and the second of which he radically rewrites to soften the stringency of its teaching.[180]

'WHO WIL ENCRECE BI VERTU MUST ASCENDE'

When in 1277 Etienne Tempier, bishop of Paris, attacked the propositions that 'the will and the intellect are not moved in act by themselves, but by an eternal cause, namely the heavenly bodies' and that 'our will is subject to the power of the heavenly bodies' among his catalogue of condemned and 'loathsome errors', he was voicing a long-standing hostility to the diminished freedom of will implicit in astrology and in theories of stellar influence.[181] Indeed, Edward Grant has said of Tempier's propositions that they

---

[176] Gathercole (1954: 250; 1967: 171); Ebin (1985: 64–5, 68).
[177] Wright (1957: 16).
[178] *Fall* IV. 2864–77; *Des Cas* fos. 88ʳ–9ᵛ (IV. ch. 13).
[179] *Des Cas* fos. 30ʳ⁻ᵛ: Laurent follows Boccaccio in his attack on Jews who falsely blame Fortune when they are punished for their indiscipline.
[180] *Des Cas* fo. 77ᵛ; cf. *Fall* IV. 939–80.
[181] Propositions 133 and 162 (renumbered by Mandonnet as 153 and 154), trans. Fortin and O'Neill, in Lerner and Mahdi (1963: 350)—see also propositions 143, 195, 206, 207, 161 (renumbered 104, 94, 106, 105, 156).

were designed 'to subvert philosophical necessitarianism and
determinism'.[182] Aquinas had attacked divination by the stars in
the *Summa*[183] and had claimed that, rather than be governed by
planetary influences, the wise man will himself dominate the
stars.[184] Robert Kilwardby (who had taught at Paris before
becoming Archbishop of Canterbury in 1272) and, later, Nicholas
d'Oresme (*c.*1320–82) both produced concerted attacks on
astrology,[185] as too did Coluccio Salutati, whose 1396 treatise *De
fato et fortuna* strenuously upholds the power of the freedom of
human will. Indeed, quoting the *Certamen* episode and Boccaccio's
exclamation 'O dura fatorum sors' from the narrative of
Croesus,[186] the modern editor of the *De fato* has suggested that
Salutati's treatise is in part a rebuttal of the arbitrarism of the
De casibus:

Certo il Salutati doveva pure cognoscere il pensiero del Boccaccio . . . sia
per la struttura dell'opera sia per l'interpretazione dei concetti di fato e
fortuna, Coluccio si monstrava assai distante dalla posizione del
Boccaccio.

(Salutati must certainly also have known the thought of Boccaccio . . .
both through the structure of his work and in his interpretation of the
concepts of fate and fortune, Coluccio shows himself to be very remote
from Boccaccio's views.)[187]

It is uncertain whether Premierfait knew of this discussion (or that
of Oresme) and deliberately followed it in his exclusion of the
influences of the stars from the *Des Cas*; however, that his own
dedicatee, Jean of Berry, had a highly developed interest in astrology is clearly attested by the *Très Riches Heures*, where zodiacal
imagery has freely been incorporated into what is in fact a prayer
book.[188] I doubt that Premierfait had access to Salutati, congenial
though the argument of the treatise would have been to him, if

[182] Grant (1979: 212).
[183] *STh* IIa. 2ae q.95 a.5. Aquinas had taught at Paris in 1256–9 and 1269–72.
[184] Ibid. Ia. q.1 a.115 ad.4 ('Are heavenly bodies the cause of human actions?').
Aquinas is here quoting Ptolemy (Aquinas 1964–6: xv. 106–7).
[185] Kilwardby, *De ortu scientarum* (*c.*1250), XII. §§ 66–76, ed. Judy (Kilwardby
1976: 31–5); Oresme, *Causa Dei* (see Tester 1987: 180).
[186] II. ch. 20: fo. 21ʳ (misnumbered 22 in the facsimile) (p. 67).
[187] *De fato et fortuna*, ed. Bianca (Salutati 1985: xxxix–xl); cf. Trinkaus (1989).
[188] Harry Bober (1948): the incongruous imagery of the *Heures* even attracted
the notice of the psychologist Jung.

only because his own treatment of the assassination of Caesar in *Des Cas* (VII. ch. 11) is so atypically insistent on the power of fickle Fortune: Salutati uses the assassination story in the *De fato* to precisely opposite effect as part of his correction of mistaken understandings of providence, will, and voluntary or contingent acts.[189] Similarly, though we have no evidence that Lydgate encountered the *De fato*, Salutati's arguments were certainly current in England in the fifteenth century: John Whethamstede, the powerful Abbot of St Albans, uses the *De fato* in his *Granarium*—which he dedicated to Lydgate's patron Humphrey of Gloucester.[190] Moreover, Humphrey owned the *De fato* in an anthology of Salutati texts which survives as a manuscript held in Chetham's library at Manchester (MS Mun. A 3.131), bearing on fo. 205ʳ the inscription 'Cest li*v*re est a *m*oy Homfrey duc de Gloucestre.'[191]

Attitudes towards astrology (or towards astronomy, for the terms have not always been as clearly distinct as they are in modern usage[192]) were not as consistently hostile as these examples might suggest. Indeed, the situation seems barely consistent at all: although Cecco d'Ascoli, Professor of Astrology at Bologna, was burned in 1327 for his views on necessary influence, just twenty-one years later the University of Paris medical faculty reported to King Philip VI that the Black Death was caused by an adverse zodiacal conjunction.[193] Augustine himself had reluctantly occupied a nuanced position towards stellar influence (in which he admitted that suggestions of its control over the body may not be 'utterly absurd',[194] while remaining fierce in his opposition to the possibility of its control over the will[195]): this position was revived

---

[189] *De fato* II. 7 (Salutati ed. Bianca, 1985: 61–4).

[190] Weiss (1957), 36; (Salutati ed. Bianca 1985: lxxviii, cv).

[191] Sammut (1980: 111); Bodleian Library, *Duke Humfrey* (1970: 9–10): the *De fato* covers fos. 91ʳ–200ᵛ and is followed by the *Declamatio Lucretiae* (fos. 200ᵛ–5ᵛ). Humphrey also owned other works on fate and astrology: Oxford, Corpus Christi College MS 243 was given to him by Whethamstede (fo. 197ᵛ) and was later owned by the astrologer John Dee (Sammut 1980: 115–16).

[192] For example, Cassiodorus uses Varro's *De astrologia* in his sketch of the quadrivium art of astronomy (*Institutes* II. 7. 2, ed. Mynors (Cassiodorus 1937: 155), and Witart, whose 1578 translation of the *De casibus* was to displace Premierfait's versions, designates Andalus an 'astrologie' (ibid.). See Tester (1987: 123).

[193] Wedel (1920: 75) and Ziegler (1969: 38).   [194] *De civitate Dei*, V. 6.

[195] *Confessiones*, IV. 3; *De civitate Dei*, V. 1–10; *De doctrina Christiana*, II. 21–3.

in the fourteenth century by Archbishop Thomas Bradwardine's *De causa Dei* (1344).[196] So, if Robert Grosseteste could in the thirteenth century be violent in his hatred of astronomers, calling their teachings 'impious and profane, written at the direction of the devil',[197] and Chaucer gently mocking of their methods in the 'Franklin's Tale' and the 'Wife of Bath's Prologue'[198] it was nonetheless also possible for Boccaccio to defy the advice of Petrarch and hold a firm belief in the influences of the stars.[199]

Although modern readers may find the claim that tragedy can function as an advisory or regiminal genre odd, medieval readers were less exercised by the tension between an ethic of human freedom and stories where misfortune is arbitrarily dealt to often undeserving victims.[200] Alain Chartier's unfinished *Traité de l'esperance* (started in about 1428) advises its readers at one stage (in the words of an English translation surviving as Bodleian MS Rawlinson A. 338, which belonged to Robert Dudley, earl of Leicester) to 'take thi leiser to reede Seneck and the tragedyes that benne in the booke of Iohn Bocasse' (fo. 96ᵛ) for the ethical teaching they contain: it is apparent that the *de casibus* tradition was quickly accepted by some readers as a collection of tragic exempla.[201] The only serious attempts to untangle the precise status of Lydgate's tragic writings and the extent of their influence on subsequent traditions of narrative and dramatic tragedy are those of Willard Farnham's highly influential 1936 study, *The Medieval Heritage of Elizabethan Tragedy*, Johannes Kleinstück's 1956 essay 'Die mittelalterliche Tragödie in England',[202] and Henry Ansgar Kelly's work in *Chaucerian Tragedy*. The issue of Lydgate's influence

---

[196] Tester (1987: 182). Cf. the references to Augustine, Boethius, and Bradwardine in the 'Nun's Priest's Tale' (*CT* VII. 3241-2/4431-2).

[197] *Hexaemeron* V. XI. 1, ed. Dales and Gieben (Grosseteste: 1982: 170). Richard Southern, however, claims that 'there is no sign that he ever rejected the theory of planetary influences, which implied the possibility of prediction' (1986, 2nd edn. 1992: 141). The earliest surviving piece of Grosseteste's handwriting occurs on a diagram of the conjunctions of Mars, Saturn, and Jupiter in 1216 (ibid. 107, 141).

[198] *CT* V. 1117-35, 1261-96 and III. 609-20, 697-710.

[199] *Commento* I. 71-2; see Wedel (1920: 88).   [200] Drew (1982: 49-54).

[201] Chartier ed. Blayney (1974: 106; 1980: 7, 124); *pace* Kelly (1997: 262) and Budra (2000: xiii, 15, and *passim*).

[202] 'Bei Lydgate ist der Mensch nicht nur Objekt der Fortuna, sondern auch handelndes und so schuldiges Subjekt' ('For Lydgate, mankind is not just Fortune's victim, but is also her agent, and so in this respect can be considered guilty') (Kleinstück 1956: 178).

will form the discussion of my last chapter; in this section we have been concerned to examine the poet's own practice. It must be admitted that Lydgate's thought is by no means that of a consistent or systematic theorist. In tracing his preferred alterations to his source materials we should not be surprised that we do not uncover any carefully formulated or consciously articulated positions; rather, we have been observing the evidence of Lydgate's habitual responses and casts of mind.

In many ways our surest guide to Lydgate's attitude towards tragedy within the *Fall of Princes* itself comes from the envoy sections he appends to many of the *Des Cas* narratives. These sections are far more than merely didactic additions. A. S. G. Edwards has remarked that the envoys provide key evidence for analysis of Lydgate's relationship with his source text.[203] Frequently, also, they reveal his attitude towards his own narrative project; it is when the *moralitas* of the envoy differs from the tenor of the preceding translated narrative that we see Lydgate's authorial preferences and prejudices most clearly. It is a well-known irony that the envoys were to become the most popular (that is, most frequently copied) parts of the *Fall*, displacing the Boccaccian material they were intended to elucidate. Given that the envoys are exactly the parts of the poem where Lydgate's hands are least tied by the constraints of fidelity to any anterior text, it is interesting that these are the very sections of the poem which use the term 'tragedye' most frequently. Examination of the fifty-seven envoy usages of the term (see Appendix II to this chapter) suggests that the word itself is not seen by Lydgate as inherently more appropriate to the sufferings of the innocent than to the deserved downfalls of the guilty. While the greater part of the narratives in the poem present the exempla of wicked princes, nearly every book also uses 'tragedie' in the envoys when virtuous sufferers are being discussed. What is even more interesting is the fact that in a large number of these envoys to innocent sufferers (here marked with an asterisk) the blame for the fall is firmly laid on Fortune rather than on other causes, such as the evil deeds or machinations of others. These innocents are Cadmus*, Gideon*, Jabin, Jocasta* and Oedipus, Hercules*, Priam*, Helen*, Paris*, Hector* and Agamemnon*, Samson, and Canace (Book I); Philip,

---

[203] Edwards (1977: 425).

Hasdrubal, Lucretia, and Virginia (Book II); Callisthenes, Eumenes*, and Arsinoe* (Book IV); Marcus Attilius Regulus and the three Scipios* (Book V); Julius Caesar* (Book VI); King Arthur* and Zenobia* (Book VIII).[204] Where Lydgate feels it is appropriate to designate the fall of an innocent as 'tragedy', then, he commonly also sees the involvement of Fortune as a factor in the experiences he records.

The ease with which Lydgate uses the term 'tragedy' remains his clearest debt to the 'Monk's Tale'; the Monk's plot-centred definitions of the genre as a move from prosperity into adversity, from joy to suffering, naturally fit well with a versified catalogue which conceives of human misfortune primarily as a *fall*.[205] The reversal-of-fortunes (or 'chauntepleure') definition occurs repeatedly in the poem. In his envoy to Cadmus, Lydgate asks:

> Who may susteene the pitous auenture
> Off this tragedie be writyng to expresse?
> Is it nat lik *onto* the chaunteplure,
> Gyn*n*yng with ioie, eendyng in wrechidnesse?—
> Al worldli blisse is meynt with bittirnesse,
> The sodeyn chaung no man theroff may knowe;
> For who sit hiest is sonest ouerthrowe.[206]

Even though the remorseless Jugurtha fully deserves his come-uppance, Lydgate's narrative at the end of Book V concludes with a similar idea:

> This may be weel callid a *tragedie*,
> Be discripciou*n* takyng auctorite;
> For tragedie, as poets spesephie,
> Gyn*n*eth with ioie, eendith with aduersite:
> From hih estat [men] cast in low degre,

---

[204] The word is used in the narrative of Zenobia (as too for Jocasta, Oedipus, and Canace) rather than in the envoy.

[205] *CT* VII. 1973-7/3163-7, 1991-4/3181-4. Laurent explicitly chooses to translate 'de casibus' as 'of the falls' rather than simply 'of the exempla ["cases"]' (see his explanation of the title of the work, *Fall* ed. Bergen vol. i, p. lvi).

[206] *Fall* I. 2157-63. This is the definition of tragedy given in the long section on classical dramatic practice in the *Troy Book*: 'It begynneth in prosperite, | And endeth e*u*er in adu*e*rsite' (II. 853-4). It is noticeable, too, that Lydgate here characteristically propounds a fortune-led understanding of tragedy (II. 855-9). The word 'chauntepleure' is used also at *Fall* VI. 8-9, IX. 3623; *Pilgrimage* ll. 30-1; *MP* ii. 429 (ll. 63-4), 612 (l. 96), 819 (l. 22). Cf. Chaucer's *Anelida* l. 320. See Whiting (1968: 77).

Exaumple taken, this story seyn ariht,
Of Iugurta, that was first a good kniht. (v. 3118–24)

The envoy to the narrative of the innocent Eumenes in Book IV
makes this same point with force; the concatenating last line of
four of the five stanzas is 'Aftir prosperite aduersite sodeyne'
(IV. 2297–331).

The term 'tragedy' is also to be found in Lydgate's other works.
Among his minor poems the lyric now called 'A Thoroughfare of
Woe' cites 'Boys in his booke of Consolacioun' and exempla from
biblical and classical sources, together with figures from recent
Lancastrian history,[207] to illustrate the power of Fortune and
uncertainty of the human condition, unstable as a 'fayre peynture
sette on a stage, | That sodainly is oft so cast aside'. The poem
concludes with a clear acknowledgement of its model: Lydgate
tells us that the 'refreyd' of the poem is borrowed from his
'mayster Chaucier, chief poete of Bretayne',

Whiche in his tragedyes made ful yore agoo,
Declared triewly and list nat for to feyne,
How this world is a thurghfare ful of woo.[208]

Although it would seem here that Lydgate thinks the line is
from the 'Monk's Tale', the refrain is in fact taken from
Egeus' consolation of Theseus after the death of Arcite in the
'Knight's Tale' and it is possible that Lydgate's use of the word
'tragedy' here shows us how he read that work.[209] The lyric 'The
World is Variable' similarly refers to 'feyned tragedyes'.[210]
Elsewhere the lyric 'As a Mydsomer Rose' refers to the 'tragedyes
divers and vnkouth | Of moral Senek': references to Senecan
models, often with explicit use of the term 'tragedy', are frequent
in the *Fall*.[211]

[207] These are Adam, David, Solomon, and Samson; Hector, Achilles, Alexander,
Julius Caesar, and Pompey; the Burgundian and Armagnac rivalries, the early death
of Henry V, and the misfortunes of the dukes of Clarence and Exeter, and the earl
of Salisbury.   [208] ll. 189–191 (*MP* ii. 828).
[209] CT I. 2847. This is the only use of this line recorded in Tatlock and
Kennedy's *Concordance* (1963).   [210] l. 10 (*MP* ii. 844).
[211] ll. 85–6 (*MP* ii. 784); references to Seneca in the *Fall* are at I. 253–4, 2384–7
(Medea), 3580 (Oedipus), 4203–4 (Atreus and Thyestes); IV. 59; VI. 3353. Other
references (without the conjunction of the idea of tragedy) are at I. 6175; II. 4490;
III. 4056; VII. 618–27, 744 (Nero); IX. 3391.

These ad hoc uses of the term tell us little of Lydgate's *understanding* of the tragic; much more useful is a passage in the lyric 'Misericordias Domini in Eternum Cantabo':

> At funeral feestys men synge tragedies
> With wooful ditees of lamentaciou*n*;
> In thorpys smale be songe Comedies
> With many vnkouth transmutaciou*n*.²¹²

The emphasis here on the qualitative aspects of tragedy as a doleful and (in contrast with rustic comedy) sophisticated category befitting funeral laments is echoed in the *Fall*:

> A furious compleynt vttrid in distresse:
> This was the maner, as poetis do descryue,
> In his tragedies when Senec was alyue.

> Lettrys of compleynt requere colour sable,
> And tragedyes in especial
> Be rad and songe at feestys fun*e*ral.²¹³

It is similarly noticeable that the second reference to ancient dramatic tragedy given in the *Troy Book* occurs in the context of a lament for the death of Hector ('wi*th* maters þat be wi*th* mournynge shent, | As tragedies, al to-tore and rent, | In compleynynge pitously in rage | In þe theatre, with a ded visage').²¹⁴ One of the most certain conclusions to be drawn from Lydgate's work is that his understanding of tragedy overlaps to a large degree with the category of the *planctus*: pathos (or 'pite') is so much a facet of the Lydgatean tragedy that it can seem (as in his use of the term for the laments of Chaucer's *Legend of Good Women*) that 'tragedy' is for him sometimes nothing more than a catch-all term meaning 'sad story'.²¹⁵

The last line of the whole poem declares that the only way to mount Fortune's wheel is by virtuous living ('Who will encrece bi virtu must ascende'), and even though it is by no means apparent that this *moralitas* logically springs from the majority of the stories that precede it, we have seen that medieval readers accepted the didactic value of the *de casibus* tradition without worrying unduly whether the intervention of Fortune weakens a coherent regiminal

---

²¹² ll. 65–8 (*MP* i. 73).   ²¹³ *Fall* VI. 3351–3; IX. 3447–9.
²¹⁴ *TB* III. 5439–42.
²¹⁵ *Fall* VI. 3620–6; for an alternative view see Kelly (1986: 107–8).

reading of the narratives. We have seen, too, that Lydgate plainly regarded Chaucer as a producer of narrative tragedies, even though the *Troy Book* shows that he knew more than did Chaucer of the conditions of the performance of classical *dramatic* tragedy. Lydgate inherits from Chaucer a broad application of the word 'tragedy' to include narratives of both deserved and undeserved falls, and also a belief that (in the case of deserved suffering) it is an appropriate term for both divine and fortunal punishment. His use of the label 'tragedie' can occasionally seem loose, but we have seen that the word did not lack coherent meaning altogether for Lydgate and that he had views about the most satisfactory *kind* of tragic action. While the demands of theological orthodoxy and, possibly, the expectations of his patron for moral clarity cause him to follow Premierfait's practice on occasion, examination of his alterations to Laurent's narratives (together with the evidence of his envoy sections) has demonstrated his characteristic presentation of the vulnerability of the *elati* to the vagaries of Fortune and other uncontrollable forces. Despite scholarly assertions to the contrary, we have seen that Lydgate's typical understanding of what constitutes a tragedy undermines any simple equation of misfortune or political downfall with just retribution for vice.[216]

When in Act III of *The Revenger's Tragedy* Vindice assures his brother Hippolito that 'When the bad bleeds, then is the tragedy good', he is locating himself in the tradition of a retributive understanding of tragedy that is closer to Premierfait's position than it is to Lydgate's. For didactic reasons the falls of wicked men may indeed make 'good' reading; however, the pathos aroused by undeserved suffering leads Lydgate to feel that narratives are much to be preferred when it is the *good* who bleeds.

APPENDIX I: ANDALUS THE BLACK

[*Des Cas* fo. 46ᵛ] Quant doncques ie remiroye en mon cueur les cas des malheureux nobles dont parauant iauoye compte les hystoires. Ie commencay a moy tresgrandement esmerueiller I et mis ensemble les cas de tous ceulx dont ie auoye compte. Et par especial ie me esmerueillay par quelles voyes I et par quelles causes soyent cheuz du hault en bas les nobles hommes que iay compte cy deuant et qui ont este tuez ius par

---

[216] Budra (2000: 51): Lydgate 'argued that fortune applied only to the wicked'.

fortune l pourtant il me semble et ne scay si ie suis deceu que les nobles
malheureux hommes do*nt* iay compte le cas ont este [fo. 47ʳ] tuez ius
pource quilz auoient appelle dame fortune contre eulx mesmes l ainsi
comme le font presque tous ceulx qui cheent par fortune. Et par ce iay
esprouue q*ue* vraye est la sentence dune fable que iadis iay ouy compter
en ieunesse l et dont il me souuient l et pource quil me semble que celle
fable fait assez proprement a ma presente intention l ie la co*m*pteray de
bon et alegre courage ta*n*dis que nous reposero*n*s la fin de nostre seco*n*d
liure. Pour lors que iestoye ieune escolier estudiant a naples soubz vng
maistre en astronomie appelle Andalus du noir qui lors estoit ho*m*me noble
en scie*n*ce 7 ho*n*norable en meurs l et ney de la cite de Gennes l 7 qui en
publicques escoles enseignoit les mouuemens du ciel et les cours 7 influences
des estoilles 7 planettes. Ie p*ar* vng iour apperceuz vne conclusion entre
celles quil lisoit qui fut telle. Le ciel 7 les estoilles ne sont point a blasmer
l Pour les malles fortunes qui aduiennent a lhomme puis que lhomme qui
est cheu du hault au bas ait procure 7 quis le cas de sa malle fortune. Si
tost que Andalus ouyt ceste parolle il qui estoit homme hastif l combien
quil fust ia vieil respondit du*n*g visage ioyeulx. Certes dist il ie vueil prou-
uer ceste co*n*clusion par vne fable tres ancie*n*ne l et de fait aucunes sie*n*s
escoliers l 7 ie mesmes priasmes 7 requismes ledit Andalus quil nous
racomptast celle fable: et il comme paisible et de doulce nature commenca
par vng langaige gracieux 7 sagement compose l ainsi cy apres senfuyt.

(III. 1 Then, when I reconsidered in my heart all that befell unfortunate nobles whose stories I had previously related, I began to wonder
very much and assembled the misfortunes of all of those I had related.
And in particular I marvelled at the means and causes by which the
noblemen whom I have treated above were thrown from their heights
and who were killed by Fortune for it seems to me, and I don't know
whether I am deceived in this, that the unhappy noblemen whose falls I
have given were justly killed because they had called Dame Fortune
against themselves, as are almost all of those who are toppled by Fortune.
And because I have found the message of a fable I remember formerly
hearing in my youth to be true and because it seems to me that this fable
fits my present intention fairly well, I shall relate it with a good and lively
spirit while we rest at the end of our second book.

III. 2 When I was a young pupil I studied at Naples under a master of
astronomy called Andalus the Black, a man gifted in science and honourable in conduct who had been born in the city of Genoa and who
taught the movements of the heavens and the courses and influences of
the stars and planets in the public schools. I one day encountered a
proposition amongst those which he read to us, which was as follows:
that the heavens and the stars are in no way to blame for the misfortunes
which come to man because anyone who is thrown down from his height

has himself brought about, and is the cause of, his bad fortune. As soon as Andalus heard this view he, being a quick man, although he was already old, replied with a happy expression: 'Indeed,' he said, 'I wish to prove this proposition with a very old fable.' And in fact certain of his pupils and I myself begged and pleaded with Andalus to tell us this tale. He began in that affable and gentle way of his to speak wisely and eloquently, as now follows.)

APPENDIX II: INSTANCES OF THE WORD 'TRAGEDY' IN THE *FALL*

Book I (31 occurrences):

248, 254, 350, 466, 944, 989 (envoy), 1380 (envoy), 1814 (envoy), 2158 (envoy), 2385, 3104 (envoy), 3125 (envoy), 3176, 3472, 3580, 3816, (envoy), 3842 (envoy), 3868, 4204, 4215 (envoy), 4544 (envoy), 4796, 5519, 5530 (envoy), 5537 (envoy), 5544 (envoy), 5551 (envoy), 5874 (envoy), 6308 (envoy), 6490 (envoy), 7040.

Book II (7):

6 (Proem), 148 (Proem), 630, 1429 (envoy), 1863 (envoy), 3068, 3931.

Book III (10):

890 (envoy), 1569 (envoy), 2166 (envoy), 2605 (envoy), 2640, 3088 (envoy), 3683 (envoy), 4019 (envoy), 4208 (envoy), 5118 (envoy).

Book IV (10):

59, 638 (envoy), 904 (envoy), 1422 (envoy), 1968 (envoy), 2297 (envoy), 2570 (envoy), 2927 (envoy), 3445 (envoy), 3717 (envoy).

Book V (9):

806 (envoy), 1590 (envoy), 1803, 1846 (envoy), 2131 (envoy), 2509 (envoy), 2844, 3118 (envoy), 3120 (envoy).

Book VI (5):

2521 (envoy), 2557, 2871 (envoy), 3353, 3620 (envoy).

Book VII (0)

Book VIII (4):

671, 678, 2321, 3130 (envoy).

Book IX (9):

477 (envoy), 1478 (envoy), 2021 (envoy), 3022 (envoy), 3055 (envoy), 3204 (envoy), 3421 (envoy to Duke Humphrey), 3448 (envoy to Duke Humphrey), 3618 (envoy unto his book).

6

The Reception and Influence
of the *Fall*

The popularity and influence of the *Fall* throughout the fifteenth and sixteenth centuries is clearly attested by the large number of extant manuscripts of the complete work, by independent fragments of *Fall* manuscripts (Brown and Robbins's *Index* lists 31 and its *Supplement* 34, but this number can be updated[1]) and of manuscripts which preserve extracts from the poem, and also by the ways in which later writers manipulate the *Fall* to form entirely new texts. Selections (and omissions) from the poem can reveal much about how contemporary readers saw the value of Lydgate's work: any act of selection is in part also one of interpretation. It has, for example, long been recognized that scribes focus on the moralizing envoy sections which Lydgate added to his translation at the request of his patron.[2] Similarly, collocations of *Fall* extracts with other manuscript material may reveal something of the reading strategies of the compilers of such anthologies and give an insight into the principles on which they excerpted stanzas from the poem in order to compile systematic anthologies. Even where no obvious rationale can be seen (that is, where manuscripts seem to be random assemblages, *collections* rather than *compilations*) we can still go some way towards examining the contexts in which later readers encountered Lydgate's poem. Marginal annotation and ownership inscriptions form important evidence for a reconstruction of who exactly was reading the *Fall*.

Seminal work has already been undertaken in the area of the reception of Lydgate's longest poem by A. S. G. Edwards, notably

---

[1] Brown and Robbins (1943: i. 732); Robbins and Cutler (1965: 52); Edwards (1977: 428 n. 17; Renoir and Benson, *Manual* vi. 2099 (in Harting and Severs 1967–93), corrected by Edwards (1985b: 451).

[2] *Fall* ii. 141–61; see Edwards (1977: 431).

in a series of notes on surviving fragments of the poem and on related matters of codicological interest, in a checklist of selections from the poem in *The Library*,[3] and in a longer 1977 article, 'The Influence of Lydgate's *Fall of Princes*, c.1440–1559: A Survey', in *Mediaeval Studies*:[4] I have benefited greatly from his insights and careful scholarship. However, room is still left for significant codicological work here: Edwards's checklist of *Fall* references offers no analysis of the make-up of the relevant manuscripts and so does not address the very interesting question of what kind of Lydgate diet the readers of these anthologized excerpts were actually getting. In the first section of this chapter, then, after a survey of later medieval developments in the *de casibus* tradition, I examine the identity of known readers of the *Fall*: later sections deal with borrowings from the *Fall* in Peter Idley's *Instructions*, evidence of manuscript ownership, and the revival of the *Fall* in the guise of the sixteenth-century *Mirror for Magistrates* tradition and related texts.

THE *DE CASIBUS* TRADITION IN THE FIFTEENTH CENTURY

Few modern readers have regretted the decision of the Knight (or, in some manuscripts, the Host)[5] to sabotage the Monk's plan to supply any more than seventeen of the hundred narratives piled in his cell: in fact, the cry 'Hoo, good sire, namore of this' and the Host's complaints of boredom have focused critical discussion to a greater degree than the narratives they interrupt.[6] However, when they echo the Host's complaint of tedium modern readers are at odds with the typical medieval response to *de casibus* literature. The copyist of the 'Paris' manuscript of the *Tales* (BN MS *fonds anglais* 39) registers that his text contains only an incomplete version of the 'Monk's Tale' in an endnote which suggests that he felt the tale to be remarkable for its emotive force rather than for its tedium: 'non plus de ista fabula quia est valde dolorosa'.[7]

---

[3] Edwards (1971*b*: 337–42).   [4] Edwards (1977: 424–39).
[5] Chaucer ed. Benson (1988: 935): the shorter and earlier version of the interruption survives in 14 manuscripts, in 10 of which it is Harry Bailey who silences the Monk.   [6] *CT* VII. 2780–805/3970–95.
[7] 'No more of this tale because it is exceedingly sorrowful' (McCormick 1933: 385 ff). The 'Paris' manuscript has only four stanzas of the tale and omits VII. 2023–766/3213–956.

The popularity of the *de casibus* tradition in the later fifteenth century is well known and there would not seem to be much doubt over the ways in which later medieval readers approached such narratives. Boccaccio may not himself have termed his tales 'tragedies', but readers (even in countries presumably untouched by Lydgate's reading of the *De casibus* as a collection of tragedies) quickly made this association for themselves. When Alfonso V of Aragon was defeated by the Genoese in 1435 and imprisoned by the Duke of Milan the Spanish poet Iñigo Lopez de Mendoza, the Marqués de Santillana, composed a dream-vision consolation for the ladies of the royal family, the *Comedieta de Ponça*, in which he clearly links Boccaccio with Senecan tragedy. In the preface he writes:

Tragedy is that which encompasses the fall of great kings and princes . . . all of whom began life happily and lived for a time until their sad downfall. And, in speaking of these individuals, Seneca the younger used the word in his *Tragedies*, as well as did Giovanni Boccaccio in his *De casibus virorum illustrium*.[8]

Caxton, too, writing his preface to Malory's Arthurian works in 1485, refers to Boccaccio when he promises the reader that 'Ye shal se also in th'ystorye of Bochas, in his book DE CASU PRINCIPUM, parte of his [Arthur's] noble actes, and also of his falle.'[9] It is plain from the tone of the preface that Caxton regards Malory's account of the Round Table as a clearly ethical work. However, in its moral confidence ('noble men may see and lerne the noble actes of chyvalrye . . . and how they that were vycious were punysshed and ofte put to shame and rebuke', 'Doo after the good and leve the evyl, and it shal brynge you to good fame and renommee') the preface offers a straightforward reading strategy which the text itself does not always sustain.[10] While it is apparent that Malory himself felt that the collapse of the Round Table and death of Arthur were tragic events, it is far from clear where he felt the cause of that tragedy to lie. Indeed, Malory's texts are characterized by a confusing variety of possible causes of the final fall of the Arthurian

[8] Frost (1971: 21); cf. Cloetta (1890: i. 43–4); Farnham (1936/56: 171). Santillana is also the author of a treatise on Fortune, *Bías contra Fortune*, written in 1448 at the request of his imprisoned cousin, the Conde de Alba (Frost, 1971: 30–1).
[9] Malory ed. Vinaver (1990: i. cxliv). Wright has noted that Caxton's Latin title is here more reminiscent of Lydgate's poem than of Boccaccio's original (1957: 21).
[10] Malory ed. Vinaver (1990: i. cxlv–cxlvi).

court: Malory blames the troublemaker Aggravain, Gawain accuses himself, Guinevere feels that she and Lancelot are at fault, while Arthur himself blames Aggravain and Mordred.[11] Malory does not use the word 'tragedy' in the *Works*, and in this he follows the thirteenth-century French *La Mort le Roi Artu*, his source for the account of the fall of the Table.[12] The French text is famously opaque on the issue of whether it is fate or human sinfulness which results in the destruction of Arthur's court, but the clearly logical causal sequence behind the *Mort* fall (in which Gawain's enmity for Lancelot persuades Arthur to pursue Lancelot into his exile in Gaunes, thereby leaving the kingdom vulnerable to the ambitions of Mordred) is obscured in Malory's version; responsibility for the ultimate tragedy is instead confused and multiple. Malory also notably diminishes the moments of more obvious set-piece pathos in the French, omitting the lament for the death of Yvain and Sagremor's strongly fortunal interpretation of the battle of Salisbury Plain. The battle itself is considerably curtailed and Malory omits Arthur's lament on the powers of Fortune after the death of Gawain. While the action of a blindly arbitrary Fortune is undercut in the English version, there is no coherent imputation of moral responsibility: even though muddled, Malory's polyphonic attribution of responsibility is skilfully realistic.[13]

In France the popularity of the *Des Cas* is attested by the large number of surviving manuscripts: forty-two are listed by Carla Bozzolo as surviving in France alone, while twenty are found in the rest of Europe; seven have been exported to the United States.[14] Bozzolo's study of surviving manuscripts of French translations of Boccaccio's works shows that Laurent's versions of the *De casibus* were by far the most popular of Boccaccio's works in French.[15] It is no surprise, either, to learn that the *Des Cas* reached some of

---

[11] Malory ed. Vinaver iii, 1154, 1230, 1252, 1184.

[12] The French *Mort* uses the term 'domage' in ways similar to later vernacular uses of the word 'tragedy' (*La Mort le Roi Artu*, ed. Frappier 1936: 68. 10 (§67), 106. 25 (§100)).

[13] For the role of Fortune in the French source see 'La Roue de Fortune' (Frappier 1961: 258–88). That Malory attempts to rationalize certain of the more enigmatic aspects of the downfall of the Table is undeniable: Lancelot's bitter taunt of Gawain with a reminder of the death of Lamorak (which is not to be found in the French text) and the killing of both Gaherys and Gareth by Malory's Lancelot (in the French he kills only Gaheriet) exemplify this.

[14] Bozzolo (1973: 49–91); Branca (1999: iii. 67–201) lists only thirty-two manuscripts in French libraries.   [15] Bozzolo (1973: 38 (facing table)).

the most powerful readers in France and England: a note in British Library MS Royal 14 E. v records that it was 'exécuté à Bruges pour Edward IV' and MS Royal 18 D. vii belonged to Mary, the second wife of Anthony Woodville, Baron Scales and the second Earl Rivers (*c*.1483).[16] The manuscript belonging to Jean of Berry, Laurent's dedicatee, survives as Geneva, Bibliothèque publique et universitaire MS fr. 190, while Paris, Bibliothèque de l'Arsenal MS 5193 spent time in the library of successive dukes of Burgundy (Jean the Fearless, Philippe the Good, and Charles the Bold).[17]

Laurent and Lydgate, of course, do not have a monopoly on the *de casibus* tradition in the fifteenth century; others engaged with it too. In the opening years of the century Froissart's extended account of the fall of Richard II at the close of the fourth book of the *Chroniques* is plainly intended to resonate as a monitory *casus*, and the text deliberately points this moral:

Now consider well ye great lordes, kynges, dukes, erles, barons, and prelates, and all men of great lynage and puissance; see and behold howe the fortunes of this worlde are marveylous, and turne diversly.[18]

Later in the century Philippe the Good's court chronicler George Chastelain dedicates his *Temple de Bocace* to Henry VI's queen, Margaret of Anjou, after her flight to the court of Burgundy in 1463. Intending to continue the *De casibus* account of fallen nobles, the *Temple* deals with the falls of over forty contemporary figures after John II, and includes Richard II, Duke Humphrey, William de la Pole, duke of Suffolk, Richard, duke of York, Edmund Beaufort, duke of Somerset, the Emperor Sigismund, the imprisoned Charles, duke of Orléans, and Margaret's uncle, Charles VII. In his *L'Exposition sur vérité mal prise* of 1459 Chastelain acknowledges his debt to the Boccaccian *de casibus* tradition:

je t'ai fait emprendre l'insécution de ce noble et ingénieux homme Bocace, et réduire à mémoire, depuis le roy Jehan où il fina, les haulx et glorieux

---

[16] Ibid. 136, 138; Woodville himself translated moral works, his *Dicts and Sayings* being among Caxton's first prints in England (1477).

[17] Ibid. 146–7; cf. Branca 1999: iii. 68–72 (Geneva MS fr. 190); 76–80 (Arsenal MS 5193); Purkis (1955: 9). See Bozzolo (1973: 40–1) for a list of the royal and noble owners of the work. Although Duke Humphrey's copy of the translated *Decameron* survives (as Paris BN MS fr. 12421, inscribed on fo. 425ʳ with the words 'du doun mon trés [*sic*] chier cousin le count de Warrewic'), his *Des Cas* (if he owned one) does not: Bozzolo (1973: 41, 107–8).

[18] Froissart trans. Berners (1903: vi. 398).

hommes de la terre succombés en fortune et venus à povre et douloreuse
termination, dont toutes-voies le nombre est grand, la hautesse de leur estat,
dangereuse, et la tractation de leur mort et infortune, à tout le monde
plorable, considéré encore les très-hautes et très-excellentes personnes,
roys et princes de nostre temps, qui y sont comprises, et dont les matières
bien traites effaceront toutes recordations anciennes

(following this noble and clever writer Boccaccio, I have set down for
you and created a record of those powerful and glorious men of this world
since King John II (which is where Boccaccio broke off) who have been
overcome by fortune and have met an impoverished and painful end; the
number of such individuals is indeed vast and their high social standing
precarious: everyone will find these accounts of death and misfortune
pitiful, particularly considering those very powerful and excellent persons,
kings, and princes of our own day who are included here: their touching
stories will outshine all previous narratives)[19]

While it is not known whether Chastelain read his 'Bocace' in
Latin or in one of the numerous manuscripts of Laurent's more
astringent version, he evidently understands the purpose of the
Temple to be consolatory and uncompromisingly didactic. The
inscription above the entrance to the temple suggests that the figures within will offer evidence for the consequences of sin and
speaks of 'vanité' and 'volupté charnele' (pp. 17–21). Later, when
Margaret addresses the 'glorieux historien Jehan Bocace' she does
so as if he were a moral counsellor: 'Tu es . . . le docteur de
pacience en adversité . . . tu incites les courages a vertu en delaiss-
ant les vices' (p. 83). Boccaccio's role is here, as it was in the
Spanish *Comedieta*, that of the Boethian *Philosophia*, but at least
one reader had no hesitation in reading the *Temple* as exemplify-
ing the acts of Fortune, for he heads the work simply: 'George,
de l'inconstance de fortune' (p. 23).

MANUSCRIPTS AND OWNERS: ANTHOLOGIZED
SELECTIONS

Cambridge, Trinity College MS R. 3. 19

Trinity College MS R. 3.19 is a clear example of the ways in which
readers seem concerned to make selections from the *Fall* which

---

[19] *L'Exposition* VI. 267 (Chastelain ed. Bliggenstorfer 1988: 13–14).

themselves produce a thematically consistent reading. This manuscript (a collection of thirteen booklets in four scribal hands) contains a variety of Chaucerian and pseudo-Chaucerian texts (*The Parliament of Fowls*, 'The Assembly of Ladies', 'La Belle Dame sans Merci', *The Legend of Good Women*, 'The Court of Love', 'The Monk's Tale'), as well as extracts from George Ashby (fos. 41ʳ–5ᵛ), from Lydgate's *Fables*, and the *Fall*.[20] However, the first text in MS R. 3. 19 is a twelve-stanza moralistic poem beginning '(T)ronos celorum continens' which Carleton Brown and Rossell Hope Robbins claim to be extant only in this version.[21] Despite its 1952 printing, the poem has received little attention. After its opening aureate stanza, the poem records a greeting from 'Senek the sage that kyng ys of desert' to 'hys brother kyng of Crystmas' and declares its regiminal purpose:

> Lettyng yow wete w`t´ hertly tendyrnes
> What longeth now vnto your astate royall

The advisory tone of the poem is predicated on the familiar need for rulers to receive good counsel:

> Hyt ys perteynyng to eny prynce and kyng
> That pepyll shall haue vnder gouernaunce
> That he haue prudent and wyse counselyng
> And to her counseyll geue attendaunce
> And that yo`r´ reame shall nat fall perchaunce
> Vnto Rewen for defaute of good counsell
> Take hede herto hit mayest avayle

In the stanzas which follow general advice is offered to this fledgling prince which could have been culled from many sections of the *Fall*. He is cautioned to act moderately, to avoid 'grete and large expence', to rule his body by diet and with relaxation ('Ye may the better labo`r´ at the long | When ye haue myrthe yo`r´ besynes among'), and is advised not to be governed in old age by his own great riches. The poet is insistent on the need for a ruler to be exemplary in behaviour and to be humble in the face

---

[20] Cf. Ashby, 'A Prisoner's Reflections', in Ashby ed. Bateson (1899: 1–12). A facsimile of the manuscript exists (*MS Trinity R. 3. 19* ed. Fletcher 1987); cf. Mooney on the manuscript in Minnis (2001: 241–66).

[21] Brown (1916–20: no. 2448); Brown and Robbins (1943: no. 3807). The poem is printed as 'A Mumming of the Seven Philosophers' in Robbins (ed.), (1952).

of the power of God:

> To preue your sylf take deliberacion
>
> . . . . .
>
> Aduertyse and here thys informacion
> How soone owre lord can set astate asyde
> Follow hym therfore and let hym be yo`r´ gyde [22]

The first excerpts from the *Fall* following this regiminal text in the Trinity manuscript are ten stanzas drawn from Books III and IV of the poem: IV. 2374–87 (fo. 2ᵛ), III. 1373–421 (fos. 2ᵛ–3ʳ), III. 78–84 (fo. 3ʳ). These lines form a thematically coherent discussion of the importance of chastity and good reputation for women. The two stanzas from Book IV (taken from the narrative of Olympias) firmly advocate the principle that 'In womanheede, as auctours alle write, | Most thyng comendid is ther chast honeste' and scorns 'princessis of hasti freelte' who 'Exceede the boundis of wifli chastite'.[23] The emphasis of the next seven stanzas is, however, subtly different: taken from the chapter on the 'extraordinary lust of princes' (III. ch. 4: 'In portentosam principum libidinem') which follows the Book III narrative of Lucretia, these lines consider not how noblewomen can be responsible for their own undoing, but instead how lecherous princes can ravish them of their virtue:

> And hard it is to rauysshe a tresour
> Which off nature is nat recuperable;
>
> . . . . .
>
> And maidenheed[e] lost off newe or yore,
> No man alyue mai it ageyn restore.   (III. 1408–9, 1413–14)

Virginity, once lost, is irrecoverable; it was for this reason, Lydgate explains, that the Romans were swifter to act against lechers than against tyrants (III. 1415–21). By way of conclusion, the redactor offers a single stanza from the Prologue to Book III in praise of lords who (by contrast) reward their servants adequately and protect them from harm.

The scribe's decision to conclude this section with the word *Explicit* makes it plain that he believes that these stanzas form a coherent unit. These ten *Fall* stanzas act as a refinement of the

[22] fo. 1ᵛ   [23] *Fall* IV. 2374–5, 2377–8.

opening and general advisory poem: where that text warned of the responsibilities of rule, the Lydgate material is used to examine one particular area of abuse—lust. Furthermore, in a neatly balanced selection, the *Fall* stanzas deal with the ways in which women are responsible for their own sexual morality before moving on to lament their victimization at the hands of predatory rulers. The Trinity redactor's moral seriousness is made clear in his careful presentation of ethical issues from a number of perspectives: men in positions of power must be virtuous, but female vice sometimes starts at home.

The preference for moralistic literature is sustained in the decision to continue the Lydgate anthology with *The Churl and the Bird* (fos. 9ʳ–11ᵛ) and with four of the *Fables* (fos. 12ʳ–16ʳ). And yet, for all this coherence, a curious love-lament (beginning 'Beauteuous braunche floure of formosyte'), for which there is no entry either in *IMEV* or its *Supplement*, is used to frame the *Fall* extracts:[24] eight stanzas are wedged in between the regiminal text and the Lydgate material (fos. 2ʳ⁻ᵛ), while a further forty-one follow the *Fall* stanzas (fos. 3ᵛ–6ᵛ). The language of courtly mannerism ('O comly creature whos colo`r´ more there ys | W`t´out faynyng than Phebus in hys spere', fo. 2ʳ) seems out of place given the nature of the material around it; moreover, the lover articulates an attitude towards Fortune which is strikingly at odds with the firm moral emphasis of both the opening regiminal poem and the Lydgate extracts:

> Fortune ys you`r´ frende ye nede nat dismay
> In glory and gladnesse yow forto guyde

These stanzas may seem bizarrely positioned, but they serve, I think, to remind us of the inadvisability of making exaggerated claims for compilers of late-medieval anthologies: personal interest certainly influences selections of material, but one such interest may just be the magpie acquisitiveness of the collector.

---

[24] The poem does not appear in Preston's *Concordance* (1975), indicating that it does not feature in the anthologies which form the corpus for this work, nor is it among the thirteen poems dealing with women in this manuscript, as recorded by Utley (1944: 336). The suggestion by Brown (1916–20: i. 239) that these lines are extracted from the *Fall* is unconvincing: even if a lover's lament were not generically at odds with the poem, the register of 'formosyte' and other terms is far too aureate for this poem.

In the eleventh booklet of the codex Trinity MS R. 3. 19 witnesses extensive selections from Lydgate's poem, as follows:

fos. 171ʳ–9ʳ:[25]   I. <u>469–1001</u>, *1380–6, 1394–400,*
                     8 unidentified stanzas, 3102–29, <u>*3788–94,*</u>
                     <u>*3431–58, 3522–8, 3529–35, 3795–801.*</u>

[fos. 179ʳ–88ᵛ: Chaucer, 'The Monk's Tale', VII.
                     3205–956/2015–766.]

fos. 188ʳ–91ᵛ: I. 1814–41, 2150–70, 3102–29, 3816–43,
                     4215–42 (om. 4238–9), 4530–57,
                     5524–51,[26] 6301–35, 7050–70.

fos. 191ᵛ–9ʳ: II. 778–805, 512–623, 1429–63, 1863–95,
                     2171–233, 2521–48, 2934–61, 3326–46,
                     <u>3536–56</u>, <u>3697–731</u>, 3935–55, <u>4222–63</u>,
                     <u>4404–59</u>.

fos. 199ʳ–202ʳ: III. 1569–638, 2164–70, 2178–91,
                     2199–205,[27] 2605–6, 2609, 2607–8,
                     2610–11, 2619–25, 2612–18, 2626–39,[28]
                     3088–115, 3683–717, 4019–60.

It is noticeable that the extracts from the *Fall* nearly all consist of Lydgate's refrained envoy passages (underlined extracts are those of narrative, rather than envoy, material); this fits the pattern of moralistic material we have seen earlier in the manuscript and, moreover (whether the redactor knew it or not), results in an anthology of those parts of Lydgate's translation which are *original* to the English poet.[29] Additionally, in the case of *Fall* II. 4222–63 the redactor displays remarkable sensitivity to Lydgate's regiminal idiom by unerringly picking out a moralizing narrative (that is, non-envoy) section of the poem, one of Lydgate's own additions to the material he found in Laurent's French text.

---

[25] Correcting Edwards (1971*a*: 341): 'fos. 171ʳ–7ʳ'. Italicized references here indicate those omitted in Edwards's checklist. For a list of corrections of selections in seven manuscripts see Mortimer (1995).   [26] Correcting '4523–5551'.

[27] The extracts III. 2164–70, 2178–91, 2199–205 represent a jumbled version of the envoy to III. ch. 5 ('Gemebundi quidam') and may reflect the condition of the redactor's exemplar text. Equally, the omission of the problematic Rome envoy (II. 4460–592, cf. *Fall* ed. Bergen vol. iv. 4, 6) suggests that the exemplar was defective here.   [28] Edwards (1971*a*: 342): italicized text correcting '2605–39'.

[29] His only omissions from the envoys to narratives in Books I to III are those to I. chs. 4, 11, 12, 17 (Samson), 18 ('In mulieres'); II. chs. 7, 23 (Rome); III. chs. 2, 16, 19.

Given the ethical seriousness we have detected in the opening compilation of texts in the manuscript, it comes as no surprise that the next sections excerpted from the *Fall* are the two chapters dealing with the Fall of Man (I. 469–1001): the Trinity redactor-scribe's focus on moral behaviour is sharpened by the collocation of his regiminal text with this biblical demonstration of the importance of personal ethical accountability. It is also interesting that the compiler perceives so strong a relationship between the *Fall* and Chaucer's 'Monk's Tale':[30] not only does he place them in close company, but he also uses them interchangeably—the omission of the Monk's first two narratives is justified by moving the Lydgatean Fall narrative so that it precedes Chaucer's text. Again, the inclusion of the non-envoy lines II. 3697–731 from the end of the Croesus story seems motivated by a desire to supply a firm moral to the last Chaucerian tragedy.

The decision to embed the Monk's tale within the *Fall* selections serves, as Edwards has noted, to modify 'the moral inadequacy of the Monk's tragedies' and counteracts the emphasis of Chaucer's text on the blindly arbitrary power of Fortune 'by placing the tale within a different context of Christian history and moral precept'.[31] However a caveat is necessary here, for the Trinity redactor is not quite so sophisticated a student of Chaucer as this claim suggests. It has been shown that the influence of Chaucer's poem on Lydgate's work is to supply a definition of tragedy which rests on the pathos generated by undeserved misfortune; in selecting precisely those passages from the *Fall* which are most nakedly didactic in their ethic of moral accountability, therefore, the redactor misrepresents the role of Fortune in Lydgate's work. Moreover, the teaching of Lydgate's envoys is ad hoc and dependent on the narratives they accompany; in severing the logical relationships between narrative and envoy the redactor produces a florilegium of passages that is uniformly moralistic in *tone*, but jarringly inconsistent in content.[32]

---

[30] A relationship which is encouraged by the emphasis on the poem's envoy sections, for it is chiefly in these passages that Lydgate uses the word 'tragedy'.

[31] Edwards (1977: 436).

[32] Namely, I. 1814–41, 2150–70, 3102–29, 4530–57; III. 2164–70, 2178–91, 2199–205 all describe an arbitrary and capricious Fortune in control of human destiny, while I. 3816–43; II. 512–623, 778–805, 1429–63, 1863–95, 3935–55 advocate moral (and pious) behaviour, discussing the falls of princes in terms of deserved punishment. Confusingly, I. 6301–35 seems to offer both possibilities for Priam and Hector.

Cambridge University Library MS Ff. i. 6 ('Findern')

The Findern manuscript, an anthology of English verse, similarly selects sections from the poem and presents them in the company of other texts so that a clearly focused reading emerges. Lydgate's poem 'A Wicked Tunge wille Sey Amys' runs from fos. 147ʳ–150ʳ[33] and is followed by three stanzas on fo. 150ʳ from the *Fall* version of Boccaccio's chapter on credulous princes (I. ch. 11: 'Adversus nimiam credulitatem') which also deal with the evils caused by the human tongue ('For there is nomore dredfull pestelens | Than is tonge that can flatre 7 fage').[34] Following these lines on fo. 150ᵛ without break are Pandarus' stanzas on the evils of boasting among lovers ('O tonge, allas! . . . ') from the third book of *Troilus*.[35] Finally, the sequence concludes on fo. 151ʳ with an unidentified stanza:

> A good god of hys high grace
> Lo what fortune is take hede
> Wher her lyketh sche marketh his chasse
> Now most j in servyse my lyffe lede
> Bothe loue serue and eke drede
> As he that is boonde and wol not be free
> Ryght so farithe hit now by me[36]

It is evident that the Findern scribe regards these several texts as coherent in message. That they should follow Lydgate's moralistic 'A Wicked Tunge' is broadly appropriate, of course, but how consistently do they work together? All seven stanzas might appropriately be described as 'ethical' in their concern, but the differences between them are important. Lydgate's lines are oriented towards more broadly *public* aspects of personal morality: his references to God's grace rewarding those who speak well of others and later to 'rihtful iuges sittyng on a rowe' serve as a reminder that outside forces constrain both personal and social behaviour.[37] Just as the individual must be mindful of the report

---

[33] *MP* ii. 839–44. A facsimile edition of the manuscript exists (Findern Manuscript ed. Beadle and Owen 1977).   [34] *Fall* I. 4621–41.

[35] *TC* III. 302–22 (here as 'O false tong . . . ').

[36] This stanza is not mentioned by Edwards in his list, nor do the editors of the facsimile acknowledge its existence in their table of the manuscript's contents (p. xxvii). I have been unable to trace it either in Brown and Robbins's *IMEV* or in Robbins and Cutler's *Supplement*.   [37] *Fall* I. 4632, 4637.

he gives of his neighbour, so too must the representatives of the public judiciary carefully weigh evidence before they pronounce judgement: in this way does Lydgate present the imperatives of personal ethics as having a correlative in wider social mechanisms.

Cambridge, Trinity College MS R. 3. 20

Extracts from the *Fall* characteristically appear in the company of broadly moral or political writings. John Shirley, the anthologist of Trinity College MS R. 3. 20 (labelled 'Lvdgati opera quedam Anglie', fo. 1*ʳ), demonstrates a preference for advisory Lydgate texts and (alongside certain religious poems)[38] presents his selections from the *Fall* in the company of Hoccleve's *Letter of Cupid* and Lydgate's own coronation ballad for Henry VI and occasional poems on the marriage of Duke Humphrey to Jacqueline of Hainault and on the Duchess's departure to Holland.[39] The interest of his readers in affairs of high politics is attested by a short prefatory note (in a later hand) to this last poem on fo. 363ʳ:

[scribe]   Complaynt for my lady of holand etc

[glossator]   Wyffe to humfrey duke of glosester howe y`e´ sayd humfrey
              ungodly maryed, she beynge y`e´ lawfull wyffe of John duke
              of brabaunt, 7 besyde her he all so y`e´ company of othar
              amongste y`e´ whiche was one Elianor Chobham, who by
              sorsere 7 wicche craftes caused hym to leave y`e´ said Jaquyl
              of holand 7 to marie hem y`e´ sayd Elianore, who afftar was
              a traytoresse to kynge henry y`e´ vj

It is interesting that when the scribe copies a section from the *Fall* later in the manuscript he should choose the ten-stanza envoy to Lydgate's version of the 'In portentosam principum libidinem' chapter in Book III: this same narrative, with its heady combination of tyranny and sexual politics, provided the material for the selection from the poem at the front of MS R. 3. 19. Whereas that manuscript selects passages from the narrative which present women as the pathetic victims of lustful princes, the envoy passage (III. 1569–638) given in MS R. 3. 20 is by comparison *anti*-feminist in tone: David may have deserved the miseries visited on him for

---

[38] Namely the *Life of Our Lady, S. Margarete (MP* i. 173), and Lydgate's poem on the Corpus Christi procession (*MP* I. 35).

[39] *MP* ii. 624, 601, 608; see Strohm (2000).

his lust for Bathsheba, but the suggestion elsewhere is that the women were themselves to blame for the lechery of Solomon, Samson, and the biblical rapist Shechem, rather than the men.[40] Lydgate observes that 'Wher women haue the dominacio*u*n' reason and virtue are defeated and sensuality has 'iuredicciou*n*'.[41] The envoy concludes with a warning to princes to be aware of 'the fals decepciou*n*' of women, their 'sugred flatrie . . . fals collusiou*n* | Lik to Sirens with vois melodious'.[42] The scribe of MS R . 3. 20, then, has a less subtle agenda than that of MS R . 3. 19; furthermore, he introduces the envoy on fo. 368ᵛ with a headnote that encourages the reader to see the extract in connection with its patron, Duke Humphrey:

Loo here my lordes begynne*þe* a balade royal nowe late made by Daun Johan Lydegate *þe* Monk of Bury ymagyned by him with in *þe* tyme of his translacon of Bocas by *þe* co*mm*andement of my lord of Gloucestre.

Immediately preceding this heading and the envoy on fo. 368ᵛ is a single wordplay stanza from the *Fall* (II. 4432–38)[43] which seems to have been popular among anthologists: the scribe of MS Sloane 1825 reproduces it in a similarly political environment alongside his copy of Hoccleve's *Regement of Princes*.[44] It is possible that the scribe of MS R. 3. 20 may here be conscripting the *Fall* envoy to make a particular comment on Humphrey's unpopular marriages and well-known misfortunes at the hands of women; certainly, the word 'Videte' in the margin of the envoy shows that it was felt to be an important inclusion in the manuscript. The explicitly contextualizing gloss on Humphrey's marriages on fo. 363ʳ shows that at least one reader tuned into the manuscript's underlying political involvement and (as if feeling it to be too subtle) supplied a blunter statement of topical reference.

The *Fall* extracts are followed in MS R .3. 20 by a list of the order of precedence of the nobles of the Order of the Garter for the visit to England of Sigismund, king of Hungary and later Holy

---

[40] Lydgate explicitly claims that Delilah assaulted Samson 'with teres plenteu-ous' and 'made hym lecherous', (*Fall* III. 1602–3); for the story of Shechem and Dinah see Gen. 34: 2.   [41] Ibid. III. 1619, 1621.

[42] Ibid. III. 1633, 1636–7.

[43] Edwards (1971b: 339): unrecorded by Edwards; note the corrected headnote.

[44] BL MS Sloane 1825, fo. 90ᵛ: the scribe, however, gives no indication that he realizes that the stanza is by Lydgate.

Roman emperor, under the heading 'Ista sunt nomina ordine sancti Georgi de Garterio Anno quo Sigismundi Rex Romanorum fuit in Anglia tempore Regis Henrici Quinti'.[45] What emerges from this otherwise unexceptional catalogue of titles is a close interest in the minutiae of diplomatic protocol; the scribe of MS R .3. 20 shares the ethical reading of Lydgate we saw in the scribe of MS R. 3. 19, but differs from the redactor of that manuscript in his more narrowly *political* concerns. The fact that the Garter list also bears the heading 'Bochas' is perhaps a significant slip, showing us something of what the scribe expected from the *De casibus*: generally proverbial or moralistic matter alone was not enough for him, and so 'Boccaccio' is made to authenticate material of a more day-to-day and pragmatic political usefulness.

Oxford, Bodleian Library MS Digby 181 and London, British Library MS Sloane 4031

Such purposive readings of Lydgate's poem also emerge in other scribal extracts: the scribe of MS Digby 181 heightens his selections from Lydgate's rendering of the moralistic 'Adversus nimiam credulitatem' chapter (1. ch. 11) by silently omitting the end of the chapter with its criticisms of women and of Theseus (1. 4663–816) and by jumping straight to the punchy envoy (1. 4817–44). In this way general satire and particular legendary involvement are jettisoned in preference for four stanzas of more focused advisory idiom, intended to be applicable to any noble reader.

A further striking example of this propensity for scribes to emphasize 'regiminal Lydgate' is seen in MS Sloane 4031, a neat copy of the *Fall* which contains in later hands a ten-stanza, rhyme-royal advisory poem at the start of the manuscript (fos. 2^r–v) and an eighty-line political prophecy pertaining to the Wars of the Roses at the end (fo. 189^v). Bergen has summarized the contents of the prophecy in the fourth volume of his edition,[46] but the reginimal poem (which is the only extant version recorded in Brown's index)[47] has not received critical attention. In interesting ways this text is a mirror image of the reginimal emphasis of the

[45] Referring to Sigismund's visit of 1416 (see Capgrave, ed. Lucas 1983: 246).
[46] *Fall* ed. Bergen vol. iv. 59–60.
[47] Brown, (1916–20: no. 2704), Brown and Robbins, (1943: *IMEV* no. 4257); printed in *Historical Poems*, ed. Robbins (1959: 233–5).

Fall envoys; whereas those passages are typically directed at princes and advise on virtuous and responsible rule, these stanzas join such advice with instructions for those who are 'comons' (counselling loyal, obedient, industrious, and pious citizenship) and for those in the spiritual estate: that the scribe regarded these stanzas as in some sense consonant with the emphases of Lydgate's poem is clear from his decision to head them 'Bocas' (fo. 2^r). Although the poem is unsystematic in structure, a broad balance is maintained between self-discipline (the 'inner kingship' evoked by the popular tag 'si rex esse velis, te rege, rex et eris'[48]) and a public virtue that finds expression in acts of social charity and restraint. By this means more explicitly political counsel (on the need for 'law concorde and vnete', for 'ryght and egvyte') is married to advice on avarice, wrath, and the corporeal deadly sins of lust, gluttony, and sloth.

London, British Library MSS Harley 2251, Additional 29729, Lansdowne 699 et al.

If Trinity College MS R. 3. 19 represents an attempt to collate the envoys of the poem, then MS Harley 2251 witnesses to a far more ambitious and disciplined engagement with the same project; whereas the Trinity redactor abandons his catalogue in the third book of the *Fall*, the Harley scribe continues to the end of the work (fos. 81^r–145^v), selecting the following extracts:[49]

I. <u>967–1001</u>,[50] 904–66.
IX. <u>2371–433</u>.[51]
I. 1380–6, 1394–400, 1338–79, 1520–33, <u>1814–24</u>,
<u>1830–4</u>, <u>1835–41</u>,[52] 2150–70, 3102–29, <u>3816–43</u>,
<u>4215–42</u> (om. 4238–9), <u>4530–43</u>,[53] <u>4551–7</u>, <u>5503–9</u>,
<u>5517–30</u>, <u>5538–51</u>, <u>6301–35</u>, <u>7050–70</u>.
II. <u>778–805</u>, 512–623, 1429–63, 1863–76, <u>1884–95</u>,[54]
<u>2171–84</u>, <u>2192–8</u>, <u>2185–91</u>, <u>2199–233</u>, <u>2346–66</u>,[55]

---

[48] 'If you wish to be a king, first rule yourself and then you will be a king'; cf. Gower, *Vox clamantis* VI. ch. 8, l. 606, (Gower ed. Macaulay 1902: 248).
[49] Correcting Edwards (1971*b*: 339): 'fos. 81^v–145^v'. Extracts which consist of or contain envoy material are here indicated by underlining.
[50] Correcting ibid.: 'I. 967–1011'.   [51] Correcting ibid.: 'IX. 2370–443'.
[52] Correcting ibid.: '1814–27, 1834–41'.   [53] Correcting ibid.: '4537–43'.
[54] Correcting ibid.: '1884–97'.   [55] Correcting ibid.: '2345–66'.

2374–464, 2472–8, 2486–527, 2234–338,[56]
2528–48, 2934–61, 3326–46, 3536–56, 3697–731,
3935–55 (om. 3949), 4222–63, 4404–59 (om. 4431).
III. 1569–638, 2164–70, 2178–91, 2199–205, 3683–717,
      4019–32, 4040–6, 4033–9, 4047–60, 3837–43,
      3851–71.
II. 4460–592 (om. 4481–7).
III. 890–931, 4208–35, 5118–52.
IV. 638–86, 904–38, 1422–49, 1968–2002, 2297–331,
      2927–68, 3445–92, 3717–44.
V. 841–75, 1590–621, 1846–85, 2131–58, 2509–36,
      3118–38.
VI. 1709–57.
VII. 775–95.
I. 2171–338.
VIII. 3137–64.
IX. 1478–512, 3022–56, 3589–604.
II. 3347–556.
I. 4845–968, 4703–4,[57] 4702–844,[58] 3788–94,
      3431–58, 3522–35, 3795–801, 4558–64, 4572–92,
      4649–62, 4971–84, 5104–31, 5195–201, 5510–16,
      5153–9, 2822–8, 2500–20, 1807–13, 4719–25,
      6511–45, 6553–87, 6595–601.
III. 2465–71.[59]
I. 2843–9, 6644–71, 6679–706, 6623–9, 6616–22,
      6609–15, 4488–94, 4663–76, 6336–56, 6371–7,
      6490–6, 6427–68, 6505–10, 6504,[60] 6707–13,
      6721–7, 6126–300.

Several significant points emerge from the Harley manuscript's selections from the *Fall*. First, the scribe's sympathy for generalized moral precept is seen in his consistent emphasis on the poem's envoys: he includes nearly every envoy in the text and demonstrates his anthologizing mentality by carefully backtracking to include omitted passages, as when he inserts the Rome envoy (II. 4460–592), the only one he had omitted of the eleven sections in

<hr/>

[56] Correcting ibid.: '2234–8'.
[57] Correcting Edwards (1971*b*: 340): 'I. 4845–72'.
[58] Correcting ibid.: '4705–844'.   [59] Correcting ibid.: 'III. 2458–64'.
[60] Correcting ibid.: '6504–10'.

Book II, in the middle of his catalogue from the third book (on fos. 107^r–109^r), and when he adds the envoy to the eleventh chapter of Book I (I. 4817–44) after the end of his catalogue of envoys.[61]

Secondly, the Harley scribe shows a sensitivity to the collocation of extracts: he moves from his treatment of the seventh book back to Book I, and inserts the first half of the Jason and Medea material from the long seventh chapter (the 'Concursus infoelicium') on fos. 121^r–123^v. This decision at first seems perplexing, for the scribe truncates the moralizing conclusion to the story (I. 2339–408) and ends with the conclusion of the narrative proper (Jason leaves Medea for Corinth where he marries Creusa, whom Medea burns in revenge) before moving quickly on to the only envoy in Book VIII (fo. 124^r). However, this envoy is that of Arthur and Mordred and deals with inter-family violence, taking variations on the moral 'Let men bewar euere of vnkynde blood' as its concatenating theme.[62] The Harley scribe's collecting impulse, then, leads him to pause before this envoy and supply earlier narrative action in evidence of the moral he finds there: Medea murdered her brother (I. 2117–18) and later persuaded the daughters of Pelias to kill their own father (I. 2262–310). The fact that the scribe omits the first stanza of the Arthur envoy (VIII. 3130–6) may further testify to his refining engagement with Lydgate's text, for it is this stanza that links the passage explicitly back to the narrative which has preceded it ('This tragedie of Arthour heer folwyng', . . . VIII. 3130); thus the scribe exploits the moral valency of the envoy by uncoupling its precepts from the Arthurian story and allowing it to reflect on the sins of Medea.

Elsewhere the scribe shows a close control of his anthology: his insertion of the Patience narrative from Book ix (IX. 2370–433) after the envoy on Adam and Eve would seem to suggest that he found the teaching of those lines particularly apposite after the story of the Fall of Man ('o noble Pacience . . . | Ground and gynnyng to stonden at diffence | Ageyns Sathanis infernal puissau*n*ce, IX. 2371, 2378–9') Later, when he selects from the material in Book I he is careful to avoid duplicating envoys he has already

---

[61] In total the Harley redactor omits only one envoy from Book I (that of ch. 12), two each from Books III–VII, and three of the six narrative envoys in Book IX.
[62] *Fall* VIII. 3143.

given.[63] For all his careful manoeuvrings, however, MS Harley 2251 does contain one repetition of material: the transcription of the envoy to the nineteenth chapter of Book II (II. 3536–56) on fos. 129[r–v] has already been included in his catalogue from the second book, even though it was not there in the company of the biblical material to which it refers (Nebuchadnezzar's restoration and the sacrilege of Belshazzar).

However, the clearest and most impressive manipulation of Lydgate's text by the Harley redactor is to be seen in the selection of largely non-envoy material from Book I with which he concludes his anthology on fos. 129[v]–45[r]. This selection begins as a collection of narrative material from chapter XII (Althaea, I. 4845–72), an omitted envoy and its relevant chapter (I. 4705–844), material from the story of Oedipus, and advice against hasty credence (I. 4572–92, 4649–62). What then follows, however, is a thoroughgoing compendium of anti-feminist material from the longest book of the *Fall.* Beginning with Lydgate's lament for Hercules ('Allas! allas! al noblesse & prudence . . . | Be sleihte off women dirkid and diffacid!', I. 5510, 5516), the collection continues with material from the Phaedra narrative, to the effect that women are liars (I. 2822–8), from Scylla, on the vice of women (I. 2500–20), and with eighteen other selections to illustrate the pride of women (I. 4719–25), their malice (I. 6511–45), feigned deceits (I. 6595–601), use of cosmetics (I. 6553–87), and their wiles (I. 6609–15), and containing lists of infamous women (I. 6623–9, 6616–22, 6609–15). The whole anthology deviates to include a few of Lydgate's defences of women from the Xerxes narrative in Book III and from Book I (III. 2458–64; I. 2843–9, 6644–71, 6679–706), but concludes with a sequence of stanzas urging men not to believe their wives and, as if as a clinching finale, with hostile material from the narrative and envoy of Samson and from Lydgate's envoy treatment of Boccaccio's anti-feminist chapter XVIII, 'In mulieres'. From a systematic gutting of Lydgate's poem, then, the Harley scribe compiles a misogynist anthology of which the Wife of Bath's Jankin might have been proud. Certainly, energetic marginal annotations (in the scribe's own hand) show that the material was felt to be unfairly partisan— the marginalia threatens 'Lydgate' with intemperate action which

---

[63] e.g. he begins a selection at I. 4558, having given two stanzas from the preceding envoy (that of Theseus, I. 4530–57).

could have been learned from Chaucer's Wife, at one point (fo. 142ʳ, alongside the rhetorically flamboyant I. 6441–7) writing: 'Be pees or j wil rende this leef out of yoʼrʼ booke'.[64]

The familiarity with the *Fall* required to produce such a reorganization of the poem is considerable, and is greater than that needed merely to collate envoy passages, for, while extant *Fall* manuscripts typically signal the envoys with sub-headings or rubrication (or both), the Harley scribe would have had no such help in his search for material in detraction of women. This awareness of the *Fall* as a 'document capable of being adapted by selection to propagandize a particular point of view'[65] may also be seen in other manuscript anthologies from the work. Other scribes share the Harley misogynist's attitudes to women and, like him, find Lydgate's poem an apt vehicle for articulating these views. John Stow's MS Additional 29729 (dated 'mdlviii' on fo. 288ᵛ) is a large Lydgate anthology copied from Trinity MS R. 3. 20 which contains several shorter texts (mummings, 'Ram's Horn', 'Tyed with a Lyne') as well as the longer *Siege of Thebes* (fos. 17ʳ–83ʳ), *Lyf of St Margarete* (fos. 170ᵛ–7ᵛ), *Reson and Sensuallyte* (fos. 184ʳ–286ᵛ), and part of the *Testament* (fos. 179ᵛ–83ʳ).[66] One of the scribes finds no difficulty in reproducing the Trinity manuscript's anti-feminist *Fall* selection from the 'In portentosam' chapter (III. 1569–638)[67] and another reader compounds this bias with an addition of his own—a one-stanza extract from the *Cato Major* by Lydgate's disciple Benedict Burgh (fo. 288ᵛ):

> Sum wemen wepyn of peure feminite
> Whan othar wyse they can not theyr intent
> Achyve but yet be ware of suche nyce pite
> Thy manly reson for þʼtʼ it be not blent
> For swiche wepyng thyn hert may not relent
> Some wemen of kynd evar wepynge
> 7 vndar þʼtʼ can they bothe pryke 7 stynge [68]

---

[64] These well-known annotations have been noted by Pearsall (1970: 75), who claims they are by Shirley, and have been printed by Edwards (1972*b*): cf. Utley (1944: 181, 193, 313); Hammond (1905); Doyle (1961). Edwards transcribes the forty-two stanzas which relate to the annotator's rebukes (i.e. fos. 138ʳ–143ʳ, I. 4719–25 onwards); however, as I have shown, the anti-feminist selection begins at least seven stanzas before this point. For a fifteenth-century use of the *Fall* as a source of anti-feminist material (in BL MS Arundel 20) see Wright (1957: 21–2).
[65] Edwards (1972*b*: 33).   [66] The Prologue (ll. 1–30) only is given.
[67] fos. 169ᵛ–170ᵛ.
[68] ll. 769–75 (st. 111) (Burgh ed. Kuriyagawa 1974.) Cf. Brown (1916–20: ii. 89), where the stanza is wrongly given as no. 104. Cf. Förster (1905).

Other selections are not as anti-feminist. The dialectally southern copyist of Bodleian MS e Musaeo 1 at first seems to share these scribes' heightened interest in anti-feminist sentiment, for he draws marginal hands pointing out the relevant sections of the poem (e.g. fo. 85ᵛ: *Fall* IV. 2449–50), but then balances them with pointers to the defences of good women (e.g. fo. 7ᵛ: *Fall* I. 8000). The scribe of MS Harley 172 (a collection of broadly regiminal material containing Peter Idley's *Instructions*[69] and an appropriate *Cato* extract on fos. 62ʳ–5ʳ beginning 'Behold my child . . .') goes one step further, however, when he opens his collection on fos. 1*ʳ–2ᵛ with the moralizing first half of Lydgate's version of the 'Adversus nimiam credulitatem' chapter (I. 4558–662), but then on fo. 2ᵛ jumps without any break from I. 4662 to the envoy to the chapter (I. 4817–44), thereby effectively and silently excising the intervening anti-feminist material (I. 4663–816).[70] MS Digby 181 does exactly the same in its brief selection from the poem on fos. 52ʳ–53ᵛ (I. 4558–662, 4817–44), raising the possibility that these two selections may be related.

The 'In portentosam' envoy (III. 1569–638) seems to have been especially popular: it has already been seen in MSS Trinity R. 3. 19 and R. 3. 20 and, of course, MS Harley 2251. It is also to be found in MS Ashmole 59 (fos. 15ʳ–16ᵛ), Stow's MS Harley 367 (which may have been copied from Shirley's Ashmole text),[71] Pierpont Morgan Library MS M. 4, and Pepys MS 2011. The section is still a favourite with copyists even when scribal inaccuracy or mechanical error alters it radically: MS Harley 4011 opens with a muddled version of Lydgate's account of the lechery of David (III. 1569–89) on fo. 1ᵛ,[72] and then moves on to offer a garbled rendition of the last two stanzas of the passage, reducing the lines on the harmful effects of female domination (III. 1625–31) to

> It taketh fro men ther cleernesse off seyng   (III. 1625)
> Shorteth ther daies, thyng dredful & pitous   (III. 1630)
> Maketh men seeme old, as be inspeccioun   (III. 1628)

---

[69] fos. 21ʳ–51ᵛ.

[70] Ironically, in omitting I. 4663–816, MS Harley 172 also excludes Lydgate's lines in defence of women (I. 4719–53).

[71] *N & Q* 214 (1969: 171)—not *N & Q* 216, as stated by Edwards (1971*b*: 339).

[72] The selection is repetitious, running as follows: III. 1569–75, 1569–82, rather than III. 1569–75, 1569–89 (Edwards 1971*b*: 340): in omitting III. 1583–9 the Harley scribe elides David's repentance.

Elsewhere, however, the bias of scribes is seen in their more ortho-dox emphasis on political material: the only selection from the *Fall* in MS Arundel 26 (fo. 32ʳ) is the 'Adversus nimiam creduli-tatem' envoy which directs 'pryncis, pryncessis . . . I Which haue lordschipe and domynaciou*n*' to be prudent and circumspect.[73] We have seen that MSS Sloane 4031, Harley 172, and Harley 4011 all present their *Fall* texts in the context of other regiminal works. These can find their way into the company of Lydgate's stanzas both systematically (as a result of having been collected by the copyist to form a 'political anthology') and casually (as later additions by readers with a regiminal interest). The Idley extract in MS Harley 172 fos. 21ʳ–51ᵛ is an example of the first of these,[74] as too is the presence of the Lancastrian 'Libelle of English Policy' in the Lydgate anthology MS Harley 4011 (fos. 120ʳ–37ʳ.) This last Harley book closes with verse precepts for Edward III (fos. 171ʳ–89ʳ) which range in their interest from mat-ters of high politics (describing the duties pertaining to the offices of 'chamburlayne', 'the warderobeȝ' and 'the state of a Pope, Emperor, kyng or Cardynall I Prynce w`t´ goldyn rodde Royall I Archebischoppe vsyng to wer þ`e´ palle')[75] to domestic advice on diet and carving meats. The attitude of MS Lansdowne 699, another Lydgate anthology, towards Lydgate's poem shows a par-ticularly specialized interest in political affairs, following the nar-rative and envoy on Arthur (VIII. 2661–3206, fos. 51ʳ–60ᵛ) immediately (and with no indication of a break) with the last stanza from Book III (III. 5146–52, fo. 61ʳ) on the mischief caused by 'blod vnkynde born of o kynreede',[76] then selecting the narrat-ive of the Emperor Constantine (VIII. 1177–463, fos. 61ᵛ–6ᵛ), and, later, the chapter and envoy on the Golden World from Book VII (VII. 1153–334, fos. 91ᵛ–4ᵛ), itself devoted to the theme of tem-perate 'gouernaunce'. The narrow focus on matters of rule is seen in several small-scale scribal decisions: for example, the scribe underlines in red the words 're publica' at VIII. 2760 and 2771

---

[73] *Fall* I. 4838–9, 4843. This envoy is also found in MSS Digby 181, Ashmole 59, St John's Cambridge 223, Harley 172, and Harley 2251.

[74] MS Harley 172 gives Book I of the poem omitting only 2 stanzas (ll. 1–420, 428–1190, 1198–470) (Idley ed. d'Evelyn 1935: 63).

[75] fos. 184ʳ, 185ʳ, 186ᵛ.

[76] *Fall* III. 5152. That his readers found the account of Arthur's fall moving is shown by frequent scribbles on fo. 61ʳ, among them 'oh false treator mordred'. The Lansdowne collocation of texts forms a variation on the treatment of the Arthur envoy by the scribe of Harley 2251.

(both fo. 52ᵛ—usually only proper nouns are so rubricated in this manuscript) and 'rem publicam' at VII. 1331 (fo. 94ᵛ); and he also omits the first stanza to the Constantine section in which Lydgate announces his intention to diverge from the text of the *Des Cas* (VIII. 1170–6), instead inserting these lines on fo. 61ᵛ:

> What thyng may be more of excellence
> Or in a prynce more for to comende
> Than is in god with a trewe pretence
> <u>Verray feith</u> that al thyng doth transcende
> My menyng is if that ye wol attende
> Off <u>Constantyne</u> in Rome Emperor
> Which to our <u>feith</u> did passand gret honor[77]

The Constantine narrative then opens at VIII. 1177 with a brief fantasia of ancient Britain's imperial authority ('This myhti prince was born in Breteyne, | So as the Brut pleynli doth vs lere') which naturally follows the nationalism of the Arthurian selections. Having drawn our attention to the relationship between imperial authority and Christian faith in his prefatory stanza, the scribe further reinforces his theme by underlining the last words of Constantine's crucial fourth-day donation of spiritual authority to the Popes which enables them 'to haue the reule and iurediccioun | Of preestis alle, <u>allone in alle thyng</u>, | <u>Of temporal lordis lich as hath the kyng</u>'.[78] A partially illegible marginal note on fo. 64ʳ here alerts us to the scribe's chosen emphasis and reads 'The Pope by the la<. . . > | of Constantyne to h<ave> | iurrisdiction above | the Spiritualtie [*sic*]'. While the focus of the Lansdowne scribe is, then, partly a churchy one (emphasizing as he does the demarcation between secular and ecclesiastical power),[79] at heart we find in his selections a generally *political* interest: elsewhere a marginal hand recognizes and continues the manuscript's specialized interest in political power by providing a dynastic gloss to the Lydgatean account on fos. 79ʳ–80ᵛ of the kings of England from William the Conqueror to Henry VI.[80]

---

[77] This stanza is only found in one other extant manuscript (Leyden, MS Vossius 9, fo. 75ʳ) (Edwards 1969: 170–1). Underlining here indicates text which is underlined in red in the MS.   [78] *Fall* VIII. 1314–16.

[79] This emphasis is found also in MS Harley 1245, which includes Lydgate's 'Defence of Holy Church' at the end of the text of the *Fall* (fos. 182ᵛ–3ʳ).

[80] Cf. *MP* ii. 710–16: the extract in MS Lansdowne 699 is ll. 106–210. The gloss on fo. 79ʳ reads 'Not þ`t´ willm ruf<us> had. 3. sonnes. <þe> first called Wil<lm> Rufus. þ`e´ seco<nd> harry the firs<t> þ`e´ thyrd was Robert duke of Normandye. Robert of Normandy dyed before his br<oþer> Harry for w`ch´ raus

Given Lydgate's own understanding of the importance of Fortune in his poem, it is interesting to ask how often scribes selecting from the *Fall* ever show signs of engaging with the poem as a collection of tragedies or of recognizing Lydgate's interest in the action of Lady Fortune. It is unlikely that readers would ever have made close comparison of the English poem with its French prose source (indeed, many headings in the extant manuscripts show that readers were prepared to believe that the work was a direct translation of Boccaccio's Latin[81]), but even without the opportunity of contrasting the poem with any predecessor, how many copyists or annotators focus on the poem's discussion of the issues of fate and human freedom of will? It is my experience that very few readers of the extant manuscripts show so sophisticated an awareness of the tragic aspects of the poem: for example, the powerful account of the meeting of Bocace and Fortuna from the start of Book VI is surprisingly *not* a popular selection from the poem; its (partial) inclusion in MS Ashmole 59 (fos. 118[r–v]) is very much an exception—even the rapacious MS Harley 2251 redactor passes over the encounter.[82] Manuscripts differ widely in their handling of the moral issues raised by a powerful Lady Fortune. The Lansdowne MS rounds off its compilation of texts dealing with political power and the morality of rule with the first three stanzas of Chaucer's 'Fortune' (fo. 81[r]): in these stanzas the 'Pleintif countre Fortune' delivers a spirited denial of the omnipotence of 'Fortunes errour' and so neatly demonstrates a recognition that ethical self-government rests on moral accountability.[83] Other scribes seem less acute. MS Royal 18 B. XXXI contains scribbled comments that illustrate an imprecise grasp of the role of

<on> theyr cosin Steph<en> was crowned kin<g>'. Verses on the kings of England are also found in Bodleian MS Rawlinson C. 448, fos. 2*[v]–1[r], 181[r–v]. MS Sloane 4031 also demonstrates such historical glossing as a reader gives the date of the English defeat of John II on fo. 4[r] ('19°. sept. 1356° was the Kyng of France takyn prisoner at the Battle of Poytiers: by Edward Prince of Wales, sonne of King Edward the 3').

[81] e.g. the Longleat MS and California University Library MS 75. Cf. Edwards (1977: 428): 'It seems quite likely that for an English audience the *Fall of Princes* and the *De casibus* were perforce synonymous, even though they were significantly different works.'

[82] MS Ashmole 59 only gives the initial description of Fortune (VI. 1–63) and ignores the debate that follows. None of the other manuscripts listed by Edwards (1971*b*) contains this section.

[83] 'Fortune' ll. 1–24 (Chaucer ed. Benson 1988: 652).

Fortune in the poem ('Arte co*m*endatio de i*n*stabili*t*ate fortune', fo. 1ʳ, 'fama no*n* est p*er*petua', fo. 9ᵛ), but it cannot be argued from these scraps alone that the scribe had a developed understanding of the way in which the Lydgatean tragedies function. In this area one must make do with the little evidence available, namely the suggestive (but inconclusive) interweaving of the 'Monk's Tale' tragedies with the *Fall* material in Trinity MS R. 3. 19, discussed above; a Chaucerian side note towards the end of the narrative of Jugurtha (v. 3062–8) on fo. 109ᵛ in MS Harley 4197 reading 'A tragide beguneth with ioye and endeth with sorowe';[84] and the choice of extracts in the Fitzwilliam McClean MS 182. The McClean manuscript contains nine brief selections from the poem,[85] opening with envoy stanzas on the role of Fortune's wheel in the 'tragedie of the duk Po*m*peie' and then balancing this fortunal envoy with the virtue-centred teaching of the envoy to the narrative of Rehoboam in Book II. Later in the manuscript the copyist acutely selects the three stanzas from the *Paupertatis et fortunae certamen* in which Poverty divests Fortune of any power:

> Sum*m*e poetis and philisophres also
> Wolde in this cas make the a goddesse,
> Which be deceyued, I dar seyn, bothe too
>
> .   .   .   .   .
>
> Thou shalt forgon thi dominaciou*n*
> To hyndre or harme any creature,
> But onli foolis, which in thi myht assure.
> Thei off ther foli may feele gret damage,
> Nat off thi power, but off ther owne outrage.[86]

It becomes clear that the McClean scribe has set out to compile an anthology that demonstrates the moral inadequacy of Fortune-led understandings of human behaviour and which finds its own conclusion in firm ethical teaching: the compilation includes the six-stanza envoy to the narrative of the tyrant Machaeus from Book III, which voices the need for princes to moderate their conduct, and

[84] Cf. *Fall* I. 2160 for a Lydgatean version of this definition.
[85] *Fall* VI. 2521–48; II. 778–805; IV. 2927–40, 2948–61, 2941–7, 2962–8; III. 365–85; IV. 624–30; III. 4019–60; I. 4817–44; III. 2164–205; III. 3088–115—these last three omitted by Edwards (1971*b* 339).
[86] Ibid. III. 624–6, 640–4. The McClean MS is the only extant manuscript to select from the *Certamen* episode.

closes with the envoy to Book III, chapter 9 on the harm done by venal judges. It comes as no surprise that the manuscript also contains Lydgate's *Serpent* (fos. 1ʳ–9ᵛ), his *Secrees* (continued by Burgh, fos. 12ʳ–49ʳ) and Hoccleve's *Regement* (fos. 54ʳ–138ʳ); but, although extracts from the *Fall* are also found with the *Regement* in St John's College Cambridge MS 223,[87] the McClean manuscript's lively interest in issues of tragedy, fortune, and ethical accountability is exceptional. The only text of the *De casibus* surviving in the British Library, the MS Harley 3565 A-version, is much more fruitful in this respect than any of the extant *Fall* manuscripts or anthologies of selections: it collocates the Boccaccian work (fos. 1ʳ–147ʳ) with Albertino Mussato's early Paduan dramatic tragedy, the *Ecerinis* (fos. 147ᵛ–57ʳ).

Manuscripts containing extracts from the *Fall*, then, are often the result of a careful selection of thematically similar passages, or of excerpts that contribute meaningfully to the other texts in the manuscript. The careful construction of these manuscript selections has been seen in the compendious MS Harley 2251, although it is by no means restricted to the extract anthologies: the second scribe of MS Royal 18 D. v, a *Fall* manuscript, scrupulously makes good the loss of leaves from the book by copying the lacking parts of the poem on fos. 185ʳ–92ᵛ and fos. 212ʳ–13ᵛ. The range and number of manuscript selections from the *Fall* attest not only to the popularity of the work in the later medieval period, but also to the characteristically *ethical* ways readers approached the poem. However, the most strikingly independent uses of the *Fall* in the fifteenth and sixteenth centuries consist not in these small-scale selections from the poem, but in rather bolder appropriations— these sometimes being adaptations of sections of the work, but elsewhere being creative assimilations of the *spirit* of the Lydgatean model. It is to Peter Idley that we first turn.

PETER IDLEY'S *INSTRUCTIONS*

The second part of Peter Idley's *Instructions to His Son* (*c.* 1445–50), a lengthy didactic poem in two books, composed in the *Fall* rhyme-royal stanza (*ababbcc*), borrows 336 lines from the

---

[87] *Regement* (fos. 1–93ᵛ), *Fall* I. 4558–64, 4551–7, 4565–711, 4768–830, 4845–51, 4831–7, 4838–44, 6350–77 (fos. 94ʳ–8ᵛ).

first three books of Lydgate's poem to supplement its rendering
of the teaching of Mannyng's *Handlyng Synne* as follows:[88]

Instructions	II. A	1791–5	*Fall*	I. 6574–9
		1798–816		I. 6581–3,
				6630–43
		2022–8		II. 36–42
		2043–56		I. 6679–85,
				6714–20
		2344–85		I. 2150–6,
				6280–93,
				II. 15–21,
				I. 3445–58
		2393–9		I. 2703–9
		2421–31		I. 3837–43,
				3522–5
		2624–37		II. 99–105, 57–63
		2638–44		II. 64–70
		2645–51		II. 113–19
	II. B	78–103, 106,		II. 533–53,
		111–19		I. 939–43,
				974–5, 980–7
		365–71		I. 806–12
		582–6, 594–6,		I. 631–5, 650–1,
		602		640, 658
		1261–7		I. 666–72
		1563–610		I. 793–819,
				825–47
		2535–604		III. 1163–95,
				1205–11,
				1296–323
		2661–74		III. 1401–14
		2682–716		III. 1107–13,
				1373–400

As with the manuscript compilations studied above, Idley's
selection of material from the *Fall* reveals an easy familiarity with
the detail of Lydgate's poem. For example, when dealing with

[88] Idley ed. d'Evelyn (1935: 49 n. 20) supplies an incomplete list of the borrowings from the *Fall*. I have underlined additions to this list and silently corrected
inaccurate references.

the seventh commandment ('Thou shalt not steal') in lines A.
2344–85 Idley draws together widely dispersed stanzas in order
to produce a mini-anthology of Lydgate material dealing with
the virtues of poverty.[89] Equally, when he discusses the sin of pride
at B. 78–119 Idley juxtaposes lines from Lydgate's version of
Boccaccio's chapter in praise of obedience (II. ch. 2: 'Obedientiae
commendatio') with portions from the thematically similar chapter 'Against Disobedience' (I. ch. 2: 'Adversus inobedientiam')
from Book I, [90] again demonstrating his sensitive reading of
the *Fall*.

Unlike the anthology compilations, Idley rarely selects lines
from Lydgate's own envoy sections (in fact, only I. 6714–20,
I. 2150–6, I. 6280–93, and I. 3837–43 originate in these passages), although, as Edwards has noted, he nonetheless shows a
preference for 'Lydgate's characteristic generalizing sententia'.[91]
He chooses stanzas from the moralizing chapter on the failings of
women (Boccaccio's I. ch.18: 'In mulieres') to accompany his
treatment of the sixth commandment ('Thou shalt not commit
adultery') at II. A. 1791–816 and lines from the preface to Book
II of the *Fall* to support the sixth and seventh commandments
(II. A. 2022–8, 2365–71, 2624–51). Similarly, when Idley later
discusses the deadly sin of pride, he co-opts material from
Lydgate's version of Boccaccio's moralizing chapter on the Fall of
Adam ('Adversus inobedientiam') at II. B. 365–71, 99–119, and
1563–610. Idley's avoidance of narrative material not only follows the pattern of the ethical readings of the *Fall* we have already
encountered, but also accords with the didactic intent of the
Instructions. Elsewhere Idley can be seen tailoring the lines he
selects from Lydgate's poem in order to increase their relevance
for his own text (and for its juvenile reader). For example, references to 'kynges & emperoures' and to 'pryncis'[92] are regularly
changed to 'lordis', 'men,' or non-specific pronouns in order to
open up the teaching of the excerpted lines to a non-royal reader;
so too, Lydgate's lines 'Pryncis, Pryncessis, which han the
souereyntee | Ouer the peeple and domynaciou*n*' begin in the

---

[89] *Fall* I. 2150–6, 6280–93; II. 15–21; I. 3445–51, 3452–8.
[90] i.e *Fall* II. 533–53 and I. 939–43, 974–5, 980–7.
[91] Edwards (1977: 435).
[92] *Fall* I. 6282; II. 20, 64; cf. *Instructions* II. A. 2353, 2370, 2638.

Instructions with the more democratic conjuration 'Therefore all ye that haue . . . '[93]

Again, Idley makes local verbal changes to the lines he culls from the *Fall* in order to eliminate unhelpful detail: when, therefore, he selects a stanza from Lydgate's envoy to the narrative of Cadmus in Book I for its moral on the power of Fortune (at A. 2344–50), he silently excises the unnecessary reference to Cadmus (in I. 2155) which would link the envoy back to its (now absent) parent narrative. Equally, when a stanza from the popular 'In portentosam' chapter of Book III is selected to contribute to his discussion of the sin of lechery at B. 2549–55, Solomon's sin of idolatry (in lines 'How for a woman prudent Solomoun | The Lord offendyng, dede ydolatrie') is altered to 'did avowtrie', the better to fit with the topic under consideration.[94]

But Idley's alterations to Lydgate's poem are not confined to small-scale refinements of this kind. Close study of the *Instructions* reveals that Idley repeatedly changes the lines he borrows from Lydgate so as to emphasize the freedom of the individual to shape his own moral behaviour and, concomitantly, to focus on the seriousness of moral failure. Not surprisingly for a work designed to inculcate basic principles of ethical behaviour in a child, Idley's selections show a preference for those parts of the *Fall* in which vice meets a justly deserved punishment: there is little room in Idley's reading of Lydgate for the tragic falls of Lady Fortune's innocent victims. Thus it is that Idley very naturally selects material from Lydgate's account of the Fall of Adam and the following moralizing section (*Fall* I. 470–1001), for in both of these chapters the strict congruence between sin and fall supports Idley's blame-driven view of misfortune. Lydgate's lines,

> Adam and Eue losten ther liberte,
> Ther fraunchise and ther blissidnesse,
> Put into exil and captyuyte
> To lyue in labour, in wo and pensifnesse,
> Thoruh fals desirs off pompous wilfulnesse,
> To the Serpent whan thei gaff credence,
> The Lord mistristyng thoruh inobedience,[95]

[93] *Fall* I. 3837–8, *Instructions* II. A. 2421.   [94] *Fall* III. 1178–9.
[95] *Fall* I. 974–80.

are woven into Idley's stanza as follows:

> Adam and Eue loste her fraunchise and liberte
> And were put from *par*adise, that noble place,
> For lak of dwe obedience and humilite,
> Perpetualli dampned *with*out merci or grace;
> And so lay in preson a longe tyme and space,
> And all was because they were disobedient
> Vnto hir sou*er*aigne and lordis co*m*maundement. [96]

The harsher tone of Idley's version of the stanza is apparent, but so too is his sharper awareness of the culpability of the sin of disobedience: it is Idley, rather than the Monk of Bury, who introduces the notion of damnation here. As a consequence of Idley's confidently ethical handling of the *Fall*, the sins and punishments of certain named figures are enhanced, as if to stress for his unsophisticated reader the justice which meets them in their downfalls. Solomon's punishment (in Idley, for adultery) at B. 2563–9 is stronger than at Lydgate's III. 1191–7, Solomon being likened to 'a best unresonable'. Similarly, Idley inserts a line into Lydgate's account of the incestuous lust of Semiramis in order to emphasize the transgressive nature of her sexual sins, even going so far as to say that she had intercourse with both her own brother and son; Lydgate's version merely follows Premierfait in saying that she lay with her son and other men.[97]

Idley's view of moral behaviour as a clear-cut area in which blame can be straightforwardly apportioned also emerges in his paraphrase of two stanzas from the prologue to Book II of the *Fall*. Lydgate here uncharacteristically undermines the category of Fortune and suggests that vicious rulers are quicker to blame Fortuna for their falls than they are to realize that they have brought their suffering upon themselves by their sinful behaviour:

> But such as list[e] nat correctid be
> Bexau*m*ple off othre fro vicious gouernau*n*ce,
> And fro ther vices list nat for to fle:
> Yiff thei be troubled in ther hih puissau*n*ce,
> Thei arette it Fortunys variau*n*ce,

---

[96] *Instructions* B. 106–12.
[97] *Fall* I. 6637–43, *Instructions* II. A. 1812–16. Cf. *Des Cas*, fo. 22ᵛ: 'quelle auoit dormy auec plusieurs ho*m*mes 7 par especial auec son propre filz yolis'.

Touchyng the giltes that thei deden vse,
Ther demerites ful falsli to excuse.

Vertu conserueth pryncis in ther glorie
And confermeth ther dominaciouns;
And vicis put ther price out off memorie,
For ther trespacis and ther transgressiouns.
And in alle such sodeyn mutaciouns,
Thei can no refut nor no bet socour,
But ageyn Fortune to maken ther clamour.[98]

Although not typical of Lydgate's usual method in the *Fall*, these lines voice exactly the kind of position Idley likes to hear. His version reads:

And suche as woll nat chastised be
By othir that be of vicious gouernaunce,
And for his vices in no wyse woll flee—
If they be trobled and haue myschaunce,
They sey it is her destonye to haue suche greuaunce.
Thus her owne synne they woll couere and excuse
And fortune falselye they wyll accuse.

Vertu kepith men in welthe and prosperite
And conserueth hym suerly to dwelle in glorie,
And vices casten hym downe into aduersitee—
This may ye rede in many a storie.
Therfore I counceill haue this in memorie,
And witeth not fortune youre myschevous falle,
But youre myslievyng whiche is cause of all. [99]

In Idley's hands the whole passage becomes rather more severe than it was in the *Fall*: the self-deception of these princes is strengthened ('her owne synne they woll couere') and their spurious arguments assume more clearly fatalistic implications ('her destonye'), while the didactic intent of the *Instructions* sharpens Lydgate's final couplet into a hard-hitting and direct accusation of moral inadequacy ('youre myslievyng whiche is cause of all'). Elsewhere, when he finds Lydgate less palatable, however, Idley is rather less subtle in his reworkings. At II. A. 2428–34 he perversely manhandles lines from Lydgate on the universal power of Fortune from the Jocasta chapter (I. ch. 8: 'De Iocasta Thebarum regina')

[98] *Fall* II. 57–70.   [99] *Instructions* II. A. 2631–44.

in order to replace the fortunal message with a firmly ethical one. Lydgate's stanza reads:

> What thyng in erthe is more deceyuable,
> Than whan a man supposith verraily
> In prosperite for to stonde stable,
> And from his ioie is remeued sodeynly?
> For wher Fortune is founde to hasty
> To trise folk, is greuous to endure,
> For sodeyn chaungis been hatful to nature.[100]

In the *Instructions* the last three lines of the stanza are replaced with a fiercely ethical conclusion:

> And if he dwelle here and doo trulie,
> In heuene shall be his habitacion,
> And if he doo the contrarie, perpetuall dampnacion.[101]

A grim ethic of blame and just deserts thus displaces Lydgate's recognition of Fortune. Later Idley also omits Lydgate's references to Fortune in his treatment of lines I. 666–72[102] in the section on the sin of sloth and, at II. B. 1563–8 (under the sin of covetousness), one of Lydgate's most obvious echoings of Chaucer ('Truth: Balade de Bon Conseyl', ll. 1–2) is reworked for the same reason, so that the stanza

> In al this world[e] thouh there were no mo,
> Texemplefie to folkis that be wise,
> How this world is a thoruhfare ful of woo,
> Lich fals Fortune, which turnyth to and fro
> To make folkis, whan thei most cleerli shyne,
> In ther estatis onwarli to declyne,[103]

is altered to contain an exhortation to 'Flee fro this synne of fals couetise | And dwelle with meane suffisauns euermoo'.[104]

While, then, Edwards is right to say that Idley's view of the *Fall* is a fragmented one which sees the poem as 'a series of isolable moral precepts', this does not do justice to the way Idley approaches the poem with a definite agenda, ransacking it for material which can be made to fit the ethical teaching of his treatise. Although Procrustean, Idley's treatment of the *Fall* is purposive and

---

[100] *Fall* I. 3522–8.   [101] *Instructions* II. A. 2432–4.
[102] Ibid. B. 1261–7.   [103] *Fall* I. 793–8; cf. CT I. 2847.
[104] *Instructions* II. B. 1564–5.

effective: he knows the poem well enough to recognize where it can support his own views, and he feels sufficiently confident in his understanding of his own project to modify lines (sometimes radically so) from Lydgate's work so that they may be assimilated into the *Instructions*.

LATER RECEPTION: THE EVIDENCE OF MANUSCRIPT OWNERSHIP

Manuscripts of the *Fall* characteristically reveal little of their original provenance; however, in inscriptions recording later owners and readers they provide valuable evidence of the early transmission of the work. Early inscriptions in manuscripts of the complete poem may be briefly recorded:[105]

Manuscript	Owners
Belvoir Castle, 'Rutland' MS	Margaret Nevill, Catherine Westmorland
Berkeley, University of California Library MS 75 (*olim* Bodmer; *olim* John Gribble; *olim* Phillipps MS 8118)	Henry Prat
Chicago UL MS 565 (*olim* Phillipps MS 4255)	John Gryffythe, Wyllyam Conkey
Glasgow University Library MS Hunterian 5	Marie Lumner, Elizabeth Lumner, Edmunde Lumner, Elizabeth, Jane, and James Calverthope, Roger Rookwoode
London, BL MS Additional 21410	Edward Sutton
London, BL MS Additional 39659	Robert Curzon
London, BL MS Harley 1245	Francis Harington, Thomas Baker, Henry Gale
London, BL MS, Harley 1766	Robert Halton (1654), John Bentley,

[105] I give thirty-one of the extant texts or independent fragments of the work here. Renoir and Benson, *Manual* vi. 2099 (in Hartung and Severs 1967–93) omit MS Sloane 2452, and give four more (nos. 22, 26, 28, 33), but see Edwards (1985*b*: 451) for corrections which reduce the number to thirty-three; Pearsall (1997: 69–71) gives thirty-four.

Manuscript	Owners
	Christopher Chapman (1654), Frechwell Holles (1654), Thomas Tyrell, John Tyrell, Jon Lyly
London, BL MS Harley 3486	——
London, BL MS Harley 4197	——
London, BL MS Harley 4203	——
London, BL MS Royal 18 B. xxxi	——
London, BL MS Royal 18 D. iv	Arms of John Tiptoft, first earl of Worcester, Marmaduke Ellerker, Julian Musgrave, Margaret Clifford, George, third earl of Cumberland
London, BL MS Royal 18 D. v	Henry Percy, fourth earl of Northumberland
London, BL MS Sloane 2452	——
London, BL MS Sloane 4031	Baron Dacre and family, Lady Elizabeth Carewes of Bedington, William Saunder, arms of Marlands of Kent
London, Lambeth Palace MS 256	Llanthony Priory
Longleat House MS 254	Robert Bell
Manchester, John Rylands Library MS Crawford English 2	——
New York, Columbia University (Bourdrillon-) Plimpton MS 255	John and Andrew McFael, Orlando Macsacrapant Macffilius
New York, Pierpont Morgan Library MS 124 (*olim* Cheney-Lee)	Simon Vorwoys, arms of Sir John Cheney
Oxford, Bodleian Library MS Bodley 263	Sir Francis Englefield, John Godsalve
Oxford, Bodleian Library MS e Musaeo 1	Lancelot Bruni, Edmund Englot (1582), Walter Clavell, Thomas and Howell Wadham, Swithune Thorpe (1570), Thomas Biddill, Elizabeth St John
Oxford, Bodleian Library MS Hatton 2 (*olim* 105)	Edmund, Alexander, and John Mather, John Pottes, William Mingeius, Henry VIII, Henry Crawthorn, Thomas Mannyng,

Manuscript	Owners
	Thomas Peade, Stephen Valinger, William Duart, Thomas King, Robert Daniellus, Phillip Fowler, William Culpeper, Runs Hildershin, Robert Hall, Thomas Waye, Thomas Willes
Oxford, Bodleian Library MS Rawlinson C. 448	——
Oxford, Corpus Christi College MS 242	Robert Loueday, Edwarde Dymmoke
Philadelphia, Rosenbach MS 439|16 (*olim* Phillipps MS 4254)	Egame Howel
Princeton UL MS Garrett 139 (*olim* Phillipps MS 8117)	Richard Reeds
Princeton University Library Robert H. Taylor Collection MS (*olim* Wollaton Hall MS)	Sir Henry Wyllogby, Thomas Meryman, Robert Tenam, Philip Hersynge, John Sharpe, Edwardus . . . Rex
San Marino, Huntington Library MS HM 268 (*olim* Ecton Hall)	——
Tokyo, Takamiya MS 40 (*olim* Houghton MS 9; *olim* Rosenbach MS 477; *olim* Mostyn-Hall MS 272)	——

By far the greater part of these inscriptions cannot be identified; however, it is still possible to see that manuscripts of the poem enjoyed a strikingly prestigious readership. Unless the inscriptions are just dating devices, two manuscripts belonged to monarchs (the Princeton Taylor MS to a 'King Edward', MS Hatton 2 to Henry VIII), and it is possible that Members of Parliament found Lydgate's moral precepts (in the form of MS Harley 1766 and the Longleat MS) congenial; 'Frechwell Holles' and 'Thomas Tyrell' may well be the Sir Frescheville Holles and Sir Thomas Tyrell who were Members for Grimsby (1667) and Aylesbury (1659–60).[106]

---

[106] If the 'Jon Lyly' who owned this book was the dramatist and author (?1554–1606), then an interesting possibility of transmission presents itself, for he was himself also MP for Aylesbury in 1593 and 1601.

The Longleat manuscript owner, again, could have been the Cambridgeshire judge and MP for King's Lynn, Sir Robert Bell (*ob.* 1577). Bergen has carefully demonstrated the intricacies of the ownership of MS Sloane 4031 by Thomas Fiennes, the unfortunate ninth Baron Dacre. [107] Nobles also show an interest in the work in the copies that survive as the Rutland MS (the Nevills), MS Additional 21410 (Edward Sutton, sixth Baron Dudley, 1482–1530),[108] and as MSS Royal 18 D. IV and 18 D. V, respectively bearing the arms of John Tiptoft, first earl of Worcester (1427–70), and of Henry Percy, fourth earl of Northumberland (1446–89).[109] That the *Fall* also gained a monastic audience beyond the Benedictine order is shown by the survival of the Lambeth MS from Llanthony Priory, the community of Augustinian canons in Monmouthshire and Gloucestershire.[110]

In this section, however, I shall examine two statements of ownership in particular detail for the evidence they supply of the readership of the *Fall* in the later years of the sixteenth century— exactly the years in which the Lydgatean *Mirror for Magistrates* tradition was at the height of its popularity. MS Bodley 263, Bergen's base text for the EETS edition of the *Fall*, contains two signed statements of ownership, the first of which is of particular interest. On fo. 225[r] is found the following quotation from the poem (written by one hand, though in a variety of scripts):

> Offise of princis | is to supporte righte
> His swerde of knyghthode fro wronges < . . . >[111]
> Sir Fraunces Englefilde knight gode
> goue you grace and Light to procede
>
> Sir Fraunces Englefielde knighte

---

[107] *Fall* ed. Bergen vol. iv. 60–1.

[108] This manuscript contains on fo. 168[v] a list of the books owned by a John Culpeper, chiefly classical works, but including Albertus Magnus (a herbal), Valla, Erasmus (*Apophthegmata, De milite Christiani, Enchiridon, Colloquium*), Vives, and Melanchthon.

[109] For details of Tiptoft's books, see Weiss (1935–7), Mitchell (1937–8), where the *Fall* is identified as one of the works Tiptoft owned before his 1458 trip to Italy (cf. Weiss 1941: 112–22); Bodleian Library (1988: 70–80).

[110] Llanthony Priory was founded in the early years of the twelfth century and colonized a daughter priory in Gloucestershire in 1136 ('Llanthony Secunda'), which itself became the mother church in 1481 (see Knowles and Hadcock 1953: 144): the Lambeth text could have belonged to either house (see Ker 1964: 119 n. 5).

[111] *Fall* III. 3774–5. Bergen fails to identify these lines in his description (*Fall* ed. Bergen vol. iv. 13).

Englefield is identifiable as the wealthy Catholic book collector and émigré who died in 1596. His career provides a significant insight into the kinds of readers the *Fall* was attracting in the latter half of the sixteenth century; at a time, that is, when, although the *Mirror for Magistrates* tradition was at its height, Lydgate's own reputation was in decline.[112]

Englefield succeeded to a considerable inheritance in Berkshire in 1537 at the age of fifteen; by the time he was twenty-four he was named High Sheriff of Oxfordshire and Berkshire and was in the same year dubbed a Knight of the Carpet at the coronation of Edward VI (20 February 1546–7). Having taken an appointment in the household of Edward's Catholic sister, in August 1551 Englefield was sent with Mary to the Tower for nine months: on Mary's accession he was rewarded for his loyalty with several offices, including that of High Steward to Reading Abbey, a Benedictine House.[113] His religious interests, therefore, were expressed both politically and also institutionally. Unsurprisingly, under Elizabeth (in 1559) he fled to the Spanish Low Countries and thence (via Padua and Rome) to Spain. That Englefield was a high-profile recusant is seen in the close interest of the English court in his activities on the Continent: when Englefield was rumoured to be among those at Trent in 1562 advocating Elizabeth's excommunication, the Queen summoned him home.[114] When he refused (he was never to return to England) the reprisal was swift: his goods and estates were sequestered by the Crown. Penniless, Englefield entered the service of Philip II and was rewarded for his loyalty to Philip's dead English queen with significant positions in Brussels and Rome: Philip himself even argued (unsuccessfully) with Elizabeth for the restoration of Englefield's estates.

Englefield's exile was, then, a highly public and favoured one: he entered into correspondence with Sixtus V (*regn.* 1585–90) and

---

[112] In the following account I draw on Loomie (1963: 14–51) and Alan Coates's work on the dispersal of the book collections of Reading Abbey (1999: 128–42). Also useful are Parmiter's two articles in *Recusant History* (1975–6, 1977–8). The manuscript is described in Branca (1999: iii. 279–81) and its owners discussed by de la Mare and Reynolds (1991–2: 46–50).

[113] Knowles and Hadcock (1953: 74).

[114] In a letter of 10 May: Elizabeth had only granted Englefield a two-year licence for absence 'over the seas', and this was now within days of expiry (Parmiter 1975–6: 162).

Philip on behalf of Mary Stuart, and in 1577 produced a list of imprisoned Catholic supporters of the Scottish queen. Although he lost his sight in 1581,[115] he devoted the last sixteen years of his life to the problem of income for recusant émigrés in Spain, becoming, in Albert Loomie's words, 'the spokesman for the needs of his countrymen' abroad.[116] Englefield's associates included radical and contentious men—chiefly, perhaps, Nicholas Sanders, the fellow of New College and Regius Professor of Canon Law under Mary, who worked in Madrid for the dethronement of Elizabeth in 1573, and William Allen, the fellow of Oriel who opened Douai seminary in 1568, founded the Jesuit College at Rome in 1579, and who was made cardinal in 1587 for his support of Philip's English claims.[117] Given Lydgate's own conservative views on matters of belief and the authority of the Church, it comes as no surprise that the *Fall* should have passed through the hands of so orthodox a Catholic, nor that evidence should survive to suggest that Englefield had a developed interest in political theory: late in life he wrote a closely argued letter to Philip (instructing that it should be opened after his death) on Anglo–Spanish relations,[118] and he also contributed to *The Conference About the Next Succession* (1595), a tract on the possible claimants to the English throne, 'the classic expression of this political theory of the English Catholic exiles'.[119] It is significant that Lydgate, who had been a bastion of Benedictine and Lancastrian interest in the fifteenth century, should become the preferred reading of not only the unfortunate, but also of the fiercely Catholic. Equally, it is significant that just a few years after Englefield's death the New College émigré John Pits praises Lydgate for his theological learning: anti-Lollard orthodoxy has evolved into anti-Protestant orthodoxy.[120]

---

[115] This failure of vision presumably lies behind the request for 'light to procede' in the manuscript inscription.

[116] Loomie (1963: 40). Englefield contributed to the report on this issue which appeared in 1596, the year of his death.

[117] Ibid. 21. Englefield went to Rome with Allen in 1576 to discuss the restoration of Catholicism in England (Parmiter 1975–6: 168).

[118] Loomie (1963: 49).

[119] Ibid. 45. One of the manuscripts taken from Reading by Englefield was an anthology of regiminal texts (Giles's *De regimine* and Vegetius), now surviving as Bodleian MS Auct. F. 3. 3.

[120] In his *Relationum historicarum de rebus Anglicis* (see ch. 1, p. 9).

Facing Englefield's verse in MS Bodley 263 (fo. 224ᵛ), and signed 'Iohannes Godsaluus. | scribebat. 1549', stands the following inscription:

> Prince desire to be honorable
> Cherishe thy folke & hate extorcion
> Suffre nothing y`t´ may be reprouable
> To thyn estate doon in thy regioun
> Shewe forth the yerde of castigac*i*on
> Drede god / do lawe / loue trouthe and worthines
> And wedd thy folke againe to stedfastnes[121]

Eldest son of Thomas Godsalve of Norwich (a noted bibliophile), John Godsalve (1505–56) had like Englefield been dubbed Knight of the Carpet at Edward VI's coronation and, furthermore, had been appointed a Crown Visitor under Edward to report on the obedience of the bishops in the reign of Henry VIII.[122] Definite links between the two owners of MS Bodley 263 exist: Godsalve was introduced to recusant circles by his second wife Elizabeth (whose uncle married Francis Englefield's aunt) and he appointed Francis Englefield executor to his will.[123]

Englefield must have written in the book before the loss of his sight in 1581, but, while it is tempting to imagine that the content of the *Fall* may have been of comfort to a man in exile (as the *De casibus* had been to the imprisoned Charles of Orléans and Chastelain's *Temple de Bocace* to Margaret of Anjou in the

---

[121] Again the choice of material is advisory: these lines form the envoy to Richard II from Chaucer's 'Lak of Stedfastnesse'.

[122] Godsalve's ownership of land in East Anglia offers the possibility that the book may have originated in Bury and been acquired by Godsalve locally. Godsalve (or his family) may not have been the first owner: although the text is itself undated, it has been dated as an early copy in various descriptions. Bergen puts it at 'about 1450' (*Fall* ed. Bergen vol. iv. 11), Saxl and Meier (1953: 292), as 'um 1450', Madan and Craster (1922: 365) put it in the third quarter of the century, while Pächt and Alexander (1973: iii. 78) suggest 'saec. xv²/⁴ (after 1439)'. Bale notes Thomas Godsalve's library in his *Index*, but no mention is made of a copy of the *Fall*.

[123] No connection has been established between John Godsalve of Norfolk and Edward Godsalve, the recusant Cambridgeshire priest and translator of Eusebius whose name appears among the original fellows of Trinity College, Cambridge; nevertheless it is interesting that this cleric was deprived of his prebend in 1559 (the year Englefield left for Louvain) and sought exile in Antwerp. Meredith Hanmer's 1577 commendation of Lydgate's 'good stories' shows that an Elizabethan translator of Eusebius could be enthusiastic about Lydgate (see ch. 1, p. 7).

1460s),[124] the manuscript shows no sign of foreign travel. Indeed, Alan Coates's work on the book collections of Reading Abbey suggests that this would be improbable: Englefield played a key role in the dispersal of the Abbey's books at its dissolution, extracting many volumes from its library and leaving them in the custody of Clement Burdett, a local priest. The books seem to have been passed into the care of Clement's brother Humphrey in the 1570s: Humphrey was married to Englefield's sister Susan and was also steward to Englefield's estates.[125] Maddan and Craster record that MS Bodley 263 was presented to Oxford by William Burdett (Humphrey's son by a second marriage and a graduate of University College) in 1608.[126] This donation was part of a presentation of thirty-four volumes to the University,[127] twenty-eight of which can be identified as belonging to the Abbey.[128] Most of these are of a biblical, late patristic, or theological nature,[129] possibly retained by Englefield for their orthodox 'Catholic' content.[130] Lydgate's vernacular *Fall* sits rather awkwardly in this academic company (even though we know that the Abbey held a copy of Marie de France's *Lais* and *Fables*),[131] and Coates has suggested that it was one of Englefield's personal books which fell into the company of the salvaged Abbey books, rather than originating from the Reading Benedictines.[132] Nonetheless, it is an important indication of the ways in which persecuted recusants and those with Catholic sympathies were reading the *Fall* at the

---

[124] Schirmer (1951: 105); Pearsall (1970: 251); Simone (1971: 21).

[125] Coates (1999: 129). Another interesting indication of the close-knit nature of the wealthier recusant families is that Clement Burdett seems to have been known by Nicholas Sanders, Englefield's associate (ibid. 132–3). On Humphrey see also Parmiter (1975–6: 163, 165)).   [126] Madan and Craster (1922: ii. 365).

[127] Macray (1890; repr. 1984: 36).

[128] Coates (1999: 135). Cf. Jamieson Hurry's much older list of Oxford manuscripts from Reading (1901; 113–22).

[129] Namely glossed books of the Bible (MSS Auct. D. 1. 19, D. 2. 12, D. 3. 12, D. 3. 15, D. 4. 18, MSS Bodley 44, 772, 781), commentaries by Augustine (MSS Bodley 241, 257), Isidore's *Etymologiae* (MSS Bodley 186, 396), Peter of Lombard's *Sentences* (MS Bodley 853) and works by Alcuin, Bernard of Clairvaux, Aquinas (commentary on *Sentences*, MS Bodley 200, and on Aristotle's *Ethics*, MS Auct. F. 3. 3), Alexander Neckam, Remigius of Auxerre, Alan of Lille (MSS Bodley 409 and 550), Peter Comestor, Robert Grosseteste, and Hugh of Saint-Victor.

[130] Coates suggests that the corpus was salvaged by Englefield in the hope of the future return of the Church to England (1999: 140–1).

[131] Now MS Harley 978, the only complete extant copy of the twelve *Lais* (Coates 1999: 74).   [132] Ibid. 139.

turn of the sixteenth century that the poem should be felt an appropriate bedfellow for serious Catholic texts: William Webbe's Protestant reservations about the Monk of Bury's influence may not have been entirely misplaced.[133]

SIXTEENTH-CENTURY RESPONSES

With the advent of printing several editions of the *De casibus* and *Des Cas* appear: Boccaccio's A-version appears twice, although the revised B-version appears just once, in 1544.[134] Laurent's literal A-version appears twice,[135] while the amplified B-version that is Lydgate's source is printed five times.[136] Hieronymus Ziegler's 1544 *De casibus* print provides an accompanying academic apparatus which is suggestive of the ways Boccaccio was being read in these years: there is an alphabetical index of characters (as there had been in the Petit A-version), a biography of the author, and explanatory footnotes at the end of each chapter. Side notes in the margins of the pages, together with the index, show that the edition was intended to help readers find their way quickly around the Latin text: the critical apparatus suggests that readers were less used to sitting down and reading the *De casibus* from cover to cover than they were accustomed to consulting it as a reference work. Certainly, Ziegler himself is in little doubt that the text yields a consistent message: his dedicatory letter speaks of the *De casibus* as if it were a dictionary of the triumphs of Fortuna 'quae quidem totius orbis imperia supera, inferaque regit, & moderat'.[137]

---

[133] See Ch. 1. For nineteenth-century Protestant readings of Boccaccio in response to the Oxford Movement see Wright (1957: 367–8).

[134] The A-version is published in Strasburg (1475) and in the Paris Petit edition reprinted in facsimile by Brewer Hall (and dated by him as 1520, although Bergen gives '1507?'; *Fall* ed. Bergen vol. iv. 125). The 1544 Augsburg printing of Hieronymus Ziegler is the only edition of the B-version until the 1983 Branca edition.

[135] Bruges (1476) and Lyons (1483).

[136] Paris 1483–4, 1494, ?1506, 1515, 1538 (see *Fall* ed. Bergen vol. iv. 129–32).

[137] 'Who indeed rules and restrains the higher and lower empires of the whole world' (Ziegler 1544: fo.xiii[r]). The Petit *De casibus* print, similarly, uses marginal pointers to highlight ethical maxims in the work. The Pynson (1494), Tottell (1554), and Wayland editions of Lydgate's *Fall* do not approach the English poem in this way: Tottell and Wayland supply a list of chapters (by heading), but it is not until Bergen's edition that Lydgate is granted the kind of academic attention Boccaccio had received in 1544.

Laurent is not the only author to translate Boccaccio's work: Ziegler produced a German prose translation of the *De casibus* in the year after his Latin edition (Augsburg, 1545), and the Spanish version of Perez Lopez da Ayala and Alfonso Garcia enjoyed a long popularity and was printed in 1495 (Seville), 1511 (Toledo), and 1552 (Mendina). Giuseppe Betussi's Italian translation *I casi degli huomini illustri* appeared four times (in Venice, 1545 and 1551, and in Florence, 1598 and 1602).[138] Perhaps most interesting is Claude Witart's decison in 1578 to supplement Laurent's translations with a version of his own, even though Laurent had been published as recently as 1538. While it may be that demand for a French *De casibus* had oustripped the supply of books available, the decision to produce another translation at this time may reflect an academic dissatisfaction with the reliability of Laurent's versions. Certainly, Witart prides himself on the accuracy of his translation and is concerned in his prefatory matter to draw attention to the fact that he has translated 'mot pour mot', even when this fidelity makes his version 'moins elegante'.[139] Furthermore, Witart's *Traité des mesaduentures de personnages signalez* is in one important respect composed in the shadow of Laurent, in that the dedicatory letter offers the text to the bishop of Soissons as a work of ethical instruction. Discussing at some length the unique power of man to regulate himself morally, Witart claims that the contemplation of virtue is 'le plus beau & digne suiect, à mon aduis, qui pourroit tomber en l'esprit' for man is born 'pour viure vertueusement & sainctement & qu'il doit auoir principalement en recommendation ce qui est eternel'.[140] He presents Boccaccio's text as a mirror

où l'homme puisse parfaictement cognoistre & voir son estre & condition descrite de toutes ses parties, c'est és [sic] discours historiques & philosophiques de ce docte Boccace . . . ie vous auray dit, Monsieur, que la seule cause qui m'a meu d'entreprendre la traduction du Latin de Boccace en nostre langue, a esté le desir . . . de faire chose qui puisse profiter au public . . . pour l'instruction de quelques vns, pour la reformation des mœurs . . . ce . . . liures de Boccace . . . tendent & seruent merueilleusement . . . a la reformation de toutes sortes d'exces . . . außi remply d'instruction tres-chrestienne & conduisant à la vie eternelle

---

[138] *Fall* ed. Bergen vol. iv. 133–6.
[139] Boccaccio trans. Witart (1578: fo. A. 4^r).
[140] Ibid. A. 2^r, A. 2^v.

(wherein a person can perfectly understand his own being and see his condition described in all its aspects: this is learned Boccaccio's historical and philosophical treatise . . . I would have said, sire, that the sole reason that led me to undertake translating Boccaccio from Latin into our own language was the desire . . . to do something that would benefit society . . . to provide instruction for some people and to improve morals . . . these books by Boccaccio are marvellously useful . . . in the correction of all kinds of excess . . . and are also full of the most Christian teaching, leading to eternal life)[141]

So uncomplicated, indeed, is Witart's belief in the regiminal value of Boccaccio's work that the concept of Fortune is not once mentioned by him in his preface.

Cavendish's *Metrical Visions*

Better known for his *de casibus* biography of Cardinal Wolsey (1554–8), George Cavendish follows Idley in the tradition of active reworkings of material from the *Fall of Princes* in his *Metrical Visions*, a rhyme-royal sequence of twenty-three post-mortem *de casibus* laments, an account of the chief victims of the Henrician police state. Unlike Idley's borrowing of lines in the *Instructions*, however, Cavendish selects passages from Lydgate in order to incorporate them into a text which is itself intended to form part of the *de casibus* tradition. The scale of his borrowings (he uses nearly two hundred lines of the *Fall*) and the ease with which he brings together lines from widely separated parts of the *Fall* witness to his close familiarity with Lydgate's poem.[142] Arguing persuasively for a slightly earlier dating of the *Visions* than has been usual, Edwards has dubbed Cavendish 'the precursor rather than the imitator' of the 1555–1610 *Mirror for Magistrates* tradition[143] and has acclaimed the *Visions* as the first example of the application of the Lydgatean model of tragic falls

---

[141] Ibid. A. 3^v, A. 4^v.

[142] Edwards has shown the extent of Cavendish's borrowings (1971*b*) and has commented on Cavendish's appropriation of material from Lydgate, in the introduction to his edition of the *Visions* (Cavendish 1980: 9–11).

[143] Edwards (1971*c*) contends that the dating of the completion of the autograph manuscript (BL MS Egerton 2402) as 24 June 1558 is the date of Cavendish's fair copy, rather than a date for the completion of his composition of the work. The *Visions* has in the past been seen as a product of the later years of the decade (see Farnham 1936/56: 273; Pearsall 1970: 252).

to contemporary politics:

> the *Metrical Visions* seem to attempt to reproduce the whole apparatus
> and ethos of the *Fall of Princes*. Cavendish introduced exhortations on
> Fortune and admonitions on the mutability of human affairs. He added
> formal envoys, made interpolations in his narrative, and varied the length
> of his tragedies. In all these respects he followed the example of Lydgate.
> Such formal and tonal appropriations from the *Fall of Princes* seem
> unique in their range and degree . . . The *Metrical Visions* are the first
> sustained attempt to write verse *de casibus* tragedy that draws its subject
> matter from contemporary history. This is Cavendish's most significant
> achievement[144]

It will be appreciated that the *Visions* represent not simply a more
ambitious response to the *Fall* than the *Instructions*, but that they
testify to an entirely different attitude to the source poem: whereas
Idley plundered the *Fall*, Cavendish uses Lydgate dynamically,
engaging in a more creative way with the *de casibus* project.
Edwards has valuably explored Cavendish's verbal borrowings
from Lydgate; here the larger imaginative debt of the *Visions* to
the *Fall*, Cavendish's participation in Lydgate's tragic project, will
be considered.

The importance of the issues of accountability and blame in
Cavendish's understanding of literary tragedy is made quickly
apparent in the work: indeed, the poet openly tussles with the
problem of human freedom of will in the prologue to the *Visions*,
saying that one June day he turned his mind to musings,

> Of ffikkellnes of ffortune and of the course of kynd

> How some are by ffortune exalted to Riches
> And ofte suche as most vnworthy be
> And some oppressed in langor and syknes
> Some wayling lakkyng welthe by wretched pouertie
> Some in bayte and bondage and some at libertie
> With other moo gyftes of ffortune Varyable
> Some pleasaunt somme mean and some onprofitable.

> But after dewe serche and better advisement
> I knewe by Reason that oonly God above
> Rewlithe thos thynges as is most convenyent
> The same devydyng to man for his behove[145]

---

[144] Cavendish ed. Edwards (1980: 10–11, 12); cf. Edwards (1977: 438).
[145] *MV* 7–18.

Later in the prologue Cavendish announces his *Visions* to be tragedies ('I onworthe this tragedy do begyne') and speaks of the 'wofull style' necessary for the laments he will present,[146] but this tells us little of what he thinks the salient characteristics of the tragic fall actually are. Having rejected the validity of the notion of a powerful Fortune in the earlier lines, Cavendish would seem to postulate a moral order in which the prevailing justice of God ensures a straightforward tit-for-tat causality between vice and misfortune. That this seems to be his understanding of the *de casibus* narratives he has read is suggested by a later stanza in the poem:

> Thes clarkes old that wrott wofull tragedies
> I pray you ware ther playntes of hyghe estates
> Recordyng ther onware falles and dayngerous ieoperdies
> Ther sodeyn chaynges and ther wofull fattes
> Ther disdaynous dispyghtes and onnaturall debattes
> Allwayes concludyng who lyst to take heade
> Howe highe estates are allwayes in most dreade.[147]

While the opening lines of this stanza suggest that Cavendish defines tragedy principally by its tonal qualities (that they are 'wofull' narratives), the later lines clearly show that his reading of *de casibus* laments is ethically sharper than a simple 'chauntepleure' reversal of fortunes: those in positions of power are always more vulnerable to the kinds of vice ('disdaynous dispyghtes') that result in misery and thus, he implies, their 'tragic' misfortunes are to some degree deserved.

These statements suggest that Cavendish sees the tragic genre as essentially retributive, but how reliable are they as a guide to the *Metrical Visions* as a whole? Do the laments of the fallen characters consistently accord with the authorial understanding of tragedy which these passages appear to offer? Remarkably few of the plaintiffs in the *Visions* come close to the sophistication of Lydgate's jostling of innocence and guilt in the *Fall* narratives: most of them readily confess their vicious pasts. Cardinal Wolsey admits the sins of fraud, self-indulgence, and vainglory, and also to having practised injustice (ll. 165–75, 127–40, 225–31, 155–61); Thomas Cromwell, earl of Essex, confesses to having abused the legal system (ll. 715–21); Edward Seymour, duke of Somerset, likewise admits his vaunting ambition and to having abused his

---

[146] Ibid. 50, 63.   [147] Ibid. ll. 1985–91; the text reads 'ware not' at l. 1986.

position as Protector (ll. 1668–9, 1698–702). Henry Grey, duke of Suffolk, confesses his treachery (ll. 2130–1) and Henry Howard, earl of Surrey, admits that he was guilty of betraying his own father (ll. 1119–25). Sir Thomas Arundell prevaricates over his guilt, but finally acknowledges that God has punished his sin of envy (ll. 1782–3, 1786–8); Thomas Culpeper (Katherine Howard's favourite) confesses a failure to respect God (ll. 941–3, 951); Henry Norris admits that he was blinded by ambition; Mark Smeaton confesses his presumption; (ll. 361, 503); William Brereton admits his malice, complicity in murder, and envy, while John Dudley, duke of Northumberland, confesses that his sins include ambition, malice, and meddling with the laws of the land.[148] By far the largest group of fallen nobles are those who confess different forms of sexual vice: George Boleyn, viscount Rochford, Sir Francis Weston, Anne Boleyn, Katherine Howard, Jane Boleyn, viscountess Rochford, and Henry VIII all recognize that suffering (or death) befell them in punishment for carnal sin.[149]

So far, so good. The retributive dynamic of these tragedies fits squarely in the ethically stringent understanding of deserved suffering as one kind of tragedy: misfortunes are for Cavendish no less 'wofull' just because they come as the punishment for past sins. However, the picture is rather less simple than this implies, for the authorial introductions and envoys to many of these laments do not always support a narrowly criminous reading of the tragic fall. For example, Cavendish introduces the narratives following Wolsey's with the claim that 'as me semed this was ther entent | On ffortune to complayn ther cause' (ll. 271–2). It could be argued that 'Fortune' here is no more than a shorthand or conceit for the regrettable habit suffering has of catching up with those who deserve it. However, the same authorial voice elsewhere goes further than this vague usage and suggests that the suffering that has visited his vicious *elati* is in part the result of the intervention of a Fortune that does not seem simply to be the deputy of divine justice. Furthermore, and with only one exception, these interpolations of Fortune pertain to figures who freely confess the blameworthiness of their behaviour, some of whom acknowledge

---

[148] MV ll. 477–83; 2006–7, 2013–15, 2020–1.
[149] Ibid. ll. 295–6, 302–8, 329; 421–41; 526–32, 593–5; 879–82, 904–10; 977–8, 984–5; 1315–26; see Rossi (1958: 63–7) for a summary of references to chastity and carnality in the work.

that their fall is the work of God's unerring justice. Cavendish puzzlingly claims that 'onhappie fortune hath brought to passe' the fall of Norris, says of Brereton that 'fortune hathe gevyn hyme a falle | Whiche sowced hyme in sorowe', and comments that the fall of Anne Boleyn allows us

> To se ffortune conceyve suche an occasion
> A quene to ouerthrowe frome hyr Royall mancion
>
> .   .   .   .
>
> Thus beyng astonyd with ffortunes mutabylitie
> Who no man fauoryth of hygh or lowe estate[150]

For Cavendish, then, it is 'tragic' when a guilty person justly meets with misfortune. The question of the *causes* of tragedy among the innocent, however, is rather different. Because their own sufferings have quite clearly not been deserved, the eight innocents of the *Metrical Visions* might be expected to voice a more Fortune-driven view of tragedy. However, it is in these laments that Cavendish most rigorously clarifies his (otherwise slightly inconsistent) position on the parts played by capricious Fortune and accountable vice in the sufferings of the guilty: in the narratives of Henry Courtenay, Marquis of Exeter, Henry Pole, Baron Montagu, Margaret Pole, countess of Salisbury, Thomas Seymour, Baron Sudeley, Sir Michael Stanhope, Sir Ralph Vane, Sir Miles Partridge, and Lady Jane Grey we find not only clear statements of innocence,[151] but, as the plaintiffs attempt to make sense of the events that led to their executions, we also see the term 'Fortune' being used to explain why it was that hostile forces conspired against them.[152] Although most of the innocent are fully aware of the direct *causes* of their falls from grace (that is, they are able to identify the figures who plotted against them) and can also adduce the *motives* of these opponents, they are typically at a loss to fathom why it should all have happened to *them*. The inexplicability and the injustice of their experiences, then, is a further part of what 'tragedy' means for Cavendish and should be considered alongside his more rigorously punitive definitions of the term.

[150] Ibid. ll. 348; 443–4; 634–5, 638–9. Cf. ll. 1034 (Lady Rochford), 1480 (Henry VIII).   [151] Ibid. ll. 790, 1558, 1621–2, 1817–18, 2223.
[152] e.g. ibid. ll. 1085–6, 1828; Rossi (1958) is rather summary on the topic of Fortune in the poem.

Oddly, it is one of Cavendish's innocents who most vigorously debunks the myth of a powerful Lady Fortune. At the end of the *Visions* sequence Lady Jane Grey bemoans the fact that her downfall and execution, although just, were not of her own deserving because it was her conniving counsellors, and not she herself, who improperly advanced her to the throne on the death of Edward VI. *She* paid the price for *their* treacherous ambition. As she lectures the men who caused her fall she argues that Fortune can not be held to have played any part in her innocent suffering:

> Nowe accuse we ffortune as cheafe ground of our falle
> And yet is she not giltie no thyng at all
>
> Yt is your pride and pevyshe presumpcion
> That hathe vs led to this myschaunce.   (ll. 2242–5)

That Cavendish's *Metrical Visions* occupy a significant place in the sixteenth-century development of the *de casibus* tradition of tragic narrative is beyond doubt; what is rather less clear, however, is what kind of tragic understanding the *Visions* embody. We have seen that Boccaccio and Premierfait do not themselves label their narratives as 'tragedies' at all, and that when Lydgate does so it is under the influence of Chaucer's extension of the term to include both innocent and criminous sufferers. But is it possible with Cavendish to capture the difference between an eclectic or 'inclusive' view of tragedy on the one hand and slapdash muddle on the other? Although his poem points in different directions, there is nonetheless a sense that he is trying to formulate an understanding of tragedy. For Cavendish misfortune is mostly retributive; but Fortune can cause bad things to happen to people who don't deserve them, and in these cases it is the *inexplicability* of their situations that lends the episodes a tragic pathos.

A Mirror for Magistrates

Cavendish is by no means the only voice in mid-Tudor England to yield, under the restoration of the old religion, to the appeal of continuing the Monk of Bury's *de casibus* project. The story of the complex publication history of the *Mirror for Magistrates* sequences has often been told, and so it need only be summarized here. In 1555 the printer John Wayland attempted to produce an edition of the *Fall of Princes* together with a continuation: this edition was abortive (having been suppressed, as Baldwin claims, by Bishop Stephen Gardiner, the Lord Chancellor) and all that survives of it are two variant title pages (one, which survives uniquely, containing Wayland's address to his reader on the verso) and a single leaf of text (the prose link between the narratives of Richard II and Owen Glendower).[153] In 1559, after the accession of Elizabeth, William Baldwin (a reformed writer who had worked for the Protestant printer Edward Whitchurch) successfully produced the first *Mirror* collection: hugely popular, the book went through several editions, and yet more narratives were added in 1563 and 1578.[154] In 1574–5 Baldwin's publisher, Thomas Marshe, printed a set of additions to the *Mirror* by John Higgins, a prequel sequence of sixteen narratives known as the 'Firste Parte', which dealt with figures from the legendary prehistory of Britain.[155] This sequence was itself supplemented in 1575 (with one narrative, that of Irenglas) and in 1587 (with twenty-three figures, fifteen of whom were Roman emperors and leaders): in this year the entire Higgins set (of forty narratives) appeared together with Baldwin's text.[156] Two further supplements were made to the Baldwin-Higgins scheme: in 1578 Thomas Blenerhasset, a soldier garrisoned on Guernsey, produced a 'Second Parte' of twelve narratives intended to make good certain omissions in the Baldwin-Higgins coverage of pre-1066 figures. That awareness of the integrity of the *Mirror* sequences was already firmly established by 1578 is perhaps shown by the fact that Blenerhasset's addition was not accepted as part of the tradition by the *Mirror* printer Marshe and was instead published by Richard Webster.[157] In 1609–10 Richard Niccols produced ten more narratives, which were printed by Felix Kyngston together with a rationalized version of the sequences

[153] The abortive *Mirror* is STC 1246: Wayland printed the *Fall* in 1554 (STC 3177.5). For an account of the failure of the Wayland print see Jackson (1932–3), *Mirror* ed. Campbell (1938: 5–7), and Budra (2000: 8–13). Baldwin claims in his 1559 dedication that the Chancellor 'hyndred' the 1555 text: for speculation on Gardiner's role see Feasey (1922–3: 177–93) and Campbell's detailed reply (1934b). An early summary of the various versions of the *Mirror* was given by Trench (1898).

[154] STC 1247 (1559), 1248 (1563), 1252.5 (1578). The 1563 edition (of 27 narratives) was popular, and reprinted in 1571 (STC 1249), 1574 (1250), 1575 (1251), and in 1578 (1252), also the year of the appearance of the 29-narrative version. For the complications attached to the delayed appearance of the Humphrey and Cobham laments, see Campbell (1934a).

[155] STC 13443 (1574).   [156] STC 13444 (1575) and 13445 (1587).
[157] STC 3131. See *Mirror* ed. Campbell (1946: 363–6).

of his predecessors.[158] Although the *Mirror* tradition spawned many imitations, Niccols's additions form the end of the textual dynasty which sprang from Baldwin's tragedies.[159]

Resolving the issue of what the various *Mirror* editors (and, in the case of Baldwin, their collaborating poets) understood themselves to be doing in their dramatic narratives is less straightforward than reconstructing the sequence of events at the presses. Wayland's address to his readers clearly suggests that he understood his composite *Fall-Mirror* as a unity, the laments of the latter being 'a continuacion of that Argument, concernyng the chefe Prynces of thys Iland, penned by the best clearkes in suche kinde of matters that be thys day lyving, not vnworthy to be matched with maister Lydgate'.[160] That Wayland understood the *Fall* itself to be a collection of tragedies is clear from the title page of his undated edition of the poem:

The trage- | dies, gathered by Iohn | Bochas, of all such Princes as | fell from theyr estates throughe | the mutability of Fortune since | the creacion of Adam, vntil his | tyme: wherin may be seen what | vices bring menne to destrucci- | on, wyth notable warninges | how the like may be auoyded.[161]

The *Fall* for Wayland is, then, a demonstration of at least two interwoven principles, the action of a changeable 'Fortune' being united with a retributive justice. Baldwin's conception of the *Mirror* seems to be close to Wayland's understanding; in his 1559 'Address to the Reader' Baldwin similarly offers the work both as a set of fortunal exempla and also as usefully regiminal in its presentation of punished vice:

the storye contynewed from where as Bochas lefte, vnto this presente time, chiefly of suche as Fortune had dalayed with here in this ylande: whiche

---

[158] The Niccols text of 1610 (STC 13446) was reprinted in 1619 (twice), 1620 (twice), and 1621 (STC 13447, 13447.5; 13448, 13448.4; 13448.7). Niccols rationalizes the whole *Mirror* corpus, partly in order to avoid duplicating narratives: he omits Blenerhasset's Guiderius, presumably because Higgins included the Briton in his 1587 extension. Campbell excludes Niccols's additions from her edition (1946: 10–13).
[159] For an account of the imitators of the *Mirror* see Farnham (1931–2: 395–410, repr. in Farnham *Medieval Heritage* (1936/56), 304–39).
[160] *Mirror* ed. Campbell (1938: 5–6).
[161] It is noticeable that it is not until the 1550s that printers designate the poem as a sequence of tragedies; Pynson's prints of 1494 (STC 3175) and 1527 (STC 3176) do not do so, although Tottell's (1554, STC 3177) and Wayland (?1554, STC 3177.5/3178) do label the poem in this way.

might be as a myrrour for al men as well noble as others, to shewe the slippery deceytes of the waueryng lady, and the due rewarde of all kinde of vices.[162]

The 1559 dedication is slightly more insistent on the didactic value of the poems:

For here as in a loking glas, you shall see (if any vice be in you) howe the like hath bene punished in other heretofore, whereby admonished, I truste it will be a good occasion to move you to the soner amendment. This is the chiefest ende, whye it is set furthe, which God graunt it may attayne.[163]

This statement would seem to provide some evidence for Willard Farnham's conviction that the tragedies in Baldwin's *Mirror* more insistently focused on issues of blame than did their Lydgatean predecessors.[164] In his 1936 study *The Medieval Heritage of Elizabethan Tragedy*, which remains the most extended discussion of the relationship between Lydgate's *Fall* and the sixteenth-century *Mirror for Magistrates* tradition, Farnham asserts that 'a good majority' of the 1559 narratives 'may be said to be primarily tragedies of retribution of sin or fault'.[165] It is certainly the case that one of the repeated emphases of the 1559 *Mirror* is a denial of the power of Fortune: typical proponents of this view are Thomas Mowbray, duke of Norfolk, Jack Cade, and Henry VI. Mowbray declares:

> I blame not Fortune though she dyd her parte,
> And true it is she can doo lytell harme,
> She gydeth goods, she hampreth not the harte,
> A vertuous mynd is safe from euery charme:
> Vyce, onely vyce, with her stoute strengthles arme,

---

[162] *Mirror* ed. Campbell (1938: 68).

[163] Ibid. 65–6. Baldwin's title pages consistently advertise the regiminal value of the texts and their emphasis on the deserved punishments of vice: (1559) 'A MYRROVRE | For Magistrates. | Wherein may be seen by | example of other, with howe gre- | uous plages vices are punished: and | howe frayle and vnstable worldly | prosperitie is founde, even of | those, whom Fortune see- | meth moste highly | to fauour' (*Mirror* ed. Campbell 1938: 62; cf. 242, 423, 425, 426, 428, 462). It is not until the composite 1587 printing that any *Mirror* title page offers its laments as 'Tragedies' (*Mirror* ed. Campbell 1938: 462; 1946: 224).

[164] Farnham (1926: 71): 'more connection of man's mortal fate with his own acts than there is in Seneca or Lydgate'. Farnham suggests that the wording of the title page of Tottell's print of the *Fall* is evidence of a shift in response to Lydgate: 'Lydgate himself had come to be magnified by his printers as a preacher of retribution' (*Medieval Heritage* (1936/56), 279); cf. *Fall* ed. Bergen vol. iv. 118–19.

[165] Farnham (1936/56: 283).

> Doth cause the harte to euyll to enclyne,
> Which I alas, doo fynde to true by myne.[166]

Equally, the rebel Cade dismisses the possibility that stellar influence governs the moral behaviour of men and, arguing that vice 'Cummeth of our selves, and so the blame [is] our owne', concludes that Fortune is nothing more than

> the folly and plage of those
> Which to the worlde their wretched willes dispose.[167]

Similarly, the unfortunate Henry VI affirms that 'god doth gide the world' and ridicules 'such doltish heades as dreame that all thinges drive by haps'.[168] Nevertheless, clear though these doctrinal statements may be, Baldwin's collection is not quite the uncomplicatedly voluntarist demonstration of accountable moral action that Farnham believes. In one of the shrewdest articles on the 1559 *Mirror* texts, William Peery in 1949 responded to Farnham's claim with an assessment of the causes of the tragedies in the 1559 *Mirror* based on a close reading of the laments.[169] Showing that Farnham had overstated his case, Peery's reading of the first Baldwin collection demonstrates that only two of the narratives (those of James I and Richard, earl of Cambridge) can clearly be said to dramatize the falls of entirely sinful protagonists.[170] Peery's work was a salutary reminder that texts should never be trusted to accomplish what their prefaces set out to achieve.

Of the thirteen narratives added to Baldwin's 1559 text over the next three decades seven may be said to dramatize the falls of criminous individuals whose misfortunes function as deserved, retributive punishment—these are those of Lord Hastings, Henry Stafford, second duke of Buckingham, Richard III, Jane Shore, the blacksmith Michael Joseph, Eleanor Cobham, duchess of Gloucester, and Cardinal Wolsey.[171] Conversely, the unambiguously innocent

---

[166] 'Mowbray', ll. 8–14, in *Mirror* ed. Campbell (1938: 102).
[167] 'Cade', ll. 35, 41–2 (ibid. 172).   [168] 'King Henry', ll. 37, 33 (ibid. 213).
[169] Other discussions of the topic include those by Budra (1988), Green (1980–1), and Kiefer (1977).
[170] It should be noted that the authors of the prose links in the 1559 *Mirror* themselves often judge their plaintiffs to be deserving of their misfortune, irrespective of the case made out for themselves by the complainants.
[171] I have excluded the account of the battle of Flodden Field from this analysis: lacking a single fallen protagonist, the narrative does not strictly function as a

victims of Fortuna number but two (Anthony Woodville, Baron Scales and second Earl Rivers, and Sir Nicholas Burdet): the remaining narratives chart falls which, although the *elati* admit their guilt, adduce accessory causes for their misfortunes (variously, those of other human agents as well as of the intervention of blind Fortune). Doctrinal statements on the relationship between destiny and personal morality are found in the mouths of both guilty and innocent: Jane Shore teaches that 'The setled minde is free from Fortunes power', while Burdet states that 'I haue . . . not Fortunes flatterie to accuse, | Nor Fate nor Destenie, nor any fancie fainde'.[172] Interestingly, only two of Baldwin's protagonists label their narratives a 'tragedie' (or 'tragicall' in their effect), and neither of these is innocent of personal responsibility for the fall.[173]

It emerges from a careful reading of the sixty-two laments in the continuations of Higgins, Blenerhasset, and Niccols that these sequences show a developing awareness of the generic status of the *de casibus* lament. In the hands of Baldwin's followers the Lydgatean fall is reworked as each of the three continuators responds to the often muddled variety of causes cited by his plaintiffs. In Higgins's forty laments there is a significant increase in the proportion of narratives charting the misfortunes of the self-confessedly guilty: twenty-six narratives fall into this category, while eight describe the falls of the innocent,[174] and only five deal with narratives of mixed causation.[175] One, that of the Roman captain Laelius Hamo, is only two stanzas long and fails to comment on the question of blame altogether. Not surprisingly, Higgins's protagonists are given to clear statements of the primacy of the human freedom of moral action. Irenglas, who is the most forthright, says:

> Som loue to boaste what Fortune they haue had:
> Som other blame, misfortune thers as fast:
> Som tell of Fortunes, there be good and bad:

de casibus narrative. Much has been written on Sackville's 'Buckingham' (see Pyle 1938, Howarth 1963). 'Shore's Wife' has also received critical attention (Hallett D. Smith 1938; Pratt 1969–70; Budra 2000: 63–4).

[172] 'Shore's Wife', l. 239, in *Mirror* ed. Campbell (1938: 381); 'Burdet', ll. 309–10 (ibid. 473).
[173] 'Richard III', l.305 (ibid. 370); 'Shore's Wife', l.56 (ibid. 375).
[174] Sabrine, Nennius, Irenglas, Brennus, Guiderius, Londricus, Fulgentius, and Septimius Geta.
[175] Albanacte, Madan, Cordelia, Stater, and Emperor Septimius Severus.

> Som fooles of Fortune make them selues agast:
> Some shewe of Fortunes comming, present, past:
> And say there is a fate that ruleth all.
> But sure it seemes their wisdome is but small:
> To talke so much, of lady Fortunes ball.
> No fortune is so bad, our selues ne frame:
> There is no chaunce at all hath vs preseru'de:
> There is no fate, whom we haue nede to blame:
> There is no destinie, but is deseru'de[176]

Lily Campbell has made clear her view that Higgins's more stringently ethical tragedies represent a shift from the political purpose of Baldwin's *Mirror*—and one which, in her opinion, diminishes the political importance of his contributions.[177] But in her insistence that Higgins reduces the *Mirror* tradition to a 'strictly literary venture' lacking in wider significance, Campbell fails to notice that Higgins's rationalization of the *de casibus* form is as much a refinement as it is a 'disintegration'.[178] In reducing the importance of arbitrary Fortune in the falls he relates, Higgins articulates a view of tragedy that has little to do with the pathos of the suffering of the innocent—indeed, none of his innocents uses the term 'tragedy' of his or her own experiences.[179] That Higgins in some sense regards himself as following the Lydgatean model of narrative tragedy emerges from his references both to the medieval poet and to 'Bochas' in his work.[180] Tragedy for Higgins quite plainly denotes sorrowful literary action, but not the kind of sorrowful action that human virtue is powerless to avert.

There is a notable shift away from Higgins's harshly retributive emphasis in the following two *Mirror* continuations: of Blenerhasset's twelve figures, only five are shown to have been entirely guilty—these being Sigebert, Alurede (the historical Alfred the Great) Egelrede (the historical Ethelred II, the 'Unready'), Edricus, and King Harold—while three are undeserving victims (Hellina, Cadwallader, and Lady Ebbe). Blenerhasset's characters seldom dilate on the theme of moral accountability (indeed, his

[176] 'Irenglas', ll. 65–76 in *Mirror* ed. Campbell (1946: 212): cf. 'Madan', l. 89 (ibid. 115), 'Manlius', ll. 92–8 (ibid. 122).

[177] *Mirror* ed. Campbell (1946: 11, 14–17): 'John Higgins . . . began the disintegration of the *Mirror* which culminated in the work of Niccols' (p. 13).

[178] Ibid. 17.

[179] Rather, the term is used by Albanacte (l. 47), Madan (l. 111), Manlius (l. 122), Mempricius (l. 131), and Cordelia (l. 146).

[180] *Mirror* ed. Campbell (1946: 279, 290).

Pinnar utters the most explicit statement when he claims, 'Men neuer reape no other than then was sowne: | If good were the gayne, the better commes the crop: | On vine growes the grape, and not the biter hop'),[181] and yet they are, conversely, rather more eager than Higgins's subjects to apply the term 'tragedie' to their laments.[182] In Niccols's 1610 sequence the retreat from Higgins's retributive accounts is continued, as pathos replaces a stringent reformist ethic: Niccols includes only three guilty protagonists (Godwin, earl of Wessex, Robert Curthose, duke of Normandy, and the villainous Richard III), while five of his ten narratives deal with the unambiguously innocent (Arthur, Edmund Ironside's brother Prince Alfred, King John, Edward II, and the 'princes in the Tower'). References to tragedy pepper his stanzas and, although Niccols's epistle 'To the Reader' commends the poems as 'paternes to shun vice and follow virtue', his 'Induction' discusses tragedy in stylistic rather than in these regiminal terms.[183] As the *Mirror* tradition evolves through the reigns of Elizabeth and James, then (years which correspondingly see the powerful emergence of dramatic tragedy on the English stage), the additions to Baldwin's original project mediate a subtly changing understanding of narrative tragedy. The arbitrarism of mid-Tudor Lydgateanism is gradually displaced (including by Baldwin himself) by a harsher and more retributive stance, which is then itself eventually supplanted by a return to a fortunal (and more emotionally sentimental) outlook.

'THE BRITISH VIRGIL AND BOCCACCIO'

Reasons for the emergence of determinedly retributive readings of the Lydgatean *Fall* tradition in the mid-Tudor period are easier to adduce than they are to substantiate. The ethical intent of the 1559 *Mirror*, while not quite as thoroughgoing as Farnham maintained, is not altogether unexpected: Baldwin's own interest in ethical enquiry is amply testified by his authorship in 1547 of the vastly popular *A Treatise of Morall Phylosophie*, a work which was reprinted twenty-three times between 1550 and 1640.[184] It is plain, however, that Baldwin, Higgins, Blenerhasset, and Niccols were children of

---

[181] 'Pinnar', ll. 5–7 in *Mirror* ed. Campbell (1946: 250).
[182] Namely at ll. 410, 425, 427, 441, 443, 448, 450, 452, 484.
[183] *Mirror* ed. Campbell (1938: 553, 555).   [184] STC 1253.

the Reformation: stinging attacks on the corruptions of the popish Church can be found in the narratives of Collingbourne, Eleanor Cobham, Humphrey of Gloucester, Cardinal Wolsey, Lady Ebbe, Cadwallader, and King John. They diverge so strongly in this respect from the Benedictine monk whose long poem inspired their tragic sequences that it would appear that the *Mirror* project gathered its force in the second half of the sixteenth century by harnessing the tragic possibilities of the *Fall* (just when the reputation of the medieval poem was sagging) and by reworking its obvious literary appeal in a new ethical and Protestant idiom.

In 1560 Jasper Heywood salutes 'Baldwin's worthy name' in the preface to his translation of Seneca's *Thyestes*; an analysis of the exact influence of the Lydgatean tradition of 'sad stories of the death of kings' on the history plays and tragedies of the Elizabethan and Jacobean stage lies well beyond the limits of my study. It suffices to say that the repeated attempts in these plays by often defiant protagonists to examine the inscrutable forces that are conspiring to bring about their ruin demonstrate not only the timeless appeal of the *de casibus* genre, but also the fertile potential the *Fall-Mirror* tradition has to be reworked and adapted for new purposes, audiences, and contexts.[185]

It is clear that the Lydgatean-*Mirror* tradition was popular: it generates at least one text of considerable power and nuance in Samuel Daniel's *Complaint of Rosamond* (1592), and the appeal of the form extends well into the seventeenth century, even being used in response to contemporary political event in the wake of the assassination of George Villiers, first duke of Buckingham, in 1628.[186] It seems that the sixteenth century, finding the literary model of the *Fall* a powerful and exciting one, ultimately allows its considerable enthusiasm for the ethical possibilities of Lydgate's poem to drown the original medieval work—the numerous progeny of Lydgate's text killing interest in the parent.[187]

The potential of the *Fall* genre for Protestant polemic, too, is quickly exploited. David Lindsay's rhyme-royal, Lydgatean 'Tragedie

---

[185] Philip Drew sketches some of the impact of the *de casibus* tradition on dramatic tragedy (1982: 47–99).

[186] *Rosamond* (STC 6243.2), cf. Primeau (1975); for the use of the *de casibus* model by Pierre Mathieu in 1617 and Thomas Hawkins in 1632 see Wright, (1957: 25–6).

[187] An example of the high esteem in which the *Mirror* tradition was held is found in Francis Mere's claim that it is among 'our best for Tragedie', *Palladis Tamia* (1598: STC 17834).

of the Late Cardinal Beaton' (1547), in which the poet is visited
by the shade of Beaton while reading 'Bochas' ('ane Buke . . . |
Quhare I fand mony Tragedie and storie'[188]), charts the deserved
fall of a villainous and ambitious prelate. The following year this
poem was translated into English by an ardent Reformer and
translator of Erasmus, Robert Burrant, who offered the poem as
an account not only of the Cardinal's fall, but also of the 'martyrdom' of one of the Reformers executed by Beaton.[189] By 1601
the *Mirror* model is being used to articulate anticatholic polemic:
Thomas Wenman's *The Legend of Mary, Queen of Scots* (which
begins with the conjuration 'Baldwyn awake, thie penn hath slept
to longe') presents the 'Churche of Rome' as an opponent of 'the
trueth of gospell'.[190] Again, John Weever exploits the form in his
*The Mirror of Martyrs, or the life and death of . . . Sir Iohn Old-
castle* (1601) in defence of Wyclif and the Lollards: in this poem
Weever's protagonist describes himself as 'a true faith-professing
Protestant', attacks 'popish charmes' and other 'manifold abuses',
and finally declares that 'Wickleues soule now beares me company'.[191] Oldcastle even contrasts his own death ('for Christs owne
quarell') with the martyrdom of Archbishop Becket, who merely
died 'in Romes defence'.[192]

The association of the printer John Wayland (who has been
described as a 'staunch Catholic') with the *Mirror* project has been
thought 'very strange':[193] certainly, in 1539 it was Wayland's press
that had produced the conservative primer commissioned by Thomas
Cromwell from John Hilsey, bishop of Rochester, and so was at
the centre of one of the most significant publishing events of the
English Reformation.[194] Such connections, however, should probably be treated with caution; the unfortunate Cromwell (himself
later to become one of Cavendish's tragic complainants) more
characteristically sponsored some of the most radically Protestant
texts of the 1530s, including William Marshall's reformed *Goodly*

---

[188] Lindsay ed. Hamer (1931: i. 129–43).   [189] *STC* 15683.
[190] *Legend* stanzas 1, 71: the text was first printed in 1810.
[191] *Martyrs* (*STC* 25226) fos. D7ᵛ, D6ʳ, D2ʳ, F2ᵛ.   [192] Ibid. fo. F3ʳ.
[193] Byrom (1931: 320, 331). Wayland is chosen in 1555 as printer for the official primer of Mary's reign, but Duffy (1992: 538) sees this as a recognition of
his career of reliable publishing rather than as a reward for his Catholic sympathies. Thompson (2001) traces the activities at Wayland's and Tottell's presses in the
1550s.
[194] *STC* 16009. Details of the *Manual of Prayers* are given in McConica (1965:
169) and Duffy (1992: 444).

Primer (1535) and the 1535 translation of Marsilius of Padua's *Defensor pacis* that was to play an important role in the Henrician legitimization of royal ecclesiastical supremacy.[195] Nonetheless, we have seen that the sixteenth-century reception of Lydgate developed along a confessional axis, and so it is no accident that the last printing of the *Fall* should occur during the reign of Mary and that the poem should appear from the house of a printer with firm Catholic sympathies. Similarly, whatever Stephen Gardiner's motives for suppressing the 1555 *Mirror*, it is intriguing that this work has to wait for a Reformist Queen before it can appear[196]— and that once it has the *Fall of Princes* (so admired by recusant Catholics) is so thoroughly eclipsed by the *Mirror* tradition it had spawned that it is not again printed until 1924.

Lydgate's fortunes at the presses have been expertly charted recently: the sudden revival of activity in the Marian period after twenty years of silence, as printers realized the opportunity for marketing the Monk of Bury in a newly conservative climate, is one of the most significant episodes in the story of Lydgate's reception into the printed canon.[197] Nonetheless, despite this fervent press activity in the 1550s, attempts in the same decade to raise a memorial tomb to Lydgate failed; we have seen, also, how the tide of Lydgate's critical fortunes was soon to turn in the first half of Elizabeth's reign. Additionally, the sheer bulk of his total output made the production of a prestige single-volume collected works both practically and economically unviable, a fact which must in part have accelerated Lydgate's eventual fall from the canon. The claim (supposedly made in the epitaph to his tomb at Bury) that Lydgate is 'Maro Britanus Boccasiousque', both the British Virgil and Boccaccio, would strike modern readers as extravagantly flattering.[198] And yet in this study we have seen that Lydgate's

---

[195] *STC* 17817. McConica (1965: 168); Loades (1991: 13–14); Rex (1993: 20). For a detailed account of the way in which Marshall's translation twists Marsilius to support his own claims of supreme temporal and ecclesiastical powers for Henry see Lockwood (1991). Marshall's works also include a translation of Valla's demonstration of the falsity of the Donation of Constantine (1534, *STC* 5641), which he commended to Cromwell as the best weapon against 'the Pope of Rome'.

[196] As, too, does the 'Protestant' *Piers Plowman*, first printed in 1550 (*STC* 19906, 19907, 19907a) under Edward, then not again appearing until 1561 (*STC* 19908) under Elizabeth.

[197] See Thompson (2001), Gillespie (D. Phil thesis, 2001a: 145–69; 2002b).

[198] Pearsall (1997: 40–1); Gillespie (D. Phil thesis, 2001a: 302–3).

careful (and frequently partisan) reworkings of his source materials, his responses to the literary, Lancastrian, and Benedictine contexts in which he found himself, and the serious manner in which readers appropriated the *Fall* in the one hundred and fifty years after his death all clearly reveal the Monk of Bury's longest poem to be a rich and rewarding text, the product of an accomplished, shrewd, and forthright poet operating at the height of his powers. Its time has now surely come.

APPENDIX: CONSPECTUS OF THE NARRATIVES

Much of the current critical resistance to the *Fall of Princes* arises not because readers (or potential readers) have strongly developed objections towards Lydgate's aims or practices in the poem, but because they feel lost in its seemingly interminable lists of unfortunate individuals. Nearly everyone will approach the *Fall* via Bergen's EETS edition, which, while first-rate, does little to alleviate the impression of the poem as nine unstructured catalogues: in some ways the medieval book, with colourful visual signals to indicate textual division (such as decorated initials and rubricated prose headnotes), offered a less daunting reading experience.

It need hardly be admitted that the *Fall* lacks the strong narrative frame found in other long poems (as, for example, *The Canterbury Tales*) and the closely wrought lyrical beauty of much shorter ones (for example, those of the *Gawain*-poet), but it need not be bewildering. Boccaccio and Premierfait subdivide their texts into chapter units which are often made internally coherent by focusing on a group of related protagonists, or by providing brief anthologies of *thematically* similar downfalls. The contours of the *Des Cas* are still there to be seen in the *Fall*; when these are uncovered it is also possible to gain some sense of the extent to which Lydgate reorganizes his material.

The reader also feels hampered by not knowing which (if any) of the constituent narratives of the *Fall* are original to Lydgate and, concomitantly, whether narratives have been silently omitted in his process of 'translating' the *Des Cas*; Bergen's notes in the fourth volume of his edition are selective in their coverage of Lydgate's treatment of his French source, and so are less helpful than one might wish.

The following pages offer a conspectus of the line numbers of the English poem alongside the chapters of the appropriate versions of the Latin and French texts. The component narratives of the French chapters have been listed and Lydgate's larger alterations to these noted; the refrained envoy sections are also indicated (allowing us, for example, to note the sharp decline in Lydgate's enthusiasm for these after Book V). The seven passages where the poem departs from its usual rhyme-royal stanza (*ababbcc*) and adopts the 'Monk's Tale' octave (*ababbcbc*) are also recorded; these sections are often codicologically interesting, in that they cause trouble for scribes by disrupting the otherwise regular *mise-en-page* of the manuscripts.

I hope that readers will now feel that it is possible to move through the *Fall* with a clearer sense of the underlying structures which informed Lydgate's composition, and without needing to have open copies of the Latin and French texts at their elbows.

De Casibus Chapters (A-Version)	Content Narratives in Des Cas (B-Version)†	Fall Reference
	Book I: 15 envoys	
*I. Prol: 'Exquirenti mihi quid ex labore'	*Boccaccio's preface, Prologue du Translateur, Dedication to Jean, duke of Berry* [L adds tributes to Chaucer and Humphrey]	I. 1–469
*I. 1: De Adam et Æva	Adam and Eve	I. 470–784
I. 2: Adversus inobedientiam	Moralizes the Fall of Man E	I. 785–1001
I. 3: De Nembroth	Nimrod	I. 1002–281
I. 4: In superbos	Moralizes Nimrod and pride of princes E	I. 1282–400
*I. 5: Nihil non absumit tempus	Vixoses, Thanaus, Zoroastres and Ninus, kings of Sodom, Pharaoh, Ogyges, Isis and Apis, Erysichthon, *Gelanor and Danaus, Tereus* E	I. 1401–841
*I. 6: De Cadmo Thebanorum rege	Cadmus, his kin (Semele, Actaeon, Pentheus, Athamus) E	I. 1842–2170
*I. 7: Concursus infoelicium	Æetes, Jason, Minos and Scylla, Theseus, Sisera, the Midianites E	I. 2171–3129
*I. 8: De Iocasta Thebarum regina	Jabin, Jocasta and Oedipus [most of Oedipus original to Lydgate], Thebes E	I. 3130–843
*I. 9: Thiestis et Atrei iurgium	Thyestes and Atreus E	I. 3844–4242
I. 10: De Theseo, Atheniensium rege	Theseus, Ariadne, Hippolytus E	I. 4243–557
*I. 11: Adversus nimiam credulitatem	Moralizes credulous princes and the wiles of women [Lydgate adds a defence of women] E	I. 4558–844
*I. 12: Conventus dolentium	Althaea and Meleager, Hercules E, Narcissus, Byblis, Myrrha [Lydgate adds Adonis], Orpheus, Marpessa and Lampedo E	I. 4845–5901

*I. 13: De Priamo et Hecuba	Priam, Troy [Lydgate abbreviates heavily and directs reader to his *Troy Book*]	I. 5902–6041
*I. 14: Contra superbos	Moralizes pride and avarice: Hector, Paris, Priam	I. 6042–104
*I. 15: De Agamemnone Mycenarum rege	*Agamemnon, Palamedes, Ulysses, Menelaus, Clytemnestra, Ægisthus* [Lydgate has absorbed this into his brief treatment of ch. 13, and therefore ignores this chapter]	—
*I. 16: Paupertati applaudit	Moralizes Poverty: Zenocrates, Clytemnestra, Diogenes, *Curius Dentatus E*	I. 6105–335
*I. 17: De Sampsone	Samson, *brief attack on women E*	I. 6336–510
*I. 18: In mulieres	Against women *E*	I. 6511–734
*I. 19: Miseri quidam	Pyrrhus [Lydgate adds Canace and Macareus] *E*	I. 6735–7070

Book II: 11 envoys

*II. Prol: 'Forsan erunt qui dicent'	[L adds the request of Duke Humphrey to supply envoys	II. 1–161
II. 1: De Saule Israelitarum rege	Saul [L adds Witch of Endor], David, *Ionothas, Abminadab, Melchis E*	II. 162–532
II. 2: Obedientiae commendatio	Moralizes obedience [L omits Agag]	II. 533–623
II. 3: Pauci flentes	*Adraazarus and Adadus*	—
II. 4: De Roboa Iudeorum rege	Rehoboam *E*	II. 624–805
*II. 5: In Fastosam Regum superbiam	Good government, Mucius Scaevola, Lucretia [L extends from a brief reference and adds passage on Chaucer], Virginia and Appius Claudius, Philip of Macedonia [L also deals with him in his envoy], Hasdrubal *E*	II. 806–1463

De Casibus Chapters (A-Version)	Content Narratives in Des Cas (B-Version)†	Fall Reference
II. 6: Concursus gementium	Jeroboam, Zerah, Adab, Zimri	II. 1464-701
II. 7: De Athalia Hierosolymae regina	Ahab and Jezebel, Athalia and Joas E	II. 1702-897
II. 8: In immoderatam rerum concupiscentiam	Moralizes the shameful deeds of the figures in ch. 7	——
II. 9: In Hebraeos	God and Fortune	——
*II. 10: De Didone regina Cartaginiensium	Dido of Tyre, the founding of Carthage, her suicide [L adds reference to Ovid]	II. 1898-2170
*II. 11: In Didus commendationem	[L treats as the E to ch. 10, then adds 5 ironic stanzas to widows]	II. 2171-233
*II. 12: De Sardanapalo rege Assyriorum	Sardanapalus	II. 2234-338
*II. 13: In Sardanapalum et eius similes	[Omitting Pythagoras and references to noble Greeks, L adds Tubal / 'Pictagoras', Seth's children, Enoch, Cam, Catacrismus, Ezra, Isis, Carmentis, Cicero] Callicrates, Mirmecides [L adds Pan, Mercury, Bacchus, Euclid, Phoebus et al., Fido¹] E	II. 2339-548
II. 14: Male fortunati plerique	Amaziah, Josiah, Uzziah, Fido, Olympic Games, [L adds exhortation], Hoshea, Sennacherib	II. 2549-814
II. 15: De Sedechia Hierosolymorum rege	Zedekiah²	II. 2815-940
II. 16: In aerumnosam mortalium conditionem	Moralizes falls [L treats as E to Zedekiah]	II. 2941-61
II. 17: De Astyage Medorum rege	Job, Tobit, Nebuchadnezzar, Astyages, Mandane, Socrates, Euripides, Demosthenes, Cyrus	II. 2962-3325

*II. 18: Pauca de sopniis	On dreams: *Simonides, Calpurnia, Artorius, Arterius*,³ *Pharaoh, Nebuchadnezzar* [L treats as E to ch. 17]	II. 3326–46
II. 19: Querelae quorumdam	Pandales [sic] and Gyges, Midas [L adds gold and ref. to Ovid], Belshazzar [L adds Daniel] E	II. 3347–556
II. 20: De Croeso Lydorum rege	Croesus and Cyrus	II. 3557–731
II. 21: Infoelices aliqui	Cyrus E, Aemilius, Numitor and Rhea, Romulus and Remus	II. 3732–4263
II. 22: De Metio Suffetio Albanorum rege	Metius Suffetius	II. 4264–403
*II. 23: In fraudem invectiva	On fraud and deceit [L adds Tullus Hostilius⁴ and Rome E]	II. 4404–592

Book III: 10 envoys

*III. Prol: 'Consueuere longum ac laboriosum'	—(Laurent incorporates into ch. 1)	III. 1–161
*III. 1: Paupertatis & Fortunae certamen	Andalus del Negro, Fortune and Poverty	III. 162–707
*III. 2: De Tullo Hostilio & Tarquinio Prisco	Tullus Hostilius, Ancus Marcius, Lucinio E, *Tarquin dynasty*	III. 708–931
*III. 3: De Tarquinio Superbo Romanorum rege novissimo	Tarquin and Lucretia	III. 932–1148
*III. 4: In portentosam principum libidinem	David, Samson, Solomon, Scipio, Cato, Drusus, lust, chastity and marriage, Jacob, Virgineus, Paris and Helen, Benjaminites, Holofernes E	III. 1149–638⁵
III. 5: Gemebundi quidam	Cambyses, Otanes and Oropastes, Darius, Coriolanus and Volumnia, Miltiades, *Themistocles at Athens* [treated in envoy] [L adds Cynaegeirus] E	III. 1639–2205
*III. 6: De Xerxe Persarum rege	Xerxes	III. 2206–534

De Casibus Chapters (A-Version)	Content Narratives in Des Cas (B-Version)†	Fall Reference
*III. 7: In lusciosam mortalium caecitatem	Xerxes E	III. 2535–639
*III. 8: Infoelices nonnulli	Artabanus, Phalanthus, Caeso Quintius, Gracchus and Cincinnatus	III. 2640–3010
*III. 9: De Appio Claudio decemviro	Appius Claudius E, on judges	III. 3011–115
*III. 10: In leguleos imperitos	Attacks corrupt judges: Phoroneus, Minos, Mercury, Solon, Lycurgus, *Sempronius, Saphyr, Cato, Censorinus* [L adds 'Exclamation']	III. 3116–283
III. 11: Flentium conventus	*Demosthenes, Nicias, Civilius, Spurius Melius, Lartes Tolumnus*	——
*III. 12: De Alcibiade Atheniensi	Alcibiades E	III. 3284–717
*III. 13: In excusationem Alcibiades	Alcibiades [L treats as 'worldly folk']	III. 3718–80
*III. 14: Auctoris purgatio, & poeseos commendatio	[L treats as a praise of industry] Retracts ch. 12, on poetry: *Homer, Virgil, Bocace* [L adds E on poets and a letter to his patron, ll. 3837–71]	III. 3781–871
III. 15: Aphri quidam queruli	Cartalus, Machaeus E, Himilco	III. 3872–4095
III. 16: De Hannone Carthaginiensi	Hanno E	III. 4096–235
*III. 17: In divitias & stolidam vulgi opinionem	[L against the covetous] *Spurius Melius, Hanno,* Amyclas, Pompey, Diogenes, [L adds Croesus], Sardanapalus, [Sophodius], *Sarranus,* Cincinnatus, Masinissa, Xerxes	III. 4236–480
III. 18: Flentium multitudo	Evagoras, Theo, Amyntas, Epaminondas, Alexander, Perdiccas *Sartas / 'Ariba',* Haman, Mordecai	III. 448–851
III. 19: De Artaxerxe Persarum rege	Artaxerxes, Cyrus, Darius E	III. 4852–5152

Book IV: 9 envoys

*IV. Prol: 'Movisse reor aliquantisper ab obstinata'	[L adds ll. 1–168 on poets] [Priam][6] Astyages, *Croesus*, [Cyrus], Tarquin, *Xerxes*, Artaxerxes	IV. 169–210
*IV. 1: De Marco Manlio Capitolino	Marcus Manlius	IV. 211–511
*IV. 2: In infidam plaebem	Disloyalty [L adds triumphs, Tarpeia, Carmentis, Marcus Manlius] *E*	IV. 512–686
IV. 3: In tyrannos	Tyranny: Nectanebes, Pausanias, Heliarchus	IV. 687–798
IV. 4: De Dionysio Syracusano inferiore	Dionysius of Syracuse *E*	IV. 799–938
IV. 5: In Dionysium & Fortunae excusationem	On Fortune and personal vice [L adds Victurbius from ch. 6]	IV. 939–80
IV. 6: De Polycrate Samiorum tyranno	*Victurbius*, Polycrates	IV. 981–1106
*IV. 7: De Callisthene philosopho	*Aribas*, Callisthenes and Alexander, Lysimachus,[7] Clytus *E*	IV. 1107–449
IV. 8: De Alexandro Epyrotarum rege	Alexander of Epirus	IV. 1450–603
IV. 9: De Dario Persarum rege	Darius, Alexander the Great *E*	IV. 1604–2002
IV. 10: Dolentium concursus	War: Leonatus, Antipater, Neptolomus and Policarpus, Perdiccas, Ariarathes, Hamilcar	IV. 2003–142
IV. 11: De Eumene Cappadociae adque Paphagoniae rege	Eumenes *E*	IV. 2143–331
IV. 12: De Olympiadae Macedonum regina	Olympias of Macedonia *E*	IV. 2332–639
IV. 13: De Agathocle Siculorum rege	Agathocles [L adds a moral on the low born] *E*	IV. 2640–968
IV. 14: Plurimus tristium concursus	Cassander and Bersane, Antipater, Demetrius, Peucestas and Amyntas, Sandrocottus, Seleuchus, Lysimachus and Callisthenes	IV. 2969–3325

De Casibus Chapters (A-Version)	Content Narratives in *Des Cas* (B-Version)[†]	*Fall* Reference
IV. 15: De Arsinoe Macedonum regina	Arsinoe and Ceraunus of Macedonia *E*	IV. 3326–492 (octaves: 3445–92)
IV. 16: Flentes plurimi	Ceraunus, Belgius, Brennus *E*, Apollo, Diana, Minerva	IV. 3493–744
IV. 17: De Pyrrho Epyrotarum rege	Pyrrhus of Epirus	IV. 3745–898
IV. 18: Arsinoe Cyrenensium regina	Aristotimus, Arsinoe and Demetrius	IV. 3899–4066
IV. 19: In pulchritudinem & amorem illecebrem	Beauty and lust: Spurina *E*	v. 1–98
Book V: 7 envoys		
v. 1: De Seleucho & Antiocho	Seleuchus, Antiochus III	v. 99–245
v. 2: Aerumnosi plures	Six nobles: Laodomeia, Cleomenes, Hiero, Cornelius, Hannibal, Xanthippus	v. 246–420
*v. 3: De Marco Attilio Regulo	Marcus Attilius Regulus	v. 421–749
*v. 4: In cives *minus* Reipublice amatores	Marcus Attilius Regulus, *attack on disloyalty E*	v. 750–840
v. 5: Grandis infoelicium turma	Ptolemy Philopator and Agathodia, Britomaris and Viridomarus of France	v. 841–1029
v. 6: De Syphace Numidiae rege	Syphax of Numidia	v. 1030–255
v. 7: Infoelicium conventus	Nabis, Punic Wars (Hasdrubal, Marcus Manlius, Lucius Censorinus, Scipio), Perseus of Sparta, Corinth, Philip Philermene and Democritus of Ætolia	v. 1156–470
v. 8: De Antiocho magno Asiae et Syriae rege	Antiochus III and Laodicea[8] *E*	v. 1471–621 (octaves: 1590–621)

v. 9: Oppressi multi	Hieronymus, *Agesipolis, Orgiagontes, Gaudotus,* Scipio Africanus, Scipio Asiaticus, Philopomen, Scipio Nasica, Gracchus *E*	v. 1622–885 (octaves: 1846–85)
*v. 10: De Annibale Carthaginiensi	Hannibal *E*	v. 1886–2158
*v. 11: De Prusia Bithyniae rege	Prusias and Nicomedes [L omits parricide]	v. 2159–214
v. 12: De Perseo Macedonum rege	Persa and Demetrius	v. 2215–98
v. 13: De Fortunae more & deiectis paucis	Azariah, Ammonius	v. 2299–340[9]
v. 14: De pseudoPhilippo Macedoniae rege	Andriscus of Macedonia	v. 2341–403
v. 15: De Alexandro Bala Syriae rege	Alexander Balas and Demetrius *E*	v. 2404–536
v. 16: Lapsi quidam	Gaius and Tiberius Gracchus, Hasdrubal's wife, Dido, *Aristonicus,* Jonathan Maccabeus and Tryphon	v. 2537–648[10]
v. 17: De Demetrio Syriae rege	Demetrius II	v. 2649–760
v. 18: De Alexandro Zebenna Syriae rege	Zebina	v. 2761–844
v. 19: Dolentes pauci	*Metellus, Caius Domicius,* Bituitus and Fabius, Cleopatra and Euergetes	v. 2845–956
v. 20: De Iugurtha Numidiarum rege	Jugurtha of Numidia *E*	v. 2957–3145

Book VI: 3 envoys

*VI. 1: Colloquutio Fortunae & auctoris et quorundam infoelicium demonstratio	Fortune and Bocace, Saturninus, Drusus, Scipio, Fanaticus, Anthonio (L's Athenion), Spartacus, Viriathus, Gaius Marius, Mithridates, Orodes of Parthia, Pompey	VI. 1–987
*VI. 2: De Caio Mario Arpinate	Gaius Marius and Sulla	VI. 988–1260

De Casibus Chapters (A-Version)	Content Narratives in Des Cas (B-Version)†	Fall Reference
*VI. 3: Pauca de nobilitate	Moralizes Marius, true nobility, *Jugurtha and Metellus Numidicus*	VI. 1261–323
VI. 4: Cleopatrae tres miserae	Three Cleopatras [L omits the second marriage of the third Cleopatra]	VI. 1324–58
VI. 5: De Mithridate Ponti rege	Mithridates of Pontus E	VI. 1359–757
VI. 6: Excussi quidam	Eucratides of Bactria, *Alexander of Egypt (son of Euergetes)*	VI. 1758–78
VI. 7: De Hyrode rege Parthorum	Herodes of Parthia	VI. 1779–925
VI. 8: Adventus flentium	Fimbria, Albinus, Adrian, Sothimus of Thrace, Thrace described, *Pompey*	VI. 1926–2023
*VI. 9: De Cneo Pompeio Magno	Pompey E	VI. 2024–548
*VI. 10: Pauca auctoris verba	*Praise of Pompey*	————
*VI. 11: Ingens certamen dolentium	*Caesar's victims*, Ptolemy of Egypt, Juba of Numidia, clothing, *Pharnaces of Pontus*, Aristobolus, Scipio, Julius Caesar's assassination, Calpurnia's dream E, Octavian, *Mark Antony, Dolabella*, and the conspirators, Cicero and Bocace	VI. 2549–3003
*VI. 12: De Marco Tullio Cicerone	Cicero and the Catiline conspiracy [L adds Cicero's works], Mark Antony	VI. 3004–276
*VI. 13: In gracculos aduersus rethoricam obstrepentes	Rhetoric and Language	VI. 3277–500
*VI. 14: Gementes plurimi	Sextus Pompey, Marcus Lepidus, Caesar Lucius, Lucius Æmilius Paullus	VI. 3501–619

*VI. 15: De Marco Antonio triumviro & Cleopatra Ægypti regina	Mark Antony and Cleopatra	VI. 3620–68
	Book VII: 3 envoys	
VII. 1: Quorundam infoelicium concursus	Antony, Caesarius, Julia, Agrippa, Cassius of Parma, Galbus	VII. 1–77
VII. 2: De Herode Iudeorum rege	Herod, *Antigonus E*	VII. 78–277 (octaves: 246–77)
*VII. 3: Tristes quidam & Tyberii Cesaris adque Caii Caligule iurgium cum Valeria Messalina	Herod Antipas, Archelaus, the quarrel of Messalina, Caligula and Tiberius	VII. 278–592
*VII. 4: De Nerone Claudio Caesare	Nero and *Seneca E*	VII. 593–795
*VII. 5: Adflicti quidam	Eleazar, Galba and *Piso Licinianus*, Otho and Vitellius	VII. 796–876
*VII. 6: De Aulo Vitellio Cesare	Vitellius	VII. 877–1103
*VII. 7: In gulam & gulosos	Gluttony, the Golden World, *the Church*, John the Baptist, *Diogenes E*[11]	VII. 1104–334
VII. 8: De excidio Hierosolymitano	The Jews, the Fall of Jerusalem, Eleazar and Masada, *Christ and the Catholic Faith, the Diaspora*	VII. 1335–565
VII. 9: In Iudaeos pauca	Christ, *the Incarnation*, the Jews, *the Passion, Pilate excused* [L adds list of portents]	VII. 1566–663, VIII. 1–7
	Book VIII: 1 envoy	
*VIII. 1: Et primo viri clarissimi Francisci Petrarche in auctorem obiurgatio	Bocace and Petrarch [L adds autobiographical comment]	VIII. 8–203

De Casibus Chapters (A-Version)	Content Narratives in Des Cas (B-Version)†	Fall Reference
VIII. 2: Imperatores miseri	A crowd of dolorous nobles, Domitian, Commodus, Clinus (L's 'Helvius Pertinax'), Julian, Septimius Severus, Postumus (L's 'Pescennius'), Albinus, Lucius Septimius Geta and Marcus Aurelius Antoninus 'Caracalla' (as the French 'Bassianus Anthonici' and L's 'Antoninus'), Martinus (L's 'Macrinus'), Antoninus Aurelius, Marcus Aurelius Alexander Severus, Maximus, Gordian, two Philips, Decius, Gallus, Volusian	VIII. 204–427
VIII. 3: De Valeriano Augusto Romanorum imperatore	Valerian and Gallienus	VIII. 428–62
VIII. 4: In Saporem Persarum regem, & Valerianum Romanorum imperatorem	Valerian and Sapor of Persia	VIII. 463–560
VIII. 5: Caterva Caesarum deiectorum	Gallienus, Quintilius, Aurelian of Denmark, Tacitus, Florianus, Probus, Clarus, Numerian and Carinus, Meontius Ballista, Æmilianus	VIII. 561–665
*VIII. 6: De Zenobia Palmyrenorum regina	Zenobia Septimia	VIII. 666–742
VIII. 7: Pauca de Diocletiano Romanorum imperatore	Diocletian [L adds St Alban and Pope Marcellus]	VIII. 743–854
VIII. 8: De Maximiano Herculeo Romanorum imperatore	Maximian	VIII. 855–903
VIII. 9: De Galerio Maximiano Romanorum imperatore	Galerius	VIII. 904–1022

VIII. 10: Nonnulli infoelices Caesares & Augusti	Maxentius, Lucinius of Denmark, Constantine and Crispus, Arius, Dalmatius, Constans and Constantius, Magnentius, *Nepotian*, Decius, Silvanus [L adds Constantine's leprosy and Donation]	VIII. 1023–463
VIII. 11: De Iuliano Apostata Romanorum imperatore	Julian Apostate	VIII. 1464–652
VIII. 12: In blasphemos	On blasphemy	VIII. 1653–708
VIII. 13: Dolentes plurimi	Valens, Hermanric, Gratian, Maximus, Andragathius, Valentinian, Arbogastes and Eugenius, Theodosius [L adds Theodosius and Ambrose]	VIII. 1709–2107
VIII. 14: De Radagaso Gothorum rege	Alaric, Radagaisus *and the Goths*	VIII. 2108–191
VIII. 15: Dolentium descriptio brevis	Rufinus, Stilicho, *Gratian*, *Maximus*, Constantine, Constans, Hieronicus (L's 'Gorontius'), Attalus, Heraclian	VIII. 2192–317
*VIII. 16: De Odoacre Rutheno Italorum rege	Odoacer	VIII. 2318–520
*VIII. 17: In presentem urbis Romae conditionem	The Fall of Rome lamented	VIII. 2521–69
VIII. 18: Deiecti quidam	Trasilla, Busar, Philete, Marcian, Leo, Symmachus, Boethius	VIII. 2570–660
*VIII. 19: De Arthuri rege Britonum	Arthur and Mordred *E*	VIII. 2661–3164[12]
VIII. 20: In scelestos filios	Unkind kindred, *Mordred moralized*	VIII. 3165–206
VIII. 21: Flentes quidam pauci	Five barbarians: Gelimer the Vandal, Vitigis the Goth, Amarales, Sindbal, Totila	VIII. 3207–55
VIII. 22: De Rosimunda Langobardorum regina	[L adds Turisund] Rosamund and Albion	VIII. 3256–381
VIII. 23: In mulieres	*On noble women*	———

De Casibus Chapters (A-Version)	Content Narratives in *Des Cas* (B-Version)†	*Fall* Reference
	Book IX: 6 narrative and 4 concluding envoys	
*IX. 1: Et primo de quibusdam miseris. Et inde de Brunichilde Francorum regina	Mauritius, Phocas, Mahomet, Brunhilde argues with Bocace E, *Brunhilde excused*	IX. 1–532
IX. 2: Quidam tristes Augusti	Heraclius, Constantine III, Constantine IV	IX. 533–651
IX. 3: De Romilda Foroiulianorum (ut loquitur) ducissa	Gisulf and Romilda	IX. 652–721
IX. 4: Imperatores plures miseri flentesque Langobardi	Five emperors and four kings: Justinian Temerarius, Leontius, Tiberius, Philippicus, Anastasius; the division of the Church, Irene; Kings Lupus, Alahis, Aribertus, *Desiderius*	IX. 722–896
IX. 5: De Desiderio rege Langobardorum	Desiderius	IX. 897–966
IX. 6: Dolentes quidam & in superbos pauca	Pope Joan, Arnulph, the Pride of Princes, *Louis*	IX. 967–1059
IX. 7: De Ioanne Papa XII	Pope John XII	IX. 1060–99
IX. 8: Concursus dolentium	Charles of Lorraine, Salomon of Hungary, Pietro of Hungary, *Leopold of Hungary*, Ernest of Swabia	IX. 1100–76[13]
IX. 9: De Diogene Romano Constantinopolitanorum imperatore	Diogenes Romanus	IX. 1177–211
IX. 10: Adflicit quidam	Robert of Normandy, Henri IV, Jocelyn of Rages	IX. 1212–337
IX. 11: De Andronico Constantinopolitanorum imperatore	Andronicus I 'Comnenus'	IX. 1338–477
IX. 12: In lascivos & sevos pauca	[L treats as an *E* to ch. 11]	IX. 1478–512

IX. 13: Infortunati alii	Isaac, Alexius, Sultans Salethus and Cathebadinus, Robert of Surrentine	IX. 1513–70
IX. 14: De Guilielmo tertio Siculorum rege	William of Sicily, Tancred	IX. 1571–640
IX. 15: Gementes aliqui	Guy of Lusignan, John of Brienne	IX. 1641–66
IX. 16: De Henrico Romanorum rege	Henry, son of Frederick II	IX. 1667–743
IX. 17: Adplaudit auctor patriae pietate	Love between kindred—six villains: Brutus, Manlius, Philip Manlius, Cassius, Herod, Frederick II	IX. 1744–99
IX. 18: Revoluti quidam	*Frederick II*, Manfred of Naples, Enzio of Sardinia, Frederick of Castile, Maumetus of Persia, Argones	IX. 1800–55
IX. 19: De Carolo Siculorum rege	Charles of Anjou, Sicily, and Jerusalem *E*	IX. 1856–2048 (octaves: 2017–48)
IX. 20: Infortunati quidam	Ugolino of Pisa, Aiton of Armenia, Boniface VIII	IX. 2049–125
IX. 21: De Iacobo magistro Templariorum	The Templars: Jacques de Molay	IX. 2126–237
IX. 22: Auctor patientiam commendatio: et ad eam summo studio amplexandam invitat unumquemque	Commends the patience of three philosophers: Theodorus of Sicily, Anaxarchus of Greece, Scaevola of Rome *E*	IX. 2238–433
*IX. 23: Numerosa querulorum turba	Philip the Fair's children: Isabell, Louis X, Philip V, Charles IV; Charles of Tarentum, *Peter, son of Charles II 'the Lame'*, Dante Alighieri, *Praise of Paris*	IX. 2434–552
*IX. 24: De Galterio Athenarum duce	Walter, duke of Athens	IX. 2553–804
*IX. 25: Excusatio auctoris ob Philippam Cathinensem	The inclusion of Philippa of Catania	IX. 2805–18[14]

De Casibus Chapters (A-Version)	Content Narratives in Des Cas (B-Version)†	Fall Reference
*IX. 26: De Philippa Cathinensi	Philippa of Catania, Jane of Calabria E	IX. 2819–3056
*IX. 27: Pauci flentes et libri conclusio	Sancho of Majorca, Louis of Jerusalem, John II of France E	IX. 3057–238 [IX. 3239–628: L adds a chapter on Fortune, in envoy form, drawing on Laurent's closing remarks, together with two envoys for Duke Humphrey and an envoy to his book] (octaves: 3239–302, 3541–604)

---

† Italicized narratives/references are those omitted by Lydgate [L]; *E* indicates an envoy supplied by Lydgate; comments in square brackets indicate major additions.

* Indicates chapters translated by Louis Brewer Hall in *The Fates of Illustrious Men* (1965).

¹ Fido is taken by Lydgate from Laurent's ch. 14 (fo. 36ᵛ).

² Note Bergen's error in claiming that II. 2584–940 'represent . . . Laurence's Chapter 14' (*Fall* ed. Bergen vol. iv. 177).

³ Laurent muddles these two figures and calls them both *Arterius*. Note Bergen's error in claiming that Lydgate's II. 3326 ff. represent Laurent's chapter 17 (ibid. IV. 178).

⁴ From Book III ch. 2 of *Des Cas*.

⁵ Note the error in Bergen's claim that the chapter ends at III. 1637 (*Fall* ed. Bergen vol. iv. 187).

6 Priam is found in Boccaccio, but not in surviving French manuscripts: possibly Lydgate's *Des Cas* had a scribal insertion at this point (see *Fall* ed. Bergen vol. iv. 205).

7 Note that the French ch. 7 says (fo. 80ʳ) only that lions killed Lysimachus in a pit, and ch. 14 (fo. 92ʳ) that Lysimachus fought with the beasts and pulled out a lion's tongue: Lydgate reverses these details, giving the fight in ch. 7 (*Fall* ed. Bergen vol. II. 510) and omitting it later (p. 564).

8 The story of Laodicea's dream of Apollo is given by Laurent at both IV ch. 14 (fo. 91ᵛ) and here (fo. 109ᵛ); Lydgate, having treated it at IV. 3248–87, ignores it here.

9 Note Bergen's error in claiming that these lines 'represent Laurence's twelfth chapter' (*Fall* ed. Bergen vol. iv. 240). Bergen has also been misled by Ziegler's reference (on p. 137 of his edn.) to Book XII, chs. 14 and 16 of Josephus, *De antiquitatibus*: the Alcimus/Joachim narrative is in fact given in XII, chs. 9 and 10.

10 Bergen claims these lines 'correspond to Laurence's chapter 21', possibly having misread XVI as XXI (*Fall* ed. Bergen vol. iv. 242).

11 Lydgate uses his refrained-envoy form for VII. 1153–313 (from the Golden World to Diogenes), anticipating the refrain of the envoy section proper (VII. 1314–34).

12 Note Bergen's erroneous claim that Lydgate treats this material as VIII. 2661–3206 (*Fall* ed. Bergen vol. iv. 326).

13 Note Bergen's error in claiming that Lydgate deals with ch. 8 in IX. 1121–69 (*Fall* ed. Bergen vol. iv. 361).

14 Wright (1957; 17 n. 1) erroneously claims that Lydgate omits this chapter.

Bibliography

I. Manuscripts†

Cambridge, Cambridge University Library	MS Ee. ii. 17	Duke Humphrey's Giles of Rome (*De regimine*) fragment and Vegetius
	MS Ff. i. 6	*Fall of Princes* extracts ('The Findern MS')
	MS Ff. ii. 29	Bury 'Registrum rubeum' (Cratfield's abbacy)
	MS Ii. iii. 21	Chaucer's copy of Boethius' *Consolation of Philosophy*
	MS Ii. vi. 39	Fragmentary English translation of Petrarch's *De remediis*
	MS Ll. ii. 8	*De casibus* A-version
Cambridge, Corpus Christi College	MS 40	Petrarch, *De remediis*
Cambridge, Fitzwilliam Museum	MS McClean 182	*Fall* extracts; *Serpent of Division*
Cambridge, Gonville and Caius College	MS 113	Bury copy of Giles of Rome, *De regimine*
Cambridge, Magdalene College	MS Pepys 2006	*Serpent of Division*
	MS Pepys 2011	*Siege of Thebes*; *Fall* extract
Cambridge, Pembroke College	MS 42*	Bury copy of Ambrose
	MS 105*	Bury copy of Valerius
	MS 119*	*Anticlaudianus*
	MS 158*	Simon Burley's copy of the *De regimine*
Cambridge, Peterhouse	MS 133	Petrarch, *De remediis* (quotation)

Cambridge, Sidney Sussex College	MS 102	Bury copy of Bede
Cambridge, St John's College	MS 223	*Fall* extracts
Cambridge, Trinity College	MS R. 3. 19	*Fall of Princes* extracts; Chaucer
	MS R. 3. 20	*Fall of Princes* extracts
	MS R. 3. 50	Curteys's copy of the *Aeneid*
Florence, Biblioteca Medicea Laurenziana	MS Plut. 49, 18	Salutati's copy of Cicero's letters
Geneva, Bibliothèque publique et universitaire	MS fr. 190	*Des Cas des nobles hommes et femmes* B-version
Glasgow, Glasgow University Library	MS Hunterian 7	Bury copy of Gower's *Confessio Amantis*
	MS Hunterian 208	*Des Cas des nobles hommes et femmes* B-version
	MSS Hunterian 371–2	*Des Cas des nobles hommes et femmes* B-version
Harvard University, Houghton Library	MS Eng. 530	*Serpent of Division*
London, British Library	MS Additional 7096	Bury Register (Curteys vol. II)
	MS Additional 11696	*Des Cas des nobles hommes et femmes* A-version
	MS Additional 14848	Bury Register (Curteys vol. I)
	MS Additional 18750	*Des Cas des nobles hommes et femmes* B-version
	MS Additional 21410	*Fall of Princes*
	MS Additional 29729	*Fall of Princes* extracts
	MS Additional 34360	Lydgate anthology
	MS Additional 35321	*Des Cas des nobles hommes et femmes* B-version
	MSS Additional 35322–3	*Cent nouvelles*
	MS Additional 39659	*Fall of Princes*

MS Additional 48031	*Serpent of Division*
MS Cotton Nero E. V	Decrees of the Council of Constance
MS Cotton Tiberius B. IX	Bury Register (Cratfield and Excetre)
MS Egerton 2402	Cavendish, *Metrical Visions* (autograph)
MS Harley 172	*Fall of Princes* extracts
MS Harley 367	*Fall of Princes* extracts
MS Harley 621	*Des Cas des nobles hommes et femmes* A-version
MS Harley 978	Marie de France, *Lais* and *Fables*
MS Harley 1245	*Fall of Princes*
MS Harley 1706	Lydgate anthology
MS Harley 1766	*Fall of Princes*
MS Harley 2202	*Fall of Princes* extracts
MS Harley 2251	*Fall of Princes* extracts
MS Harley 2255	*Fall of Princes* extracts
MS Harley 3426	Duke Humphrey's copy of translated Plutarch's *Lives*
MS Harley 3486	*Fall of Princes*
MS Harley 3565	*De casibus* A-version
MS Harley 4011	*Fall of Princes* extracts
MS Harley 4197	*Fall of Princes*
MS Harley 4203	*Fall of Princes*
MS Lansdowne 699	*Fall of Princes* extracts
MS Royal 8 C. IV	Bury copy of *Legenda aurea* (fragment)
MS Royal 11 B. III	Bury collection
MS Royal 12 C. VI	Bury collection; *Secreta*
MS Royal 14 E. V	*Des Cas des nobles hommes et femmes* B-version
MS Royal 18 B. XXXI	*Fall of Princes*
MS Royal 18 D. IV	*Fall of Princes*
MS Royal 18 D. V	*Fall of Princes*
MS Royal 18 D. VII	*Des Cas des nobles hommes et femmes* B-version

	MS Royal 19 C. IV	Duke Humphrey's copy of *Songe du Vergier*
	MS Royal 19 E. I	*Cent nouvelles*
	MS Royal 20 C. IV	*Des Cas des nobles hommes et femmes* B-version
	MS Sloane 1825	*Fall of Princes* extract
	MS Sloane 2452	*Fall of Princes* (fragmentary text)
	MS Sloane 2577	Catalogue of Lydgate's works
	MS Sloane 4031	*Fall of Princes*
London, Westminster Cathedral Library	MS B. 2. 8	Register of Bishop William Alnwick
Manchester, Chetham's Library	MS 27929	Duke Humphrey's copy of Salutati's *De fato et fortuna*
	MS Mun. A 3.131	Duke Humphrey's anthology of Salutati texts
Manchester University, John Rylands Library	MS Crawford English 2	*Fall of Princes*
Munich, Bayerische Staatsbibliothek	MS Gallicus 6	*Des Cas des nobles hommes et femmes* B-version
New York, Pierpont Morgan Library	MS M. 4	*Siege of Thebes*, minor verse selections
Oxford, Bodleian Library	MS Arch. Selden B. 10	*Fall of Princes* fragment
	MS Arch. Selden B. 24	Chaucer, *Troilus* and *Cressida*
	MS Ashmole 59	*Fall of Princes* extract
	MS Auct. F. 3. 3	Reading Abbey anthology of regiminal texts
	MS Bodley 181	Giles of Rome, *De regimine*
	MS Bodley 240	Bury miscellany
	MS Bodley 263	*Fall of Princes*
	MS Bodley 265	*Des Cas des nobles hommes et femmes* B-version
	MS Bodley 294	Duke Humphrey's copy of *Confessio Amantis*
	MS Bodley 544	Giles of Rome, *De regimine*
	MS Bodley 589	Giles of Rome, *De regimine*
	MS Bodley 686	Chaucer, *Canterbury Tales*

	MS Bodley 716	Bury copy of Wyclif's *postilla* on the New Testament
	MS Digby 102	Verse anthology
	MS Digby 181	*Fall* extract
	MS Digby 233	Giles of Rome, *De regimine*
	MS Douce 213	*Cent nouvelles*
	MS Fairfax 16	Chaucer and Lydgate collection
	MS Hatton 2	*Fall of Princes*
	MS Hatton 73	Lydgate collection
	MS Holkham Hall misc. 37	Guido delle Colonne
	MS Lat. misc. d. 34	Duke Humphrey's Boccaccio/Petrarch
	MS Laud Misc. 702	Giles of Rome, *De regimine*
	MS Laud Misc. 721	*De casibus* (extract)
	MS e Musaeo 1	*Fall of Princes*
	MS Rawlinson A. 338	English translation of Chartier's *Le Traité de l'esperance*
	MS Rawlinson C. 448	*Fall of Princes*
Oxford, All Souls College	MS 182	Letter from Henry V to abbot of Bury
Oxford, Balliol College	MS 329	Lydgate selections
Oxford, Corpus Christi College	MS 242	*Fall of Princes*
	MS 243	Duke Humphrey's copies of astrological texts
Oxford, Lincoln College	MS Latin 32*	*De casibus* B-version
	MS 69*	Giles of Rome, *De regimine*
Oxford, Magdalen College	MS 172	Bury copy of Geoffrey of Monmouth
	MS 198	*De casibus* B-version
	MS Lat. 37	Duke Humphrey's copy of translated Plutarch's *Lives*
Oxford, New College	MS 263*	*De casibus* B-version
Oxford, Oriel College	MS 32 (membr.)*	Duke Humphrey's copy of Capgrave on Genesis

Paris, Bibliothèque de l'Arsenal	MS 5070	Philippe the Good's copy of *Cent nouvelles*
	MS 5193	*Des Cas des nobles hommes et femmes* B-version
Paris, Bibliothèque Nationale	MS *fonds anglais* 39	Chaucer, *Canterbury Tales* ['Paris' MS]
	MS fr. 226	*Des Cas des nobles hommes et femmes* B-version
	MS fr. 231	*Des Cas des nobles hommes et femmes* B-version
	MSS fr. 264–6	Bersuire's translation of Livy
	MS fr. 1120	*Des cleres et nobles femmes*
	MS fr. 1122	*Cent nouvelles*
	MS fr. 12421	*Cent nouvelles*
	MS fr. 24289	*Des Cas des nobles hommes et femmes* A-version
	MS lat. 5690	Petrarch's copy of Livy
	MS lat. 6498	Petrarch, *De remediis*
	MS lat. 8537	Duke Humphrey's copy of Cicero's letters
	MS lat. 10209	Duke Humphrey's copy of Petrarch's *De remediis*
Paris, Bibliothèque Mazarine	MS 3880	*Des Cas des nobles hommes et femmes* extracts, A-version
Paris, Bibliothèque Sainte-Geneviève	MS fr. 777	Duke Humphrey's copy of Bersuire's Livy
Vatican, Biblioteca Apostolica Vaticana	MS Capponi 147	Salutati's copy of Giles of Rome
	MS Pal. lat. 1989	*Cent nouvelles*
	MS Urb. lat. 694	Duke Humphrey's copy of Salutati's *De laboribus Herculis*
	MS Vat. lat. 10669	Duke Humphrey's copy of Decembrio's translation of Plato's *Republic*

† the manuscript contents listed here only include those texts pertinent to study of Lydgate.

* denotes a manuscript deposited in the Bodleian Library or CUL.

II. Unpublished Doctoral Theses

Barr, Helen, 'A Study of *Mum and the Sothsegger* in its Political and Literary Contexts', 2 vols. (University of Oxford, 1989).

Beutner, Hans, 'Lydgate's *Testament*: Textkritische Ausgabe' (Munich University, 1914).

Cavanagh, Susan H., 'A Study of Books Privately Owned in England: 1300–1450', 2 vols. (University of Pennsylvania, 1980).

Childs, Herbert E., 'A Study of the Unique Middle English Translation of the *De regimine principum* of Aegidius Romanus (MS Digby 233)' (University of Washington, 1932).

Dinn, Robert B., 'Popular Religion in Late Medieval Bury St Edmunds', 2 vols. (University of Manchester, 1990).

Dougherty, D. M., 'Political Literature in France During the Reigns of Charles V and Charles VI' (Harvard University, 1932).

Elston, John W., 'William Curteys, Abbot of Bury St Edmunds (1429–46)' (University of California, Berkeley, 1979).

Gillespie, Alexandra, 'Chaucer and Lydgate in Print: The Medieval Author and the History of the Book, 1476–1579', 2 vols. (University of Oxford, 2001). [2001*a*]

Hauvette, Henri, 'De Laurentio Primofato qui primus Joannis Boccacci opera quaedam Gallice transtulit ineunte seculo XV' (Paris, 1903). [1903*a*]

Heale, Nicholas J., 'Religious and Intellectual Interests at St Edmunds Abbey at Bury and the Nature of English Benedictinism, *c.*1350–1450' (University of Oxford, 1994).

Herold, Christine, 'Chaucer's Tragic Muse: The Paganization of Christian Tragedy' (University of Massachusetts, Amherst, 1994).

Howlett, D. R., 'Studies in the Works of John Whethamstede' (University of Oxford, 1975).

Kekevich, Margaret L., 'Books of Advice for Princes in Fifteenth Century England with Particular Reference to the Period 1450–85' (Open University, 1987).

Koeppel, Emil, 'Laurents de Premierfait und John Lydgates Bearbeitungen von Boccaccios *De casibus virorum illustrium*: Ein Beitrag zur Litteraturgeschichte des 15. Jahrhunderts' (Munich University, 1885).

McCay, Christa T., 'Narrative Technique in John Lydgate's *Fall of Princes*' (University of Wisconsin, Madison, 1972).

Mapstone, Sally L., 'The Advice to Princes Tradition in Scottish Literature, 1400–1500' (University of Oxford, 1986).

Miller, James Ivan, 'John Lydgate's *St Edmund and St Fremund*: An Annotated Edition' (Harvard University, 1967).

Perzl, Wilhelm, 'Die Arthur-Legende in Lydgate's Fall of Princes
[*sic*]: Kritische Neuausgabe mit Quellenforschung' (Munich
University, 1911).
Scanlon, Larry, 'Literal Authority: the Exemplum and its Traditions in
Middle English Literature' (Johns Hopkins University, 1986).
Werner, Fritz, 'Ein Sammelkapitel aus Lydgates *Fall of Princes*:
Kritische Neuausgabe mit Quellenforschung' (Munich University,
1914).
White, H. R. B., 'Nature and the Natural Man in some Medieval
English Writers' (University of Oxford, 1986).

III. Material Printed Before 1640

Baldwin, William, *A Myrroure for Magistrates* (1559; 1563; 1571).
—— *The Last Parte of the Mirour for Magistrates* (1574; 1575; 1578).
Boccaccio, Giovanni, *Traité des mesaduentures de personnages signalez*,
trans. Claude Witart (Paris, 1578).
—— *Bocace des nobles maleureux*, trans. Laurent de Premierfait (Paris:
Nicholas Couteau, 1538).
—— *De casibus virorum*, ed. Hieronymus Ziegler (Augsburg, 1544).
—— *Boccace des dames de renom*, trans. Denis Sauvage (Lyon, 1551).
—— *I casi degli huomini illustri*, trans. Giuseppe Betussi (Venice, 1545,
1551/Florence, 1598, 1602).
Burrant, Robert, *The Tragical Death of Dauid Beaton* (?1548).
Chastelain, George, *Le Temple de Bocace* (Paris, 1517).
Covell, William, *Polimanteia, or, The meanes lawfull and vnlawfull
to Iudge of the Fall of A Common wealth . . . Whereunto is
added, A Letter from England to her three daughters* (Cambridge,
1595).
Freeman, Thomas, *Rvbbe, And A great Cast: Epigrams* (London,
1614).
Hanmer, Meredith, *The Auncient Ecclesiasticall Histories of the First
Six Hundred Yeares After Christ* (London, 1577).
Higgins, John, *The firste parte of the mirour for magistrates* (1574).
The Life and Death of Hector (London, 1614).
Lydgate, John, *Here begynnethe the boke calledde John
Bochas . . .* (Pynson, 1494).
—— *This lytell treatyse compendiously declareth the damage . . . caused
by the serpente of diuision* (n.p.: c.1535).
—— *A Treatise excellent and compendious shewing the falles of sondry
most notable princes* (London: Tottell, 1554).
—— *The Tragedies, gathered by Ihon Bochas, of all such princes as
fell from theyr estates* (Wayland, ?1554).

Matthieu, Pierre, *The Powerful favourite* (1628).

Niccols, Richard, *A Mirour for Magistrates* (1610).

Pits, John, *Ioannis Pitsei, Relationum historicarum de rebus Anglicis* (Paris, 1619).

Sherry, Richard, *A Treatise of Schemes and Tropes very profytable for the better vnderstanding of good authors* (London, 1550–1).

Vaughan, William, *The Golden-grove, moralized in three books*, 2nd edn. (London: Stafford, 1608).

Webbe, William, *A Discourse of English Poetrie* (London, 1586).

Weever, John, *The Mirror of Martyrs, or the life and death of . . . Sir John Old-castle* (1601).

IV. Primary Texts

Amundesham, John, *Annales monasterii S. Albani*, ed. H. T. Riley, RS 28/5a–b, 2 vols. (London, 1870–1).

Anstey, Henry (ed.), *Epistolae Academicae Oxon. (Registrum F)*, Oxford Historical Society, 35–6, 2 vols. (Oxford: Clarendon, 1898).

Ante-Nicene Christian Library, 23 vols. (Edinburgh: Clark, 1867–72).

Aquinas, Thomas, *Summa Theologiae*, Blackfriars edn., 60 vols. (London: Eyre and Spottiswoode, 1964–6).

—— *Aquinas: Selected Political Writings*, ed. A. P. D'Entrèves, trans. J. G. Dawson (Oxford: Blackwell, 1948).

Arderne, John, *Treatises of Fistula in Ano*, ed. D'Arcy Power, EETS OS 139 (1910).

Ashby, George, *George Ashby's Poems*, ed. Mary Bateson, EETS ES 76 (1899).

Augustine, Saint, *The City of God*, trans. Henry Bettenson (Harmondsworth: Penguin, 1972).

—— *Confessions*, trans. Henry Chadwick (Oxford: Oxford University Press, 1991).

Bale, John, *Index Britanniae scriptorum: John Bale's Index of British and Other Writers*, ed. Reginald Lane Poole, with Mary Bateson (Oxford: Clarendon, 1902; repr. Cambridge: Brewer, 1990).

Becket, Thomas, *Materials for the History of Thomas Becket, Archbishop of Canterbury*, ed. J. C. Robertson and J. Brigstocke Sheppard, RS 67A–G, 7 vols. (London, 1875–85).

Bekynton, Thomas, *Official Correspondence, Thomas Bekynton*, ed. George Williams, RS 56A–B, 2 vols. (London, 1872).

Bennett, J. A. W., *Devotional Pieces in Verse and Prose from MS Arundel 285 and MS Harleian 6919*, STS 3rd ser., 23 (Edinburgh and London: Blackwood, 1955).

Boccaccio, Giovanni, *Genealogie deorum gentilium libri*, ser. Scrittori d'Italia, 200–1, ed. Vincenzo Romano, 2 vols. (Bari: Laterza, 1951).
—— *De casibus virorum illustrium* (Paris 1520 A-version); repr. Louis Brewer Hall, Scholars' Facsimiles and Reprints (Gainesville, Fla.: 1962).
—— *Concerning Famous Women*, trans. Guarini A. Guarino (New Brunswick, NJ.: Rutgers University Press, 1963).
—— *The Fates of Illustrious Men*, trans. and abr. Louis Brewer Hall (New York: Ungar, 1965).
—— *De mulieribus claris*, ed. Vittorio Zaccaria, *Tutte le opere di Giovanni Boccaccio X*, gen. ed. Vittore Branca (Milan: Mondadori, 1967).
—— *Boccaccio in Defence of Poetry*, trans. Jeremiah Reedy (Toronto: PIMS, 1978).
—— *De casibus virorum illustrium*, ed. Vittorio Zaccaria and Pier Giorgio Ricci, *Tutte le Opere di Giovanni Boccaccio IX*, gen. ed. Vittore Branca (Milan: Mondadori, 1983).
Boethius, *The Consolation of Philosophy*, trans. V. E. Watts (Harmondsworth: Penguin, 1969).
—— *The Theological Tractates*, trans. H. F. Stewart, E. K. Rand, and S. J. Tester, Loeb Classical Library (London: Heinemann and Harvard University Press, 1973).
Bokenham, Osbern, *Legendys of Hooly Wummen*, ed. Mary S. Serjeantson, EETS OS 206 (1938).
Borges, Jorge Luis, 'Averroes's Search', in *Labyrinths* (1964; repr. Harmondsworth: Penguin, 1970), 180–8.
Burgh, Benedict, *Parvus Cato-Magnus Cato*, ed. Fumio Kuriyagawa, Seijo English Monographs, 13 (Tokyo: Seijo University, 1974).
[Bury St Edmunds, Abbey Community of], *The Chronicle of Bury St Edmunds 1212–1301*, ed. Antonia Gransden (London: Nelson, 1964).
—— *The Customary of the Benedictine Abbey of Bury St Edmunds in Suffolk*, ed. Antonia Gransden, Henry Bradshaw Society, 99 (London: Henry Bradshaw Society, 1973).
—— *The Chronicle of the Election of Hugh, Abbot of Bury St Edmunds and Later Bishop of Ely*, ed. Rodney M. Thomson, Oxford Medieval Texts (Oxford: Clarendon, 1974).
—— *The Archives of the Abbey of Bury St Edmunds*, ed. Rodney M. Thomson, Suffolk Records Society, 21 (Woodbridge: Boydell, 1980).
Capgrave, John, *John Capgrave's Abbreuiacion of Chronicles*, ed. Peter J. Lucas, EETS OS 285 (1983).
Cassiodorus, *Cassiodori Senatoris Institutiones*, ed. R. A. B. Mynors (Oxford: Clarendon, 1937).

Cavendish, George, *Metrical Visions*, ed. A. S. G. Edwards, RETS 5th ser. 9 (Columbia, SC.: University of South Carolina Press, 1980).

Caxton, William, *The Book of Courtesye*, ed. Frederick J. Furnivall, EETS ES 3 (1868).

—— *The Prologues and Epilogues of William Caxton*, ed. W. J. B. Crotch, EETS OS 176 (1928).

Chartier, Alain, *Fifteenth-Century English Translations of Alain Chartier's 'Le Traité de l'Esperance' and 'Le Quadrilogue Invectif'*, ed. Margaret S. Blayney, EETS OS 270 (1974) and OS 281 (1980).

Chastelain, George, *Le Temple de Bocace*, ed. Susanna Bliggenstorfer, Romanica Helvetica 104 (Berne: Éditions Francke, 1988).

Chatterton, Thomas, *The Complete Works of Thomas Chatterton: A Bicentenary Edition*, ed. Donald S. Taylor with Benjamin B. Hoover, 2 vols. (Oxford: Clarendon, 1971).

Chaucer, Geoffrey, *The Facsimile Series of the Works of Geoffrey Chaucer, vi: Pepys 2006, Magdalene College, Cambridge* ed. A. S. G. Edwards (Norman, Okla.: Pilgrim/Woodbridge: Boydell and Brewer, 1985). [1985a]

—— *The Riverside Chaucer*, gen. ed. L. D. Benson (Boston, Mass.: Houghton Mifflin, 1988).

—— *Troilus and Criseyde*, ed. B. A. Windeatt (London: Longman, 1984).

The Chronicle of Battle Abbey, trans. and ed. Eleanor Searle (Oxford: Clarendon, 1980).

Chronicon Angliae, RS 64, ed. E. M. Thompson (London, 1874).

Collins, John Churton, *Ephemera critica, Or Plain Truths about Current Literature* (Westminster: Constable, 1901).

Cusa, Nicholas of, *De concordantia catholica*, trans. Paul E. Sigmund, *The Catholic Concordance*, Cambridge Texts in the History of Political Thought (Cambridge: Cambridge University Press, 1991).

Daniel, Samuel, *The Complete Works in Verse and Prose of Samuel Daniel*, ed. Alexander B. Grosart, 5 vols. (London, 1885–96).

Dante, *Dante Alighieri: Opere Minori*, ed. Cesare Vasoli and Domenico Robertis (Milan and Naples: Riccardo, n.d.).

Dictionnaire de Droit Canonique, ed. R. Naz, 7 vols. (Paris, 1931–65).

Dorsch, T. S. (ed.), *Classical Literary Criticism* (Harmondsworth: Penguin, 1965).

Dunbar, William, *The Poems of William Dunbar*, ed. James Kinsley (Oxford: Clarendon, 1979).

An English Chronicle of the Reigns of Richard II, Henry IV, Henry V, and Henry VI, ed. John Sylvester Davies, CS 64 (London, 1856).

English Historical Documents, IV. 1327–1485, ed. A. R. Myers (London: Eyre and Spottiswoode, 1969).

Fantosme, Jordan, *Chronique de Jordan Fantosme*, ed. Richard
  Howlett, *Chronicles of the Reigns of Stephen, Henry II and
  Richard I*, RS 82.A–D, 4 vols. (London, 1884–9).
Feylde, Thomas, *The Complaint of a Lover's Life (Llouer and a Jay)*,
  ed. T. F. Dibdin, The Roxburghe Club (London, 1818).
The Findern Manuscript, ed. Richard Beadle and A. E. B. Owen
  (London: Scolar, 1977).
Förster, Max, 'Die Burghsche Cato-Paraphrase', *Archiv*, 115 (1905),
  298–323.
Fortescue, John, *De laudibus legum Anglie* and *The Governance of
  England*, trans. Shelley Lockwood, *On the Laws and Governance of
  England*, Cambridge Texts in the History of Political Thought
  (Cambridge: Cambridge University Press, 1997).
Froissart, Jean, *The Chronicle of Froissart translated out of the French
  by Sir John Bourchier, Lord Berners*, ed. W. P. Ker, Tudor
  Translations, 27–32, 6 vols. (London, 1901–3).
Gerson, Jean, *Oeuvres Complètes*, ed. P. Glorieux, 10 vols. (Paris,
  1960–73).
Gower, John, *John Gower's English Works*, ed. G. C. Macaulay, EETS
  ES 81–2 (1900–1).
—— *The Complete Works of John Gower: The Latin Works*,
  ed. G. C. Macaulay (Oxford: Clarendon, 1902).
Gray, Thomas, *The Works of Thomas Gray in Prose and Verse*, ed.
  Edmund Gosse, 4 vols. (London: Macmillan, 1884).
Grosseteste, Robert, *Hexaemeron*, ed. R. C. Dales and Servus Gieben,
  Auctores Britannici Medii Aevi vi (for The British Academy,
  London, at Oxford: Oxford University Press, 1982).
Hall's Chronicle; Containing the History of England (London, 1809).
Hammond, Eleanor Prescott, *English Verse between Chaucer and
  Surrey* (Durham, NC./London: Cambridge University Press, 1927).
Hardison, O. B. et al. (eds.), *Medieval Literary Criticism: Translations
  and Interpretations* (New York: Ungar, 1974).
Hawes, Stephen, *The Passetyme of Pleasure*, ed. William E. Mead,
  EETS OS 173 (1928).
—— *Stephen Hawes: The Minor Poems*, ed. Florence W. Gluck and
  Alice B. Morgan, EETS OS 271 (1974).
Hoccleve, Thomas, *Works, i. The Minor Poems*, ed. Frederick J.
  Furnivall, EETS ES 61 (1892).
Horstmann, Carl, *Altenglische Legenden: neue Folge* (Heilbronn, 1881).
Hugh [de Avalon], Saint, *Magna Vita S. Hugonis Episcopi
  Lincolniensis*, ed. James F. Dimock, RS 37 (London, 1864).
Hus, John, *De ecclesia: The Church*, trans. David Schaff (New York:
  Scribner, 1915).

308   *Bibliography*

Idley, Peter, *Peter Idley's Instructions to His Son*, ed. Charlotte
D'Evelyn, Modern Languages Association of America Monograph vi
(Boston, Mass./London: Oxford University Press, 1935).

Jacobus de Voragine, *Legenda aurea: vulgo historia lombardica dicta*,
ed. Th. Graesse (Leipzig, 1850).

—— *Jacobus de Voragine, The Golden Legend: Readings on the Saints*,
trans. William Granger Ryan, 2 vols. (Princeton, NJ.: Princeton
University Press, 1993).

Jean de Tuim, *Li Hystore de Julius Cesar: Eine altfranzösische
Erzählung in Prosa, von Jehan de Tuim*, ed. F. Settegast (Halle:
Niemeyer, 1881).

Jocelin of Brakelonde, *Cronica de electione Hugonis Abbatis*, in
Memorials of St Edmunds Abbey, ed. Arnold (1892), ii.

John of Salisbury, *Joannes Saresberiensis . . . Politcratici*, ed. C. I. Webb,
2 vols. (Oxford: Clarendon, 1909).

—— *Policraticus. Of the Frivolities of Courtiers and the Footprints of
Philosophers*, trans. Cary J. Nederman, Cambridge Texts in the
History of Political Thought (Cambridge: Cambridge University
Press, 1990).

Jonson, Ben, *Ben Jonson*, ed. C. H. Herford, Percy and Evelyn
Simpson, 11 vols. (Oxford: Clarendon, 1925–52).

Josephus, Flavius, *Works*, trans. W. Whiston, rev. A. R. Shilleto, 5 vols.
(London, 1900–3).

Journal d'un Bourgeois de Paris sous Charles VI et Charles VII, ed.
André Mary (Paris: Jonquières, 1929).

Kemble, J. M., *Codex diplomaticus aevi Saxonici*, 6 vols. (London,
1839–48).

Kilwardby, Robert, *De ortu scientarum*, ed. Albert G. Judy, *Auctores
Britannici Medii Aevi* iv (for The British Academy, London, and
PIMS, Toronto, at Oxford: Oxford University Press, 1976).

Lactantius, *The Divine Institutes*, i–vii, trans. M. F. McDonald, *Fathers
of the Church*, 49 (Washington, DC.: Catholic University of
America Press, 1964).

Langland, William, *The Vision of Piers Plowman: A Complete Edition
of the B-Text*, ed. A. V. C. Schmidt (London: Dent, 1978).

Legaré, Anne-Marie et al., *Le Livre des Échecs Amoureux* (Paris:
Chêne, 1991).

Legge, M. Dominica, *Anglo-Norman Letters and Petitions from All
Souls MS 182*, ANTS 3 (1941).

Leland, John, *Commentarii de scriptoribus Britannicis auctore Joanne
Lelando Londinate* (Oxford, 1709).

[*The Middle French*] *'Liber Fortunae'*, ed. John L. Grigsby (Berkeley,
Calif.: California University Press, 1967).

Lille, Alan of [Alanus de Insulis], *Anticlaudianus*, trans. J. J. Sheridan (Toronto: PIMS, 1973).

Lindsay, David, *The Works of Sir David Lindsay of the Mount*, ed. Douglas Hamer, STS 3rd ser., 1, 2, 6, 8 (Edinburgh/London: Blackwood, 1931–6).

Livy, *Ab urbe condita*, trans. B. O. Foster et al., Loeb Classical Library, 14 vols. (London: Heinemann/Cambridge, Mass.: Harvard University Press, 1919–59).

Lombard, Peter, *Petri Lombardi, Sententiarum Libri Quatuor* (Paris, 1892).

Lorris, Guillaume de, and Meun, Jean de, *The Romance of the Rose*, trans. Charles Dahlberg (Hanover, NH.: University Press of New England, 1971; rev. 1983).

—— *The Romance of the Rose*, trans. Frances Horgan (Oxford: Oxford University Press, 1994).

Lucan, *The Civil War ('Pharsalia')*, trans. J. D. Duff, Loeb Classical Library (London/Cambridge, Mass.: Harvard University Press, 1928).

Lydgate, John, *SS Edmund and Fremund*, ed. Carl Horstmann, *Altenglische Legenden: neue Folge* (Heilbronn, 1881), 376–445.

—— *S. Albon und Amphabel, ein Legendenepos*, ed. Carl Horstmann (Berlin, 1882).

—— *Temple of Glas*, ed. J. Schick, EETS ES 60 (1891).

—— *Lydgate and Burgh's Secrees of Old Philosoffres*, ed. Robert Steele, EETS ES 66 (1894).

—— *The Assembly of Gods*, ed. O. L. Triggs, EETS ES 69 (1896).

—— *Lydgate's Fabula duorum mercatorum*, ed. Julius Zupitza and G. Schleich (Strasburg, 1897).

—— *Pilgrimage of the Life of Man*, ed. F. J. Furnivall and K. B. Locock, EETS ES 77, 83, 92 (1899, 1901, 1904).

—— *Two Nightingale Poems*, ed. O. Glauning, EETS ES 80 (1900).

—— *Reson and Sensuallyte*, ed. E. Sieper, EETS ES 84 and 89 (1901, 1903).

—— *Troy Book*, ed. H. Bergen, EETS ES 97, 103, 106, 126 (1906, 1908, 1910, 1935).

—— *The Serpent of Division*, ed. H. N. MacCracken (London: Oxford University Press/New Haven, Conn.: Yale University Press, 1911). [1911a]

—— *Minor Poems*, ed. Henry Noble MacCracken, EETS ES 107 [1911b] and OS 192 (1911, 1934).

—— *Siege of Thebes*, ed. A. Erdmann, EETS ES 108 [1911c] and 125 (1911, 1930).

—— *Fall of Princes*, ed. Henry Bergen, EETS ES 121–4 (1924, 1924, 1924, 1927).

Lydgate, John, *The Dance of Death*, ed. Florence Warren, EETS ES
181 (1931).
—— *A Critical Edition of John Lydgate's 'Life of Our Lady'*, ed.
Joseph A. Lauritis, Ralph A. Klinefelter, and Vernon F. Gallagher,
Duquesne Studies, Philological Series 2 (Pittsburgh, Penn.: Duquesne
University, 1961).
—— *Poems*, ed. John Norton-Smith (Oxford: Clarendon, 1966).
—— *Saint Albon and Saint Amphibalus*, ed. George F. Reinecke,
Garland Medieval Texts 11 (New York: 1974; repr. 1985).
—— *The Life of Saint Albon and Saint Amphibal*, ed. J. E. van der
Westhuizen (Leiden, 1974).
Machiavelli, Niccolò, *The Discourses of Niccolò Machiavelli*, trans.
and ed. Leslie J. Walker and Cecil H. Clough, 2nd edn., 2 vols.
(London/Boston, Mass.: Routledge and Kegan Paul, 1975).
Malory, Thomas, *The Works of Sir Thomas Malory*, ed. Eugène Vinaver,
rev. P. J. C. Field, 3rd edn., 3 vols. (Oxford: Clarendon, 1990).
Memorials of St Edmund's Abbey, ed. T. Arnold, RS 96A–C, 3 vols.
(London: 1890, 1892, 1896).
Metham, John, *The Works of John Metham*, ed. Hardin Craig, EETS
OS 132 (1916).
The Mirror for Magistrates, ed. Lily B. Campbell (Cambridge:
Cambridge University Press, 1938).
—— *Parts added to 'The Mirror for Magistrates' by John Higgins and
Thomas Blenerhasset*, ed. Lily B. Campbell (Cambridge: Cambridge
University Press, 1946).
Monstrelet, Enguerrand de, *The Chronicles of Enguerrand de Monstrelet*,
trans. Thomas Johnes, 13 vols. (London: Longman et al., 1810).
La Mort le Roi Artu. Roman du XIIIᵉ Siècle, ed. Jean Frappier (Paris:
Droz, 1936).
MS Trinity R. 3. 19, ed. B. Y. Fletcher (Norman, Okla.: Pilgrim, 1987).
[Nicene], *A Select Library of Nicene and Post-Nicene Fathers of the
Christian Church*, 2nd ser., ed. Philip Schaff and Henry Wace,
14 vols. (New York: 1890–1900).
Norton, Thomas, and Sackville, Thomas, *Gorboduc, or Ferrex and
Porrex, A Tragedy*, ed. Lucy Toulmin Smith (Heilbronn, 1883).
Pantin, W. A. (ed.), *Documents Illustrating the Activities of the
General and Provincial Chapters of the English Black Monks,
1215–1540*, 3 vols., CS 3rd ser., 45, 47, 54 (1931, 1933, 1937).
Paterson, Samuel, *Bibliotheca Westiana: A Catalogue of the Curious
and truly Valuable Library of the late James West* (London, 1773).
Petrarch, Francesco, *A Dialogue between Reason and Adversity: A Late
Middle English Version of Petrarch's* De remediis, ed.
F. N. M. Diekstra (Assen: Van Gorcum, 1968).

Petrarch, Francesco, *Petrarch's 'Bucolicum carmen'*, trans. Thomas G. Bergin (New Haven, Conn.: Yale University Press, 1974).

Phillips, Edward, *Theatrum Poetarum, or a Compleat Collection of the Poets* (London, 1675).

Pisan, Christine de, *The Epistle of Othéa*, trans. Stephen Scrope, ed. Curt F. Bühler, EETS OS 264 (1970).

—— *The 'Livre de la Paix' of Christine de Pisan*, ed. Charity Cannon Willard (The Hague, 1958).

—— *Le Livre de la Mutacion de Fortune*, ed. Suzanne Solente, SATF, 4 vols. (Paris, 1959, 1959, 1964, 1966).

—— *Treasure of the City of Ladies*, trans. Sarah Lawson (Harmondsworth: Penguin, 1985).

Premierfait, Laurent de, *Laurent de Premierfait's 'Des Cas des nobles hommes et femmes'*, Book One, translated from Boccaccio: A Critical Edition based on Six Manuscripts, ed. Patricia M. Gathercole, University of North Carolina Studies in the Romance Languages and Literatures 74 (Chapel Hill, NC.: University of North Carolina Press, 1968).

Proceedings and Ordinances of the Privy Council of England, ed. N. H. Nicolas, 7 vols. (London, 1834–7).

Puttenham, George, *The Arte of English Poesie*, ed. Gladys D. Willcock and Alice Walker (Cambridge: Cambridge University Press, 1936).

Ritson, Joseph, 'A Historical Essay on the Origin and Progress of National Song,' in *A Select Collection of English Songs*, 3 vols. (London, 1783), vol. i, pp. i–lxxii.

—— *Bibliographia Poetica: A Catalogue of English Poets* (London: 1802).

Robbins, Rossell Hope (ed.), *Secular Lyrics of the XIVth and XVth Centuries* (Oxford: Clarendon, 1952).

—— (ed.), *Historical Poems of the XIVth and XVth Centuries* (New York: Columbia University Press, 1959).

Rotuli parliamentorum, ed. J. Strachey et al., 6 vols. and index (London: 1767–77, 1832).

Russell, D. A., and Winterbottom, M. (eds.), *Ancient Literary Criticism: The Principal Texts in New Translations* (Oxford: Oxford University Press, 1972).

Rymer, Thomas, *Foedera, Conventiones, Litterae . . . Acta Publica*, 4 vols. (London, 1816–30).

Salutati, Coluccio, *Epistolario di Coluccio Salutati*, ed. Francesco Novati, 4 vols. (Rome, 1891–1911).

—— *Coluccio Salutati: Editi e inediti latini dal MS 53 della Biblioteca communale di Todi*, ed. Enrico Menestò, Res Tudertine 12 (Todi, 1971).

Salutati, Coluccio, *De fato et fortuna*, ed. Concetta Bianca, Instituto Nazionale di Studi sul Rinascimento: Studi e Testi x (Florence: Solschki, 1985).

Samson, Abbot, *The Kalendar of Abbot Samson of Bury St Edmunds and Related Documents*, ed. R. H. C. Davis, CS 3rd ser., 84 (London: Royal Historical Society, 1954).

Seneca, *Moral Essays*, trans. John W. Basore, Loeb Classical Library, 3 vols. (London/Cambridge, Mass.: Harvard University Press, 1928–35).

—— *Ad Lucilium Epistulae Morales*, trans. Richard M. Gummere, Loeb Classical Library (London/Cambridge, Mass.: Harvard University Press, 1953).

The Septuagint Version of the Old Testamant, with an English Translation (London, 1879).

Sidney, Philip, *An Apology for Poetry*, ed. Geoffrey Shepherd (London: Thomas Nelson, 1965; reissued Manchester: Manchester University Press, 1973).

Skelton, John, *John Skelton: The Complete English Poems*, ed. John Scattergood (Harmondsworth: Penguin, 1983).

Stow, John, *A Survey of London*, ed. C. L. Kingsford, 2 vols. (Oxford: Clarendon, 1908; repr. 1971).

Stratford, Jenny, *The Bedford Inventories: The Worldly Goods of John, Duke of Bedford, Regent of France*, Reports of the Research Committee of the Society of Antiquaries 49 (London, 1993).

Suetonius, *Lives of the Caesars*, trans. J. C. Rolfe, Loeb Classical Library, rev. edn., 2 vols. (London/Cambridge, Mass.: Harvard University Press, 1997–8).

Suffolk Archaeological Society (anon.), 'Abstracts of Gild Certificates, Suffolk', 'Abstracts of Chantry Certificates, Suffolk, 1546', 'Notes Concerning Suffolk Chapels, Chantries and Gilds', *Proceedings of the Suffolk Archaeological Society*, 12 (1904), 24–9, 30–71, 72–87.

Tanner, Norman P. (ed.), *Heresy Trials in the Diocese of Norwich, 1428–31*, CS 4th ser., 20 (London: Royal Historical Society, 1977).

—— (ed.), *Decrees of the Ecumenical Councils*, 2 vols. (London: Sheed and Ward, 1990).

Tatian, *Oratio ad Graecos, The Writings of Tatian and Theophilus; and the Clementine Recognitions*, trans. B. P. Pratten, Ante-Nicene Christian Library iii (Edinburgh: T. and T. Clark, 1867).

Trevisa, John, *Polychronicon*, ed. Churchill Babington and J. L. Lumby, RS 41. I–IX, 9 vols. (London, 1865–86).

Twenty-six Political and Other Poems, ed. J. Kail, EETS OS 124 (1904).

Valla, Lorenzo, *The Treatise of Lorenzo Valla on the Donation of Constantine: Text and Translation into English*, trans. Christopher B. Coleman (New Haven, Conn.: Yale University Press, 1922).

Wales, Gerald of (Giraldus Cambrensis), *Concerning the Instruction of Princes*, trans. Joseph Stevenson (London: 1858; repr. Felinfach: J. M. F. Books, 1991).

Walsingham, Thomas, *Thomae Walsingham, quondam monachi S. Albani, Historia Anglicana*, ed. H. T. Riley, RS 28/1a–b, 2 vols. (London: 1863–4).

Webster, John, *The Complete Works of John Webster*, ed. F. L. Lucas, 4 vols. (London: Chatto and Windus, 1927).

Wenman, Thomas, *The Legend of Mary, Queen of Scots, and other Ancient Poems*, ed. J. Fry (London, 1810).

Wright, Thomas, *Political Poems and Songs relating to English History*, RS 14a–b, 2 vols. (London, 1859, 1861).

Wyclif, John, *Tractatus de civile dominio*, ed. Reginald Lane Poole, Wyclif Society, 4 vols. (London, 1885–1904).

—— *Dialogus sive speculum ecclesie militantis*, ed. A. W. Pollard, Wyclif Society (London, 1886).

—— *Tractatus de ecclesia*, ed. Johann Loserth, Wyclif Society (London, 1886).

V. Secondary Texts

Aers, David (ed.), *Medieval Literature and Historical Inquiry: Essays in Honour of Derek Pearsall* (Woodbridge: Brewer, 2000).

Aiken, Pauline, 'Vincent of Beauvais and Chaucer's Monk's Tale', *Speculum*, 17 (1942), 56–68.

Allmand, C. T., 'Normandy and the Council of Basle', *Speculum*, 40 (1965), 1–14.

Angulo, Lucy de, 'Charles and Jean d'Orléans: An Attempt to Trace the Contacts between them during their Captivity in England', in Franco Simone (1967) (ed.), 61–92.

Aston, Margaret, 'William White's Lollard Followers', *Catholic Historical Review*, 68 (1982), 469–97.

Atkins, J. W. H., '*The Serpent of Division*', [review] *MLR* 7 (1912), 253–4.

Audollent, A., Beranger, H. et al., *Entre Camarades*, Société des Anciens Élèves de la Faculté des Lettres de l'Université de Paris (Paris, 1901).

Ayers, Robert W., 'Medieval History, Moral Purpose, and the Structure of Lydgate's *Siege of Thebes*', *PMLA* 73 (1958), 463–74.

Babcock, R. W., 'The Mediaeval Setting of Chaucer's Monk's Tale', *PMLA* 46 (1931), 205–13.

Bacquet, Paul, *Un contemporain d'Elisabeth I: Thomas Sackville. L'Homme et l'œuvre*, Travaux d'humanisme et renaissance, 76 (Geneva: Droz, 1966).

Barnes, Timothy D., *Tertullian: A Historical and Literary Study* (Oxford: Clarendon, 1971).

Baron, Hans, *Humanistic and Political Literature in Florence and Venice at the Beginning of the Quattrocento* (Cambridge, Mass.: Harvard University Press, 1955). [1955a]

—— *The Crisis of the Early Italian Renaissance*, 2 vols. (Princeton, NJ.: Princeton University Press, 1955). [1955b]

—— 'Chronology and Historical Certainty: The Dates of Bruni's *Laudatio* and *Dialogi*', in Baron (ed.), *From Petrarch to Leonardo Bruni: Studies in Humanistic and Political Literature* (Chicago, Ill.: Chicago University Press, 1968), 102–37.

—— 'Imitation, Rhetoric, and Quattrocento Thought in Bruni's *Laudatio*', in Baron (ed.), *From Petrarch to Leonardo Bruni* (1968), 151–71.

Barr, Helen, 'The Treatment of Natural Law in *Richard the Redeless* and *Mum and the Sothsegger*', *Leeds Studies*, NS, 23 (1992), 49–80.

Beer, Jeanette M. A., *A Medieval Caesar*, Études de philologie et d'histoire 30 (Geneva: Droz, 1976).

Bennett, H. S., 'Notes on English Retail Book-prices, 1480–1560', *The Library*, 5th ser., 5 (1950–1), 172–8.

Bennett, J. A. W., and Gray, Douglas, *Oxford History of English Literature: Middle English Literature, 1100–1400* (Oxford: Clarendon, 1986).

Benskin, Michael, and Samuels, M. L. (eds.), *So meny people longages and tonges: Philological Essays in Scots and Mediaeval English Presented to Angus McIntosh* (Edinburgh: Benskin and Samuels, 1981).

Benson, C. David, 'Incest and Moral Poetry in Gower's *Confessio Amantis*', *ChauR* 19 (1984), 100–9.

Bergin, Thomas G., *Boccaccio* (New York: Viking, 1981).

Berlin, Normand, *Thomas Sackville*, TEAS 165 (New York: Twayne, 1974).

Bernardo, Aldo S. (ed.), *Francesco Petrarca, Citizen of the World: Proceedings of the World Petrarch Congress, Washington DC., April 6–13 1974*, *Studi sul Petrarca*, 8 (Padua: Antenore, 1980).

Bertolet, Craig, 'From Revenge to Reform: The Changing Face of "Lucrece" and its Meaning in Gower's *Confessio Amantis*', *PhilQ* 70 (1991), 403–21.

Billanovich, Giuseppe, and Frasso, Giuseppe (eds.), *Il Petrarca ad Arquà: atti del Convegno di studi nel VI Centenario (1370–1374)* (Arquà Petrarca, 6–8 nov. 1970), Studi sul Petrarca 2 (Padua: Antenore, 1975).

Black, A. J., 'The Political Ideas of Conciliarism and Papalism, 1430–50', *JEH* 20 (1969), 45–65.

Blake, N. F., *Caxton and His World*, Language Library Series (London: Andre Deutsch, 1969).

—— 'John Lydgate and William Caxton', *Leeds Studies*, NS, 16 (1985), 272–89.

Bober, Harry, 'The Zodiacal Miniature of the *Très Riches Heures* of the Duke of Berry—its Sources and Meaning', *JWCI* 11 (1948), 1–34.

[Bodleian Library], *Duke Humfrey and English Humanism in the Fifteenth Century: A Catalogue of an Exhibition held in the Bodleian Library* (Oxford: Bodleian Library, 1970).

[Bodleian Library], *Duke Humfrey's Library and the Divinity School 1488–1988: An Exhibition at the Bodleian Library, June–August 1988* (Oxford: Bodleian Library, 1988).

Boitani, Piero, 'The Monk's Tale: Dante and Boccaccio', *Medium Ævum*, 45 (1976), 50–69.

—— (ed.), *Chaucer and the Italian Trecento* (Cambridge: Cambridge University Press, 1983).

—— and Torti, Anna (eds.), *Genres, Themes, and Images in English Literature from the Fourteenth to the Fifteenth Century: The J. A. W. Bennett Memorial Lectures, Perugia, 1986* (Tübingen: Gunter Narr, 1988).

Borsa, Mario, 'Correspondence of Humphrey Duke of Gloucester and Pier Candido Decembrio', *EHR* 19 (1904), 509–26.

Bozzolo, Carla, *Manuscrits des Traductions Françaises d'Œuvres de Boccace, XVᵉ Siècle*, Medioevo e umanesimo, 5 (Padua: Antenore, 1973).

Braden, Gordon, *Renaissance Tragedy and the Senecan Tradition: Anger's Privilege* (New Haven, Conn.: Yale University Press, 1985).

Branca, Vittore (ed.), *Boccaccio Visualizzato: Narrare per parole e per immagini fra Medioevo e Rinascimento*, Biblioteca di storia dell'arte 30, 3 vols. (Turin: Einaudi, 1999).

Brewer, Derek (ed.), *Chaucer and Chaucerians* (London: Nelson, 1966).

Brie, Friedrich, [obituary for Emil Koeppel] *Englische Studien*, 51 (1917–18), 469.

—— 'Mittelalter und Antike bei Lydgate', *Englische Studien*, 64 (1929), 261–301.

[British Library], *The British Library Catalogue of Additions to the Manuscripts. The Yelverton Manuscripts: Additional 48000–48196*, 2 vols. (London: British Library, 1994).

Brown, Carleton, *A Register of Middle English Religious and Didactic Verse*, 2 vols. (Oxford: Oxford University Press, 1916–20).

—— and Robbins, R. H., *The Index of Middle English Verse* (New York: Columbia University Press, 1943).

Browning, Elizabeth Barrett, *The Greek Christian Poets and the English Poets* (London: Chapman, 1863).

Brusendorff, A., *The Chaucer Tradition* (Copenhagen: Pio/London: Oxford University Press, 1925).

Bryan, W. F., and Dempster, Germaine (eds.), *Sources and Analogues of Chaucer's 'Canterbury Tales'* (Chicago, Ill.: University of Chicago Press, 1941; repr. London: Routledge and Kegan Paul, 1958).

Brydges, Samuel Egerton, *Censura Literaria*, 10 vols. (London, 1805–9).

Budra, Paul, '*The Mirror for Magistrates* and the Shape of *De casibus* Tragedy', *English Studies*, 69 (1988), 303–12.

—— 'The *Mirror for Magistrates* and the Politics of Readership', *Studies in English Literature* (Rice), 32 (1992), 1–13.

—— '*A Mirror for Magistrates*' and the de casibus *Tradition* (Toronto: University of Toronto Press, 2000).

Bughetti, P. Benvenutus, 'Statutum concordiae inter quatuor ordines mendicantes . . .', *Archivum Franciscum historicum*, 25 (1932), 241–56.

Bühler, Curt F., 'A Survival from the Middle Ages: Baldwin's Use of the *Dictes and Sayings*', *Speculum*, 23 (1948), 76–80.

Butt, Ronald, *A History of Parliament: The Middle Ages* (London: Constable, 1989).

Byrom, H. J., 'John Wayland—Printer, Scrivener, and Litigant', *The Library*, 4th ser., 11 (1930–1), 312–49.

Callu, Florence, and Avril, François, *Boccace en France: De l'humanisme à l'érotisme* (Paris: Bibliothìque Nationale, 1975).

Campbell, Lily B., 'Humphrey Duke of Gloucester and Elianor Cobham his Wife in the *Mirror for Magistrates*', HLB 5 (1934), 119–55. [1934*a*]

—— 'The Suppressed Edition of *A Mirror for Magistrates*', HLB 6 (1934), 1–16. [1934*b*]

—— *Tudor Conceptions of History and Tragedy in 'A Mirror for Magistrates'* (Berkeley, Calif.: University of California Press, 1936).

—— *Shakespeare's Tragic Heroes: Slaves of Passion* (Cambridge: Cambridge University Press, 1930; repr. London: Methuen, 1961).

Cappelli, Adriano, *Dizionario di abbreviature latine ed italiane*, 6th edn. (Milan: Ulrico Hoepli, 1990).

Catholic Encyclopedia, 16 vols. (London/New York, 1907–14).

Chadwick, Henry, *Boethius: The Consolations of Music, Logic, Theology, and Philosophy* (Oxford: Clarendon, 1981).

Chambers, R. W., 'Long Will, Dante, and the Righteous Heathen', *Essays and Studies*, 9 (1923), 50–69.

Chrimes, S. B., 'The Pretensions of the Duke of Gloucester in 1422', *EHR* 45 (1930), 101–3.

Clark, James M., 'The Dance of Death in Medieval Literature: Some Recent Theories of its Origin', *MLR* 45 (1950), 336–45.

Cloetta, Wilhelm, *Beiträge zur Litteraturgeschichte des Mittelalters und der Renaissance*, 2 vols. (Halle: Niemeyer, 1890–2).

Coates, Alan, *English Medieval Books: The Reading Abbey Collections from Foundation to Dispersal* (Oxford: Clarendon, 1999).

Connolly, James L., *John Gerson: Reformer and Mystic*, Recueil de travaux publiés par les membres des conférences d'histoire et de philologie, 2nd ser., xii (Louvain/London: Librairie universitaire, Uystpruyst, 1928).

Coogan, Robert, 'Petrarch's Latin Prose and the English Renaissance', *SP* 68 (1971), 270–91.

Cooper, Helen, *The Structure of 'The Canterbury Tales'* (London and Athens, Ga.: University of Georgia Press, 1984).

—— *Oxford Guides to Chaucer: 'The Canterbury Tales'*, 2nd edn. (Oxford: Oxford University Press, 1996).

—— 'The Four Last Things in Dante and Chaucer: Ugolino in the House of Rumour', in David Lawton, Wendy Scase, and Rita Copeland (1999) (eds.), 39–66.

—— and Mapstone, Sally (eds.), *The Long Fifteenth Century: Essays in Honour of Douglas Gray* (Oxford: Clarendon, 1997).

Coville, Alfred, 'Le Véritable Texte de la Justification du duc de Bourgogne', *Bibliothèque de l'École des Chartes*, 72 (1911), 57–91.

—— *Jean Petit: La Question du Tyrannicide au Commencement du XVᵉ Siècle* (Paris: A. Picard, 1932; repr. Geneva: Slatkine, 1974).

Cox, Jeffrey N., and Reynolds, Larry J. (eds.), *New Historical Study: Essays on Reproducing Texts, Representing History* (Princeton, NJ.: Princeton University Press, 1993).

Cucchi, Paolo, 'The First French *Decameron*: Laurent de Premierfait's Translation and the Early French *Nouvelle*', *French Literature Studies*, 2 (1975), 1–14.

—— and Lacy, Norris J., 'La tradition manuscrit des *Cent Nouvelles* de Laurent de Premierfait', *Le Moyen Âge*, 80, 4th ser., 29 (1974), 483–502.

Cuming, G. J., and Baker, Derek (eds.), *Councils and Assemblies*, SCH 7 (Cambridge: Cambridge University Press, 1971).

Dane, Joseph A., and Beesemyer, Irene Basey, 'The Denigration of John Lydgate: Implications of Printing History', *English Studies*, 81 (2000), 117–26.

Davies, Brian, *The Thought of Thomas Aquinas* (Oxford: Clarendon, 1992).

Davies, Richard G., 'Martin V and the English Episcopate, with Particular Reference to his Campaign for the Repeal of the Statute of Provisors', *EHR* 92 (1977), 309–44.

318 *Bibliography*

Davis, G. R. C., *Medieval Cartularies of Great Britain: A Short Catalogue* (London: Longman, 1958).

Davis, Herbert, and Gardner, Helen (eds.), *Elizabethan and Jacobean Studies Presented to Frank Percy Wilson in Honour of his Seventieth Birthday* (Oxford: Clarendon, 1959).

Davis, H. W. C., 'The Liberties of Bury St Edmunds', EHR 24 (1909), 417–31.

Davis, R. H. C., 'The Monks of St Edmund, 1021–1148', *History*, NS, 40 (1955), 227–49.

De la Mare, A. C., and Reynolds, C., 'Illustrated Boccaccio Manuscripts in Oxford Libraries', *Studi sul Boccaccio*, 20 (1991–2), 1–72.

Dean, Ruth J., 'The Earliest Medieval Commentary on Livy—by Nicholas Trevet', *Medievalia et humanistica*, 3 (1945), 86–98.

Delisle, Léopold V., *Recherches sur la Librairie de Charles V*, 2 vols. (Paris, 1907).

Dobson, R. B. (ed.), *The Church, Politics and Patronage in the Fifteenth Century* (Gloucester: Sutton, 1984).

Donaldson, Ian, *The Rapes of Lucretia: A Myth and its Transformations* (Oxford: Clarendon, 1982).

Dorsten, J. A. van, 'The Leyden "Lydgate Manuscript" ', *Scriptorium*, 14 (1960), 315–25.

Douce, Francis, *The Dance of Death* (London, 1833).

Doyle, A. I., 'More Light on John Shirley', *Medium Ævum*, 30 (1961), 93–101.

—— and Pace, George B., 'Further Texts of Chaucer's Minor Poems', *Studies in Bibliography*, 28 (1975), 41–61.

Drew, Philip, *The Meaning of Freedom* (Aberdeen: Aberdeen University Press, 1982).

DuBruck, Edelgard E., 'Another Look at "Macabre" ' *Romania*, 79 (1958), 536–43.

Duffy, Eamon, *The Stripping of the Altars: Traditional Religion in England, c.1400–c.1580* (New Haven, Conn. and London: Yale University Press, 1992).

Durrieu, Paul, *Le Boccace de Munich* (Munich: Rosenthal, 1909).

Dwyer, Richard, 'Some Readers of John Trevisa', N&Q 212 (1967), 291–2.

—— *Boethian Fictions: Narratives in the Medieval French Versions of the 'Consolatio Philosophiae'*, Medieval Academy of America Publications 83 (Cambridge, Mass.: 1976).

—— 'Arthur's Stellification in the *Fall of Princes*', PhilQ 57 (1978), 155–71.

Ebin, Lois, 'Lydgate's Views on Poetry', *Annuale medievale*, 18 (1977), 17–105.

—— 'Poetics and Style in Late Medieval Literature', in Ebin (ed.), *Vernacular Poetics in the Middle Ages*, Studies in Medieval Culture 16 (Kalamazoo, Mich.: Medieval Institute Publications, 1984), 263–93.

——*John Lydgate*, TEAS 407 (Boston, Mass.: Twayne, 1985).

Edwards, A. S. G., 'Lydgate's *Fall of Princes*: Unrecorded Readings', *N&Q* 214 (1969), 170–1.

—— 'A Lydgate Bibliography, 1928–68', *Bulletin of Bibliography and Magazine Notes*, 27 (1970), 95–8. [1970*a*]

—— 'Lydgate's Attitudes to Women', *English Studies*, 51 (1970), 436–7. [1970*b*]

—— 'A Missing Leaf from the Plimpton *Fall of Princes*', *Manuscripta*, 15 (1971), 29–31. [1971*a*]

—— 'Selections from Lydgate's *Fall of Princes*: A Checklist', *The Library*, 5th ser., 26 (1971), 337–42. [1971*b*]

—— 'Some Borrowings by Cavendish from Lydgate's *Fall of Princes*', *N&Q* 216 (1971), 207–9. [1971*c*]

—— 'The Huntington *Fall of Princes* and Sloane 2452', *Manuscripta*, 16 (1972), 37–40. [1972*a*]

—— 'John Lydgate, Medieval Antifeminism and Harley 2251', *Annuale medievale*, 13 (1972), 32–44. [1972*b*]

—— 'Stow and Lydgate's *Edmund*', *N&Q* 218 (1973), 365–9.

—— 'The Date of George Cavendish's *Metrical Visions*', *PhilQ* 53 (1974), 131. [1974*a*]

—— 'Douglas's *Palice of Honour* and Lydgate's *Fall of Princes*', *N&Q* 219 (1974), 83. [1974*b*]

—— 'The McGill Fragment of Lydgate's *Fall of Princes*', *Scriptorium*, 28 (1974), 75–7. [1974*c*]

—— 'The Influence of Lydgate's *Fall of Princes*, c. 1440–1559: A Survey', *Mediaeval Studies*, 39 (1977), 424–39.

—— 'Lydgate's *Fall of Princes*: A "Lost" Manuscript Found', *Manuscripta*, 22 (1978), 176–8.

—— 'Lydgate Manuscripts: Some Directions for Future Research', in Derek Pearsall (1983) (ed.), 15–26.

—— 'Lydgate Scholarship—Progress and Prospects', in R. F. Yeager (1984) (ed.), 29–47.

—— 'Additions and Corrections to the Bibliography of John Lydgate', *N&Q* 230 (1985), 450–2. [1985*b*]

—— (ed.), *Middle English Prose: A Critical Guide to Major Authors and Genres* (New Brunswick, NJ.: Rutgers University Press, 1986).

—— 'An Unidentified Extract from Lydgate's *Troy Book*', *N&Q* 234 (1989), 307–8.

—— 'Introduction', *MLQ* 53 (1992), 1–4.

Edwards, A. S. G., and Pearsall, Derek, 'The Manuscripts of the Major English Poetic Texts', in Jeremy Griffiths and Derek Pearsall (1989) (eds.), 257–78.

Eisler, Robert, 'Danse Macabre', *Traditio*, 6 (1948), 187–225.

Ellis, George, *Specimens of the Early English Poets*, 4th edn., 3 vols. (London, 1811).

Ellis, Roger, *Patterns of Religious Narrative in 'The Canterbury Tales'* (London: Croom Helm, 1986).

Emerton, Ephraim, *Humanism and Tyranny: Studies in the Italian Trecento* (Cambridge, Mass.: Harvard University Press, 1925).

Encyclopaedia Judaica, 16 vols. (Jerusalem: Encyclopaedia Judaica, 1972).

Evans, Joan, *Life in Medieval France* [1925] 3rd edn. (London: Phaidon, 1969).

Famiglietti, R. C., 'Laurent de Premierfait: The Career of a Humanist in Early Fifteenth-Century Paris', *Journal of Medieval History*, 9 (1983), 25–42.

Farnham, Willard, '*The Mirror for Magistrates* and Elizabethan Tragedy', *JEGP* 25 (1926), 66–78.

—— 'The Progeny of *A Mirror for Magistrates*', *ModPhil* 29 (1931–2), 395–410; repr. in *The Medieval Heritage of Elizabethan Tragedy* (1936/56), 304–39.

—— *The Medieval Heritage of Elizabethan Tragedy* (Berkeley, Calif.: University of California Press, 1936; rev. edn. Oxford: Blackwell, 1956).

Feasey, Eveline, 'The Licensing of the *Mirror for Magistrates*', *The Library*, 4th ser., 3 (1922–3), 177–93.

Fisher, J. L., 'The Harlow Cartulary: Seals of the Abbots and Convents of Bury St Edmunds', *Transactions of the Essex Archaeological Society*, NS, 22 (1936–40), 239–70.

Flutre, Louis-Fernand, *Les Manuscrits des Faits des Romains* (Paris: Hachette, 1932).

Förster, Max, 'Boccaccio's De casibus virorum illustrium in englischer Bearbeitung', *Deutsche Literaturzeitung* 45, Heft 27 (1924), cols. 1943–6.

Frappier, Jean, *Étude sur La Mort le Roi Artu, Roman du XIIIᵉ Siècle*, 2nd edn. (Paris and Geneva: Droz, 1961).

Frost, David William, *The Marqués de Santillana*, TWAS 154 (New York: Twayne, 1971).

Fry, D. K., 'The Ending of the Monk's Tale', *JEGP* 71 (1972), 355–68.

Gage, John, 'Letters from Henry VI to the Abbot of St Edmundsbury', *Archaeologia*, 23 (1831), 339–43.

Galbraith, V. H., 'The East Anglian See and the Abbey of Bury St Edmunds', *EHR* 40 (1925), 222–8.

Galigani, Giuseppe, *Il Boccaccio nella cultura inglese e anglo-americana* (Florence: Olschki, 1974).

Galinsky, Hans, *Der Lucretia-Stoff in der Weltliteratur*, Sprache und Kultur der Germanisch-romanischen Völker, B: Germanistische Reihe 3 (Breslau, 1932).

Galpin, Stanley L., 'Les Eschez Amoureux: A Complete Synopsis, with Unpublished Extracts', *The Romanic Review*, 11 (1920), 283–307.

Gathercole, Patricia M., 'Laurent de Premierfait: The Translator of Boccaccio's *De casibus virorum illustrium*', *The French Review*, 4 (1954), 245–52.

—— 'The Manuscripts of Laurent de Premierfait's *Du Cas des Nobles* (Boccaccio's *De casibus virorum illustrium*)', *Italica*, 32 (1955), 14–21.

—— 'Two Old French Translations of Boccaccio's *De casibus virorum illustrium*', *MLQ* 17 (1956), 304–9.

—— 'The Manuscripts of Laurent de Premierfait's Works', *MLQ* 19 (1958), 262–70.

—— 'Fifteenth-Century Translation: The Development of Laurent de Premierfait', *MLQ* 21 (1960), 365–70.

—— 'Illuminations on the French *Decameron*', *Italica*, 38 (1961), 314–18.

—— 'The Manuscripts of Laurent de Premierfait's Works: Additions and Changes', *MLQ* 23 (1962), 225–8.

—— 'Manuscript no. 290 in the Free Library, Philadelphia, Pennsylvania: A Boccaccio Manuscript', *Romance Notes*, 3 (1962), 40–3.

—— 'A Frenchman's Praise of Boccaccio', *Italica*, 40 (1963), 225–30.

—— 'Illuminations on *Des Cas des Nobles* (Boccaccio's *De casibus*)', *Studi sul Boccaccio*, 2 (1964), 343–56.

—— 'Illuminations on the French Manuscripts of Boccaccio's *De claris mulieribus*', *Italica*, 42 (1965), 213–17.

—— 'Lydgate's *Fall of Princes* and the French version of Boccaccio's *De casibus*', in Franco Simone (1967) (ed.), 167–78.

—— 'Boccaccio in French', *Studi sul Boccaccio*, 5 (1968), 275–97.

—— 'Boccaccio in English', *Studi sul Boccaccio*, 7 (1973), 353–68.

Gibson, Margaret (ed.), *Boethius: His Life, Thought and Influence* (Oxford: Blackwell, 1981).

Gill, Joseph, *The Council of Florence* (Cambridge: Cambridge University Press, 1959).

Gillespie, Alexandra, 'Caxton's Chaucer and Lydgate Quartos: Miscellanies from Manuscripts to Print', *TCBS* 12 (2000), 1–25. [2000a]

—— 'The Lydgate Canon in Print from 1476 to 1534', *JEBS* 2000, 59–93. [2000b]

Gillespie, Alexandra, 'Framing Lydgate's *Fall of Princes*: The Evidence of Book History', *Mediaevalia*, 20 (2001), 153–78. [2001*b*]

—— ' "These proverbs yet do last": Lydgate, the Fifth Earl of Northumberland, and Tudor Miscellanies from Print to Manuscript', *YES* 33 (2003), 215–32.

—— *Print Culture and the Medieval Author: Chaucer, Lydgate, and their Books, 1473–1559* (Oxford: Oxford University Press, forthcoming).

Godman, Peter, 'Chaucer and Boccaccio's Latin Works', in Piero Boitani (1983) (ed.), 269–95.

Gordon, D. J., 'Giannotti, Michelangelo and the Cult of Brutus', in D. J. Gordon (ed.), *Fritz Saxl, 1890–1948: A Volume of Memorial Essays from his Friends in England* (London/New York, NY.: Nelson, 1957), 281–96.

Gradon, Pamela, '*Trajanus Redivivus*: Another look at Trajan in *Piers Plowman*', in Douglas Gray and E. G. Stanley (1983) (eds.), 93–114.

Gransden Antonia, 'The Alleged Rape by Edward III of the Countess of Salisbury', in Gransden (ed.), *Legends, Traditions and History in Medieval England* (London: Hambledon, 1992), 267–78.

Grant, Edward, 'The Condemnation of 1277, God's Absolute Power and Physical Thought in the Late Middle Ages', *Viator*, 10 (1979), 211–44.

Gray, Douglas, 'Humanism and Humanisms in the Literature of Late Medieval England', in Sergio Rossi and Daniella Savoia (1989) (eds.), 26–44.

—— and Stanley, E. G. (eds.), *Middle English Studies Presented to Norman Davis in Honour of his Seventieth Birthday* (Oxford: Clarendon, 1983).

Green, Lawrence D., 'Modes of Perception in the *Mirror for Magistrates*', *HLQ* 44 (1980–1), 117–33.

Green, R. F., *Poets and Princepleasers: Literature and the English Court in the Late Middle Ages* (Toronto: Toronto University Press, 1980).

Grennen, J. E., ' "Sampsoun" in *The Canterbury Tales*: Chaucer Adapting a Source', *NeuphilMitt* 67 (1966), 117–22.

Gresham, Stephen, 'William Baldwin: Literary Voice of the Reign of Edward VI', *HLQ* 44 (1980–1), 101–16.

Griffiths, Jeremy, and Pearsall, Derek (eds.), *Book Production and Publishing in Britain 1375–1475* (Cambridge: Cambridge University Press, 1989).

Griffiths, Ralph A., 'The Trial of Eleanor Cobham: An Episode in the Fall of Duke Humphrey of Gloucester', *BJRL* 51 (1968–9), 381–99.

—— *The Reign of Henry VI: The Exercise of Royal Authority,*
1422–61 (London: Benn, 1981).

Guenée, Bernard, *Un Meurtre, une Société: L'assassinat du Duc*
d'Orléans, 23 novembre 1407 (Paris: Gallimard, 1992).

Haas, Renate, 'Chaucer's *Monk's Tale*: An Ingenious Criticism of Early
Humanist Conceptions of Tragedy', *Humanistica Lovaniensia*, 36
(1987), 44–70.

Hagen, Susan K., *Allegorical Remembrance: A Study of the 'Pilgrimage*
of the Life of Man' as a Medieval Treatise on Seeing and
Remembering (Athens, Ga./London: University of Georgia Press,
1990).

Hammond, Eleanor Prescott, 'Two British Museum Manuscripts: A
Contribution to the Bibliography of John Lydgate', *Anglia*, 28
(1905), 1–28.

—— 'Ashmole 59 and other Shirley Manuscripts', *Anglia*, 30 (1907),
320–48.

—— 'Poet and Patron in the *Fall of Princes*: Lydgate and Humphrey of
Gloucester', *Anglia*, 38 (1914), 121–36.

—— 'Lydgate and Coluccio Salutati', *ModPhil* 25 (1927–8), 49–57.

Hardison, O. B., 'The Place of Averroes' Commentary on the *Poetics*
of Aristotle in the History of Medieval Criticism', in J. Lievsay
(1970) (ed.), 57–81.

Harriss, G. L., 'Cardinal Beaufort—Patriot or Usurer?', *TRHS*, 5th ser.,
20 (1970), 129–48.

—— *Cardinal Beaufort, A Study of Lancastrian Ascendancy and*
Decline (Oxford: Clarendon, 1988).

—— 'Cardinal Beaufort', in Judith Loades (1991) (ed.), 81–92.

—— 'Good Duke Humfrey', *BLR* 15 (1995), 119–23.

Hartung, Albert E., and Severs, J. Burke (gen. eds.), *A Manual of the*
Writings in Middle English, 1050–1500, 9 vols. (New Haven,
Conn.: Connecticut Academy of Arts and Sciences, 1967–93), vol. vi,
ed. A. Renoir and C. D. Benson (1980), 1835–40, 2099–106.

Hauvette, Henri, 'Recherches sur le *De casibus virorum illustrium* de
Boccace', in A. Audollent, H. Beranger *et al.* (1901) (eds.), 279–97.

—— 'Un chapitre de Boccace et sa Fortune dans la Littérature
Française', *Bulletin Italien*, 3 (1903), 1–6. [1903*b*]

—— 'Les plus anciennes traductions françaises de Bocace', *Bulletin*
Italien, 7 (1907), 281–313; 8 (1908), 1–17, 189–211, 285–311;
9 (1909), 1–26, 193–211.

—— *Boccace, Étude biographique et littéraire* (Paris, 1914).

Hogg, James, *Zeit, Tod und Ewigkeit in der Renaissance Literatur*,
Analecta Cartusiana 117, 3 vols. (Salzburg: Institut für Anglistik
aund Amerikanistik, Universität Salzburg, 1986–7).

Holmes, G. A., 'Cardinal Beaufort and the Crusade against the Hussites', *EHR* 88 (1973), 721–50.

Horner, Patrick J., ' "The King taught us the Lesson": Benedictine Support for Henry V's Suppression of the Lollards', *Mediaeval Studies*, 52 (1990), 190–220.

Horrall, Sarah M., 'Lydgate's "Verses on the Kings of England": A New Manuscript', *N&Q* 233 (1988), 441.

Hortis, Attilio, *Studij sulle opere latine del Boccaccio* (Trieste, 1879).

Howarth, R. G., 'Thomas Sackville and *A Mirror for Magistrates*', *English Studies in Africa*, 6 (1963), 77–100.

Hudson, Anne, 'The Examination of Lollards', *BIHR* 46 (1973), 145–59.

—— 'The Debate on Bible Translation, Oxford 1401', *EHR* 90 (1975), 1–18, repr. in (1985), 67–84.

—— 'A Lollard Sect Vocabulary?', in Michael Benskin and M. L. Samuels (1981) (eds.), 15–30; repr. in Anne Hudson (1985), 165–80.

—— 'Lollardy: The English Heresy?', in Stuart Mews (1982) (ed.), 261–83.

—— *Lollards and their Books* (London/Ronceverte, WVa.: Hambledon, 1985).

—— *The Premature Reformation: Wycliffite Texts and Lollard History* (Oxford: Clarendon, 1988).

Huizinga, Johan, *The Waning of the Middle Ages* (London: Arnold, 1924).

Hurry, Jamieson B., *Reading Abbey: Illustrated by Plans, Views and Facsimiles* (London, 1901).

Jackson, William Alexander, 'Wayland's Edition of *The Mirror for Magistrates*', *The Library*, 4th ser., 13 (1932–3), 155–7.

James, M. R., 'Bury St Edmunds Manuscripts', *ELH* 41 (1926), 251–60.

Jed, Stephanie, *Chaste Thinking: The Rape of Lucretia and the Birth of Humanism* (Bloomington, Ind.: Indiana University Press, 1989).

Jochums, Milford C., 'The Legend of the Voice from Heaven', *N&Q* 209 (1964), 44–7.

Johnson, Dudley R., 'The Biblical Characters of Chaucer's Monk', *PMLA* 66 (1951), 827–43.

Jordan, W. C., McNab, B., and Ruiz, T. F. (eds.), *Order and Innovation in the Middle Ages: Essays in Honor of Joseph R. Strayer* (Princeton, NJ.: Princeton University Press, 1976).

Kaske, R. E., 'The Knight's Interruption of the Monk's Tale', *ELH* 24 (1957), 249–68.

Kato, Tomomi (ed.), *A Concordance to the Works of Sir Thomas Malory* (Tokyo: University of Tokyo Press, 1974).

Keiser, George R., '*Ordinatio* in the Manuscripts of John Lydgate's *Lyf of Our Lady*: Its Value for the Reader, its Challenge for the Modern Editor', in Tim W. Machan (1991) (ed.), 139–57.

Kelly, Douglas, '*Translatio studii*: Translation, Adaptation, and Allegory in Medieval French Literature', *PhilQ* 57 (1978), 287–310.

Kelly, Henry Ansgar, 'Aristotle-Averroes-Alemannus on Tragedy: The Influence of the *Poetics* on the Middle Ages', *Viator*, 10 (1979), 161–209. [1979*a*]

—— 'Tragedy and the Performance of Tragedy in Late Roman Antiquity', *Traditio*, 35 (1979), 21–44. [1979*b*]

—— 'The Non-Tragedy of Arthur', in Gregory Kratzmann and James Simpson (1986) (eds.), 92–114.

—— 'The Croyland Chronicle Tragedies', *The Ricardian*, 7/99 (1987), 498–515.

—— *Tragedy and Comedy from Dante to Pseudo-Dante* (Berkeley, Calif./London: University of California Press, 1989). [1989*a*]

—— 'Chaucer and Shakespeare on Tragedy', *Leeds Studies in English*, NS, 20 (1989), 191–206. [1989*b*]

—— *Ideas and Forms of Tragedies from Aristotle to the Middle Ages*, Cambridge Studies in Medieval Literature 18 (Cambridge: Cambridge University Press, 1993).

—— *Chaucerian Tragedy*, Chaucer Studies 24 (Cambridge: Brewer, 1997).

Ker, N. P., *Medieval Libraries of Great Britain: A List of Surviving Books*, 2nd edn., Guides and Handbooks 3 (London: Royal Historical Society, 1964).

Kiefer, Frederick, 'Fortune and Providence in the *Mirror for Magistrates*', *Studies in Philology*, 74 (1977), 146–64.

Kleineke, Wilhelm, *Englische Fürstenspiegel vom Policraticus Johanns von Salisbury bis zum Basilikon Doron König Jakobs I*, Studien zur Englischen Philologie 90 (Halle: Niemeyer, 1937).

Kleinstück, Johannes, 'Die mittelalterliche Tragödie in England', *Euphorion*, 50 (1956), 177–95.

Knowles, David, *The Religious Orders in England*, 3 vols. (Cambridge: Cambridge University Press, 1948–59).

—— and Hadcock, R. Neville, *Medieval Religious Houses: England and Wales* (London: Longman, 1953).

Kratzmann, Gregory, and Simpson, James (eds.), *Medieval English Religious and Ethical Literature: Essays in Honour of G. H. Russell* (Cambridge: Brewer, 1986).

Kuczynski, Michael P., *Prophetic Song: The Psalms as Moral Discourse in Later Medieval England* (Philadelphia, Penn.: University of Pennsylvania Press, 1995).

Kurose, Tamotsu, 'Notes on John Lydgate's Character Drawings of the Goddess Fortune in the *Fall of Princes*', *Studies in English Literature*, 52 (1975), 79–100.

Lambert, Malcolm, *Medieval Heresy: Popular Movements from the Gregorian Reform to the Reformation* (Oxford: Blackwell, 1977; rev. edn. 1992).

Lancashire, Ian, *Computer-Based Chaucer Studies*, Centre for Computing in the Humanities Working Papers 3 (Toronto: University of Toronto, 1993), 161–76.

Lander, J. R., *The Limitations of English Monarchy in the Later Middle Ages: The 1986 Joanne Goodman Lectures* (Toronto/London: University of Toronto Press, 1989).

Lawton, David, *Chaucer's Narrators*, Chaucer Studies 13 (Cambridge: Brewer, 1985).

—— 'Dullness and the Fifteenth Century', *ELH* 54 (1987), 761–99.

—— Scase, Wendy, and Copeland, Rita (eds.), *New Medieval Literatures* 3 (Oxford: Oxford University Press, 1999).

Lepley, Douglas L., 'The Monk's Boethian Tale', *ChauR* 12 (1977–8), 162–70.

Lerer, Seth, *Chaucer and his Readers: Imagining the Author in Late Medieval England* (Princeton, NJ.: Princeton University Press, 1993).

Lerner, Ralph, and Mahdi, M., *Medieval Political Philosophy: A Sourcebook* (New York: Free Press of Glencoe, 1963).

Lewis, C. S., *The Allegory of Love: A Study in Medieval Tradition* (Oxford: Oxford University Press, 1936).

—— *Oxford History of English Literature: The Sixteenth Century, excluding Drama* (Oxford: Clarendon, 1954).

Lewis, N. B., 'The Last Medieval Summons of the English Feudal Levy, 13 June 1385', *EHR* 73 (1958), 1–26.

Lewis, P. S., 'Two Pieces of Fifteenth-Century Political Iconography', *JWCI* 27 (1964), 317–20.

—— 'Jean Juvenal des Ursins and the Common Literary Attitude towards Tyranny in Fifteenth-Century France', *Medium Ævum*, 34 (1965), 103–21.

Lievsay, J. (ed.), *Medieval and Renaissance Studies* 4 (Durham, NC., 1970).

Loades, David, *Politics, Censorship and the English Reformation* (London: Pinter, 1991).

Loades, Judith (ed.), *Medieval History I* (Bangor: 1991).

Lobel, M. D., *The Borough of Bury St Edmunds: A Study in the Growth and Development of a Monastic Town* (Oxford: Clarendon, 1935).

Lockwood, Shelley, 'Marsilius of Padua and the Case for the Royal Ecclesiastical Supremacy', *TRHS* 6th ser., 1 (1991), 89–119.

Loomie, Albert J., *The Spanish Elizabethans: The English Exiles at the Court of Philip II* (London: Burns and Oates, 1963).

Loomis, L. R., *The Council of Constance: The Unification of the Church*, ed. J. H. Mundy and K. M. Woody, Records of Civilisation 63 (New York/London: Columbia University Press, 1961).

Lucas, Robert H., 'Mediaeval French Translations of the Latin Classics to 1500', *Speculum*, 45 (1970), 225–53.

Lyall, R. J., and Riddy, Felicity (eds.), *Proceedings of the Third International Conference on Scottish Language and Literature (Medieval and Renaissance), University of Stirling, 2–7 July 1981* (Glasgow: University of Glasgow, 1981).

McCabe, Herbert, *God Matters* (London: Chapman, 1987).

McCann, Justin, *Saint Benedict* (London: Sheed and Ward, 1937).

McConica, James Kelsey, *English Reformation Politics under Henry VIII and Edward VI* (Oxford: Clarendon, 1965).

McCord Adams, Marilyn, *William Ockham*, 2 vols. (Notre Dame, Ind.: University of Notre Dame Press, 1987).

McCormick, William, *The Manuscripts of the Canterbury Tales* (Oxford: Oxford University Press, 1933).

MacCracken, H. N., 'Lydgate's *Serpent of Division*', *MLR* 8 (1913), 103–4.

McFarlane, K. B., 'Henry V, Bishop Beaufort and the Red Hat', *EHR* 40 (1945), 316–48.

Machan, Tim W. (ed.), *Medieval Literature: Texts and Interpretation* (Binghamton, NY.: Center for Medieval and Early Renaisance Studies, 1991).

McHardy, A. K., 'Clerical Taxation in Fifteenth-Century England: The Clergy as Agents of the Crown', in R. B. Dobson (1984) (ed.), 168–89.

McKenna, J. W., 'Henry VI of England and the Dual Monarchy: Aspects of Royal Political Propaganda', *JWCI* 28 (1965), 145–62.

McLeod, Enid, *Charles of Orleans: Prince and Poet* (London: Chatto and Windus, 1969).

McLeod, W., 'Alban and Amphibal: Some Extant Lives and a Lost Life', *Mediaeval Studies*, 42 (1980), 407–30.

McLynn, Neil B., *Ambrose of Milan: Church and Court in a Christian Capital* (Berkeley, Calif.: California University Press, 1994).

Macray, W. D., *Annals of the Bodleian Library, Oxford*, 2nd edn. (Oxford: Clarendon, 1890; repr. Oxford: Bodleian Library, 1984).

Madan, F., and Craster, H. H. E., *Summary Catalogue of Western Manuscripts in the Bodleian Library at Oxford*, 11 vols. (Oxford: Clarendon, 1922–4).

Mâle, Emile, *L'Art religieux de la fin du Moyen Âge en France: étude sur les origines de l'iconographie du Moyen Âge*, 2nd edn. (Paris: Colin, 1922).

Mann, Nicholas, 'La fortune de Pétrarque en France: Recherches sur le *De remediis*', *Studi francesi*, 13 (1969), 1–15.

—— 'The Manuscripts of Petrarch's *De remediis*: A Checklist', *Italia medioevale e umanistica*, 14 (1971), 57–90. [1971*a*]

—— 'Petrarch's Role in Humanism', *Apollo*, 94 (1971), 176–83. [1971*b*]

—— 'Petrarch Manuscripts in the British Isles', *Italia medioevale e umanistica*, 18 (1975), 139–509. [1975*a*]

—— 'La Prima Fortuna del Petrarca in Inghilterra', in Giuseppe Billanovich and Giuseppe Frasso (1975) (eds.), 279–89. [1975*b*]

—— 'Petrarch and Humanism: The Paradox of Posterity', in Aldo S. Bernardo (1980) (ed.), 287–97.

Martin, Henry, *Le Boccace de Jean sans Peur: Des Cas des nobles hommes et femmes* (Brussels, 1911).

Matheson, Lister M., 'Historical Prose', in A. S. G. Edwards (1986) (ed.), 209–48.

Meerseman, A., 'Concordia inter Quatuor Ordines mendicantes', *Archivum fratrum predicatorum*, 4 (1934), 75–97.

Mews, Stuart (ed.), *Religion and National Identity, SCH 18* (Oxford: Blackwell, 1982).

Meyendorff, John, *Imperial Unity and Christian Divisions: The Church 450–680 A.D.*, The Church in History 2 (New York: St Vladimir, 1989).

Meyerstein, E. H. W., *A Life of Chatterton* (London: Ingpen and Grant, 1930).

Minnis, A. J., 'Aspects of the Medieval French and English Traditions of the *De Consolatione Philosophiae*', in Margaret Gibson (1981) (ed.), 312–61.

—— *Chaucer and Pagan Antiquity*, Chaucer Studies 8 (Cambridge: Brewer, 1982).

—— *Medieval Theory of Authorship: Scholastic Literary Attitudes in the Later Middle Ages*, 2nd edn. (Aldershot: Wildwood House, 1988).

—— *Chaucer's 'Boece' and the Medieval Tradition of Boethius*, Chaucer Studies 18 (Cambridge: Brewer, 1993).

—— *Middle English Poetry: Texts and Traditions. Essays in Honour of Derek Pearsall* (York: York Medieval Press, 2001).

—— and Scott, A. B. (eds.), with Wallace, D., *Medieval Literary Theory and Criticism c.1100–c.1375: The Commentary Tradition* (Oxford: Oxford University Press, 1988; rev. edn. 1991).

Mitchell, Bruce, and Robinson, Fred C., *A Guide to Old English*, 6th edn. (Oxford: Blackwell, 2001).

Mitchell, R. J., 'A Renaissance Library: The Collection of John Tiptoft, Earl of Worcester', *The Library*, 4th ser., 18 (1937–8), 67–83.

Molho, Anthony, and Tedeschi, John A. (eds.), *Renaissance: Studies in Honor of Hans Baron*, Biblioteca storica Sansoni, NS, 49 (Florence: Sansoni, 1971).

Mooney, Linne R., 'Lydgate's "Kings of England" and Another Verse Chronicle of the Kings', *Viator*, 20 (1989), 255–89.

—— 'Scribes and Booklets of Trinity College Cambridge, Manuscripts R. 3. 19 and R. 3. 21', in A. J. Minnis (2001) (ed.), 241–66.

Morrell, J. B., *Gerson and the Great Schism* (Manchester: Manchester University Press, 1960).

Morse, Ruth, 'Historical Fiction in Fifteenth-Century Burgundy', *MLR* 75 (1980), 48–64.

Mortimer, Nigel, 'Selections from Lydgate's *Fall of Princes*: A Corrected Checklist', *The Library*, 6th ser., 17 (1995), 342–4.

Mynors, R. A. B., 'The Latin Classics known to Boston of Bury', in D. J. Gordon (1957) (ed.), 199–217.

Neuse, Richard, *Chaucer's Dante* (Berkeley, Calif.: 1991).

Nicholson, Peter (ed.), *Gower's* Confessio Amantis: *A Critical Anthology*, John Gower Society 3 (Cambridge: Brewer, 1991).

Norton, Glyn P., 'Laurent de Premierfait and the Fifteenth-Century French Assimilation of the *Decameron*: A Study in Tonal Transformation', *Comparative Literature Studies*, 9 (1972), 376–91.

Oakley, Francis, *The Political Thought of Pierre d'Ailly: The Voluntarist Tradition* (New Haven, Conn.: Yale University Press, 1964).

Oberman, Heiko Augustinus, *The Harvest of Medieval Theology: Gabriel Biel and Late Medieval Nominalism* (Cambridge, Mass.: Harvard University Press, 1963).

—— trans. Paul L. Nyhus, *Forerunners of the Reformation: The Shape of Late Medieval Thought* (London: Lutterworth, 1967).

O'Connor, D. J., *Aquinas and Natural Law* (London: Macmillan, 1967).

Olson, Glending, *Literature as Recreation in the Later Middle Ages* (Ithaca, NY: Cornell University Press, 1982).

Ord, Craven, 'Account of the Entertainment of King Henry the Sixth at the Abbey of Bury St Edmunds', *Archaeologia*, 15 (1806), 65–71.

Orwen, William R., 'Spenser and the Serpent of Division', *SP* 38 (1941), 198–210.

Pächt, Otto, and Alexander, J. J. G., *Illuminated Manuscripts in the Bodleian Library, Oxford* (Oxford: Clarendon, 1973).

Pantin, W. A., 'Gloucester College', *Oxoniensa*, 11–12 (1946–7), 65–74.

Parmiter, Geoffrey de C., 'Plowden, Englefield and Sandford, i. 1558–85', *Recusant History*, 13 (1975–6), 9–25.

—— 'Plowden, Englefield and Sandford, ii. 1585–1609', *Recusant History*, 14 (1977–8), 159–77.

Pascoe, Louis B., *Jean Gerson: Principles of Church Reform*, Studies in Medieval and Reformation Thought 7 (Leiden: Brill, 1973).

—— 'Gerson and the Donation of Constantine: Growth and Development within the Church', *Viator*, 5 (1974), 469–85.

Patch, Howard, *The Tradition of the Goddess Fortuna in Medieval Philosophy and Literature*, Smith College Studies in Modern Languages 3 (Northampton, Mass./Paris: Champion, 1922).

—— *Fortuna in Old French Literature*, Smith College Studies in Modern Languages 4 (Northampton, Mass.: Smith College, 1923).

—— *The Goddess Fortuna in Mediaeval Literature* (Cambridge, Mass.: Harvard University Press, 1927).

Patterson, Lee, *Negotiating the Past: The Historical Understanding of Medieval Literature* (Madison, Wisc.: University of Wisconsin Press, 1987).

—— 'Making Identities in Fifteenth-century England: Henry V and John Lydgate', in Jeffrey N. Cox and Larry J. Reynolds (1993) (eds.), 69–107.

Pearsall, Derek, 'The English Chaucerians', in Derek Brewer (1966) (ed.), 201–39. [1966a]

—— 'Gower's Narrative Art', *PMLA* 81 (1966), 475–84; repr. in Peter Nicholson (1991) (ed.), 62–80. [1966b]

—— *Gower and Lydgate: Writers and their Work* 211 (Harlow: Longman, for the British Council, 1969).

—— *John Lydgate* (London: Routledge and Kegan Paul, 1970).

—— *Old and Middle English Poetry* (London: Routledge and Kegan Paul, 1977).

—— (ed.), *Manuscripts and Readers in Fifteenth Century England: The Literary Implications of Manuscript Study. Essay from the 1981 Conference at the University of York* (Cambridge: Brewer, 1983).

—— *The Canterbury Tales*, Unwin Critical Library (London: Allen and Unwin, 1985).

—— 'Signs of Life in Lydgate's *Dance Macabre*', in James Hogg (1986–7) (ed.), iii. 58–71.

—— 'Lydgate as Innovator', *MLQ* 53 (1992), 5–22.

—— *John Lydgate (1371–1449): A Bio-bibliography*, English Literary Studies Monograph Series 71 (Victoria, BC.: University of Victoria, 1997).

Peery, William, 'Tragic Retribution in the 1559 *Mirror for Magistrates*', *SP* 46 (1949), 113–30.

Pellegrin, Elisabeth, 'Manuscrits de Pétrarque dans les bibliothèques de France: I', *Italia medioevale e umanistica*, 4 (1961), 341–431.

Petriberg, M., 'Some Literary Correspondence of Humphrey, duke of Gloucester', *EHR* 10 (1895), 99–104.

Pratt, Karen (ed.), *Shifts and Transpositions in Narrative: A Festschrift for Dr Elspeth Kennedy* (Woodbridge: Brewer, 1994).

Pratt, Samuel M., 'Jane Shore and the Elizabethans: Some Facts and Speculations', *Texas Studies in Literature and Language*, 11 (1969–70), 1293–306.

Preston, Michael J. (ed.), *A Concordance to the Middle English Shorter Poem* (Leeds: Maney, 1975).

Primeau, Ronald, 'Daniel and the *Mirror* Tradition', *Studies in English Literature*, 15 (1975), 21–36.

Purkis, G. S., 'Laurent de Premierfait. The First French Translator of the *Decameron*', *Italian Studies*, 4 (1949), 22–36.

—— 'A Bodleian *Decameron*', *Medium Ævum*, 19 (1950), 67–9.

—— 'Laurent de Premierfait's Translation of the *Decameron*', *Medium Ævum*, 24 (1955), 1–15.

Pyle, Fitzroy, 'Thomas Sackville and *A Mirror for Magistrates*', *RES* 14 (1938), 315–21.

Rashdall, Hastings, *The Universities of Europe in the Middle Ages*, ed. F. M. Powicke and A. B. Emden, 3 vols. (London: Oxford University Press, 1936).

Reiss, Edmund, 'Boccaccio in English Culture of the Fourteenth and Fifteenth Centuries', in Giuseppe Galigani (1974) (ed.), 15–26.

Renoir, Alain, 'Chaucerian Character Names in Lydgate's *Siege of Thebes*', *MLN* 71 (1956), 249–56.

—— 'A Note on Saintsbury's Criticism of Lydgate', *NeuphilMitt* 58 (1957), 69–71.

—— 'Attitudes Towards Women in Lydgate's Poetry', *English Studies*, 42 (1961), 1–14. [1961*a*]

—— 'The Immediate Source of Lydgate's *Siege of Thebes*', *Studia Neophilologica*, 33 (1961), 86–95. [1961*b*]

—— *The Poetry of John Lydgate* (London: Routledge and Kegan Paul, 1967).

Reuss, Franz, 'Das Naturgefühl bei Lydgate', *Archiv für das Studium der neueren Sprachen und Literaturen*, 122 (1909), 269–300.

Rex, Richard, *Henry VIII and the English Reformation* (London: Macmillan, 1993).

Reynolds, Catherine, 'Illustrated Boccaccio Manuscripts in the British Library (London)', *Studi sul Boccaccio*, 17 (1988), 113–81.

Reynolds, Catherine, 'I codici del Boccaccio illustrati in Inghilterra', in Vittore Branca (1999) (ed.), iii. 267–86.

Ricci, Pier Giorgio, 'Le due Redazioni del *De casibus*', *Studi sulla vita e le opere del Boccaccio* (Milan/Naples: Ricciardi, 1985), 179–88; first printed as part of 'Studi sulle opere latine e volgari del Boccaccio', *Rinascimento*, 2nd ser., 2 (1962), 3–29.

Riddy, Felicity, 'Dating *The Buke of the Howlat*', *RES* 37 (1986), 1–11.

Ringler, William, 'Lydgate's *Serpent of Division*, 1559, edited by John Stow', *Studies in Bibliography*, 14 (1961), 201–3.

Robbins, Rossell Hope, 'An Epitaph for Duke Humphrey', *NeuphilMitt* 56 (1955), 241–9.

—— 'A New Lydgate Fragment', *ELN* 5 (1967–8), 243–7.

—— and Cutler, John L., *Supplement to the Index of Middle English Verse* (Lexington, Ky: University of Kentucky Press, 1965).

Roberts, Phyllis B., *Thomas Becket in the Medieval Latin Preaching Tradition: An Inventory of Sermons about St Thomas Becket, c.1170–c.1400*, Instrumenta patristica 25 (The Hague: Nijhoff, 1992).

Robertson, D. W., 'Chaucerian Tragedy', *ELH* 19 (1952), 1–37.

Robinson, F. N., 'On Two Manuscripts of Lydgate's *Guy of Warwick*', *Harvard Studies and Notes in Philology and Literature*, 5 (1896), 177–220.

Root, Robert K., 'The Monk's Tale', in W. F. Bryan and Germaine Dempster (1941) (eds.), 615–44.

Rosenfeld, Hellmut, *Der Mittelalterliche Totentanz*, 2nd edn. (Cologne: Böhlau, 1968).

Rosenmeyer, Thomas G., *Senecan Drama and Stoic Cosmology* (Berkeley, Calif./London: University of California Press, 1989).

Roskell, J. S., 'The Office and Dignity of Protector in England, with Special Reference to its Origins', *EHR* 68 (1953), 193–233; repr. in *Parliament and Politics in Late Medieval England*, 3 vols. (London: Hambledon, 1981–3), i. 193–234.

Rossi, Sergio, 'George Cavendish e il tema della Fortuna', *English Miscellany*, 9 (1958), 51–76.

—— 'Goodly histories, Tragicall Matters and other Morall Argument: La novella italiana nel cinquecento inglese', *Contributi dell'Istituto di filologia moderna: Serie inglese*, Scienze Filologiche e Letteratura 5 (Milan: Vita e Pensiero, 1974), 39–112.

—— and Savoia, Dianella (eds.), *Italy and the English Renaissance* (Milan: Unicopli, 1989).

Rouse, Charles A., 'Thomas Heywood and *The Life and Death of Hector*', *PMLA* 43 (1928), 779–83.

Rowe, B. J. H., 'King Henry VI's Claim to France in Picture and Poem', *The Library*, 4th ser., 13 (1932–3), 77–88.

Rubin, Miri, *Corpus Christi: The Eucharist in Late Medieval Culture* (Cambridge: Cambridge University Press, 1991).

Rubinstein, Nicolai, 'The Beginnings of Political Thought in Florence: A Study in Medieval Historiography', *JWCI* 5 (1942), 198–227.

Ruggiers, Paul G., 'Notes Towards a Theory of Tragedy in Chaucer', *ChauR* 8 (1973–4), 89–99.

Salter, Elizabeth, 'The Timeliness of *Wynnere and Wastoure*', *Medium Ævum*, 47 (1978), 40–65.

Sammut, Alfonso, *Unfredo duca di Gloucester e gli umanisti italiani*, Medioevo e umanesimo 41 (Padua: Antenore, 1980).

Sarton, George A. L., *Introduction to the History of Science*, Carnegie Institution of Washington Publication 376, 3 vols. (Baltimore, Md.: Williams and Wilkins, 1927–48).

Saxl, Fritz, and Meier, Hans, *Verzeichnis astrologischer und mythologischer illustrierter Handschriften des lateinischen Mittelalters*, ed. Harry Bober, 3 vols. (London: Warburg Institute, 1953).

Scanlon, Larry, *Narrative, Authority, and Power: The Medieval Exemplum and the Chaucerian Tradition*, Cambridge Studies in Medieval Literature 20 (Cambridge: Cambridge University Press, 1994).

—— and Simpson, James (eds.), *John Lydgate: Poetry, Culture, and Lancastrian England* (Notre Dame, Ind.: Notre Dame Press, forthcoming).

Scase, Wendy, Copeland, Rita, and Lawton, David (eds.), *New Medieval Literatures*: IV (Oxford: Oxford University Press, 2001).

Scattergood, V. J., *Politics and Poetry in the Fifteenth Century, 1399–1485* (London: Blandford, 1971).

Schanzer, Ernest, 'Dante and Julius Caesar', *Medium Ævum*, 24 (1955), 20–2.

Schibanoff, Susan, 'Avarice and Cerberus in Coluccio Salutati's *De laboribus Herculis* and Lydgate's *Fall of Princes*', *ModPhil* 71 (1974), 390–2.

Schirmer, Walter, 'Lydgate's *Fall of Princes*', *Anglia*, 69 (1950), 301–34.

—— 'The Importance of the Fifteenth Century for the Study of the English Renaissance with Special Reference to Lydgate', in C. L. Wrenn and G. Bullough (1951) (eds.), 104–10.

—— *John Lydgate: ein Kulturbild aus dem 15. Jahrhundert* (Tübingen: Niemeyer, 1952), trans. Ann E. Keep, as *John Lydgate: A Study in the Culture of the XVth Century* (London: Methuen, 1961).

Schofield, A. N. E. D., 'The First English Delegation to the Council of Basle', *JEH* 12 (1961), 167–96.

Schofield, A. N. E. D., 'The Second English Delegation to the Council of Basle', *JEH* 17 (1966), 29–64.

—— 'Some Aspects of the English Representation at the Council of Basle', *SCH* 7 (1971), 219–27.

—— 'England and the Council of Basel', *Annuarium historiae Conciliorum*, 5 (1973), 1–117.

Scott, Kathleen, 'A Mid-Fifteenth-Century English Illuminating Shop and its Customers', *JWCI* 31 (1968), 170–96.

Serafini-Sauli, Judith Powers, *Giovanni Boccaccio*, TWAS 644 (Boston, Mass.: Twayne, 1982).

Seymour, M. C., 'The Manuscripts of Hoccleve's *Regement of Princes*', *Edinburgh Bibliographical Society Transactions*, 4 (1974), 253–97.

—— 'Some Lydgate Manuscripts: *Lives of SS Edmund and Fremund* and *Danse Macabre*', *Edinburgh Bibliographical Society Transactions*, 5 (1985), 10–24.

Sieper, Ernst, 'Les Échecs Amoureux, eine altfranzösische Nachahmung des Rosenromans und ihre englische Übertragung', *Litterarhistorische Forschungen*, Heft 9 (Weimar: Felber, 1898).

Simone, Franco (ed.), *Miscellanea di studi e ricerche sul quattrocento francese* (Turin: Giappichelli, 1967).

—— 'La Présence de Boccace dans la Culture Française du XVe Siècle', *JMRS* 1 (1971), 17–32.

Simpson, James, ' "Dysemol daies and fatal houres": Lydgate's *Destruction of Thebes* and Chaucer's *Knight's Tale*', in Helen Cooper and Sally Mapstone (1997) (eds.), 15–33.

—— 'The Other Book of Troy: Guido delle Colonne's *Historia destructionis Troiae* in Fourteenth-century England', *Speculum*, 73 (1998), 397–423.

—— 'Bulldozing the Middle Ages: The Case of "John Lydgate" ', in Wendy Scase, Rita Copeland, and David Lawton (2001) (eds.), 213–42.

—— 'The Energies of John Lydgate', *The Oxford English Literary History, ii. 1350–1547: Reform and Cultural Revolution* (Oxford: Oxford University Press, 2002), 34–67.

Smalley, Beryl, 'John Wyclif's Postilla super totam Bibliam', *BLR* 4 (1953), 186–205.

—— *English Friars and Antiquity in the Early Fourteenth Century* (Oxford: Blackwell, 1960).

Smith, David M., *Guide to Bishops' Registers of England and Wales: A Survey from the Middle Ages to the Abolition of Episcopacy in 1646*, Royal Historical Society Guides and Handbooks 11 (London: Royal Historical Society, 1981).

—— Florence A., 'Laurent de Premierfait's French Version of the *De casibus virorum illustrium*, with some Notes on its Influence in France', *Revue de Littérature Comparée*, 14 (1934), 512–26.

Smith, Hallett D., 'A Woman Killed with Kindness', *PMLA* 53 (1938), 138–47.

Socola, Edward M., 'Chaucer's Development of Fortune in the Monk's Tale', *JEGP* 49 (1950), 159–71.

Southern, R. W., *Robert Grosseteste: The Growth of an English Mind in Medieval Europe* (Oxford: Clarendon, 1986; 2nd edn. 1992).

Spearing, A. C., *Medieval to Renaissance in English Poetry* (Cambridge: Cambridge University Press, 1985).

Spencer, H. Leith, *English Preaching in the Late Middle Ages* (Oxford: Clarendon, 1993).

Spencer, Theodore, 'The Story of Ugolino in Dante and Chaucer', *Speculum*, 9 (1934), 295–301.

Spurgeon, Caroline F. E., *Five Hundred Years of Chaucer Criticism and Allusion, 1357–1800*, 3 vols. (Cambridge: Cambridge University Press, 1920; rev. 1925).

Stieber, Joachim W., *Pope Eugenius IV, the Council of Basel and the Secular and Ecclesiastical Authorities in the Empire*, Studies in the History of Christian Thought 13 (Leiden: Brill, 1978).

Straker, Scott-Morgan, 'Rivalry and Reciprocity in Lydgate's *Troy Book*', in David Lawton, Wendy Scase, and Rita Copeland (1999) (eds.), 119–47.

—— 'Difference and Deference: Lydgate, Chaucer, and the *Siege of Thebes*', *RES* 52 (2001), 1–21.

Strange, W. C., 'The Monk's Tale: A Generous View', *ChauR* 1 (1966–7), 167–80.

Strohm, Paul, 'Chaucer's Audience', *Literature and History*, 3 (1977), 26–41.

—— 'Chaucer's Fifteenth-Century Audience and the Narrowing of the "Chaucer Tradition" ', *Studies in the Age of Chaucer*, 4 (1982), 3–32.

—— 'Fourteenth- and Fifteenth-Century Writers as Readers of Chaucer', in Piero Boitani and Anna Torti (1988) (eds.), 90–104.

—— *England's Empty Throne: Usurpation and the Language of Legitimation, 1399–1422* (New Haven, Conn./London: Yale University Press, 1998).

—— 'Hoccleve, Lydgate and the Lancastrian Court', in David Wallace (1999) (ed.), 640–61.

—— 'John Lydgate, Jacque of Holland, and the Poetics of Conspiracy', in David Aers (2000) (ed.), 115–32.

Summit, Jennifer, ' "Stable in Study": Lydgate's *Fall of Princes* and Duke Humphrey's Library', in Larry Scanlon and James Simpson (forthcoming) (eds.).

Sutherland, Stewart R., 'Christianity and Tragedy', *Literature and Theology*, 4 (1990), 157–68.

Swanson, R. N., *Church and Society in Late Medieval England* (Oxford: Blackwell, 1989).

Tatlock, John S., and Kennedy, Arthur G. K., *A Concordance to the Complete Works of Geoffrey Chaucer* (Gloucester, Mass.: Smith, 1963).

Taylor, Jane H. M., 'Translation as Reception: *La Danse macabré*', in Karen Pratt (1994) (ed.), 181–92.

Tesnière, Marie-Hélène, 'Un Remaniement du "Tite-Live" de Pierre Bersuire par Laurent de Premierfait', *Romania*, 107 (1986), 231–81.

Tester, S. J., *A History of Western Astrology* (Woodbridge: Boydell and Brewer, 1987).

Thaler, Alwin, 'Literary Criticism in *A Mirror for Magistrates*', *JEGP* 49 (1950), 1–13.

Thompson, John J., 'Reading Lydgate in Post-Reformation England', in A. J. Minnis (2001) (ed.), 181–209.

Thomson, J. A. F., 'A Lollard Rising in Kent: 1431 or 1438?', *BIHR* 37 (1964), 100–2.

—— *The Later Lollards, 1414–1520*, Oxford Historical Series (London: Oxford University Press, 1965).

Thomson, Rodney M., 'The Library of Bury St Edmunds Abbey in the Eleventh and Twelfth Centuries', *Speculum*, 47 (1972), 617–45.

Tillyard, E. M. W., '*A Mirror for Magistrates* Revisited', in Herbert Davis and Helen Gardner (1959) (eds.), 1–16.

Tokunaga, Satoko, 'The Sources of Wynkyn de Worde's version of *The Monk's Tale*', *The Library*, 7th ser., 2 (2001), 223–35.

Trapp, J. B., 'Verses by Lydgate at Long Melford', *RES*, NS, 6 (1955), 1–11.

—— *The Iconography of Petrarch in the Age of Humanism* (Florence: Casa Editrice le Lettere, 1996).

Trench, W. F., *A Mirror for Magistrates: Its Origin and Influence* (n.p.: 1898).

Trenholme, Norman M., 'The English Monastic Boroughs', *University of Missouri Studies*, 2 § 3 (1927).

Trinkaus, Charles, 'Coluccio Salutati's Critique of Astrology in the Context of his Natural Philosophy', *Speculum*, 64 (1989), 46–68.

Ullman, Berthold L., 'Leonardo Bruni and Humanistic Historiography', *Medievalia et humanistica*, 4 (1946), 45–61; repr. in Ullman (1973), 321–43.

—— *The Humanism of Coluccio Salutati*, Medioevo e umanesimo 4 (Padua: 1963).

—— 'Coluccio Salutati on Monarchy', *Mélanges Eugène Tisserant* 5, Archives Vaticanes Histoire Ecclesiastique, Studi e Testi 235 (Vatican City: Biblioteca Apostolica Vaticana, 1964), 401–11; repr. in Ullman (1973), 461–73.

—— *Studies in the Italian Renaissance*, Storia e letteratura raccolta di studi e testi 51, 2nd edn. (Rome: Edizioni di storia e letteratura, 1973).

—— 'Manuscripts of Duke Humphrey of Gloucester', in Ullman (1973), 345–56.

—— 'The Post-Mortem Adventures of Livy', in Ullman (1973), 53–77.

Utley, F. L., *The Crooked Rib: An Analytical Index to the Argument about Women in English and Scots Literature to the end of the year 1568* (Columbus, Ohio: Ohio State University, 1944).

Vaughan, Richard, *John the Fearless: The Growth of a Burgundian Power* (London: Longman, 1966; repr. Woodbridge: Boydell, 2002).

—— *Philip the Good: The Apogee of Burgundy* (London: Longman, 1970; repr. Woodbridge: Boydell, 2002).

Vickers, R. H., *Humphrey Duke of Gloucester, a Biography* (London: Constable, 1907).

Wallace, David, *Chaucerian Polity: Absolutist Lineages and Associational Forms in England and Italy* (Stanford, Calif.: Stanford University Press, 1997).

—— (ed.), *The Cambridge History of Medieval English Literature* (Cambridge: Cambridge University Press, 1999).

Ward, A. W., and Waller, A. R., *The Cambridge History of English Literature*, 14 vols. (Cambridge: Cambridge University Press, 1907–16).

Warton, Thomas, *The History of English Poetry from the close of the Eleventh to the commencement of the Eighteenth Century*, 3 vols. (London, 1774–81).

Watts, John, *Henry VI and the Politics of Kingship* (Cambridge: Cambridge University Press, 1996).

Wedel, Theodore O., *The Mediaeval Attitude Toward Astrology, Particularly in England*, Yale Studies in English 60 (New Haven, Conn./London: Yale University Press, 1920).

Weiher, Carol, 'Chaucer's and Gower's Stories of Lucretia and Virginia', *ELN* 14 (1976–7), 7–9.

Weiss, Roberto, 'The Library of John Tiptoft, Earl of Worcester', *BQR* 8 (1935–7), 157–64.

—— *Humanism in England During the Fifteenth Century*, 2nd edn. (Oxford: Blackwell, 1957). [1957*a*]

Weiss, Roberto, 'Humphrey, duke of Gloucester, and Tito Livio
    Frulovisi', in D. J. Gordon (1957) (ed.), 218–27. [1957*b*]
Welch, Edwin, 'Some Suffolk Lollards', *Proceedings of the Suffolk
    Institute of Archaeology*, 29 (1962–4), 154–65.
Whatley, Gordon, 'The Uses of Hagiography: The Legend of Pope
    Gregory and the Emperor Trajan in the Middle Ages', *Viator*, 15
    (1984), 25–63.
White, Hugh R. B., 'Nature and the Good in Gower's *Confessio
    Amantis*', in R. F. Yeager (1989) (ed.), 1–20.
Whiting, Bartlett Jere, *Proverbs, Sentences and Proverbial Phrases from
    English Writings, Mainly before 1500* (Cambridge, Mass.: Harvard
    University Press/London: Oxford University Press, 1968).
Wilken, Robert L., *The Christians as the Romans Saw Them*
    (New Haven, Conn.: Yale University Press, 1984).
Wilkins, Ernest Hatch, 'An Introductory Boccaccio Bibliography',
    PhilQ 6 (1927), 111–22.
—— *Life of Petrarch* (Chicago, Ill./London: University of Chicago
    Press, 1961).
Windeatt, B. A., *Oxford Guides to Chaucer: 'Troilus and Criseyde'*
    (Oxford: Oxford University Press, 1992).
Witt, Ronald G., 'The *De tyranno* and Coluccio Salutati's view of
    Politics and Roman History', *Nuova rivistica storica*, 53 (1969),
    443–8.
—— 'The Rebirth of the Concept of Republican Liberty in Italy', in
    Anthony Molho and John A. Tedeschi (1971) (eds.), 173–99.
—— 'Toward a Biography of Coluccio Salutati', *Rinascimento*, 2nd
    ser., 16 (1976), 19–34.
—— *Hercules at the Crossroads: The Life, Works, and Thought of
    Coluccio Salutati*, Duke Monographs in Medieval and Renaissance
    Studies 6 (Durham, NC.: Duke University Press, 1983).
Wolffe, Bertram, *Henry VI* (London: Eyre Methuen, 1981).
Wood, Charles T., 'Queens, Queans, and Kingship: An Inquiry into
    Theories of Royal Legitimacy in Late Medieval England and
    France', in W. C. Jordan, B. McNab, and T. F. Ruiz (1976) (eds.),
    387–400.
Wrenn, C. L., and Bullough, G. (eds.), *English Studies To-day, Papers
    read at the International Conference of University Professors of
    English, held in Magdalen College, Oxford, August 1950* (London:
    Oxford University Press, 1951).
Wright, Herbert G., *Boccaccio in England from Chaucer to Tennyson*
    (London: Athlone, 1957).
Wurtele, Douglas J., 'Chaucer's Monk: An Errant Exegete', *Literature
    and Theology*, 1 (1987), 191–209.

Yeager, R. F. (ed.), *Fifteenth Century Studies: Recent Essays* (Hamden, Conn.: Archon, 1984).

—— (ed.), *John Gower, Recent Readings: Papers Presented at the Meetings of the John Gower Society at the International Congress on Medieval Studies, Western Michigan University, 1983–1988*, Studies in Medieval Culture 26 (Kalamazoo, Mich.: Medieval Institute Publications, Western Michigan University, 1989).

Zaccaria, Vittorio, 'Le due Redazioni del *De casibus*', *Studi sul Boccaccio*, 10 (1977–8), 1–26.

Zeller, Hubert van, *The Benedictine Idea* (London: Burns and Oates, 1959).

Ziegler, Philip, *The Black Death* (Harmondsworth: Penguin, 1969).

General Index

A supplementary index lists references made to characters in the *Fall of Princes* and other texts in the *de casibus* tradition.

Sutton, Edward, sixth Baron Dudley
251, 254
Sweyn 'Forkbeard', king of England
and Denmark 135
Sylvius Piccolomini, Aeneas (Pope
Pius II) 57 n. 26
synderesis, see natural law

Talbot, Margaret, countess of
Shrewsbury 46
Tatian, Christian apologist 131
Tempier, Etienne, bishop of Paris 179
n. 112, 208–9
temptation, *see* freedom of
human will
Tertullian 65, 131, 161
Thessalonika, massacre at (390 AD)
103, 105–7
Tiptoft, John, Baron 56 n. 20
Tiptoft, John, first earl of Worcester
252, 254
Tottell, Richard 259 n. 137, 268 n. 161,
269 n. 164, 275 n. 193
Toulmin Smith, Lucy 80, 88
tragedy:
patristic understandings of
161–2
use of word 'tragedy' in European
vernaculars 155–7
see also Boccaccio, Giovanni;
Cavendish, George; Chaucer,
Geoffrey, 'Monk's Tale';
Lydgate, John, *Fall of Princes*;
Premierfait, Laurent de, *Des Cas
des nobles hommes et femmes*
Trajan, Roman emperor 91
Trent, Council of (1545–63) 255
Trevet, Nicholas 31 n. 33, 166–7
Trevisa, John 156, 199 n. 152
triumvirate of English poets, *see*
Lydgate, John
tyrannicide 27–8, 46 n. 98
Tyrell, Sir Thomas 252, 253

undeserved misfortune, *see* freedom of
human will
Uprisings of 1381 ('Peasants'
Revolt') 138

Valentinian II, Roman emperor
107 n. 27
Valerius Maximus 85
Valla, Lorenzo 108 n. 28, 254
n. 108, 276 n. 195
Valois dynasty 38
Varro, Marcus Terentius 210 n. 192
Vegetius (Flavius Vegetius Renatus)
256 n. 119
Vere, Elizabeth de, countess of Oxford
141 n. 132
vice, *see* freedom of human will
Villiers, George, first duke of
Buckingham 274
Vincent of Beauvais, *Speculum
historiale* 41, 83
Virgil 30, 276
Aeneid 41, 157 n. 23
virtue, *see* freedom of human will
virtuous pagans, canonists' debate
over 91–2
Visconti, *signori* of Milan 44, 77
Vives, Juna Luis 34, 254 n. 108

Walsingham, Thomas 139 n. 126, 156
Warton, Thomas 10, 153
Warwick, earls and countesses of, *see*
Beauchamp, Isabella, Margaret,
and Richard
Watts, John 55
Wayland, John 7, 11, 154 n. 8, 259
n. 137, 266–7, 268 n. 161, 275
Webbe, William 8, 259
Webster, John 9
Webster, Richard 267
Weever, John 275
Wenman, Thomas 275
West, James, sale of library of (1773)
10–11
West Stow (Suffolk) 143
Whethamstede, John, abbot of
St Albans 78 n. 99, 118,
132 n. 100, 140, 147, 151
n. 172, 210
Whitchurch, Edward 498, 267
William I ('the Conqueror'), king of
England 141, 149, 241
William of Conches 174 n. 91

Subjects of Narratives Index

Key: [CA]   *Confessio Amantis*
      [DC]   *Des Cas* material omitted by Lydgate
      [FP]   *Fall of Princes*
      [Idl] Idley's *Instructions*
      [MM]   *Mirror for Magistrates*
      [MT]   *The Monk's Tale*
      [MV]   *Metrical Visions*
      [TB]   *Temple de Bocace*
      [TW]   'Thoroughfare of Woe'

Achilles [TW] 214 n. 207
Adam (and Eve) [MT, FP, TW, Idl] 167,
      170, 182–3, 204–6, 214 n. 207,
      229, 236, 246, 247–8
Æolus [FP] 203
Agamemnon, king of Mycenae and
      Argos [FP] 212
Agathocles, king of Syracuse [FP]
      59–60, 208
Albanacte, legendary first king of Albany
      [MM] 271 n. 175, 272 n. 179
Alcibiades, Athenian general [FP]
      60 n. 41
Alexander III ('the Great'), king of
      Macedonia [MT, FP, TW] 130,
      169, 170, 177, 214 n. 207
Alfred, prince [MM] 273
Althaea and Meleager of Calydon [FP]
      195, 237
Alurede (Alfred 'the Great'), king of the
      West Saxons [MM] 272
Ambrose, St, bishop of Milan [FP] 103,
      105, 107, 115
Anastasius II ('Artemius'), Eastern
      Roman emperor [FP] 60, 116,
      128–30
Andalus 'the Black' of Genoa ('Andalò
      del Negro') [FP] 188–93, 210
      n. 192
Antiochus III ('the Great'), king of Syria
      [FP] 116, 170 n. 76

Antiochus IV (Epiphanes, 'the
      Illustrious'), king of Syria [MT]
      168, 170
Arbogastes, Frankish general [FP] 103,
      104
Argus, king [FP] 199–200
Arsinoe, queen of Macedonia [FP] 60
      n. 41, 213
Arthur, legendary British king (and
      Mordred) [FP, MM] 213, 236,
      240–1
Arundell, Sir Thomas [MV] 264
Astyages, last king of the Medes [FP]
      156 n. 19
Athalia(h), queen of Judah [FP] 99–100
Atreus and Thyestes, legendary kings of
      Mycenae and Argos [FP] 41
      n. 70, 204 n. 168, 206, 214 n. 211
Aurelius (Marcus Aurelius Antoninus
      'Caracalla'), Roman emperor
      [FP] 149 n. 164
Azariah, *see* 'Iosias'

Bathsheba [FP] 232
Beaufort, Edmund, duke of Somerset
      [TB] 223
Beaufort, Thomas, duke of Exeter [TW]
      214 n. 207
Belshazzar ('Balthasar') [MT, FP] 116,
      124–5, 130, 168, 170, 237
'Bochas' and Fortuna [FP] 184–5, 242

CPSIA information can be obtained at www.ICGtesting.com
Printed in the USA
BVOW080457191012

303392BV00003B/14/P